North Carolina Capital Case Law Handbook

Third Edition, 2013

Jeffrey B. Welty

UNC
SCHOOL OF
GOVERNMENT

The School of Government at the University of North Carolina at Chapel Hill works to improve the lives of North Carolinians by engaging in practical scholarship that helps public officials and citizens understand and improve state and local government. Established in 1931 as the Institute of Government, the School provides educational, advisory, and research services for state and local governments. The School of Government is also home to a nationally ranked graduate program in public administration and specialized centers focused on information technology and environmental finance.

As the largest university-based local government training, advisory, and research organization in the United States, the School of Government offers up to 200 courses, webinars, and specialized conferences for more than 12,000 public officials each year. In addition, faculty members annually publish approximately fifty books, book chapters, bulletins, and other reference works related to state and local government. Each day that the General Assembly is in session, the School produces the *Daily Bulletin*, which reports on the day's activities for members of the legislature and others who need to follow the course of legislation.

The Master of Public Administration Program is a full-time, two-year program that serves up to sixty students annually. It consistently ranks among the best public administration graduate programs in the country, particularly in city management. With courses ranging from public policy analysis to ethics and management, the program educates leaders for local, state, and federal governments and nonprofit organizations.

Operating support for the School of Government's programs and activities comes from many sources, including state appropriations, local government membership dues, private contributions, publication sales, course fees, and service contracts. Visit www.sog.unc.edu or call 919.966.5381 for more information on the School's courses, publications, programs, and services.

Printed in the United States of America

22 21 20 19 18 2 3 4 5 6

ISBN 978-1-56011-731-5

Contents

Chapter 3

Selected Trial Issues

Chapter 4
The Capital Sentencing Hearing

Chapter 5
Aggravating Circumstances

Chapter 6

Mitigating Circumstances

Chapter 7

The Racial Justice Act

Preface

This book is intended as a reference for North Carolina judges and lawyers handling capital cases. It focuses mainly on the unique aspects of capital proceedings, rather than on elements common to all criminal cases.

The name of the book comes from the fact that it contains many summaries of appellate cases. For this edition, the summaries have been updated with decisions rendered through the end of 2012. Of course, the book also addresses relevant statutory law, and that treatment, too, has been updated. Furthermore, this edition contains somewhat more analysis and discussion than previous versions, and it contains an entirely new chapter on the Racial Justice Act.

This edition builds on the work of my colleague Bob Farb, who wrote the previous editions, published in 1996 and 2004. He also read and commented on a draft of this edition. Jessie Smith, Jamie Markham, and other School of Government faculty members also reviewed this book, and research attorney Tom Tyner helped me sift through recent court decisions. The Publications Division of the School of Government turned my manuscript into this polished final product, and my editor, Melissa Twomey, was efficient, patient, and unflappable.

Finally, I am deeply grateful to the prosecutors and defense attorneys who reviewed and commented on a draft of this book. They did so notwithstanding their already busy schedules, and the book is much better for their contributions. Obviously, whatever errors remain are my own.

I welcome comments, positive or negative, on the structure, organization, or content of this book. I may be reached at (919) 843-8474, or by email at welty@sog.unc.edu.

Jeff Welty
Chapel Hill
Spring 2013

Chapter 1

Introduction

Chapter 1

Introduction

This chapter provides a brief overview of North Carolina's capital punishment statute and court procedures.

A. Origins of the Current Capital Punishment Statute

In 1976 the United States Supreme Court ruled that North Carolina's death penalty law was unconstitutional.[1] As a result of that ruling, the North Carolina General Assembly enacted legislation in 1977 that restored the death penalty as an authorized punishment for first-degree murders committed on or after June 1, 1977.[2] That legislation, with a few substantive changes, remains the law today.

B. Constitutionality of the Current Capital Punishment Statute

Generally, the constitutionality of North Carolina's death penalty statute has been upheld by the courts.[3] Specific constitutional objections to the statute are addressed at appropriate points throughout this book.

---

1. Woodson v. North Carolina, 428 U.S. 280 (1976) (holding that North Carolina's death penalty law, which mandated capital punishment for all cases of first-degree murder, violated the Eighth Amendment; the character of the offender and the circumstances of the offense must be considered before the death penalty may be imposed).

2. 1977 N.C. Sess. Laws ch. 406; *see also* State v. Detter, 298 N.C. 604 (1979) (death penalty could not be imposed on a defendant whose murderous acts were committed before June 1, 1977, even though the victim died after June 1, 1977).

3. *See, e.g.*, State v. Elliott, 360 N.C. 400, 423–24 (2006) ("The constitutionality of North Carolina's capital punishment statute has been affirmed numerous times by this Court, and we find no reason to overrule our precedent.").

C. Scope of the Current Capital Punishment Statute

Included and Excluded Offenses

First-degree murder is a capital felony.[4] There are no other capital felonies in North Carolina. The United States Supreme Court has held that the Eighth Amendment does not permit the death penalty to be imposed for non-homicide crimes against individuals.[5]

Included and Excluded Defendants

Generally, a death sentence may be imposed on any defendant who commits first-degree murder if the jury makes appropriate findings regarding the balance of aggravating and mitigating circumstances, as discussed later in this chapter. However, there are several categorical exceptions, which are listed immediately below. A defendant who is convicted of first-degree murder and is not eligible for the death penalty must be sentenced to life imprisonment without the possibility of parole, except for certain defendants under 18 years old, as explained in the following paragraph.

Defendants under 18

A defendant who was under 18 years old when he or she committed first-degree murder is not eligible for the death penalty.[6] In fact, as a result of the ruling of the United States Supreme Court in *Miller v. Alabama*,[7] juveniles sentenced for murder after July 12, 2012, must be sentenced under a special statutory scheme that provides for possible sentences of life without parole or life with the possibility of parole after 25 years.[8]

Mentally Retarded Defendants

The Eighth Amendment and North Carolina statutory law prohibit the imposition of the death penalty on a defendant who is, to quote the statutes, "mentally retarded."[9] Under North Carolina's statutory procedures, a judge may determine before trial—or a jury may determine at a capital sentencing hearing—that a defendant is mentally retarded and not eligible for the death penalty.[10] These procedures are discussed in more detail in Chapters 2 and 4.

---

4. Section 14-17 of the North Carolina General Statutes (hereinafter G.S.) (providing that first-degree murder may be punished by "death or imprisonment . . . for life without parole").

5. Kennedy v. Louisiana, 554 U.S. 407, 437 (2008) (holding that the Eighth Amendment precludes the imposition of the death penalty for raping a child and stating that "the death penalty should not be expanded to [crimes against individuals] where the victim's life was not taken").

6. Roper v. Simmons, 543 U.S. 551 (2005) (holding that the Eighth Amendment precludes the imposition of the death penalty on defendants who were under 18 at the time of their crimes); G.S. 14-17 (any person convicted of first-degree murder "who was under 18 years of age at the time of the murder shall be punished with imprisonment . . . for life without parole").

7. __ U.S. __, 132 S. Ct. 2455 (2012) (holding that the mandatory imposition of a sentence of life without parole on a juvenile convicted of murder is cruel and unusual punishment in violation of the Eighth Amendment).

8. S.L. 2012-148. The sentencing scheme is codified at G.S. 15A-1476 *et seq.* Whether *Miller* has retroactive effect has not been decided as of this writing.

9. Atkins v. Virginia, 536 U.S. 304 (2002); G.S. 15A-2005. The legislation enacted in 2001 to prohibit the execution of mentally retarded defendants also provided a procedure for defendants already sentenced to death to file motions for appropriate relief to seek relief from their death sentences on the ground that they were mentally retarded when they committed their crimes. S.L. 2001-346, sec. 3. That provision set deadlines for the filing of such motions. In most cases, the deadline was January 31, 2002. The provision, which was codified at G.S. 15A-2006, expired on October 1, 2002.

10. G.S. 15A-2005.

Enmund Defendants

The United States Supreme Court has held that the death penalty may not be imposed on a defendant who "aids and abets a felony in the course of which a murder is committed by others but who does not himself kill, attempt to kill, or intend that a killing take place or that lethal force will be employed."[11] In other words, certain defendants who are convicted of first-degree murder only as aiders or abettors of a felony murder are ineligible for the death penalty. This issue is discussed in more detail in Chapter 4.

D. Prosecutorial Discretion in Seeking the Death Penalty

Before 2001, our appellate courts held that the state was required to seek the death penalty in all cases of first-degree murder in which there was evidence of an aggravating circumstance that might warrant its imposition. The state was not permitted to forego pursuit of the death penalty even in exchange for a defendant's guilty plea to first-degree murder. However, in 2001, the General Assembly enacted legislation giving prosecutors the discretion to try first-degree murder cases without seeking the death penalty, even where one or more aggravating circumstances exist. This issue is discussed in more detail in Chapter 2.

E. Life Imprisonment

For an offense committed on or after October 1, 1994, an adult defendant who is convicted of first-degree murder and sentenced to life imprisonment must be sentenced to life imprisonment without parole.[12]

However, as noted above, as of July 12, 2012, defendants who were under 18 at the time they committed first-degree murder may be sentenced to life without parole or life with the possibility of parole after 25 years.

Applicable only to a first-degree murder committed before December 1, 1998, G.S. 15A-1380.5 provides that a defendant who is sentenced to life imprisonment without parole is entitled to a review of that sentence by a resident superior court judge for the county in which the defendant was convicted after the defendant has served 25 years in prison.[13] After conducting the specified review set out in the statute, the judge must recommend to the governor (or to any executive agency or board designated by the governor) whether or not the sentence should be altered or commuted. This recommendation may be reviewed by an appellate court on appeal only for an abuse of discretion. The governor or the agency or board must consider the judge's recommendation but is not bound by it.

---

11. Enmund v. Florida, 458 U.S. 782, 797 (1982).

12. G.S. 15A-2002. The issue of parole eligibility is addressed in greater detail in Chapter 4. A sentence of life imprisonment without parole does not violate the constitution of North Carolina. State v. Allen, 346 N.C. 731 (1997).

13. G.S. 15A-1380.5 was repealed by S.L. 1998-212, effective for first-degree murders committed on or after December 1, 1998.

For an offense committed before October 1, 1994, a defendant who is convicted of first-degree murder and sentenced to life imprisonment is eligible for parole for that offense after serving 25 years in prison for that offense.[14]

F. Overview of Capital Case Procedures

Generally, capital cases are governed by the same procedures that apply to other criminal cases. However, capital cases have several unique features, which are summarized below.

Pretrial

There are several pretrial procedures unique to capital cases. If the state decides to pursue the death penalty in a first-degree murder case, it must inform the defendant of that fact.[15] The state must also ask for, and a superior court judge must schedule, a pretrial conference in order to attempt to simplify the issues in the case, to ensure that the defendant is appropriately represented, and to consider "such other matters as may aid in the disposition of the action."[16] An indigent defendant is entitled to the assistance of two lawyers, with the second being appointed "in a timely manner," generally at or before the pretrial conference.[17] Under certain circumstances, a defendant who asserts that he or she is mentally retarded may be entitled to a pretrial hearing on the matter.[18] Pretrial proceedings are examined in detail in Chapter 2.

Bifurcated Trial

A capital trial is conducted under a bifurcated procedure. In the first phase—commonly known as the *guilt phase* or the *guilt-innocence phase*—the guilt or innocence of the defendant is determined. Unless the defendant pleads guilty, this requires a jury trial. Issues that commonly arise at this stage of a capital trial are discussed in Chapter 3.

If the defendant is convicted of first-degree murder, either by a jury or by a plea of guilty, and there is evidence of at least one aggravating circumstance that could support a sentence of death, then a separate sentencing hearing is conducted.[19] That is the second phase of the trial, commonly known as the sentencing phase or the penalty phase.

---

14. *See* former G.S. 15A-1371(a1). Although this statute was repealed by 1994 N.C. Sess. Laws, ch. 21 Ex. Sess., a savings clause in that chapter continues to make the provision applicable to these sentences.

15. G.S. 15A-2004(b).

16. Gen. R. Prac. Super. & Dist. Cts. 24. The rule requires such a conference "in every case in which the defendant stands charged with a crime punishable by death." Because first-degree murder is "a crime punishable by death," the rule may call for a pretrial conference in every first-degree murder case, even if the state has made clear that it will not seek the death penalty in a particular matter.

17. G.S. 7A-450(b1).

18. G.S. 15A-2005(c). This issue is discussed in greater detail in Chapter 2.

19. G.S. 15A-2000(a)(1).

The Capital Sentencing Hearing

Procedures for the penalty phase of a capital trial are considered in Chapter 4. If the defendant pled guilty to first-degree murder, a jury is empaneled for this phase.[20] If the defendant was found guilty of first-degree murder, the same jury that determined guilt normally participates in the sentencing phase.[21] The purpose of the sentencing phase is for the jury to issue a sentencing recommendation, either of death or of life imprisonment. The jury's recommendation is binding upon the court.[22]

At the sentencing hearing, all evidence presented at the guilt-innocence phase is automatically available for the jury's consideration without the need to introduce it again.[23] Both the state and the defendant may introduce additional evidence.

After the evidence has been submitted and the lawyers have made their closing arguments, the trial judge instructs the jury on the law. Trial judges generally adhere closely to North Carolina Pattern Jury Instruction (hereinafter N.C.P.I.)—Crim. 150.10. Likewise, judges normally use a verdict sheet closely modeled after the verdict sheet contained in the pattern instruction.

Among the first issues considered by the sentencing jury is whether any aggravating circumstances exist.[24] This is commonly known as *Issue One.* An aggravating circumstance is a "fact or group of facts which tend to make a specific murder particularly deserving" of a death sentence.[25] Aggravating circumstances are discussed further in Chapter 5. They are limited to those listed in G.S. 15A-2000(e). They include such circumstances as the defendant previously had been convicted of a violent felony; the murder was especially heinous, atrocious, or cruel; the murder was committed for pecuniary gain; or the murder was committed during a course of conduct that included violent crimes against people other than the murder victim. The state must prove the existence of aggravating circumstances beyond a reasonable doubt, and the jury's finding of an aggravating circumstance must be unanimous. If the jury unanimously[26] finds no aggravating circumstances, it must recommend a sentence of life

---

20. G.S. 15A-2000(a)(2).

21. *Id.* In *State v. Berry*, 356 N.C. 490, 498 (2002), the court stated that "a trial court may not select for the guilt-innocence phase of a trial a panel of jurors, some of whom oppose the death penalty while others are not so opposed, with the understanding that different jurors, all of whom are unopposed to the death penalty, will be substituted for the sentencing proceeding." *See also* State v. Bondurant, 309 N.C. 674, 682 (1983) (holding that such a proposed procedure "contravenes G.S. 15A-2000(a)(2), which contemplates that the same jury which determines guilt will recommend the sentence").

22. G.S. 15A-2002.

23. G.S. 15A-2000(a)(3).

24. In some cases, the jury must first deliberate on additional issues. The first is whether the defendant is ineligible for the death penalty under *Enmund v. Florida*, 458 U.S. 782 (1982), discussed briefly above and in more detail in Chapter 4. Only if the jury finds in favor of the state on this issue will it consider whether aggravating and mitigating circumstances exist. If the jury finds in favor of the defendant, the defendant automatically will be sentenced to life imprisonment. The second issue that the jury may be required to consider before determining the existence of aggravating and mitigating circumstances is whether the defendant is mentally retarded. A person who is mentally retarded may not be sentenced to death, as noted above and discussed in more detail in Chapters 2 and 4.

25. N.C.P.I.—Crim. 150.10.

26. G.S. 15A-2000(b) ("The sentence recommendation must be agreed upon by a unanimous vote of the 12 jurors"). In *State v. McCarver*, 341 N.C. 364, 389 (1995), the court ruled that "any jury recommendation requiring a sentence of death or life imprisonment must be unanimous." In other words, the answer "no" as well as the answer "yes" to Issues One, Three, and Four, must be unanimous. (Issues Three and Four are discussed in the main text below.) The court stated that requiring unanimity for either yes or no answers for these issues "ensures that the jury *properly* fulfills its duty to deliberate *genuinely* for a *reasonable* period of time . . . in reaching a unanimous sentencing recommendation, as required by the Constitution of North Carolina and by our death penalty statute itself." *Id.* at 392 (emphases in original). The court also stated that if the jury is unable to agree unanimously as to one of these issues, it should simply report that fact to the trial judge whose duty

imprisonment. If it finds one or more aggravating circumstances, it uses the verdict form to indicate which aggravating circumstances it found and continues to the next issue.

The next issue normally considered by the jury, commonly known as *Issue Two*, is whether any mitigating circumstances exist. Mitigating circumstances consist of facts or conditions "which may be considered as extenuating or reducing the moral culpability of [a] killing or make it less deserving of [a death sentence] than other first-degree murders."[27] Mitigating circumstances are separated into two categories: *statutory* and *nonstatutory*. Statutory mitigating circumstances are those specifically described in G.S. 15A-2000(f). Examples of statutory mitigating circumstances include the following: the defendant had no significant history of prior criminal activity; the murder was committed while the defendant was under the influence of mental or emotional disturbance; the defendant's capacity to appreciate the criminality of his or her conduct or to conform that conduct to the requirements of the law was impaired; or the defendant's age at the time of the murder. Nonstatutory mitigating circumstances include any aspects of the defendant's character or record or the murder itself that may call for a sentence other than death.[28] For example, the defendant showed remorse for committing the murder; the defendant was a victim of childhood abuse; the defendant was honorably discharged from the military; or the defendant was well-behaved while in jail awaiting trial. Mitigating circumstances are addressed in Chapter 6.

A defendant must prove a statutory or nonstatutory mitigating circumstance by a preponderance of evidence. However, the jury need not unanimously find the existence of a mitigating circumstance in order to consider that circumstance in its sentence recommendation. Instead, each individual juror may find a mitigating circumstance to exist and must then consider that circumstance when deliberating with the other jurors.[29] The jury uses the verdict form to indicate whether any jurors found each of the mitigating circumstances submitted to the jury.

If any jurors found any mitigating circumstances, the jury then considers *Issue Three*, which asks whether the state has proven beyond a reasonable doubt that the mitigating circumstances are insufficient to outweigh the aggravating circumstances.[30] If the jury unanimously[31] answers "no" to this question—in other words, if the jury concludes that the mitigating circumstances *are* sufficient to outweigh the aggravating circumstances—it must recommend that the defendant be sentenced to life imprisonment.[32]

If no jurors found any mitigating circumstances, or if the jury unanimously agrees that the mitigating circumstances are insufficient to outweigh the aggravating circumstances, the jury then proceeds

---

would then be to impose a sentence of life imprisonment. However, the jury should not initially be made aware of the law about the consequences of their inability to agree unanimously because revealing such information "would be an open invitation to the jury—or a single juror—to avoid its responsibility to *fully* deliberate and to force a recommendation of life [imprisonment] by the simple expedient of disagreeing." *Id.* at 394 (emphasis in original). Instead, the judge—if and only if the jury makes an inquiry about the issue—must inform the jurors that their inability to reach unanimity "should not be their concern but should simply be reported to the court." *Id.* (citation, internal quotation marks omitted). Otherwise, no instruction is warranted.

27. N.C.P.I.—Crim. 150.10.

28. *Id.*

29. *Id.*; McKoy v. North Carolina, 494 U.S. 433, 444 (1990) (holding that the rule in effect at that time, which required the jury to be unanimous regarding mitigating circumstances, "impermissibly limit[ed] jurors' consideration of mitigating evidence"); State v. Lee, 335 N.C. 244 (1994).

30. In answering this issue, each individual juror considers any mitigating circumstances he or she found under Issue Two, but a juror who did not find a particular mitigating circumstance is not required to consider a mitigating circumstance found by another juror. State v. Skipper, 337 N.C. 1 (1994); *Lee*, 335 N.C. 244.

31. *See supra* note 26.

32. N.C.P.I.—Crim. 150.10.

Figure 1. Determining the Jury's Recommendation

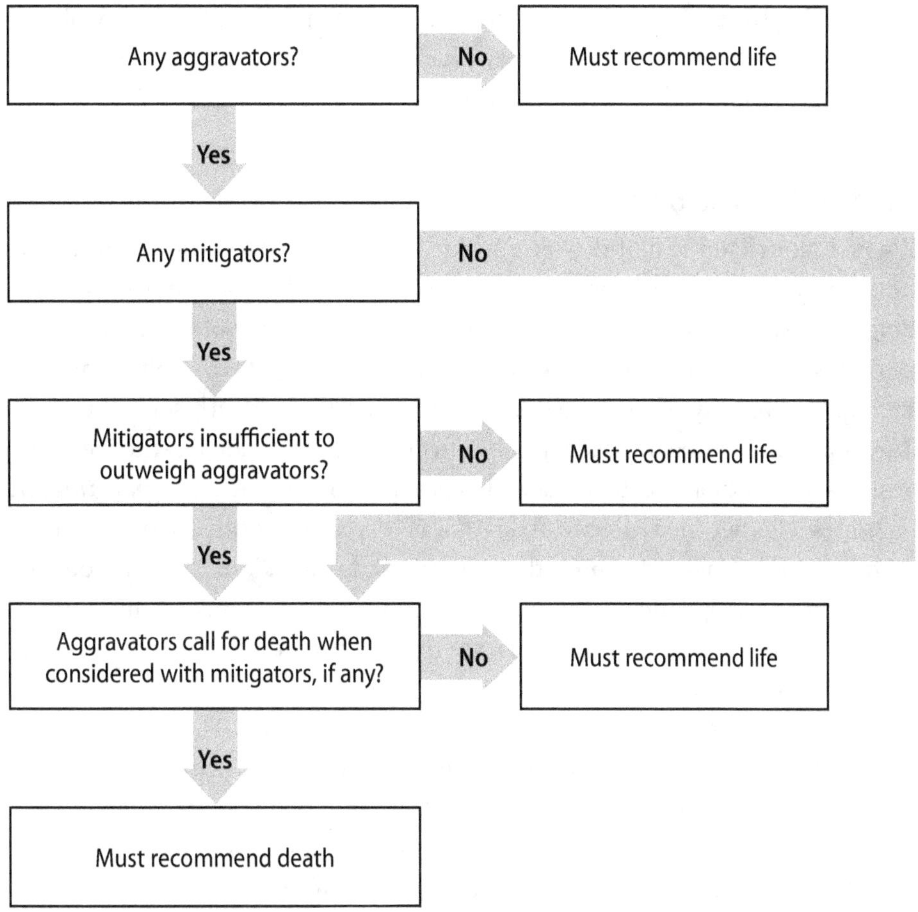

to the final issue, generally known as *Issue Four*: whether the aggravating circumstances, when considered with the mitigating circumstances, are sufficiently substantial to impose the death penalty. If the jury unanimously[33] answers "no" to this question, it must recommend that the defendant be sentenced to life imprisonment. If the jury unanimously answers "yes" to this question, it must recommend that the defendant be sentenced to death.[34]

If the jury does not unanimously agree to a sentence recommendation within a reasonable time, G.S. 15A-2000(b) requires the trial judge to impose a sentence of life imprisonment.[35] If the jury unanimously agrees to a sentence recommendation, the trial court then must poll the jurors individually to make sure that the jury's recommendation is each individual juror's recommendation.[36]

33. *See supra* note 26.

34. A jury instruction that imposes a duty on a jury to recommend a death sentence is constitutional. State v. McDougall, 308 N.C. 1 (1983); State v. DeCastro, 342 N.C. 667 (1996).

35. In *State v. Kirkley*, 308 N.C. 196 (1983), the court ruled that what constitutes a reasonable time for jury deliberations is left to the trial judge's discretion, subject to appellate review for abuse of that discretion.

36. In *State v. Lee*, 335 N.C. 244 (1994), the court ruled that the trial court must poll the jury only on their final recommendation—death or life imprisonment—not the subsidiary issues leading to that recommendation.

As noted above, the trial judge is bound by the jury's recommendation and must impose the recommended sentence of death or life imprisonment.[37]

Figure 1, above, illustrates the decisions to be made by the jury at the penalty phase of a capital case. (It depicts the basic process of the penalty phase but does not include decisions that must be made by some capital juries, such as whether the defendant is mentally retarded.)

Appellate and Other Postconviction Review

A defendant who is convicted of first-degree murder and sentenced to death is entitled to automatic review of the case by the North Carolina Supreme Court.[38] If the court finds no error in the trial and sentencing phases, it must then determine whether the sentence of death "was imposed under the influence of passion, prejudice, or any other arbitrary factor."[39] If the court finds that the death sentence was imposed for any of these reasons, it must vacate the death sentence and order that a sentence of life imprisonment be imposed. If the court finds that the death sentence was not imposed for any of those reasons, it then must conduct what is commonly known as *proportionality review*, in which it determines whether the sentence of death was "excessive or disproportionate to the penalty imposed in similar cases, considering both the crime and the defendant."[40] If the court finds that the death penalty was not disproportionate, it must affirm the death sentence. If the court finds that the death penalty was disproportionate, it must vacate the death sentence and order that a sentence of life imprisonment be imposed.[41]

If the North Carolina Supreme Court affirms the death sentence, that completes a defendant's automatic right to direct appellate review of the case. What follows is a discussion of the typical path a defendant may take in seeking further review of his or her case.

A defendant may file a petition for a writ of certiorari to the United States Supreme Court to review any questions of federal law addressed in the ruling of the North Carolina Supreme Court that affirmed the defendant's conviction and death sentence.

A defendant may then file a motion for appropriate relief in the state superior court where the trial was conducted.[42] That motion is generally limited to issues that were not required to be asserted in the initial appeal to the North Carolina Supreme Court.[43] Grounds that are commonly asserted in this motion include, among others, the alleged ineffective assistance of counsel who represented the defendant at trial, the state's failure to disclose exculpatory evidence to the defendant for use at the

37. State v. Smith, 305 N.C. 691 (1982); State v. Hutchins, 303 N.C. 321 (1981). *See also* State v. Johnson, 298 N.C. 355 (1979) (trial judge has no authority to grant a defendant's motion to set aside a death sentence on the ground that the sole aggravating circumstance found was not supported by the evidence; only the supreme court decides that issue).

38. G.S. 15A-2000(d)(1).

39. G.S. 15A-2000(d)(2).

40. *Id.* See *State v. Bacon*, 337 N.C. 66 (1994), for the court's ruling on what cases are included in the proportionality pool from which the court makes this determination. The most recent case in which the supreme court found the death penalty disproportionate was *State v. Kemmerlin*, 356 N.C. 446, 488 (2002) (finding that the death penalty was a disproportionate punishment for a wife convicted of the first-degree murder of her husband, in part because the evidence of the sole aggravating circumstance was "weak," the jury found multiple mitigating circumstances, and the wife's co-defendant was not sentenced to death).

41. *See, e.g.*, State v. Benson, 323 N.C. 318 (1988).

42. For an overview of motions for appropriate relief, see Jessica Smith, *Motions for Appropriate Relief*, Admin. of Just. Bull. No. 2010/03 (UNC School of Government, June 2010), www.sog.unc.edu/pubs/electronicversions/pdfs/aojb1003.pdf.

43. *See generally* G.S. 15A-1419.

trial or sentencing hearing, and the discovery of new evidence that would entitle the defendant to a new trial. If the motion for appropriate relief is denied, the defendant may seek appellate review by filing a writ of certiorari with the North Carolina Supreme Court. If that review is unsuccessful, the defendant may file a petition for a writ of certiorari to the United States Supreme Court to review the denial of the motion.

A defendant who has exhausted his or her state remedies may file a petition for a writ of habeas corpus in the appropriate federal district court (the eastern, middle, or western district of North Carolina, depending on where the trial was held) to review the case for federal constitutional errors. If the district court denies the petition, the defendant may seek review of the district court's decision in the United States Court of Appeals for the Fourth Circuit. If the Fourth Circuit denies relief, the defendant may file a petition for a writ of certiorari to the United States Supreme Court to review that ruling.

If the review discussed above has been unsuccessful, a defendant may have additional opportunities for state and federal court review, depending on the law and facts in the case, including filing a claim under the Racial Justice Act,[44] discussed in Chapter 7. A defendant may also seek relief through the North Carolina Innocence Inquiry Commission.[45]

Finally, the governor of North Carolina has the authority under Section 5(6) of Article III of the Constitution of North Carolina to grant reprieves (delays in the execution of a sentence), commutations (for example, a reduction in the punishment from death to life imprisonment), and pardons (which may include a release from punishment or guilt or both).[46] Although this authority may be exercised at any time after a conviction, the governor will usually make a decision on a request for a commutation of a death sentence, for example, near the time of execution and after legal challenges to the conviction and sentence have been exhausted.

Manner of Execution

G.S. 15-187 provides that the execution of a defendant is by the administration of lethal drugs.[47] There has been recent litigation concerning the state's execution protocol,[48] though the details of that litigation are beyond the scope of this book. G.S. 15-188 requires that the execution be carried out at Central Prison in Raleigh.[49]

---

44. G.S. 15A-2010 *et seq.*

45. *See generally* G.S. 15A-1460 *et seq.*

46. For cases on the exercise of the clemency power, see *Bacon v. Lee*, 353 N.C. 696 (2001) (court upheld constitutionality of Governor Easley's exercise of clemency power), and *Ohio Adult Parole Authority v. Woodard*, 523 U.S. 272 (1998) (court ruled that Ohio's clemency proceedings for death-row inmate did not violate due process).

47. State v. Hunt, 357 N.C. 454 (2003) (G.S. 15-187 and G.S. 15-188 do not limit the drugs or chemicals that can be used during execution by lethal injection).

48. Conner v. N.C. Council of State, 365 N.C. 242, *reh'g denied*, 365 N.C. 367 (2011). The course of this litigation may be affected by S.L. 2012-136, which removes from G.S. 15-188 the requirement that the Council of State approve the execution protocol. Additional legislative changes are under consideration at the time of this writing.

49. The statute states that the execution is to be carried out at the "North Carolina penitentiary at Raleigh, North Carolina." That facility is commonly known as Central Prison.

Chapter 2

Selected Pretrial Issues

Chapter 2

Selected Pretrial Issues

This chapter discusses selected pretrial issues that commonly arise in North Carolina capital cases. While some issues are unique to first-degree capital murder cases, others are common to all criminal cases.

A. Indictment for First-Degree Murder

A defendant may not be tried for first-degree capital murder unless he or she has been indicted by a grand jury. An information may not be used to charge this offense.[1]

Charging Language

G.S. 15-144 states that when charging murder, "it is sufficient . . . to allege that the accused person feloniously, willfully, and of his malice aforethought, did kill and murder" the victim. This charging language is sufficient to charge "both first-degree and second-degree murder,"[2] and it is sufficient to charge first-degree murder even if the caption of the indictment does not indicate the degree of murder being charged.[3] An indictment that contains this charging language is commonly known as a *short-form indictment,* since it does not specifically allege all the elements of first-degree murder. The sufficiency of the short-form indictment has been upheld.[4] The Administrative Office of the Courts has promulgated an indictment form for murder that uses the short-form language and contains a checkbox to indicate whether first-degree or second-degree murder is being charged.[5]

---

1. Section 15A-642(b) of the North Carolina General Statutes (hereinafter G.S.).
2. State v. Braxton, 352 N.C. 158, 174 (2000).
3. State v. King, 311 N.C. 603 (1984).
4. In *State v. Hunt,* 357 N.C. 257 (2003), the defendant argued that the use of the short-form indictment was unconstitutional under *Ring v. Arizona,* 536 U.S. 584 (2002), and that it violated the command in G.S. 15A-924(a)(5) that an indictment must contain allegations concerning "every element of a criminal offense." The Supreme Court of North Carolina rejected both arguments, noting that the sufficiency of the short-form indictment has repeatedly been challenged and upheld.
5. The form is AOC-CR-124. Omitting the word "aforethought" may be another way of limiting the charge to second-degree murder. *See* State v. McGee, 47 N.C. App. 280 (1980). *But cf.* State v. Smith, 221 N.C. 278 (1942) (stating that "malice aforethought" does not connote premeditation and deliberation). For another charging form for murder, see Jeffrey B. Welty, Arrest Warrant and Indictment Forms (UNC School of Government, 6th ed. 2010).

A short-form indictment is legally sufficient to allege all theories of first-degree murder,[6] which include:

1. A murder committed with premeditation and deliberation.
2. Felony murder, that is, a murder committed in the perpetration or attempted perpetration of any arson, rape, sex offense, robbery, kidnapping, burglary, or other felony committed or attempted with the use of a deadly weapon.
3. A murder perpetrated by means of poison, lying in wait, imprisonment, starving, or torture.
4. A murder perpetrated by means of a nuclear, biological, or chemical weapon of mass destruction as defined in G.S. 14-288.21.[7]

If the indictment contains all of the short-form language but also contains additional allegations concerning a particular theory of first-degree murder, the indictment does not limit the state to the particular theory but, rather, remains sufficient to support any theory of first-degree murder.[8] By contrast, if the state elects not to use the short-form language but instead to charge the defendant *only* using allegations concerning a particular theory of first-degree murder, the state is limited to the theory alleged.[9]

When the state indicts a defendant for first-degree murder under the felony murder rule, it is not also required to indict the defendant for the underlying felony or felonies.[10] The murder indictment need not specify the predicate felony on which the state intends to rely, nor is the defendant entitled to that information through a bill of particulars, for it constitutes the state's "theory of the case."[11]

A first-degree murder indictment need not allege the aggravating circumstances that the state will seek to prove to support the death penalty.[12]

Amendments to the Indictment and Variances

Amendments to, and variances from, murder indictments are comprehensively addressed in another publication, and that discussion will not be repeated here.[13]

---

6. *See, e.g.*, State v. Garcia, 358 N.C. 382, 388 (2004) (stating that "this Court has consistently held that [short-form] murder indictments . . . are sufficient to charge first-degree murder on the basis of *any theory*" of first-degree murder) (emphasis in original); *Braxton*, 352 N.C. at 174 ("[T]he short-form indictment is sufficient to charge first-degree murder on the basis of any of the theories, including premeditation and deliberation, set forth in [G.S.] 14-17."); State v. Brown, 320 N.C. 179, 191–92 (1987) (noting that the short-form indictment is sufficient to charge premeditation and deliberation, felony murder, and lying in wait).

7. G.S. 14-17 (establishing four theories of first-degree murder); Jessica Smith, North Carolina Crimes 83–90 (UNC School of Government, 7th ed. 2012) (summarizing each theory).

8. State v. Moore, 284 N.C. 485, 495–96 (1974) ("[A]n indictment drawn under G.S. 15-144 will support a verdict of murder in the first degree without any further allegation of premeditation and deliberation or in the perpetration or attempt to perpetrate a felony. If the bill does allege a malicious killing after premeditation and deliberation, nevertheless the conviction will be sustained if the evidence shows and the jury finds the killing was done in the perpetration or in the attempt to perpetrate a felony.").

9. State v. Davis, 253 N.C. 86 (1960) (when the state alleged felony murder specifically rather than using the short-form language, it was bound to its theory).

10. State v. Carey, 288 N.C. 254 (1975); State v. Williams, 305 N.C. 656 (1982); State v. Scott, 150 N.C. App. 442 (2002); State v. Dudley, 151 N.C. App. 711 (2002).

11. *Garcia*, 358 N.C. at 390.

12. State v. Hunt, 357 N.C. 257 (2003).

13. Jessica Smith, *The Criminal Indictment: Fatal Defect, Fatal Variances, and Amendment*, Admin. of Just. Bull. No. 2008/03 (UNC School of Government, July 2008), www.sog.unc.edu/pubs/electronicversions/pdfs/aojb0803.pdf.

Lesser-Included Offenses of Short-Form Indictment

As discussed in greater detail in Chapter 3, a defendant is entitled to an instruction on a lesser-included offense when there is evidence from which the jury could find that the defendant committed the lesser offense and not the greater.[14] On the other hand, if the evidence is positive as to each element of the greater offense and there is no conflicting evidence, an instruction on a lesser-included offense is not warranted.[15]

Lesser-included offenses of first-degree murder charged in a short-form indictment are second-degree murder, voluntary manslaughter, and involuntary manslaughter.[16] Attempted first-degree murder is also a lesser-included offense,[17] though an instruction on attempted first-degree murder will be required only in unusual circumstances.[18]

Felony and misdemeanor assaults are not lesser-included offenses of first-degree murder charged in a short-form indictment.[19] If the state wants assault offenses to be submitted to the jury, it must charge those offenses in additional counts of the indictment or in additional indictments.

B. Theories of First-Degree Murder

Generally

As noted above, first-degree murder is the unlawful killing of another living human being taking any of the following forms:

1. A murder committed with premeditation and deliberation.
2. Felony murder, that is, a murder committed in the perpetration or attempted perpetration of any arson, rape, sex offense, robbery, kidnapping, burglary, or other felony committed or attempted with the use of a deadly weapon.
3. A murder perpetrated by means of poison, lying in wait, imprisonment, starving, or torture.

---

14. *See, e.g.*, Beck v. Alabama, 447 U.S. 625 (1980) (federal Due Process Clause requires a lesser-included offense instruction in a capital case when there is evidence to support such an instruction); State v. Conaway, 339 N.C. 487, 514 (1995) (stating that a judge must instruct on a lesser-included offense if "there is any evidence in the record which would support" a conviction of the lesser rather than the greater).

15. *See, e.g.*, State v. Taylor, 362 N.C. 514, 530–31 (2008); State v. Rose, 339 N.C. 172, 194 (1994); State v. Thomas, 325 N.C. 583, 592 (1989) (reversing first-degree murder conviction for failure to instruct on involuntary manslaughter where some evidence supported the latter).

16. *See, e.g.*, State v. Muhammad, 186 N.C. App. 355, 361 (2007) ("[T]he jury received instructions on possible lesser included offenses of second degree murder, voluntary manslaughter, and involuntary manslaughter in addition to first degree murder"); North Carolina Pattern Jury Instruction (hereinafter N.C.P.I.)—Crim. 206.10 (listing lesser-included offenses as possible verdicts).

17. State v. Collins, 334 N.C. 54, 59 (1993). In *State v. Coble*, 351 N.C. 448, 451 (2000), the court ruled that attempted second-degree murder is not a crime under North Carolina law.

18. For example, in *Collins*, 334 N.C. at 57, there was evidence that "tended to show that the gunshot wound inflicted upon the victim did not in any way contribute to his death," so that the jury might conclude that the defendant shot the victim in an attempt to kill him but that the victim actually died for unrelated reasons.

19. State v. Gibson, 333 N.C. 29, 38 (1992) (holding that assaults are not lesser-included offenses of first-degree murder charged by short-form indictment "because such [a] murder indictment does not specify a murder accomplished by assault"), *overruled on other grounds by* State v. Lynch, 334 N.C. 402 (1993); State v. Whiteside, 325 N.C. 389 (1989) (similar). *Cf.* State v. Garris, 191 N.C. App. 276 (2008) (assault with a deadly weapon with intent to kill is not a lesser-included offense of attempted first-degree murder); State v. Rainey, 154 N.C. App. 282, 285 (2002) ("[A]ssault with a deadly weapon inflicting serious injury is not a lesser-included offense of attempted first-degree murder.").

4. A murder perpetrated by means of a nuclear, biological, or chemical weapon of mass destruction as defined in G.S. 14-288.21.[20]

Attempt, solicitation, conspiracy, and being an accessory after the fact to first-degree murder are not Class A felonies and therefore are not capital felonies.[21]

By contrast, one who aids and abets, or acts in concert with another to commit,[22] first-degree murder is guilty of first-degree murder, a Class A capital felony.[23] However, as discussed briefly in Chapter 1 and in greater detail in Chapter 4, certain defendants who are guilty of first-degree murder only as aiders or abettors of a felony murder are ineligible for the death penalty under United States Supreme Court precedent.

Finally, G.S. 14-5.2 provides that a person who "heretofore would have been . . . an accessory before the fact" to a felony is a principal. Therefore, a person who, under prior law, would have been an accessory before the fact to first-degree murder is in fact guilty of first-degree murder, a Class A capital felony. However, if such a person is convicted and "the jury finds that his conviction was based solely on the uncorroborated testimony of one or more principals, coconspirators, or accessories to the crime," the person is guilty only of a Class B2 felony.[24] The death penalty could not be imposed on such a person since it is not an authorized punishment for a Class B2 felony.[25] Also, if all the principals to a first-degree murder are acquitted, an accessory before the fact may not be convicted.[26] A few additional cases on accessories before the fact are set out in the margin.[27]

---

20. G.S. 14-17 (establishing four theories of first-degree murder); JESSICA SMITH, NORTH CAROLINA CRIMES 83–90 (UNC School of Government, 7th ed. 2012) (summarizing each theory).

21. *See generally* SMITH, *supra* note 20, at 67–75, 76–78 (discussing these offenses and the punishment for each).

22. There is little difference between these two theories. *See, e.g.*, State v. Williams, 299 N.C. 652, 656 (1980) (stating that "[t]he distinction between aiding and abetting and acting in concert, however, is of little significance"). Both theories are discussed in SMITH, *supra* note 20, at 29–34.

23. *See, e.g.*, State v. Kemmerlin, 356 N.C. 446, 475 (2002) (one who acts in concert to commit a crime is guilty "as a principal") (quoting G.S. 14-5.2); State v. Bond, 345 N.C. 1, 24 (1996) (a defendant may be "convicted of first-degree murder under a theory of aiding and abetting").

24. G.S. 14-5.2.

25. G.S. 15A-1340.17.

26. SMITH, *supra* note 20, at 35. *But cf.* State v. Wilson, 338 N.C. 244 (1994) (defendant may be convicted of first-degree murder on the theory of accessory before the fact even though all the principals had pled guilty to second-degree murder; a principal's plea to a lesser crime is different from a jury's acquittal); State v. Larrimore, 340 N.C. 119 (1995).

27. State v. Davis, 319 N.C. 620 (1987) (noting that the elements of accessory before the fact to murder are (1) the defendant counseled, procured, commanded, encouraged, or aided the principal to murder the victim; (2) the principal murdered the victim; and (3) the defendant was not present when the murder was committed; and holding that the judge must instruct the jury to determine whether there was the necessary causal connection between the accessory's actions and the principal's commission of the murder); State v. Marr, 342 N.C. 607 (1996) (holding that the trial judge erred in submitting only the theory that the defendant was an accessory before the fact to first-degree murder committed with premeditation and deliberation and not the theory that the defendant was an accessory before the fact to first-degree felony murder; although on appeal, the state conceded that there was insufficient evidence to support the former theory, there was sufficient evidence to support the latter, and retrial on the latter theory was permissible). *See also* N.C.P.I.—CRIM. 202.30 (providing pattern jury instructions for cases in which the defendant allegedly acted as an accessory before the fact).

Premeditation and Deliberation

Generally, "[p]remeditation means that the act was thought out beforehand for some length of time, however short, but no particular amount of time is necessary for the mental process of premeditation."[28] And "[d]eliberation means an intent to kill, carried out in a cool state of blood . . . and not under the influence of a violent passion, suddenly aroused by lawful or just cause or legal provocation."[29] Deliberation does not require "a total absence of passion or emotion,"[30] so long as the defendant's anger or passion does not overcome his or her reason.[31]

Circumstances, among others, to consider in determining whether a killing was committed with premeditation and deliberation are

1. the absence of provocation by the deceased,
2. the defendant's conduct and statements before and after the killing,
3. the defendant's threats and declarations before and during the occurrence that led to the death of the deceased,
4. ill will or prior difficulties between the defendant and the deceased,
5. lethal blows to the deceased after the deceased has been felled and rendered helpless,
6. the brutality of the killing, and
7. the nature and number of the deceased's wounds.[32]

A large number of recent cases have found sufficient evidence of premeditation and deliberation. A few are cited in the margin,[33] but there are many more.

In a few cases, North Carolina's appellate courts have found insufficient evidence of premeditation. Examples include the following:

State v. Reese, 319 N.C. 110 (1987). Although the defendant was guilty of first-degree murder based on the felony murder rule for planning an armed robbery with his accomplice and being constructively present during the robbery, there was insufficient evidence of premeditation and deliberation when the defendant did not participate in the killing, did not intend that a killing take place, and did not know that his accomplice intended to kill the victim. The law does not impute premeditation and deliberation from the person who actually kills the victim to another person who is responsible for the murder because of his or her participation in the underlying felony. Note, however, that *Reese* has been substantially overruled by *State v. Barnes*, 345 N.C. 184 (1997).

State v. Corn, 303 N.C. 293 (1981). The court stated that all the evidence tended to show that the defendant shot the victim "after a quarrel, in a state of passion, without aforethought or calm consideration."

---

28. State v. Conner, 335 N.C. 618, 635–36 (1994).

29. *Id.* at 636.

30. N.C.P.I.—Crim. 206.10.

31. *See generally* Smith, *supra* note 20, at 85.

32. State v. Crandell, 208 N.C. App. 227, 232 (2010). These factors have been listed in countless opinions of North Carolina's appellate courts; virtually all of them can be traced back at least as far as *State v. Williams*, 308 N.C. 47 (1983).

33. State v. Taylor, 362 N.C. 514, 531 (2008) (sufficient evidence in part because the defendant entered a store "armed with a semiautomatic weapon and joined by an [armed] accomplice . . . [suggesting] [t]hat defendant was prepared to fire his weapon in the event of a confrontation"); State v. Robinson, 355 N.C. 320 (2002); *Crandell*, 208 N.C. App. at 233; State v. Blue, 207 N.C. App. 267 (2010) (sufficient evidence even though defendant may have been high on drugs).

State v. Williams, 144 N.C. App. 526 (2001), *aff'd per curiam*, 355 N.C. 272 (2002). There was no evidence that the defendant and the victim knew each other before their altercation; no evidence of animosity or that the defendant had made threatening remarks to the victim; the evidence showed that the defendant was provoked by the victim's assault, to which the defendant immediately retaliated by firing one shot resulting in immediate cessation of the altercation after the victim fell; and the defendant's actions before and after the shooting did not show planning or forethought.

A trial judge may submit the case to the jury on the theory of premeditation and deliberation over the state's objection if the evidence supports the theory.[34]

Felony Murder

Under G.S. 14-17, a murder "committed in the perpetration or attempted perpetration of any arson, rape or a sex offense, robbery, kidnapping, burglary, or other felony committed or attempted with the use of a deadly weapon" is first-degree murder. Murders committed in this manner are called felony murders. A felony murder need not be committed with premeditation and deliberation, or even intentionally.[35] However, the killing must be done by the defendant or one of his or her accomplices; if an accomplice or a bystander is killed "at the hands of an adversary to the crimes," the death is not felony murder.[36]

Predicate Felonies

Sometimes questions arise about whether a particular crime qualifies as one of the six offenses listed in the statute: arson, rape, sex offense, robbery, kidnapping, and burglary. For example, in *State v. Williams*,[37] the court held that burglary with explosives under G.S. 14-57 is a "burglary" as that term is used in G.S. 14-17. A similar issue might arise if, for example, the state sought to argue that the offense of taking indecent liberties with a child under G.S. 14-202.1 was a "sex offense" or that certain of the burning offenses in Article 15 of Chapter 14 of the General Statutes qualified as "arson." No cases address the latter examples.

Another issue that arises with respect to felony murder is which crimes fall within the statutory residual clause, "or other felony committed or attempted with the use of a deadly weapon." Generally, any intentional felony fits within the statute, so long as a deadly weapon is involved.[38] Among others, appellate cases have found that the following crimes fit: murder;[39] felony child abuse, where

34. In *State v. Hales*, 344 N.C. 419 (1996), the court held that a trial judge properly submitted the case on the theory of premeditation and deliberation despite the prosecutor's announcement at a pretrial conference as well as at a charge conference that the state would not seek a conviction based on that theory but, rather, would pursue only felony murder. The court said that the judge "was not deprived of [his] right and duty to determine what bases for the offense the evidence would support because the district attorney had a different opinion" and asserted that "[t]he evidence and defense tactics should have been the same whether the theory of premeditation and deliberation was or was not submitted to the jury." *Id.* at 423.

35. *See generally* SMITH, *supra* note 20, at 86–88.

36. State v. Bonner, 330 N.C. 536, 537 (1992) (no felony murder where the defendant's accomplices were killed by a security guard working at the restaurant the defendant and the accomplices sought to rob).

37. 334 N.C. 440 (1993).

38. In *Hales*, the defendant used gasoline and fire to burn an occupied mobile home, killing a person who was inside the mobile home. The defendant was convicted of first-degree murder based on felony murder, the theory being the commission of a felony with a deadly weapon. The court ruled that the use of gasoline and fire to burn an occupied mobile home was sufficient evidence of a deadly weapon.

39. State v. Weeks, 322 N.C. 152 (1988); State v. Hutchins, 303 N.C. 321 (1981).

the defendant's hands were deadly weapons;[40] discharging a firearm into occupied property or an occupied vehicle;[41] larceny, where the defendant carried a gun;[42] burning a building used for trade, where the defendant used fire bombs to burn the building;[43] escape from prison;[44] crime against nature;[45] and attempted sale of cocaine.[46]

An important limitation on the residual clause is that felony murder may only be based on crimes committed intentionally. Crimes committed only by culpable negligence cannot support felony murder. For example, in *State v. Jones*,[47] the defendant, driving while impaired by alcohol and drugs, recklessly collided with another vehicle and killed two of its occupants and seriously injured three others. The defendant was convicted of two counts of felony murder, with the predicate felonies being the assaults with a deadly weapon inflicting serious injury against the three injured occupants. The state supreme court ruled that the defendant was improperly convicted of felony murder because the felonious assaults were only committed through culpable negligence. The court stated that a defendant must purposely resolve to commit the underlying felony in order to use that felony as a predicate for felony murder.

Another limitation on felony murder was expressed in *Jones*: In "cases involving a single assault victim who dies of his injuries . . . the assault on the victim cannot be used as an underlying felony for purposes of the felony murder rule. Otherwise, virtually all felonious assaults . . . that result in . . . death would be first-degree murders via felony murder, thereby negating lesser homicide charges such as second-degree murder and manslaughter."[48] This can be called the part-and-parcel assault rule because it precludes assaults that are part and parcel of a homicide from being used as felony murder predicates.[49]

Just how closely related must the assault and the homicide be in order for the part-and-parcel assault rule to apply? Very closely, under *State v. Carroll*.[50] In *Carroll*, the defendant struck the victim with a machete, then strangled her. He was convicted of felony murder, with assault with a deadly weapon inflicting serious injury—based on the blow with the machete—as the underlying felony. The

40. State v. Pierce, 346 N.C. 471 (1997) (2-year-old victim; defendant's behavior also qualified as murder by torture). *Cf.* State v. Ridgeway, 185 N.C. App. 423 (2007).

41. State v. Cook, 334 N.C. 564 (1993); State v. Wall, 304 N.C. 609 (1982).

42. State v. Fields, 315 N.C. 191 (1985) (the defendant and his accomplices entered a storage shed, removed items, and were checking to see if the house was occupied when the victim approached to investigate; the defendant then shot and killed the victim; the court found no error with a felony murder conviction because the defendant carried a gun during the commission of the larceny, even though he did not use it to commit the larceny). *But see* State v. Pakulski, 319 N.C. 562 (1987) (evidence was insufficient to support felony murder based on breaking or entering where the defendants did not possess a deadly weapon during the initial breaking but instead later obtained the deadly weapon from the murder victim, a security guard, who was in the building).

43. State v. Avery, 315 N.C. 1 (1985).

44. State v. Lee, 277 N.C. 205 (1970).

45. State v. Doss, 279 N.C. 413 (1971), *death sentence vacated*, 408 U.S. 939 (1972). The conduct at issue in *Doss*—forcible anal sex—would today normally be charged as a first-degree sexual offense under G.S. 14-27.4.

46. State v. Freeman, 202 N.C. App. 740 (2010). *Cf.* State v. Squires, 357 N.C. 529 (2003) (affirming conviction but focusing on the sufficiency of the evidence of the underlying felony, not on whether it fell within the scope of G.S. 14-17).

47. 353 N.C. 159 (2000).

48. *Id.* at 170 n.3.

49. It is sometimes also called the merger rule because the assault and the homicide are said to merge together, but that name is confusing because of the *other* felony murder merger rule, which requires the sentencing judge to arrest judgment on the predicate felony. *See, e.g.*, State v. Millsaps, 356 N.C. 556, 560 (2002) ("When a defendant is convicted of felony murder only, the underlying felony constitutes an element of first-degree murder and merges into the murder conviction.").

50. 356 N.C. 526 (2002).

state supreme court affirmed, holding that "[t]he victim . . . did not die as a result of the assault with the machete. The blow to her head was not fatal. Rather, the cause of death was strangulation. As such, the assault was a separate offense from the murder. Accordingly, the trial court did not err in submitting a felony murder instruction to the jury because the felonious assault did not merge into the homicide."[51] *Carroll* appeared to involve a slight time gap between the blow with the machete and the strangulation, and perhaps the result would be different if the non-fatal assault were followed immediately by the fatal one—for example, if A stabbed B during a fight then immediately shot him.

Whether and how *Jones* applies to felonies that are not denominated as assaults but involve similar conduct is unclear. For example, is felony child abuse subject to the part-and-parcel assault rule? We have very little law in this important area. Several pre-*Jones* cases affirmed felony murder convictions based on felonies that are similar to assaults.[52] And while the court of appeals has continued to follow these precedents for the specific offenses involved,[53] the holding of *Jones* calls the reasoning of these cases into question.

Continuous Transaction Doctrine

Under the continuous transaction doctrine, "a person may commit felony murder when the felony . . . occurs before, during, or soon after the victim's death, as long as the felony and the murder form one continuous transaction."[54] The doctrine often comes up when the predicate felony is armed robbery; in such cases, it does not matter whether the robbery takes place before or after the killing.[55] In fact, it is immaterial "whether the intention to commit the taking of the victim's property was formed before or after the killing,"[56] so long as the robbery and the homicide are part of a single series of events. The continuous transaction doctrine is not, of course, limited to robberies, and it has been applied to a range of predicate felonies including arson,[57] discharging a firearm into occupied property,[58] attempted sale of cocaine,[59] larceny,[60] felony assault,[61] sexual offense,[62] and others. The doctrine has also been applied to reject the arguments of defendants who claimed that they could not be criminally responsible for would-be predicate felonies because their victims were already dead at the time of their actions.[63]

---

51. *Id.* at 535.

52. *See, e.g.*, State v. Wall, 304 N.C. 609 (1982) (discharging a firearm into an occupied vehicle); State v. Pierce, 346 N.C. 471 (1997) (felony child abuse).

53. *See, e.g.*, State v. Jackson, 189 N.C. App. 747 (2008) (discharging a firearm into an occupied vehicle).

54. Smith, *supra* note 20, at 87.

55.*See, e.g.*, State v. Campbell, 359 N.C. 644 (2005).

56. State v. Handy, 331 N.C. 515, 529 (1992).

57. *See, e.g.*, State v. Jaynes, 342 N.C. 249 (1995).

58. State v. Moore, 339 N.C. 456 (1994) (the defendant shot into a house occupied by the victim and others; when the victim came outside to confront the defendant, the defendant shot him; homicide was part of a continuous transaction with the discharging offense).

59. State v. Freeman, 202 N.C. App. 740 (2010).

60. In *State v. Fields*, 315 N.C. 191 (1985), the court ruled that the murder victim's death occurred during the perpetration of a felony larceny when the defendant and his accomplices entered a storage shed, removed items, and were checking to see if the house was occupied when the victim approached to investigate; the defendant then shot and killed the victim.

61. State v. Abraham, 338 N.C. 315 (1994); State v. Terry, 337 N.C. 615 (1994).

62. State v. Thomas, 329 N.C. 423 (1991); State v. Williams, 308 N.C. 47 (1983).

63. State v. Cook, 334 N.C. 564, 575 (1993) ("Given that the victim was mortally wounded during a volley of gunfire from defendants' firearms, the temporal order of the fatal shot by [the] defendant . . . and other shots fired by [a co-defendant] . . . is immaterial. The underlying felony and the murder occurred in a time frame that can be perceived as a single transaction," making it irrelevant whether the victim was already dead when the defendant fired at him); *Thomas*, 329 N.C. at 434 ("Because the sexual act was committed during a continuous

There is no bright-line test for whether a predicate felony and a homicide are part of the same transaction or series of events. In *State v. Jaynes,*[64] an accomplice and the defendant murdered the victim in his mobile home, left the scene, and returned several hours later to burn the mobile home (with the murder victim's dead body inside) to destroy the evidence. The court ruled that the defendant was properly convicted of first-degree felony murder, with the predicate felony being first-degree arson. The time interval between the murder and arson was short enough so that both crimes were part of one continuous transaction.[65] In *State v. Freeman,*[66] the defendant and an accomplice delivered cocaine to the victim in exchange for a promise of future payment. When the victim had not paid a week later, they shot and killed her. The court of appeals ruled that the attempted sale of cocaine was ongoing and that the homicide was part of the continuing transaction.

Murder by Torture

Under G.S. 14-17, murder "perpetrated by means of . . . torture" is first-degree murder. The pattern jury instruction states that in order to convict the defendant on this theory, the state must prove that the defendant intentionally tortured the victim and that the torture proximately caused the victim's death.[67] "Torture" is defined in the instruction as a course of conduct involving the intentional infliction of "grievous pain and suffering,"[68] and this is consistent with the case law.[69] The state need not prove malice,[70] premeditation and deliberation,[71] or a specific intent to kill[72] in order to prove murder by torture.

Fact patterns that have been deemed sufficient to qualify as torture include: forcing a child to drink large amounts of water as a method of discipline;[73] repeatedly beating and battering a child over a period of one week[74] or several weeks;[75] and repeatedly beating, cutting, binding, and gagging an adult victim over a period of several days.[76] Though no challenge to the sufficiency of the evidence was raised, a conviction for murder by torture was also affirmed where the defendant beat the victim, his girlfriend, apparently striking dozens of blows over the course of several hours and causing extensive bruising and lacerations as well as multiple broken ribs.[77]

Murder by Poisoning

Under G.S. 14-17, murder "perpetrated by means of . . . poison" is first-degree murder. The pattern jury instruction states that in order to convict the defendant on this theory, the state must prove that the defendant "intentionally caused a substance known to him to be poison to . . . enter the body of

---

transaction that began when the victim was alive, we conclude the evidence was sufficient to support defendant's conviction for first-degree sexual offense."). *See also Williams* 308 N.C. 47 (similar to *Thomas*).

64. 342 N.C. 249 (1995).

65. *See also* State v. Campbell, 332 N.C. 116 (1992) (similar).

66. 202 N.C. App. 740 (2010).

67. N.C.P.I.—CRIM. 206.20.

68. *Id.*

69. *See, e.g.,* State v. Pierce, 346 N.C. 471 (1997); State v. Anderson, 346 N.C. 158 (1997); State v. Crawford, 329 N.C. 466 (1991).

70. *Crawford,* 329 N.C. 466.

71. State v. Lee, 348 N.C. 474 (1998); State v. Phillips, 328 N.C. 1 (1991); State v. Johnson, 317 N.C. 193 (1986).

72. *Pierce,* 346 N.C. 471.

73. *Crawford,* 329 N.C. 466.

74. *Lee,* 348 N.C. 474.

75. *Pierce,* 346 N.C. 471; *Phillips,* 328 N.C. 1.

76. State v. Anderson, 346 N.C. 158 (1997).

77. State v. Stroud, 345 N.C. 106 (1996).

the victim" and that the poisoning was a proximate cause of the victim's death.[78] As with murder by torture, the state need not prove malice, intent to kill, or premeditation and deliberation in order to prove murder by poisoning.[79] The pattern jury instruction defines poison as "a substance . . . likely to cause death (by a chemical reaction) when . . . caused to enter the body."[80] The reported cases have generally involved substances that unquestionably qualify as poisons, such as arsenic[81] and pesticides.[82] Unintended deaths resulting from the distribution of controlled substances are generally second-degree murders,[83] though it is possible to imagine an extreme case in which a first-degree murder case could be brought.

Murder by Lying in Wait

Under G.S. 14-17, murder "perpetrated by means of . . . lying in wait" is first-degree murder. The pattern jury instruction provides that in order to convict the defendant on this theory, the state must prove that the defendant "waited and watched for the victim in ambush for a private attack on him," intentionally assaulted the victim, and proximately caused the victim's death.[84] As with the theories discussed immediately above, the state need not prove malice, intent to kill, or premeditation and deliberation in order to prove murder by lying in wait.[85]

Although the archetype of lying in wait may be a case in which the defendant hides him or herself for a protracted period of time in a location likely to be visited by the victim, then springs out to launch an assault,[86] the theory is not limited to such cases. The defendant need not be in position for any particular period of time,[87] nor must the victim be unaware of the defendant's presence, so long as the victim is unaware of the defendant's murderous purpose.[88] However, there must be "some sort of ambush and surprise of the victim," and the state supreme court has found insufficient evidence of lying in wait where the defendant had threatened the victim, then went to her workplace, chased her across the parking lot, forced her into a car, and stabbed her.[89]

---

78. N.C.P.I.—Crim. 206.12.

79. State v. Smith, 351 N.C. 251 (2000); State v. Johnson, 317 N.C. 193 (1986).

80. N.C.P.I.—Crim. 206.12.

81. State v. Lanier, 165 N.C. App. 337 (2004); State v. Moore, 335 N.C. 567 (1994); State v. Detter, 298 N.C. 604 (1979).

82. *Smith,* 351 N.C. 251.

83. G.S. 14-17 (providing that murders proximately caused by the distribution of specified drugs is second-degree murder); Smith, *supra* note 20, at 92–93 (discussing this fact pattern).

84. N.C.P.I.—Crim. 206.16. The use of the phrase "private attack" may be misleading, insofar as "a person may lie in wait in a crowd as well as behind a log or a hedge." State v. Allison, 298 N.C. 135, 148 (1979). So long as the attack is a surprise on the victim, it may constitute lying in wait, as discussed below.

85. State v. Leroux, 326 N.C. 368 (1990).

86. *See, e.g.,* State v. Baldwin, 330 N.C. 446 (1992) (closet); State v. Battle, 322 N.C. 69 (1988) (behind a clothes dryer).

87. State v. Brown, 320 N.C. 179, 193 (1987) (the defendant snuck up to the victim's window, waited for the victim to bend down, then shot him; "[t]he duration of the pause before the kill is . . . irrelevant.").

88. *Leroux,* 326 N.C. 368; *Allison,* 298 N.C. 135.

89. State v. Lynch, 327 N.C. 210, 217 (1990). *See also* State v. Camacho, 337 N.C. 224, 229 (1994) (evidence conflicted regarding whether the defendant was lying in wait before he killed the victim, so the jury should have been instructed on lesser-included offenses; although the state's evidence was that the defendant hid in the victim's closet and waited for her, the defendant's evidence was that he was in the victim's room to retrieve some personal belongings when he was overcome with "head rushes" resulting from his excessive use of alcohol and cocaine, dropped some tools, and was attacked by the victim before he killed her); State v. Holcombe, 203 N.C. App. 530, 536 (2010) (analogizing the crimes of secret assault and murder by lying in wait and finding the following commonalities in murder by lying in wait cases: "For most of the victims, their first awareness of potential danger occurred simultaneously with the assaults themselves. Also, most of the defendants were concealed and

C. Prosecutor's Decision to Seek the Death Penalty

Before 2001, our appellate courts held that the state was required to seek the death penalty in all cases of first-degree murder in which there was evidence of an aggravating circumstance that might warrant its imposition.[90] The state was not permitted to forego pursuit of the death penalty even in exchange for a defendant's guilty plea to first-degree murder.[91] This was principally a matter of statutory interpretation.[92] The version of G.S. 15A-2000 in effect prior to 2001 said that "[u]pon conviction or adjudication of guilt of a defendant of a capital felony . . . the court shall conduct a separate sentencing proceeding to determine whether the defendant should be sentenced to death or life imprisonment." The appellate courts interpreted the word "shall" to mean that a penalty phase was mandatory and likewise interpreted the version of G.S. 15A-2001 then in effect to require a penalty phase even in guilty plea cases.

In 2001, the General Assembly enacted legislation to give prosecutors the discretion to try a first-degree murder case without seeking the death penalty, even where one or more aggravating circumstances exist.[93] The legislation effectively reversed the rulings referenced above, though it may be argued that it did not reverse the cases' requirement that *if* the state chooses to seek the death penalty, it must submit all the aggravating circumstances supported by the evidence.[94]

---

waiting for their victims prior to the victims' arrival at the scene. Finally, each defendant took some deliberate action to disguise either his presence or his purpose from the victim. All of these factors indicate that the victims were taken by surprise and were unable to defend themselves from the assaults.").

90. *See, e.g.,* State v. Case, 330 N.C. 161 (1991).

91. *See, e.g.,* State v. Johnson, 298 N.C. 355 (1979).

92. However, on at least two occasions, the appellate courts su ggested that the lack of discretion might be a constitutional imperative. For example, in *Case,* 330 N.C. 161, the court said: "The decision as to whether a case of murder in the first degree should be tried as a capital case is not within the district attorney's discretion. . . . This is so in order to prevent capital sentencing from being . . . arbitrary. If our law permitted the district attorney to exercise discretion . . . our death penalty scheme would be arbitrary and, therefore, unconstitutional." *Id.* at 163. If the court were correct on this point, then the General Assembly's subsequent statutory authorization of discretion would be ineffective. But the court's remark, offered without citation, is inconsistent with *Gregg v. Georgia,* 428 U.S. 153, 199 (1976), which upheld Georgia's death penalty scheme despite the defendant's argument that "the state prosecutor has unfettered authority to select those persons whom he wishes to prosecute for a capital offense and to plea bargain with them" and stated that "[t]he existence of these discretionary stages is not determinative of the issues before us. . . . Nothing in any of our cases suggests that the decision to afford an individual defendant mercy violates the Constitution." Therefore, the comment in *Case,* like a somewhat similar remark in *State v. Johnson,* 298 N.C. 47 (1979), is probably best viewed as dicta.

93. S.L. 2001-81, codified at G.S. 15A-2004.

94. *See, e.g., Case,* 330 N.C. at 163 ("If our law permitted the district attorney to exercise discretion as to when an aggravating circumstance supported by the evidence would or would not be submitted, our death penalty scheme would be arbitrary and, therefore, unconstitutional."). *Case* and other decisions tend to conflate (1) the issue of whether a prosecutor has discretion regarding whether to seek the death penalty and (2) the issue of whether a prosecutor who is seeking the death penalty has discretion regarding whether to submit an aggravating circumstance that is supported by the evidence. To the extent that these issues are viewed as inseparable or indistinguishable, the enactment of G.S. 15A-2004 arguably reversed the courts' holdings on both. However, G.S. 15A-2004 by its terms addresses only the former issue, not the latter. As to the implementation of the *Case* "all aggravators" rule, see *State v. Prevatte,* 356 N.C. 178 (2002) (where the state requested the submission of aggravating circumstance G.S. 15A-2000(e)(3) (prior violent felony conviction) rather than G.S. 15A-2000(e)(2) (prior capital felony conviction) based on the defendant's prior murder conviction, the rule of *Case* was not violated because "[w]hether it was styled as a capital felony or as a violent felony, the fact that defendant had been convicted previously of murder was submitted to the jury for its consideration." *Prevatte,* 356 N.C. at 256); *State v. McNeil,* 350 N.C. 657 (1999) (the state sought to join three murders for trial, but the trial judge refused to join one of them; the defendant then pled guilty to the two joined murders; the state agreed that it would not seek to introduce evidence of the third murder; the rule of *Case* was not violated because the

Under G.S. 15A-2004, a prosecutor who wishes to seek the death penalty must give notice of the state's intent to do so by the later of arraignment or the Rule 24 conference, which is discussed below. If notice is not timely given, the case may only be tried noncapitally. This procedure appears to provide sufficient notice to the defendant to satisfy the requirements of due process.[95]

Sometimes, a defendant may argue that the prosecutor has abused his or her discretion in seeking the death penalty. "The prosecutor has discretion to consider numerous factors in determining whether a murder case should be tried capitally,"[96] including the number of aggravating circumstances, the seriousness of the case, and the treatment of similar cases. The prosecutor may also consider the wishes of the victim's family.[97] It is not inherently arbitrary "for a prosecutor to ask the jury for the death penalty in one case and not in another despite evidence of an aggravating circumstance in both."[98] However, if the defendant can establish that the decision to proceed capitally was based on the defendant's race, religion, or other improper consideration, the defendant will be entitled to relief.[99] The issue of racial discrimination in charging decisions is discussed further in Chapter 7 in connection with the Racial Justice Act.

Finally, it is worth noting that when a defendant is charged using a short-form indictment, a prosecutor also has discretion regarding whether to seek a conviction of first-degree murder or only second-degree murder. The state may change its position and prosecute a defendant for first-degree murder even though it had previously announced that it would only prosecute the defendant for second-degree murder.[100] However, the state must give the defendant sufficient notice of its change of position to ensure that the defendant's rights to due process and effective assistance of counsel are not violated.[101] A trial judge may grant a continuance of the trial to make sure that these rights are protected. (Of course, even if the state may prosecute the defendant for first-degree murder, it will not be able to seek the death penalty if it failed to give timely notice under G.S. 15A-2004, discussed above.)

---

evidence of the third murder was inadmissible as a result of the joinder ruling; the court also stated, citing G.S. 15A-1443(c), that the defendant, by opposing joinder, could not be prejudiced by a ruling he had requested).

95. Lankford v. Idaho, 500 U.S. 110 (1991) (finding a due process violation where the state indicated prior to sentencing that it was not seeking the death penalty but the trial judge nonetheless elected to impose it).

96. State v. Barden, 356 N.C. 316, 385 (2002).

97. State v. Wilson, 311 N.C. 117, 124 (1984) ("We find nothing impermissible about the district attorney's consideration of the wishes of the family as *one factor* in determining which defendants will be prosecuted for murder in the first degree and thereby subjected to the death penalty.") (emphasis in original).

98. State v. Jones, 327 N.C. 439, 451 (1990).

99. State v. Garner, 340 N.C. 573, 588 (1995) ("[T]he decision to prosecute capitally may not be deliberately based upon an unjustifiable standard such as race, religion, or other arbitrary classification."); *Wilson*, 311 N.C. at 124 (suggesting that if the defendant had been able to show that "the district attorney's decision to prosecute him for murder in the first degree and seek the death penalty was based upon 'an unjustifiable standard such as race, religion, or other arbitrary classification,'" he would have established an equal protection violation.).

100. State v. Hickey, 317 N.C. 457 (1986). *See also* State v. Wallace, 345 N.C. 462 (1997) (the state's offer of a second-degree murder plea, which was rejected by a judge after hearing evidence of the murder at the plea hearing, did not bar a later trial on first-degree murder; the defendant's double jeopardy rights were not violated because jeopardy does not attach until a plea is accepted by a judge). The state's change of position must be made before jeopardy attaches, i.e., before the jury is sworn and impaneled. Of course, if the state changes its position near the beginning of a trial, a defendant ordinarily would be entitled to a continuance. Note also that G.S. 7A-451(b1) states that an indigent defendant in a case when the state is seeking the death penalty is entitled to the appointment of a second defense lawyer in a "timely manner."

101. *Hickey*, 317 N.C. 457. *See also* Lankford v. Idaho, 500 U.S. 110 (1991) (defendant's due process rights were violated because he did not have adequate notice at the time of the sentencing hearing that the trial judge might sentence him to death); State v. Jones, 317 N.C. 487 (1986) (although the defendant was arguably indicted for first-degree rape, the prosecutor arraigned the defendant for second-degree rape and failed thereafter to give any notice to the defendant of an intent to prosecute for first-degree rape until after the jury had been sworn and impaneled; the conviction of first-degree rape was vacated).

D. Rule 24 Mandatory Pretrial Conference

Rule 24 of the General Rules of Practice for the Superior and District Courts requires a pretrial conference in every "case in which the defendant stands charged with a crime punishable by death."[102] The Rule 24 hearing is "the pivotal point in the pretrial proceedings when the court may declare the case capital, triggering appointment of second counsel and making public resources available to aid an indigent accused in preparing his defense."[103]

Not later than ten days after the superior court obtains jurisdiction—typically when an indictment is returned—the district attorney must apply to a superior court judge, who then must order the prosecutor and defense counsel to appear before the court within forty-five days for the conference, although a continuance is permitted. Among the matters to be discussed at this conference are the nature of the charges against the defendant, the existence of aggravating circumstances, and timely appointment of assistant counsel for an indigent defendant if the state is seeking the death penalty.

At the hearing, the state need not identify the particular aggravating circumstances on which it intends to rely.[104] Similarly, the North Carolina Supreme Court has ruled that a judge does not err in denying a defendant's motion for a bill of particulars requiring the state to disclose the aggravating circumstances on which it will rely in sentencing.[105] Nonetheless, at the Rule 24 hearing, the state will normally be asked to forecast at least a part of the evidence it intends to present at sentencing. If, after the hearing, the court finds that "there exists no evidence of an aggravating circumstance," it may declare the case noncapital.[106]

If the state fails to request a timely Rule 24 hearing, the court may enforce the Rule's mandates "through the contempt power or disciplinary action."[107] The state supreme court has ruled that trial courts also "have inherent authority to declare a case noncapital as a sanction for the State's violation of Rule 24," but only if "the State's noncompliance caused sufficient prejudice to warrant declaring the

---

102. First-degree murder is the only crime punishable by death. As to whether there must be a Rule 24 hearing in first-degree murder cases in which the state is not seeking the death penalty, the better reading of the rule seems to require such a hearing. First-degree murder remains a "crime punishable by death" even when the state has elected not to pursue that punishment in a particular case. Further, Rule 24(2) states that an issue to be considered at the conference is "appointment of assistant counsel . . . when the State is seeking the death penalty." The reference to "when the State is seeking the death penalty" would be superfluous if the conference were to be held only in cases to be tried capitally. In practice, however, Rule 24 hearings are not always held in noncapital first-degree murder cases.

103. State v. Defoe, 364 N.C. 29, 36 (2010). The reference to "public resources" appears to mean "funds for second counsel and mitigation experts." However, as the court's opinion notes, a defendant may seek the appointment of second counsel and the assistance of a mitigation specialist before the Rule 24 hearing.

104. State v. Chapman, 342 N.C. 330, 339 (1995) ("[N]othing in the rule intimates that the prosecution must enumerate with finality all aggravating circumstances it will pursue at trial. . . . In fact, a trial court cannot require the prosecution to declare which aggravating circumstances it will rely upon at the punishment phase.").

105. State v. Baker, 338 N.C. 526 (1994). *See also* State v. Brown, 306 N.C. 151 (1982) (state's failure to list the (e)(11) aggravating circumstance (murder part of violent course of conduct) in response to trial judge's pretrial order did not bar the submission of that circumstance based on the facts in this case; judge had no authority to order state to disclose its aggravating circumstances under G.S. 15A-925); State v. Hill, 331 N.C. 387 (1992) (indictment need not list aggravating circumstances on which state will rely).

106. State v. Seward, 362 N.C. 210, 211 (2008). However, the court may not declare a case noncapital based upon its conclusion that there is insufficient evidence of first-degree murder. *Id.* at 216 (reasoning that probable cause has already been established by the grand jury).

107. *Defoe*, 364 N.C. at 36. *See also* State v. Rorie, 348 N.C. 266 (1998) (decided prior to the 2001 amendments to G.S. 15A-2000 and superseded by that statute as stated in *Defoe*).

case noncapital."[108] However, the General Assembly recently amended G.S. 15A-2004(b) to provide that "[a] court may discipline or sanction the State for failure to comply with the time requirements in Rule 24, but shall not declare a case as noncapital as a consequence of such failure."[109] How this legislative enactment will be reconciled with the inherent authority of trial judges remains to be resolved.

The defendant does not have a right to be present at this conference, either under the defendant's unwaivable state constitutional right to be present at his or her trial (see the discussion of this issue in Chapter 3) or the provisions of Rule 24.[110]

E. Pretrial Hearing to Determine Sufficiency of Evidence of Aggravating Circumstances

The state or the defendant may make a motion for a pretrial hearing, commonly known as a *Watson* hearing,[111] to determine whether there is sufficient evidence of an aggravating circumstance to try the case as first-degree capital murder. A judge has the discretion whether to conduct such a hearing,[112] which in some cases may be an efficient way to determine whether a case is properly capital. If the judge decides to conduct a *Watson* hearing, he or she considers the evidence presented at the hearing and rules whether there is sufficient evidence of an aggravating circumstance to try the case capitally.[113] In ruling on the motion, the judge must use the same standard applied in determining a motion to dismiss a criminal charge at the end of the presentation of evidence, which means that the state is entitled to every reasonable inference arising from the evidence.[114] Neither the state nor the defendant has a right to appeal the judge's ruling, but either could file a writ of certiorari (a discretionary writ) with the North Carolina Supreme Court requesting the court to review the trial judge's ruling.[115] Although "the duty of the trial court in Rule 24 conferences is similar to that of a *Watson* hearing," Rule 24 has not supplanted *Watson* hearings, which remain available.[116]

108. *Defoe*, 364 N.C. at 36. The court does not state in its opinion what type of showing might suffice, but it did reject the defendant's argument that a two-and-a-half-year delay prejudiced the defendant because it prevented him from obtaining second counsel or a mitigation specialist. *Id.* at 37.

109. S.L. 2012-136 (effective for Rule 24 hearings scheduled on or after July 2, 2012).

110. State v. Chapman, 342 N.C. 330, 338 (1995) (noting that "a defendant's right to be present at all stages of his trial does not arise prior to the commencement of trial")).

111. In *State v. Watson*, 310 N.C. 384 (1984), the court commented with approval that a trial judge had conducted such a pretrial hearing. Thereafter, this type of hearing became known as a *Watson* hearing.

112. State v. Wilds, 133 N.C. App. 195 (1999) (judge did not abuse discretion in denying defendant's motion for *Watson* hearing).

113. It is not clear whether the rules of evidence apply at such a hearing. *See generally* G.S. 8C-1 (North Carolina Rules of Evidence), Rules 104(a), 1101.

114. State v. Gaines, 332 N.C. 461 (1992).

115. In *Gaines*, 332 N.C. 461, the court granted the state's petition for a writ of certiorari and reversed the trial judge's ruling that an aggravating circumstance did not exist.

116. State v. Seward, 362 N.C. 210, 215 (2008).

F. Pretrial Hearing on Mental Retardation

The Eighth Amendment[117] and North Carolina statutory law[118] prohibit the imposition of the death penalty on a defendant who is mentally retarded. Mental retardation is defined in G.S. 15A-2005(a)(1)a to require "[s]ignificantly subaverage general intellectual functioning, existing concurrently with significant limitations in adaptive functioning, both of which were manifested before the age of 18." Generally, a defendant is considered mentally retarded if his or her IQ is 70 or below and he or she is significantly limited in two or more of the adaptive skill areas listed in the statute, such as communication, self-care, social skills, and the like.[119]

G.S. 15A-2005(c) provides that when the defendant's motion is supported by appropriate affidavits, the court *may* order a pretrial hearing to determine whether the defendant is mentally retarded. If the state consents, the court *must* hold a pretrial hearing. At this hearing, the defendant has the burden of proving mental retardation by clear and convincing evidence. If the court determines that the defendant is mentally retarded, it must declare the case to be noncapital. If the court determines that the defendant is not mentally retarded, the defendant has the right to present the issue of mental retardation to the jury at the capital sentencing hearing, as discussed in Chapter 4.

G. Joinder and Severance

Because it is efficient to handle related cases at the same time, the state may move to join for trial two or more charges against a defendant if they are transactionally connected. A sufficient connection exists if the offenses are based (a) on "the same act or transaction" or (b) on "a series of acts or transactions connected together or constituting parts of a single scheme or plan."[120] Among the factors that courts consider when determining whether there is a sufficient connection to warrant joinder are the time lapse between the offenses and whether the offenses involve a common *modus operandi*.[121]

A defendant may move to sever offenses that have been joined for trial. Such a motion normally must be made before trial begins.[122] If a pretrial motion to sever is denied, the defendant may renew that motion "before or at the close of all the evidence."[123] Any right to sever offenses is waived if the defendant fails to renew the motion,[124] though the judge's initial joinder decision remains subject to appellate review.[125]

---

117. Atkins v. Virginia, 536 U.S. 304 (2002).

118. G.S. 15A-2005(b).

119. Such circumstances satisfy, respectively, the "significantly subaverage general intellectual functioning" and "significant limitations in adaptive functioning" components of the statutory definition of mental retardation. The *Atkins* Court noted the definitions used by the American Association of Mental Retardation and the American Psychiatric Association. 536 U.S. at 308 n.3. All three definitions are quite similar, so there is little reason to believe that the constitutional and statutory requirements for death eligibility are significantly different.

120. G.S. 15A-926(a).

121. State v. Williams, 355 N.C. 501 (2002).

122. G.S. 15A-927(a)(1).

123. G.S. 15A-927(a)(2).

124. G.S. 15A-927(a). *See also* State v. Mitchell, 342 N.C. 797 (1996).

125. In *State v. Silva*, 304 N.C. 122 (1981), the court stated that the correctness of the trial judge's decision to join offenses for trial must be determined at the time of the judge's decision and not in light of subsequent developments in the case. If later developments show the joinder to have been improper, a defendant may protect his or her rights by moving to sever. A defendant who fails to make and to renew a motion for severance waives his or her right to severance. *See also* State v. McDonald, 163 N.C. App. 458, 463–64 (2004) (stating that after a defendant forfeits his or her right to severance by failing to renew a motion to sever, an appellate court may still

Just as related cases against a single defendant may be joined for trial, so, too, may the related cases of multiple defendants be joined for trial. Indeed, "[p]ublic policy supports consolidation of trials where defendants are alleged to be responsible for the same behavior."[126] The state may move to join two or more defendants for trial when:

1. Each of the defendants is charged with accountability for each offense, or
2. The charged offenses were
    a. Part of a common scheme or plan,
    b. Part of the same act or transaction, or
    c. So closely connected in time, place, and occasion that it would be difficult to separate proof of one charge from proof of the other charges.[127]

A defendant may object to joinder or make a pretrial motion to sever his or her case from the other defendant or defendants on the ground that joinder of defendants would deny the defendant a fair trial; the defendant may renew that motion during trial.[128] A common ground for opposing joinder is that defendants have mutually antagonistic defenses that would deny each a fair determination of his or her guilt or innocence, especially if joinder would deny a defendant the opportunity to introduce evidence on his or her behalf.[129] Where a non-testifying defendant has made a statement incriminating a co-defendant, the state must either forego the use of the statement, sever the cases, or offer a redacted or sanitized version of the statement that omits references to the co-defendant.[130]

Case Summaries: Joinder of Offenses or Denial of Severance Was Error

State v. Weathers, 339 N.C. 441 (1994). The court ruled that the trial judge erred by joining for trial a 1989 murder charge and a later 1991 charge of willful failure to appear for the murder trial. The charges were not transactionally related under G.S. 15A-926(a). However, the court found the error to be harmless.

Case Summaries: Joinder of Offenses or Denial of Severance Was Proper

State v. Williams, 355 N.C. 501 (2002). The trial court properly joined the charges against the defendant, notwithstanding his argument that "there were fourteen separate charges [including two murders] involving seven different victims over a fifteen-month span, and the crimes themselves differed significantly." All the offenses were committed in a one-square-mile area; all involved black victims who were drug users and prostitutes; and most or all of the assaults involved strangulation and the use of an edged weapon.

State v. Hyatt, 355 N.C. 642 (2002). Joinder of two murders for trial was proper. They were committed four months apart and had many similarities: "[B]oth victims were females traveling alone on public roads; both victims were taken to isolated areas of Buncombe County; both were robbed, raped, and killed by stabbing in the left chest area; and both victims were abandoned in isolated areas."

---

review "whether the trial court abused its discretion in ordering joinder at the time of the trial court's decision to join"; note that *McDonald*, apparently improperly, applies the waiver rule for motions to sever *offenses* to the issue of severance of *defendants*).

126. State v. Tirado, 358 N.C. 551, 564 (2004).

127. G.S. 15A-926(b)(2).

128. G.S. 15A-927(c).

129. *See, e.g.*, State v. Boykin, 307 N.C. 87 (1982).

130. G.S. 15A-927(c)(1). *See also generally* Bruton v. United States, 391 U.S. 123 (1968).

State v. Chapman, 342 N.C. 330 (1995). The trial judge did not err in allowing two murders committed about two months apart to be joined for trial when the facts underlying the murders shared a common *modus operandi* and the temporal proximity was sufficient to establish a transactional connection. Both murder victims were young women with drug habits and the defendant knew both and had smoked crack with each. One victim was nude when found, and the other was nude from the waist down. Both victims suffered blunt-force trauma injuries to their heads and one victim died of strangulation and the pathologist could not exclude the possibility that the other victim had also been strangled. Both bodies were found in the lowest part of vacant houses and the houses were within two blocks of each other. The defendant exhibited a misogynistic attitude toward women. The court rejected the defendant's argument that there must be a commonality of witnesses as prerequisite to join two murder cases for trial.

State v. McNeil, 324 N.C. 33 (1989). The trial judge did not err in allowing two murders committed two days apart to be joined for trial when they were part of the defendant's plan to obtain money for rent and other bills. The defendant carried out his plan by luring each victim into his car and then driving to another location and killing her. *See also* State v. Oxendine, 303 N.C. 235 (1981) (proper joinder of murder and felonious assault committed about six to eight hours after another murder); State v. Clark, 301 N.C. 176 (1980) (proper joinder of kidnapping of victim A and kidnapping and murder of victim B that occurred only hours apart).

Case Summaries: Joinder of Defendants or Denial of Severance Was Error

State v. Hucks, 323 N.C. 574 (1988). First-degree murder charges were joined for trial against a co-defendant and the defendant. The defendant objected and made a timely motion for severance, which was denied. After the jury was impaneled and the co-defendant changed his plea from not guilty to guilty, the defendant again moved for severance and a mistrial, which was denied. The trial proceeded for the defendant after the trial judge instructed the jury that (1) the co-defendant had entered a guilty plea to the first-degree murder for which both the defendant and co-defendant were charged and (2) the jury was simultaneously to consider the evidence to be introduced at trial on the appropriateness of death or life imprisonment for the co-defendant and on the issue of the defendant's guilt or innocence. (The court noted that the initial joinder of the defendant and co-defendant was proper. It also noted that the mere fact that a defendant pleads guilty after a jury has been impaneled to determine his or her guilt or innocence in a capital case does not by itself prohibit using the same jury for the sentencing hearing for that defendant.) The court ruled that it was unfair to the defendant to require the jury to determine whether one admittedly guilty co-defendant should receive the death sentence and, based on the same evidence, simultaneously determine the defendant's guilt and innocence. On these facts, the cases against the defendants should have been severed, with one of the cases removed from the jury and another jury impaneled for either the co-defendant's sentencing or the defendant's trial.

State v. Boykin, 307 N.C. 87 (1982). The trial judge erred in joining the trials of two defendants for murder and felonious assault charges when the defense of defendant A was antagonistic toward the defense of defendant B. Joinder denied defendant B the opportunity to introduce evidence that would have explained his admissions (for example, that defendant B made these admissions to protect his brother, defendant A, who had previously been convicted of murder), which were some of the strongest evidence against him. Therefore, defendant B was denied a fair trial.

Case Summaries: Joinder of Defendants or Denial of Severance Was Proper

State v. Bell, 359 N.C. 1 (2004). The defendant's case was joined with a co-defendant's for trial. Both were charged with the same murder and related offenses. Because the charges "arose from the same series of events involving the same victim and witnesses, and the evidence tended to indicate a common scheme," joinder was proper. The fact that the co-defendant struck a juror that the defendant would have kept did not require severance. Nor was severance required because the co-defendant presented alibi witness and argued to the jury that the defendant and a third person committed the crimes.

State v. Tirado, 358 N.C. 551 (2004). Two defendants' cases were joined for trial. Both were charged with committing two murders. One had confessed, implicating both himself and the other. To avoid problems under *Bruton v. United States,* 391 U.S. 123 (1968) (holding that the Confrontation Clause precludes the admission of a non-testifying co-defendant's confession that incriminates a defendant), the state introduced a redacted version of the confession that omitted any mention of the other defendant. After the defendants were convicted, the trial judge split the case into two separate sentencing hearings, both of which were held before the same jury that determined guilt. This allowed the defendant who had confessed to introduce a complete, unredacted version of his confession during the penalty phase to show that he had been completely honest with investigators. This procedure sufficiently protected both defendants' interests and merited denial of a motion to sever by the defendant. The fact that the defendants may have disagreed during trial about whether to remove an empaneled juror who was under criminal investigation similarly failed to provide a basis for severance.

State v. Golphin, 352 N.C. 364 (2000). A defendant moved to sever his case from his co-defendant's because of *Bruton* issues and allegedly antagonistic defenses, which he was allowed to explain to the trial judge in an ex parte hearing. However, he later expressly waived any *Bruton* claim, and the state supreme court held that the defendants' positions were not so antagonistic as to deprive them of a fair trial; the state presented substantial evidence of the guilt of both defendants and so was not a "mere witness to an evidentiary battle" between the defendants.

State v. Hunt, 323 N.C. 407 (1988). The consolidation of the murder charges against the defendant and two co-defendants was not error. The court noted that even if all the defendants were tried separately, each could assert his Fifth Amendment privilege to prevent questioning by the other defendants. The court ruled that the defendants' defenses were not so antagonistic to each other to require severance.

State v. Green, 321 N.C. 594 (1988). Three first-degree murder charges were joined for trial against the co-defendant and the defendant. The court ruled that joinder of the defendants was proper and rejected the defendant's argument that the co-defendant's testimony at trial was so antagonistic to his defense that he was denied his right to a fair trial. The court noted that although the co-defendant's testimony was inimical to the defendant's defense in important respects, it was not entirely antagonistic to the defendant. The defendant was not prevented from giving exculpatory testimony or deprived of the opportunity to present inculpatory testimony of his co-defendant. *See also* State v. Lowery, 318 N.C. 54 (1986) (proper to allow joinder of defendant's trial for murder and conspiracy to commit murder with co-defendant who solicited defendant to commit murder and was charged with murder and conspiracy to commit murder; there were no antagonistic defenses); State v. Lake, 305 N.C. 143 (1982) (motion to sever based on antagonistic defenses was properly denied; although defenses were antagonistic, defendant had opportunity at trial to vigorously cross-examine co-defendant and state offered other sufficient evidence of defendant's guilt).

State v. Rasor, 319 N.C. 577 (1987). The defendant's motion to sever his trial from his co-defendant, based on *Bruton*, was properly denied because the co-defendant's statements were properly redacted and, in any event, the co-defendant testified at trial and was subject to cross-examination by the defendant. *See also* State v. Hayes, 314 N.C. 460 (1985) (joinder of charges against defendants and denial of motions for severance were proper; admission of extrajudicial statements of each defendant did not prejudice the other defendants).

State v. Oliver, 309 N.C. 326 (1983). The defendant and his co-defendant were tried jointly, and both were convicted of the first-degree murders of A and B. At a joint capital sentencing hearing, the defendant was sentenced to death for both murders and his co-defendant was sentenced to death for the murder of A and sentenced to life imprisonment for the murder of B. The North Carolina Supreme Court ordered (for reasons not related to joinder) new sentencing hearings for both death sentences of the defendant and the one death sentence of the co-defendant. Over the defendant's objection, the defendant and co-defendant were joined together for the resentencing hearing. The defendant and co-defendant received the same death sentences at the resentencing hearing. The court reviewed the facts in this case and ruled that joinder was proper.

State v. Barnett, 307 N.C. 608 (1983). The charges of first-degree murder and armed robbery were properly joined against the three defendants when the evidence showed that each defendant participated in the robbery and the victim was killed with a deadly weapon during the commission of the robbery. Each defendant was subject to conviction for the first-degree felony murder of the victim. *See also* State v. Rinck, 303 N.C. 551 (1981) (joinder of defendants for first-degree murder charge was proper; there were no antagonistic defenses).

H. Defendant's Capacity to Proceed

The Due Process Clause of the United States Constitution prohibits the state from prosecuting a defendant who is mentally incompetent.[131] Similarly, G.S. 15A-1001(a) provides that "[n]o person may be tried, convicted, sentenced, or punished for a crime" while incompetent.

The statutory test of a defendant's capacity to proceed is whether the defendant, by reason of mental illness or defect, is unable to

1. Understand the nature and object of the proceedings against him or her,
2. Comprehend his or her own situation concerning the proceedings, or
3. Assist in his or her defense in a rational or reasonable manner.[132]

The constitutional standard of competence is similar.[133]

---

131. *See, e.g.*, Godinez v. Moran, 509 U.S. 389, 396 (1993) ("A criminal defendant may not be tried unless he is competent.").

132. G.S. 15A-1001(a). *See also* State v. Jenkins, 300 N.C. 578 (1980).

133. *Godinez*, 509 U.S. at 396 ("[T]he standard for competence to stand trial is whether the defendant has sufficient present ability to consult with his lawyer with a reasonable degree of rational understanding and has a rational as well as factual understanding of the proceedings against him.") (citations, internal quotation marks omitted).

Although the issue is often raised before trial, the defendant's capacity to proceed may be raised by a judge, prosecutor, defense counsel, or the defendant at any time during a criminal case.[134] A motion raising this issue must specify the conduct of the defendant that calls into question his or her capacity to proceed.[135] Form AOC-CR-208 is sometimes used for such motions.[136] A defendant has the burden of proving that he or she lacks the capacity to proceed.[137]

A defendant's failure to raise the issue of competence waives his or her statutory right to a determination of his or her capacity to proceed. However, constitutional due process considerations mandate that a trial judge conduct a competency hearing sua sponte if there is "substantial evidence" that the defendant is not competent.[138]

G.S. 15A-1002 sets out the procedures for ordering an examination of the defendant, if appropriate, and for conducting a hearing on this issue. One significant point about which the statue is unclear is the state's right of access to the report prepared by the expert who examined the defendant. The statute states that any report

> shall be forwarded to the clerk of superior court in a sealed envelope addressed to the attention of a presiding judge, with a covering statement to the clerk of the fact of the examination of the defendant and any conclusion as to whether the defendant has or lacks capacity to proceed. A copy of the full report shall be forwarded to defense counsel, or to the defendant if he is not represented by counsel provided, *if the question of the defendant's capacity to proceed is raised at any time, a copy of the full report must be forwarded to the district attorney.*[139]

Although one could argue that the report exists only because "the question of the defendant's capacity to proceed [has been] raised," and so the report must *always* be provided to the state, the intent of the statute may be to allow the state access to the report only if the defendant persists in questioning his or her competence *after* the report has been returned.[140]

When a proper foundation has been laid, both expert and lay opinion testimony is admissible at the hearing to determine the defendant's capacity to proceed.[141]

A defendant who is competent only by virtue of medication is, nonetheless, competent to proceed.[142] There is a small body of case law regarding whether and when a defendant may be forced to take medication to restore his or her competence.[143]

---

134. G.S. 15A-1002(a).

135. *Id.*; State v. Bowie, 340 N.C. 199 (1995); State v. Taylor, 298 N.C. 405 (1979).

136. This form is available online at www.nccourts.org/Forms/Documents/1023.pdf.

137. State v. Gates, 65 N.C. App. 277 (1983). A state may constitutionally place the burden of proof on the defendant. Medina v. California, 505 U.S. 437 (1992). Although the defendant's standard of proof has not been stated in North Carolina appellate cases, it probably is proof by a preponderance of evidence. A higher standard of proof would not be constitutionally permissible. Cooper v. Oklahoma, 517 U.S. 348 (1996).

138. *See generally, e.g.,* State v. Badgett, 361 N.C. 234 (2007).

139. G.S. 15A-1002(d) (emphasis supplied).

140. Assuming that the state should not be given a copy of the report automatically, the presiding judge may still have the authority to order that the report be disclosed to the state even absent a continuing dispute about the defendant's competence. *See* G.S. 15A-1002(d) (stating that the report "shall not be revealed *except as directed by the court*" (emphasis supplied)); McCarver v. Lee, 221 F.3d 583, 596 (4th Cir. 2000) (interpreting this language as allowing the court "the discretion to reveal the contents of the reports" to the state, even in the absence of a contested competency hearing).

141. State v. Silvers, 323 N.C. 646 (1989).

142. State v. Buie, 297 N.C. 159, 161 (1979).

143. The leading case is *Sell v. United States,* 539 U.S. 166, 179 (2003), which held that the state is permitted "involuntarily to administer antipsychotic drugs to a mentally ill defendant facing serious criminal charges in

A defendant who is mentally retarded is not necessarily incompetent. The issue of a defendant's mental retardation is discussed elsewhere in this chapter and this book.

G.S. 15A-1003 through -1009 set out the process for handling a defendant who is found incapable of proceeding. G.S. 15A-1003 sets out procedures for the civil commitment of such a defendant. G.S. 15A-1004 prescribes judicial orders for safeguarding the defendant and possible return for trial. G.S. 15A-1005 sets out the clerk's duty to maintain a docket listing defendants who have been determined to be incapable of proceeding. G.S. 15A-1006 requires an institution or person who has custody of a defendant found incapable of proceeding to notify the clerk of superior court if the defendant gains the capacity to proceed. G.S. 15A-1007 describes when supplemental hearings may be held on whether the defendant has gained the capacity to proceed. G.S. 15A-1008 and -1009 set out the conditions for the dismissal, or the dismissal with leave, of charges against a defendant who has been determined to lack the capacity to proceed.

Case Summaries: Defendant's Capacity to Proceed

State v. Goode, 197 N.C. App. 543 (2009). The defendant was taking anti-anxiety medication, but one morning during the defendant's trial, the jail nurse failed to dispense the medication to the defendant before she was taken to court. Defense counsel informed the court that the defendant's mental state had deteriorated throughout the day and questioned the defendant's competence. The trial judge recessed court for the day, and trial resumed the next day without further discussion of the issue. Although "[u]nder normal circumstances," a judge must conduct a competency hearing when the issue is raised, here, "when Defendant failed to object to the trial court resuming the trial without a competency hearing, she effectively waived" her right to such a review.

State v. Coley, 193 N.C. App. 458 (2008). At the defendant's competency hearing, both sides presented expert witnesses. The trial judge found the defendant to be competent and adopted the state's expert's report as the court's findings of fact. The court of appeals ruled that "[w]hile the better practice is to make independent detailed findings of fact," it could "find no authority prohibiting the court from making findings of fact by incorporating a factual summary from a detailed report" and "adopting facts set forth in the report was not prejudicial." Furthermore, the trial court was not required to conduct a competency hearing sua sponte during trial simply because the defendant rambled in his testimony; such behavior was not new for the defendant, and the state's expert had already concluded that it did not render the defendant incompetent.

State v. Badgett, 361 N.C. 234 (2007). The trial court did not err in failing to conduct a sua sponte competency hearing during trial. No one called for such a hearing, and a defendant's "statutory right to a competency hearing [is] waived by the failure to assert that right at trial." However, a judge has a constitutional obligation to conduct a competency hearing where there is "substantial evidence" suggesting incompetence. Here, although the defendant "wrote numerous letters to the trial court and the district attorney expressing his desire for a speedy trial resulting in a death sentence," implicitly asked the jury to sentence him to death, and had an emotional outburst during sentencing, this did not constitute substantial evidence when weighed

---

order to render that defendant competent to stand trial, but only if the treatment is medically appropriate, is substantially unlikely to have side effects that may undermine the fairness of the trial, and, taking account of less intrusive alternatives, is necessary significantly to further important governmental trial-related interests." For a discussion of *Sell* and a Fourth Circuit case interpreting it, see Jeff Welty, *Fourth Circuit Decides Involuntary Medication Case*, N.C. CRIM. L., UNC SCH. OF GOV'T BLOG (Sept. 23, 2010), http://nccriminallaw.sog.unc.edu/?p=1618.

against the defendant's appropriate and intelligent interactions with his lawyers and the court and the fact that none of the defendant's three mental health experts raised doubts about his competence.

State v. King, 353 N.C. 457 (2001). The defendant did not request a competency hearing and so waived any statutory right to such a hearing. He argued that the trial judge was constitutionally required to conduct a hearing sua sponte. The state supreme court disagreed, stating that although the "defendant had received precautionary treatment for depression and suicidal tendencies several months before trial[,] . . . this evidence of past treatment, standing alone, does not constitute 'substantial evidence'" that the defendant was not competent; accordingly, the court did not mandate a hearing.

State v. Grooms, 353 N.C. 50 (2000). Defense counsel twice raised the issue of the defendant's capacity to proceed based on the defendant's refusal to present mitigating evidence at his capital sentencing hearing. The court ruled that the trial judge did not err in declining to order a psychiatric evaluation of the defendant's capacity to proceed. The court stated that the record disclosed that the defendant was adamant and unequivocal about not wanting a mental health examination; the defendant fully understood the proceedings and his rights; the defendant assisted in his own defense throughout the trial by directing the filing of motions, the questioning of witnesses, and the presentation of evidence; the defendant fully understood the ramifications of his decision not to present mitigating evidence during the sentencing hearing; and the defendant's outbursts during trial, specifically, during the voir dire of five Rule 404(b) witnesses, indicated the defendant's deliberate intent to intimidate these witnesses. In the absence of any evidence suggesting that defendant may have been incapable of proceeding, the court concluded that the trial judge did not err in deciding not to order the evaluation.

State v. Shytle, 323 N.C. 684 (1989). The court examined the evidence introduced at the hearing on the defendant's capacity to proceed and ruled that, although the defendant suffered brain damage that impaired her emotional response to situations in which she found herself, the defendant had the capacity to proceed because she had an IQ within the normal range, knew what the charges against her were, and understood what could happen to her if she were to be convicted.

State v. Silvers, 323 N.C. 646 (1989). The defendant made a pretrial motion to determine her capacity to proceed under G.S. 15A-1001. The trial judge erred in excluding testimony of two sheriff's department employees (who had an opportunity to observe the defendant during her incarceration) concerning whether the defendant understood the nature and object of the proceedings against her and was able to assist in her defense in a rational or reasonable manner. It was proper lay opinion testimony.

State v. Avery, 315 N.C. 1 (1985). The court upheld the trial judge's ruling that the defendant was competent to be tried despite some memory impairment. The court also rejected the defendant's proposed rule that when the defense is insanity and the defendant's amnesia hampers the preparation of the defense in a "crucial way," then the defendant is incompetent to stand trial. *See also* State v. Jenkins, 300 N.C. 578 (1980) (similar ruling); State v. Heptinstall, 309 N.C. 231 (1983) (defendant was competent to be tried despite diagnosis of paranoid schizophrenia); State v. Clark, 300 N.C. 116 (1980) (similar ruling).

I. Defendant's Right to Counsel and Related Issues

The Sixth Amendment to the United States Constitution guarantees a criminal defendant the right to counsel. How this guarantee is implemented depends on whether the defendant is indigent or not. A defendant is indigent if he or she "is financially unable to secure legal representation and to provide all other necessary expenses of representation."[144]

Generally, a defendant who is not indigent must hire a lawyer if he or she wants one. (Alternatively, a defendant may choose to represent him or herself, as discussed below.) Every defendant is entitled to "retain an attorney of [his or her] choice."[145] Because the General Assembly has expressed a policy preference for capital defendants having two lawyers, the North Carolina Court of Appeals has held that if such a defendant is able to afford only one attorney, a second attorney must be appointed unless the defendant waives his or her right to a second lawyer.[146] Failure to appoint a second attorney is "error *per se*," automatically requiring a new trial.[147] A defendant who exhausts his or her financial resources paying for counsel is also entitled to have the state pay necessary collateral expenses, such as expert witness fees. This subject is discussed later in this chapter.

A defendant who is indigent is generally entitled to a court-appointed lawyer if one is desired.[148] Indigent *capital* defendants are, as mentioned above, entitled to have two attorneys appointed.[149] The right to a second lawyer is statutory, not constitutional.[150] However, again as noted above, failure to appoint a second attorney is automatically reversible error.

An indigent defendant is "not entitled to counsel of his [or her] choice."[151] Rather, the Director of the Office of Indigent Defense Services (IDS) decides who will represent the defendant.[152] (In practice, the Capital Defender normally functions as the designee of the IDS Director with respect to decisions concerning the appointment of counsel in capital cases.) The first attorney should be appointed "as soon as feasible after the [defendant] is taken into custody or service is made upon him of the charge."[153] The second attorney must be appointed "in a timely manner,"[154] which the North Carolina Supreme Court has stated normally means "as soon as practicable after indictment of the

---

144. G.S. 7A-450(a).

145. State v. Taylor, 155 N.C. App. 251, 254 (2002).

146. State v. Davis, 168 N.C. App. 321 (2005) (reasoning that a second attorney is a "necessary expense[] of representation" under G.S. 7A-450(a)). By contrast, in *State v. McDowell*, 329 N.C. 363, 372–73 (1991), the defendant expressly accepted a single retained lawyer to represent him and agreed to waive "any other rights that [he] may have [had] to an additional court appointed lawyer." Under such circumstances, it was not necessary to appoint a second lawyer.

147. *Davis*, 168 N.C. App. at 330. *See also* State v. Brown, 325 N.C. 427 (1989).

148. *See generally, e.g.*, G.S. 7A-451.

149. G.S. 7A-450(b1).

150. State v. Locklear, 322 N.C. 349, 357 (1988) (noting that the right to the "appointment of additional counsel in capital cases is statutory, not constitutional" (emphasis omitted)).

151. State v. Williams, 363 N.C. 689, 699 (2009). *See also* State v. Cunningham, 344 N.C. 341 (1996) (defendant's refusal to accept all available attorneys did not require the court to appoint the out-of-state lawyer that defendant wanted).

152. G.S. 7A-498.3(c) (stating that "appointment of counsel . . . shall be in accordance with rules and procedures adopted by" IDS); Office of Indigent Defense Servs., N.C. Ct. Sys., Rules for Providing Legal Representation in Capital Cases, Part 2, § 2A.2 (amended Dec. 9, 2011), www.ncids.org/Rules%20&%20Procedures/IDS%20Rules/IDS%20Rules%20Part%202.pdf (assigning the responsibility of appointing counsel in capital cases to the IDS Director).

153. G.S. 7A-451(b). *See also* Office of Indigent Defense Servs., *supra* note 152, at § 2A.2(a) (allowing for the provisional appointment of counsel as early as when the IDS Director "learn[s] that a defendant has been charged with a capital offense").

154. G.S. 7A-450(b1).

indigent defendant on a capital charge."[155] Relevant IDS rules provide for appointment of the second lawyer upon completion of the Rule 24 hearing, although, upon request by the first lawyer, the IDS Director may appoint a second attorney at an earlier stage.[156] If two lawyers have been appointed to a case that is subsequently declared noncapital, one of the two normally must move to withdraw.[157]

IDS rules establish certain experience requirements for lead counsel and for associate counsel, positions that are sometimes also called "first chair" and "second chair."[158] The requirements may be waived by the IDS Director.[159] Even if associate counsel examines more witnesses, interposes more objections, and the like, he or she does not thereby become *de facto* lead counsel, and so is not subject to the experience requirements for lead counsel.[160]

Although a capital defendant is entitled to the assistance of two lawyers, both lawyers need not be present for every minute of the proceedings.[161] Furthermore, in the interest of maintaining an orderly courtroom, a trial judge may require that certain activities be conducted by a single lawyer—for example, making objections during jury selection,[162] conducting jury selection,[163] or objecting during a witness's testimony.[164]

Whether indigent or not, a defendant retains the right to represent him or herself. Under *Faretta v. California*,[165] part of the right to counsel is the "constitutional right to proceed without counsel."[166] However, the right to self-representation may be limited for defendants of limited competency.[167] A defendant's request to represent him or herself must be unequivocal.[168] If a defendant clearly expresses a desire to represent him or herself, the trial judge must make a "thorough inquiry" and must be satisfied that the defendant understands (1) his or her right to counsel, (2) the consequences of representing him or herself, and (3) "the nature of the charges and proceedings and the range of

---

155. State v. Hucks, 323 N.C. 574, 577 (1988).

156. Office of Indigent Defense Servs., *supra* note 152, at § 2A.2(d).

157. *Id.* at § 2A.5(c). The rule contains an exception for "exceptional circumstances."

158. *Id.* at Appendix 2A, §§ 2A.1 (App.)(a), (b), online at www.ncids.org/Rules%20&%20Procedures/IDS%20Rules/IDS%20Rules%20Part%202%20Appendix.pdf.

159. *Id.* at § 2A.1 (App.)(c).

160. State v. Howell, 335 N.C. 457 (1994) (decided with reference to the North Carolina State Bar's then-effective five-year experience requirement). In any event, it does not appear that IDS's experience requirements confer any legal rights on the defendant or, if not observed, create a legal issue for appeal.

161. State v. Thomas, 350 N.C. 315 (1999) (brief absences by associate counsel at various points during the trial did not deprive the defendant of his right to two attorneys). *See also* State v. Parker, 350 N.C. 411 (1999) (court found it was acceptable to conduct preliminary stages of jury selection in the absence of lead counsel, who was ill, where the defendant and associate counsel consented).

162. State v. Frye, 341 N.C. 470, 493 (1995) (noting that "[t]he second attorney remained present and could prompt the first when he thought objections should be made").

163. State v. Fullwood, 343 N.C. 725 (1996).

164. State v. Call, 353 N.C. 400 (2001).

165. 422 U.S. 806 (1975).

166. *Id.* at 807.

167. Indiana v. Edwards, 554 U.S. 164 (2008) (holding that a state court may, consistent with the Sixth Amendment, require a defendant to be represented where the court concludes that the defendant is competent to stand trial but not capable of representing him or herself). *See also* State v. Lane, 365 N.C. 7 (2011) (holding that a defendant was properly allowed to represent himself and noting that *Edwards* only *permits*, and does not *require*, that so-called "gray area defendants" be barred from self-representation).

168. State v. Williams, 334 N.C. 440, 455 (1993) (holding that a defendant has no right to represent him or herself if there is "any ambiguity" about his or her desire to do so); State v. Thomas, 331 N.C. 671 (1992).

possible punishments."[169] If the defendant is indigent, IDS rules require a written waiver of the right to appointed counsel.[170]

When a defendant elects to represent him or herself, a lawyer may be appointed to serve as standby counsel. Under G.S. 15A-1243, the discretion to appoint standby counsel rests with the trial judge, while under IDS rules, the determination is to be made by the IDS Director.[171] A defendant must represent him or herself or have a lawyer do so; the defendant is not entitled to participate as co-counsel along with an attorney.[172]

Generally, the role of standby counsel is "to assist the defendant when called upon and to bring to the judge's attention matters favorable to the defendant upon which the judge should rule upon his own motion."[173] Consider the following cases regarding the participation of standby counsel:

> **McKaskle v. Wiggins, 465 U.S. 168 (1984).** The defendant was charged with robbery and chose to represent himself. The court appointed standby counsel to assist him. Counsel consulted with the defendant throughout the trial and performed other tasks, such as conducting a voir dire of a witness and making an opening statement, generally with the defendant's consent. Counsel also made motions and expressed counsel's disagreement with the defendant on various issues, usually outside the presence of the jury. On appeal, the defendant argued that counsel's actions interfered with his right to represent himself, but the United States Supreme Court disagreed. It found "no absolute bar on standby counsel's unsolicited participation" in a trial. Rather, so long as the defendant retains "actual control over the case he chooses to present to the jury" and counsel's participation does not "destroy the jury's perception that the defendant is representing himself," counsel's actions are permissible. The Court noted that it is particularly "problematic" when standby counsel participates in a trial while the jury is present, but it declined to impose a categorical rule even against such participation. Measured against these standards, counsel's participation was permissible as it was often with the defendant's consent and was principally outside the jury's presence.

> **State v. Thomas, 346 N.C. 135 (1997).** The defendant requested that he be allowed to represent himself. A judge questioned the defendant in accordance with G.S. 15A-1242, obtained a written waiver of counsel, granted defendant's motion, and appointed two standby counsel. Standby counsel, acting without the defendant's consent, filed a motion requesting that they be appointed counsel to represent the defendant for the limited purpose of litigating his capacity to knowingly and intelligently waive his right to counsel and to choose to represent himself and for authorization to obtain a professional evaluation of the defendant's mental health. A judge (not the one who had originally allowed the defendant to represent himself) heard the motion ex parte and entered an order, over the defendant's objection, granting standby counsel's motion.

---

169. G.S. 15A-1242. Likewise, North Carolina case law provides that "[b]efore a defendant is allowed to waive appointed counsel, the trial court must insure that . . . the defendant . . . clearly and unequivocally waive[s] his right to counsel and instead elect[s] to proceed *pro se* . . . [and] knowingly, intelligently, and voluntarily waive[s] his right to in-court representation." State v. LeGrande, 346 N.C. 718, 722–23 (1997) (citations, internal quotation marks omitted). *See also* State v. Moore, 362 N.C. 319 (2008) (finding that the trial judge's informal colloquy with the defendant did not encompass the required inquiries).

170. Office of Indigent Defense Servs., *supra* note 152, at § 2A.3(a).

171. *Id.* at § 2A.3(b). *See generally* Jessica Smith, "Counsel Issues," *in* The Survival Guide: Superior Court Judges' Benchbook (UNC School of Government, Jan. 2010), www.sog.unc.edu/sites/www.sog.unc.edu/files/Counsel%20Issues_January%202010%20Cite%20Checked.pdf.

172. *See, e.g.,* State v. Williams, 319 N.C. 73 (1987); State v. Porter, 303 N.C. 680 (1981).

173. G.S. 15A-1243.

A hearing was held on the issue of the defendant's mental competence to execute a waiver of counsel. The judge entered an order appointing standby counsel to represent the defendant as his trial counsel. The order did not contain findings or conclusions of law that the defendant was or ever had been unable to properly waive his right to counsel under G.S. 15A-1242. The defendant was tried and convicted of first-degree murder and received a life sentence.

On appeal, the court noted that at the time standby counsel's motion was filed, a judge had found that the defendant knowingly and voluntarily waived his right to counsel and was representing himself. The court ruled that when the second judge allowed standby counsel to intervene by motion in this case, over the defendant's objection, the filing of the motion exceeded the authority of standby counsel granted under G.S. 15A-1243. The court also stated that allowing standby counsel to advocate any position over a pro se defendant's objection also interferes with the exercise of a defendant's right to self-representation. In addition, the judge's appointment of standby counsel for a limited purpose violated the rule against a defendant proceeding both pro se and by counsel, citing *State v. Thomas*, 331 N.C. 671 (1992). Due to this prohibition against hybrid representation, a judge cannot allow a defendant to proceed pro se while also appointing counsel to represent the defendant, even for a limited purpose.

State v. Rich, 346 N.C. 50 (1997). The defendant was charged with first-degree murder and was appointed counsel to represent him. The defendant asked a judge to remove his appointed counsel because he wanted to represent himself. The judge told the defendant that before he would consider removing appointed counsel he would want to have the defendant evaluated to determine his competence both to stand trial and to represent himself. The defendant told the judge that there was "nothing wrong with [his] head" and he would not cooperate with any mental health evaluation. After additional inquiry, the judge granted the defendant's request to represent himself but also appointed standby counsel.

About two months later, at trial, standby counsel made a motion for the trial judge to find that the defendant was incompetent to waive counsel and requested that the trial judge review the defendant's mental health records. The trial judge questioned the defendant thoroughly about his decision not to cooperate with a mental health evaluation and explained the capital sentencing procedure. The judge ruled that the defendant could represent himself with the help of standby counsel. The next day, the judge thoroughly questioned the defendant about his decision to plead guilty to first-degree murder and accepted his plea. The defendant represented himself at the capital sentencing hearing and received a death sentence.

The defendant argued on appeal that the judge erred in failing to appoint an expert to inquire into the defendant's capacity to waive counsel or to represent himself. The court noted that if a defendant demonstrates or if information before the judge indicates that there is a significant possibility that a defendant is incompetent to waive counsel or to proceed to trial, the judge must appoint an expert or experts to inquire about the defendant's mental health in accord with G.S. 15A-1002(b)(1). However, the court ruled that nothing in the record in the present case tended to indicate that the defendant was incompetent to waive his right to counsel, to plead guilty, or to represent himself. The court also ruled that the trial judge properly granted the defendant's request to represent himself and honored that decision throughout the proceedings.

The court stated that "[w]e take this opportunity to reiterate that so long as a trial court follows these guidelines [referring to the inquiry mandated by G.S. 15A-1242] in determining the validity of a defendant's waiver of [the] right to counsel, this Court will [respect] that defendant's right to proceed pro se."

State v. Thomas, 134 N.C. App. 560 (1999). The defendant was charged with murder and elected to represent himself. The judge appointed standby counsel, then ruled that standby counsel could not "make any statement[s] in front of the jury." Counsel was permitted to argue legal issues outside the jury's presence and to approach the bench with the defendant. The defendant was convicted. On appeal, he argued that counsel's role was excessive and amounted to a prohibited "hybrid" representation, but the court of appeals disagreed: "[T]he record shows that such involvement occurred either when the jury was absent from the courtroom or at bench conferences outside of the jury's hearing. . . . [I]n all instances, defendant expressly requested the assistance of the standby counsel."

When difficulties arise between a defendant and his or her appointed lawyers, one of two things typically takes place. First, the defendant may elect to discharge his or her lawyers and to represent him or herself, as described above. Second, the defendant may ask the court to discharge his or her lawyers and to replace them, or one or both lawyers may make a similar request. A court has the authority to remove defense counsel if, for example, a conflict of interest arises or if irreconcilable differences exist between counsel and the defendant such that the defendant would be denied the effective assistance of counsel.[174] Of course, a court is not required to act on generalized complaints about a poor working relationship and may require defense counsel to continue representing the defendant unless discharged by him or her.[175]

Tactical decisions at trial, other than what plea to enter and whether the defendant will testify, are generally left to the defense attorney's discretion. Such decisions include how to conduct jury selection, which jurors to challenge and which to accept, whether and how to cross-examine witnesses, and what motions to make during trial.[176] Of course, counsel may permit the defendant to offer his or her views about these decisions.[177] And if counsel and a fully informed defendant reach an absolute impasse about a tactical decision, the defendant's wishes must control because the attorney is the defendant's agent.[178] This principle does not apply if the record merely shows a temporary disagreement between

---

174. In such a case, replacement counsel would be appointed by the IDS Director. *See supra* note 152; State v. Williams 363 N.C. 689 (2009) (discussing, without objection, trial court's conclusion that IDS was responsible for appointing successor counsel).

175. State v. Robinson, 330 N.C. 1 (1991) (finding no error in trial judge's refusal to remove counsel despite a lack of trust between the defendant and counsel arising from counsel's questioning defendant's mental health); State v. Kuplen, 316 N.C. 387 (1986) (finding no error in trial judge's refusal to remove counsel despite a strained working relationship, defendant's hiring of a private investigator, and defendant's frequent statements that he was considering retaining counsel); State v. Hutchins, 303 N.C. 321 (1981) (recognizing the trial court's broad discretion in addressing difficulties between defendants and their lawyers and finding no error in trial judge's refusal to remove counsel despite the defendant's complaints that counsel did not visit him frequently enough in jail and did not keep him abreast of developments in his case).

176. *See generally* State v. Brown, 339 N.C. 426 (1994); State v. McDowell, 329 N.C. 363, 380 (1991) ("Tactical decisions at trial, other than the right to testify and plead, are generally left to attorney discretion.").

177. *See, e.g.*, *McDowell*, 329 N.C. at 381 ("We find that defense counsel, simply by consulting with defendant regarding potential jurors, did not relinquish his authority as 'attorney' but merely gave deference to his client's wishes in making his tactical decision . . .").

178. State v. Mitchell, 353 N.C. 309 (2001) (trial judge properly followed the defendant's wishes, over the protestations of defense counsel, in removing a juror for cause without any attempt at rehabilitation); State v. Grooms, 353 N.C. 50 (2000) (trial judge properly ordered defense counsel to defer to the defendant's decision not to present mitigating evidence at sentencing); State v. White, 349 N.C. 535 (1998) (trial judge properly permitted the defendant to forbid the introduction of mitigating evidence about the history of domestic violence and abuse in his family when he was a child); State v. Ali, 329 N.C. 394 (1991) (trial judge properly permitted the defendant to have the final say on whether to exercise a peremptory challenge during jury selection); State v. Freeman, 202 N.C. App. 740, 746 (2010) (trial judge erred when, after being informed of an impasse between the defendant and his attorney regarding jury selection, he told the lawyer "you decide how to proceed" and allowed

the defendant and counsel[179] or if the defendant wants to pursue a course of action that is impossible or unlawful.[180] If an impasse is reached, counsel should make a record of the circumstances, counsel's advice to the defendant, the reasons for the advice, the defendant's decision, and the conclusion reached.[181]

J. Defendant's Right to the Assistance of Investigators and Experts

Capital defendants and their attorneys often seek the assistance of a variety of investigators and experts. Defendants who are not indigent must pay for such assistance themselves. Defendants who are indigent have a right, under certain circumstances, to have such assistance provided at state expense.[182]

The first source of an indigent defendant's right to the assistance of investigators and experts is federal constitutional law. In *Ake v. Oklahoma*,[183] the United States Supreme Court ruled that an indigent defendant has a due process right to the assistance of a mental health expert when the defendant makes a threshold showing that his or her mental state is likely to be a significant factor in the defendant's defense at trial or at a sentencing hearing. The North Carolina Supreme Court has interpreted *Ake* to mean that an indigent defendant must show a "particularized need" for expert assistance.[184]

---

the lawyer to override his client's desires). The rule that the attorney must yield to the client on tactical matters is not uniformly accepted across the country, and it can create difficult ethical issues for attorneys in some instances. For further discussion, see Jeff Welty, *Jury Selection and Attorneys as Agents of Their Clients*, N.C. Crim. L., UNC Sch. of Gov't Blog (Mar. 2, 2010), http://sogweb.sog.unc.edu/blogs/ncclaw/?p=1108, and Jessica Smith, "Absolute Impasse," *in* The Survival Guide: Superior Court Judges' Benchbook (UNC School of Government, Nov. 2011), www.sog.unc.edu/sites/www.sog.unc.edu/files/Absolute%20Impasse_November%20 2011%20Cite%20Checked.pdf.

179. State v. Williams, 191 N.C. App. 96 (2008) (although the defendant claimed that he and his lawyer were at an impasse about the exercise of peremptory challenges, and the defendant loudly voiced various demands and objections regarding his attorney's proposed course of action, the defendant ultimately allowed counsel to make the final decision regarding the use of the challenges).

180. State v. Prevatte, 356 N.C. 178, 213 (2002) (although the defendant claimed that he and his lawyers were at an impasse regarding "whether or not to have venue changed to Stanly County," there was actually no impasse because both the defendant and counsel agreed to seek a change of venue and "[a] defendant may not condition a motion for a change of venue upon the trial court's agreeing to transfer the case to a particular county specified by the defendant"); *Williams*, 191 N.C. App. 96 (although the defendant claimed that he and his lawyer were at an impasse about the exercise of peremptory challenges, the defendant's only specific request was to remove more jurors than the number of peremptory challenges he had remaining; for this reason and others, there was no impasse, and the defendant ultimately allowed counsel to make final decisions).

181. *Ali*, 329 N.C. 394.

182. A defendant is indigent if he or she cannot afford counsel "and . . . all other necessary expenses of representation." G.S. 7A-450(a). In *State v. Boyd*, 332 N.C. 101, 109 (1992), the court explained that "whenever a defendant's personal resources are depleted and he can demonstrate indigency, he is eligible for state funding of the remaining necessary expenses of representation," including the assistance of expert witnesses. The level of funding presumably must be sufficient to allow the defendant to secure the necessary assistance. *Cf. generally* State v. Coffey, 326 N.C. 268 (1990) (rejecting the defendant's argument that the $250 allowed by the trial judge for an expert in textile science was insufficient, where the defendant already had an expert in hair and fiber analysis and where the defendant's attorney told the trial court that $250 would be sufficient).

183. 470 U.S. 68 (1985). By contrast, the Court later ruled in *Caldwell v. Mississippi*, 472 U.S. 320 (1985), that a trial judge did not err in denying a defendant's requests for the assistance of a criminal investigator, a fingerprint expert, and a ballistics expert where the requests "were accompanied by no showing as to their reasonableness" and were supported only by general assertions to the effect that the experts would be helpful or necessary. *Caldwell*, 472 U.S. at 323 n.1.

184. State v. Robinson, 327 N.C. 346, 354 (1990).

State statutory law is a second source for providing an indigent defendant with the assistance of investigators and experts. Under G.S. 7A-450(b), an indigent defendant is entitled not only to counsel, but also to the "necessary expenses of representation." The North Carolina Supreme Court has ruled that assistance under this statute will be provided if the defendant shows that there is a "reasonable likelihood that it will materially assist the defendant in the preparation of his defense or that without such help it is probable that [the] defendant will not receive a fair trial."[185] It is unclear whether this statutory provision provides a right to expert assistance that is more expansive than the federal constitutional right recognized in *Ake*.

At one time, indigent capital defendants sought assistance by applying directly to the trial court. However, since the Office of Indigent Defense Services (IDS) was created, the "use of funds for experts and other services related to legal representation" is governed by IDS rules and procedures.[186] And those rules provide that, in capital cases, defense counsel "shall make application to the IDS Director for authorization to retain experts or for other substantial expenses necessary to the defense," such as investigators.[187] Under the rules, the IDS Director[188] applies the same standards "as would be required by a fair but exacting trial judge applying G.S. 7A-450(a) and *Ake v. Oklahoma* and its progeny."[189] IDS has issued a policy emphasizing the importance of making an adequate showing of necessity.[190] Further, IDS has promulgated a number of specific policies regarding, for example, the use of mental health experts[191] and the use of investigators and mitigation specialists.[192] The details of those policies will not be repeated here, as they are available on the IDS website.[193]

Only if IDS denies a defendant's application may the defendant ask a court to approve the request.[194] There is a dearth of recent North Carolina appellate cases addressing courts' handling of such requests, suggesting that it may be uncommon for defense counsel to request assistance from IDS, for IDS to

---

185. State v. Gray, 292 N.C. 270, 278 (1977).

186. G.S. 7A-498.3(c).

187. Office of Indigent Defense Servs., *supra* note 152, at § 2D.1.

188. In practice, an initial determination regarding requests of this nature will be made by a designee rather than the IDS Director him or herself. As of this writing, for cases at the trial level, the designee is normally the Capital Defender.

189. Office of Indigent Defense Servs., *supra* note 152, at § 2D.1.

190. Office of Indigent Defense Servs., N.C. Ct. Sys., Expert Requests & Spending (updated Apr. 15, 2011), www.ncids.org/Rules%20&%20Procedures/Policies%20By%20Case%20Type/CapCases/Expert%20 requests%20&%20spending,%20trial.pdf (emphasizing that counsel must make a "particularized showing of need").

191. Office of Indigent Defense Servs., N.C. Ct. Sys., Effective Use of Mental Health Experts in Potentially Capital Cases (effective July 31, 2008), www.ncids.org/Rules%20&%20Procedures/Policies%20 By%20Case%20Type/CapCases/MentalHealthExperts.pdf (stating that "[c]ounsel generally will not be in a position to select mental health experts until after a mitigation specialist and investigator have explored the facts of the case and the background of the defendant").

192. Office of Indigent Defense Servs., N.C. Ct. Sys., Exceptional Capital Cases (updated Apr. 6, 2011), www.ncids.org/Rules%20&%20Procedures/Policies%20By%20Case%20Type/CapCases/Exceptional%20 case%20policy.pdf (establishing presumptive limits of $10,000 in compensation to an investigator and $10,000 in compensation to a mitigation specialist, prior to jury selection, unless a case is designated "exceptional," *see id.* § (B)(2); requests within those limits remain subject to the approval process described above).

193. Web address: www.ncids.org.

194. Office of Indigent Defense Servs., *supra* note 152, at § 2D.4. A request submitted to a court may not "include[] information not contained in the application made to the IDS Director unless exceptional or extraordinary circumstances necessitate submitting such new or additional information directly to a court." *Id.* The request must include a copy of the application submitted to IDS, as well as a copy of the IDS Director's written notice of disapproval. *Id.*

deny the request, and for counsel to seek review from a court. However, a court considering such a request should apply the constitutional and statutory standards described above.

One issue that arises from time to time is whether a request for expert assistance, when made to a court, may be made ex parte (that is, without notice to the state and conducted without the presence of a prosecutor). The North Carolina Supreme Court has ruled that a judge must grant an indigent defendant's motion for an ex parte hearing to present evidence in support of the defendant's request for the appointment of a mental health expert to assist the defendant.[195] The court reasoned that a defendant has a Fifth Amendment right not to be compelled to make statements revealing his or her mental condition or other defense strategy in the presence of the prosecution. Also, an ex parte hearing protects the indigent defendant's Sixth Amendment right to the effective assistance of counsel, which includes counsel's access to expert witnesses. However, not all hearings must be conducted ex parte. For example, the North Carolina Supreme Court has recognized that, under some circumstances, a hearing on a motion for the appointment of a fingerprint identification expert need not be conducted ex parte.[196]

Case Summaries: Failure to Appoint Mental Health Expert Was Error

Ake v. Oklahoma, 470 U.S. 68 (1985). The Court ruled that an indigent defendant has a constitutional right to the assistance of a mental health expert when the defendant makes a threshold showing that his or her sanity is likely to be a significant factor in the defendant's defense at trial or at a sentencing hearing. In this case, the defendant was entitled to such expert assistance at both the trial and the capital sentencing hearing.

State v. Jones, 344 N.C. 722 (1996). The court ruled that a judge erred in failing to grant the defendant's pretrial ex parte motion for psychiatric assistance. The defendant's counsel clearly demonstrated that the only defense he intended to raise or could raise was that at the time of the killing the defendant suffered from diminished capacity and therefore may not have acted with premeditation and deliberation or the specific intent to kill. The attorney also presented a doctor's statement about the defendant's treatment for depression and suicidal tendencies in the months before the murder. In addition, evidence showed that the defendant had no history of violence or criminal activity. The lawyer presented his own affidavit that the defendant admitted that he was not in control of his mental processes at the time of the murder and had advised counsel that he did not have a premeditated intent to kill.

State v. Parks, 331 N.C. 649 (1992). Although evidence of the defendant's psychiatric problems during the interval between his arrest and his motion for a court-appointed psychiatrist may be considered by the trial judge in determining whether to grant the motion, the lack of such evidence is not dispositive against granting the motion. The court ruled that the trial judge erred in not granting the defendant's motion.

---

195. State v. Ballard, 333 N.C. 515 (1993). *See also* State v. Greene, 335 N.C. 548 (1994).

196. State v. Phipps, 331 N.C. 427, 451 (1992) (holding that while there are "strong reasons" for allowing the defendant to proceed ex parte, such a procedure is "not constitutionally required in every case" and that the defendant was not prejudiced by not being allowed to proceed ex parte regarding the assistance of a fingerprint expert). *See also* State v. White, 340 N.C. 264, 277 (1995) (concluding that "the request for an investigator is more analogous to a request for a fingerprint expert as in *Phipps* than to a request for a psychiatrist as in *Ballard*," so the trial court did not err in denying an ex parte hearing); State v. Garner, 136 N.C. App. 1 (1999) (defendant not entitled to ex parte hearing regarding request for the assistance of an eyewitness identification expert).

State v. Moore, 321 N.C. 327 (1988). The trial judge erred in denying the defendant's motion for appointment of a psychiatrist for the mentally retarded defendant, who had an IQ of 51, to assist in challenging the legality of his waiver of rights before he gave a statement and the believability of a confession he had made. The forensic psychiatrist who had examined the defendant to determine his competence to stand trial was not sufficient assistance on this issue.

State v. Gambrell, 318 N.C. 249 (1986). Two months after the murder being tried, physicians concluded that the defendant needed psychiatric examination and treatment. The defendant's behavior in court was bizarre, and he was ordered to undergo psychiatric examination. He experienced hallucinations and delusions, was suffering from depression and anxiety, and was thought to have acute psychosis. He was administered a high dose of a psychotropic drug. The court concluded that this evidence (and additional facts set out in the opinion) was a sufficient showing that the defendant's sanity was likely to be a significant factor at trial and that, therefore, the trial judge erred in denying the defendant's motion to be furnished with a psychiatrist to assist in his defense at trial. The court, however, rejected the defendant's contention that he had the right to choose his own psychiatrist or to receive funds to hire a private psychiatric expert. The employment of state-employed psychiatrists may fulfill the state's constitutional obligation.

Case Summaries: Failure to Appoint Mental Health Expert Was Proper

State v. Brown, 357 N.C. 382 (2003). The trial judge approved the defendant's initial ex parte application for the assistance of a mental health expert, a psychologist, to review the defendant's mental health status. This expert concluded that the defendant was suffering from a substance-induced mood disorder that precipitates psychosis. The expert stated that he was only generally familiar with this diagnosis and suggested that the defendant retain a specialist. The trial judge denied the defendant's ex parte motion for a specialist. The court ruled that the trial judge did not err because the defendant failed to show what the specialist could have contributed to the confirmation of the psychologist's diagnosis. The court noted that the defendant also had as a witness at his sentencing hearing a Virginia psychologist who had reached a similar diagnosis at the defendant's 1986 Virginia prosecution for malicious wounding.

State v. Page, 346 N.C. 689 (1997). The court ruled that the trial judge did not err in failing to appoint a forensic psychiatrist. The court noted that the defendant had both a psychiatric and psychological expert present evidence for him at trial. Both had treated the defendant over an extended period before the murder being tried and had made similar diagnoses. The state's psychiatrist was in accord with their diagnoses except she did not believe that the defendant suffered from post-traumatic stress disorder. The court concluded that the defendant had substantial assistance from mental health experts in preparing and conducting his defense. The court stated that mere suspicion that the state psychiatrist's classification as a forensic psychiatrist made her better equipped than the defendant's psychiatrist was insufficient to require that the defendant be given a court-appointed forensic expert. *See also* State v. Pierce, 346 N.C. 471 (1997) (trial judge did not err in denying motions for psychiatrist, pathologist, and medical expert in child abuse).

State v. Rose, 339 N.C. 172 (1994). When the defendant was furnished with two competent psychiatrists (one of whom was paid with state funds) who had examined him and were available to assist in evaluating, preparing, and presenting his defense at trial and sentencing, the trial judge did not abuse his discretion in denying the defendant's motion for funds for an evaluation by a neuropsychologist.

State v. Reeves, 337 N.C. 700 (1994). The court ruled that because the defendant's appointed forensic psychiatrist offered testimony about how the defendant's sexual disorder affected his behavior, the trial judge properly refused to appoint a psychiatrist who specialized in sexual disorders. In addition, the defendant's psychiatrist had consulted with a psychologist who specialized in this field and that psychologist was in the courtroom—the defendant simply chose not to call her to testify.

State v. Hood, 332 N.C. 611 (1992). The defendant failed to make a sufficient showing for the appointment of a psychiatrist when the evidence submitted with the motion, a psychiatric report, affirmatively showed that the defendant's mental state at the time of the offenses being tried would not be a factor at trial.

State v. Bearthes, 329 N.C. 149 (1991). The defendant was not entitled to another state-funded mental health expert simply because his mental health expert inadvertently mailed a copy of his report to the district attorney.

State v. Robinson, 327 N.C. 346 (1990). The defendant failed to make a sufficient preliminary showing for a state-funded psychiatrist because the state psychiatrist's report, on which the defendant's motion relied, did not show that the defendant's sanity would be a significant factor at trial. And the state psychiatrist's assistance was sufficient to offer evidence of the defendant's mental state as a mitigating circumstance.

State v. McLaughlin, 323 N.C. 68 (1988). The defendant failed to show a particularized need for a second independent psychiatric evaluation at the state's expense. *See also* State v. Jones, 342 N.C. 523 (1996) (similar ruling).

State v. Lloyd, 321 N.C. 301 (1988). The trial judge did not err in denying the defendant's motion for state funds to hire a private psychologist or psychiatrist to assist in investigating potential mitigating circumstances for the sentencing hearing. In support of his motion, defense counsel offered a psychiatric evaluation that noted the defendant's episodic alcohol abuse. Defense counsel also asserted that the evaluation was inadequate. The court ruled that the defendant's showing was insufficient to support the motion.

State v. Smith, 320 N.C. 404 (1987). Before the sentencing hearing began, the defendant made a motion for funds to hire a psychiatrist. Defense counsel admitted that there was no indication that the defendant had a mental illness, but there might be some mental defect of which they were unaware. The court ruled that the trial judge properly denied the motion, since the defendant had failed to make a sufficient showing to support his motion.

State v. Massey, 316 N.C. 558 (1986). The trial judge did not err in denying the defendant's motion to appoint a private psychiatrist. Although the defendant was mildly retarded, the defendant had already been examined by a state psychiatrist and there was no serious contention that the defendant's sanity would be a significant factor at trial. The trial judge also did not err in denying the defendant's motion to appoint a social psychologist when the defendant offered no evidence to support the motion.

Case Summaries: Failure to Appoint Fingerprint Expert Was Error

State v. Bridges, 325 N.C. 529 (1989). The trial judge erred in denying an indigent defendant's motion for funds to hire an independent fingerprint expert when the defendant demonstrated that fingerprint evidence was the only direct evidence linking him to the murder and the experts who testified about the preparation and identification of the latent prints found at the crime scene were witnesses for the state, not independent parties. Without the assistance of a fingerprint expert, the defendant was unable to assess adequately the state experts' conclusion that the latent prints from the crime scene were the defendant's.

State v. Moore, 321 N.C. 327 (1988). When the victim of a sexual assault and burglary could not identify her attacker, and the state's identification of the defendant as the attacker rested largely on the defendant's alleged palm print left at the crime scene, the trial judge erred in denying the defendant's motion for funds to hire a fingerprint expert. (The mentally retarded defendant could provide only limited assistance to his attorney.) The court rejected the state's argument that the defendant, to show the necessity for state funds to hire a fingerprint expert, must present a specific basis for questioning the accuracy of the state's conclusion that the palm print was the defendant's.

Case Summaries: Failure to Appoint Fingerprint Expert Was Proper

State v. Tucker, 329 N.C. 709 (1991). The trial judge did not err in denying the indigent defendant's motion for the appointment of a fingerprint (as well as hair and blood) expert. The court noted, distinguishing *Bridges* and *Moore*, summarized above, that this case was based largely on eyewitness testimony.

State v. Wilson, 322 N.C. 117 (1988). The trial judge properly denied the defendant's motion for state assistance to hire an expert in fingerprints (as well as pathology and psychology) because the defendant failed to make a particularized showing for the expert. He merely indicated that an expert might be helpful in preparing his defense.

Case Summaries: Failure to Appoint Pathologist Was Proper

State v. Moseley, 338 N.C. 1 (1994). The court ruled that the trial judge properly denied a defense motion for funds to employ a forensic pathologist. The court stated that a review of the record, slides, and photographs showed that the similarities between the location and types of wounds of the murder victim in this case and the victim of another murder (evidence of which was admitted under Rule 404(b)) were obvious and self-explanatory, even to the ordinary lay juror; expert interpretation was not required. And there was substantial additional evidence that demonstrated the similarities between the two murders, so the jury could find, based on this evidence, that the same person committed them. The defendant failed to demonstrate that the assistance of a pathologist would have materially aided him in the preparation of his defense or that lack of such an expert deprived him of a fair trial.

State v. Penley, 318 N.C. 30 (1986). The trial judge did not err in denying the defendant's motion for the appointment of a pathologist (cause of death was an issue in this case) since the defendant did not show what, if anything, an additional pathologist could have offered in his defense. In addition, two medical experts testified for the defense on the issue of cause of death.

State v. Johnson, 317 N.C. 193 (1986). In a prosecution for first-degree murder committed by poisoning, the trial judge did not err in denying the defendant's motion for a medical expert to aid in the investigation and preparation of his case for his trial by evaluating medical reports, autopsy results and samples, and prevailing scientific data on organophosphate poisons. The defendant failed to set out any facts showing a specific or particularized need for a medical expert. The court also noted that the defendant did in fact receive some expert assistance on these issues before trial.

Case Summaries: Failure to Appoint Private Investigator Was Proper

State v. Barnes, 333 N.C. 666 (1993). The defendant failed to make a sufficient showing for the appointment of a private investigator. For similar rulings, see *State v. McCullers*, 341 N.C. 19 (1995); *State v. Jones*, 339 N.C. 114 (1994); *State v. Phipps*, 331 N.C. 427 (1992); *State v. Roper*, 328 N.C. 337 (1991); *State v. Eason*, 328 N.C. 409 (1991); *State v. McLaughlin*, 323 N.C. 68 (1988); *State v. Crandell*, 322 N.C. 487 (1988); *State v. Locklear*, 322 N.C. 349 (1988); *State v. Zuniga*, 320 N.C. 233 (1987); *State v. Hickey*, 317 N.C. 457 (1986); and *State v. Massey*, 316 N.C. 558 (1986).

Case Summaries: Failure to Appoint Jury Selection Expert or Statistician Was Proper

State v. McLaughlin, 323 N.C. 68 (1988). The defendant failed to make a sufficient showing for the appointment of a jury selection expert. *See also* State v. Artis, 316 N.C. 507 (1986); State v. Zuniga, 320 N.C. 233 (1987).

State v. Massey, 316 N.C. 558 (1986). The trial judge did not err in denying the defendant's motion for the appointment of a statistician to determine whether the jury commissioners had performed their duties in compiling the jury venire. The defendant offered no evidence to show any statutory violations committed by the commissioners.

Case Summaries: Failure to Appoint Other Experts Was Proper

Caldwell v. Mississippi, 472 U.S. 320 (1985). A defendant's undeveloped assertions that expert assistance (in this case, a criminal investigator, fingerprint expert, and ballistics expert) would be beneficial did not satisfy the necessary threshold showing to obtain assistance.

State v. Abraham, 338 N.C. 315 (1994). The court ruled that the trial judge did not err in denying the defendant's motion for the appointment of an expert on eyewitness identification. The defendant failed to show how an expert would have materially assisted him. His pretrial motion was based solely on his perceived need to show the unreliability of the identification of him and a co-defendant at an earlier shooting offered under Rule 404(b), not the shooting that was being tried. The court also noted that this was not a case involving the uncorroborated identification of a single eyewitness. Victims of an earlier shooting and the shooting being tried knew the defendant and his co-defendant. Further, the identification issues for which the defendant sought expert assistance involved matters within the scope of the jury's general capability and understanding.

State v. Mills, 332 N.C. 392 (1992). The defendant did not show a particularized need for the appointment of a DNA expert (or nine other kinds of experts) at the time of his pretrial motion, and so the trial judge properly denied the motion. Although the defendant contended that the need for a DNA expert became evident during trial, he did not then renew the motion for appointment of an expert, nor did he tell the court of specific circumstances showing a particularized need.

State v. Speight, 166 N.C. App. 106 (2004). The trial court did not err in denying defendant's request for a medical expert and an accident reconstruction expert in second-degree murder case arising out of impaired driving. The defendant "alleged no specific facts or circumstances" about his need for a reconstructionist beyond a desire to have one "review the State's evidence" and likewise offered only "speculation" and "unsupported assertions" regarding his need for a medical expert.

K. Discovery

Discovery issues are not unique to capital cases, and the law of discovery has been detailed elsewhere.[197] Therefore, this book will not attempt a comprehensive discussion of discovery but, rather, will offer a brief overview of the subject, then focus on issues that are especially likely to arise in capital cases at the trial level. Different rules apply to post-conviction litigation,[198] and those rules are not discussed in this book at all.

Overview of Statutory Discovery

In 2004, the General Assembly enacted what is commonly called open file discovery, which provides defendants in capital cases—and many other defendants—with broad access to the state's evidence.[199] The statutory discovery laws are codified beginning at G.S. 15A-901. They provide generally that upon request, the state must "[m]ake available to the defendant the complete files of all law enforcement agencies, investigatory agencies, and prosecutors' offices involved in the investigation of the crimes committed or the prosecution of the defendant."[200] The statutes also mandate that the state provide the defendant notice of its expert witnesses[201] and give certain other information to the defense, but the state is permitted to withhold some work product of the prosecutor and his or her staff.[202] The discovery statutes also impose certain obligations on the defendant[203] and give trial judges broad authority to regulate and limit discovery and to sanction discovery violations.[204]

In addition to these statutory provisions, the state has a constitutional obligation to disclose material exculpatory or mitigating evidence to the defendant. Constitutional discovery is addressed separately below.

Statutory Discovery Procedures

Need for Request

Neither party has any obligation to provide statutory discovery to the other absent a written request, unless the parties enter into a written agreement to provide voluntary discovery, a practice which does not appear to be widespread. Once a request is made, the party receiving the request may provide discovery (in which case, the discovery is deemed to be made pursuant to a court order and must be made to the same extent as a court would order if asked) or may refuse to respond or to make discovery (in which case, the party seeking discovery may file a motion to compel discovery and thereby obtain a court order requiring complete statutory discovery).[205]

---

197. *See, e.g.,* Robert L. Farb, North Carolina Prosecutors' Trial Manual 47–68 (4th ed. 2007); John Rubin, *2004 Legislation Affecting Criminal Law and Procedure,* Admin. of Just. Bull. No. 2004/06 2–8 (UNC School of Government, Oct. 2004), www.sog.unc.edu/sites/www.sog.unc.edu/files/aoj200406.pdf.

198. *See generally* G.S. 15A-1415(f).

199. S.L. 2004-154.

200. G.S. 15A-903(a)(1).

201. G.S. 15A-903(a)(2).

202. G.S. 15A-904(a).

203. G.S. 15A-905.

204. G.S. 15A-908 through -910.

205. *See generally* G.S. 15A-902(a)–(b); 15A-903(a)–(b). *See also* State v. Flint, 199 N.C. App. 709, 715 (2009) (stating that "the defendant must make a motion in order for the State's obligation to provide discovery prior to trial [to arise]").

Timing of Request

Under G.S. 15A-902(d), a defendant who is represented by counsel may request voluntary discovery from the state "not later than the tenth working day after" the earliest of the following:

- The date of the probable cause hearing
- The date the defendant waives his or her right to a probable cause hearing
- The date the defendant consents to the filing of a bill of information (though this provision does not apply to capital cases, which may not be prosecuted by information)[206]
- The date the defendant is served with notice of an indictment

In the presumably unusual situation that a defendant is not represented by counsel by the time of the probable cause hearing or the defendant's waiver of his or her right to a probable cause hearing, the defendant may request voluntary discovery from the state "not later than the tenth working day after" the later of the following:

- The date the defendant is served with notice of an indictment (or, in a noncapital case, the date he or she consents to the filing of a bill of information[207])
- The date that counsel is appointed

The state may request voluntary discovery from the defendant within ten working days of "disclosure by the State with respect to the category of discovery in question."[208]

Timing of Discovery

G.S. 15A-903 does not provide a precise timetable for the disclosure by the state of the contents of the state's file, nor does G.S. 15A-905 provide a timetable for the disclosure by the defense of documents and tangible objects that the defendant intends to introduce at trial. Presumably, disclosure must be made in time to allow the opposing party to review and analyze the material provided before trial begins. The timing of expert discovery is discussed in the section on expert discovery, below. The parties must exchange witness lists "at the beginning of jury selection."[209] The statutes provide specific time limits within which the defendant must give notice of his or her intent to offer certain defenses, including alibi, self-defense, entrapment, and insanity and other mental health defenses.[210]

If discoverable material comes to the attention of a party after that party has provided discovery, the new material is subject to an ongoing duty to disclose.[211] Trial judges have substantial authority to regulate the timing of discovery.[212]

---

206. G.S. 15A-642(b).

207. Again, capital cases may not be prosecuted by information. *Id.*

208. G.S. 15A-902(e).

209. G.S. 15A-903(a)(3); 15A-905(c)(3).

210. G.S. 15A-905(c)(1).

211. G.S. 15A-907.

212. *See generally* G.S. 15A-908(a) (authority to "order that discovery or inspection be denied, restricted, or deferred"); 15A-910(a)(1) (authority to order that discovery be permitted). The court's authority is also recognized in connection with expert discovery, which, as noted above, must be made "within a reasonable time prior to trial, as specified by the court." G.S. 15A-903(a)(2); 15A-905(c)(2).

Remedies for Violations

If a party fails to provide discovery as required, the presiding judge has the discretion to impose a variety of remedies,[213] from granting a continuance to allow the opposing party additional time to examine or meet the evidence,[214] to excluding the evidence, to granting a mistrial or even a dismissal.[215] The court may also, in appropriate cases, exercise its contempt powers.[216] When the discovery violation relates to a prosecutor's failure to disclose information contained in an officer's file, and the court is considering the imposition of "personal sanctions," the court must presume that the prosecutor acted in good faith if he or she acted with reasonable diligence.[217] A court imposing any "sanction," apparently meaning a personal sanction against a prosecutor, must make specific findings justifying its action.[218] Certain willful discovery violations are also criminal offenses.[219]

Scope of Statutory Discovery for the Defendant

As noted above, the scope of statutory discovery available to the defendant is quite broad. Generally, the defendant is entitled to three things: open file discovery, expert discovery, and a witness list. The witness list provision is self-explanatory, and expert discovery is discussed separately below, so this section focuses on open file discovery.

The defendant is entitled to access "the complete files of all law enforcement agencies, investigatory agencies, and prosecutors' offices involved in the investigation of the crimes committed or the prosecution of the defendant."[220] That includes the statements of the defendant, any co-defendants, and other witnesses; officers' notes and reports; "results of tests and examinations"; and "any other matter or evidence obtained during the investigation of the offenses alleged to have been committed by the defendant."[221] It does not include legal research, correspondence, and similar items belonging to the prosecutor, nor does it include certain trial preparation materials, such as the prosecutor's draft witness examinations.[222]

Witness statements must be in writing or recorded, though "oral statements made by a witness to a prosecuting attorney outside the presence of a law enforcement officer or investigatorial assistant"

---

213. The judge also has the discretion *not* to impose any remedy. *See, e.g.*, State v. Ellis, 205 N.C. App. 650 (2010).

214. *See, e.g.*, State v. Remley, 201 N.C. App. 146 (2009) (brief recess was sufficient remedy where state did not disclose defendant's incriminating statement until after trial began).

215. These more severe sanctions likely should be imposed only if less serious sanctions are insufficient to address the violation.

216. G.S. 15A-910.

217. G.S. 15A-910(c).

218. G.S. 15A-910(d).

219. G.S. 15A-903(d).

220. G.S. 15A-903(a)(1).

221. G.S. 15A-903(a)(1)a. Occasionally, questions may arise about whether relevant information in the state's possession was acquired in connection with the investigation of the offenses allegedly committed by the defendant. For example, in *State v. Tuck*, 191 N.C. App. 768 (2008), the state alleged that the defendant and a co-defendant committed a carjacking together, though only the co-defendant was apprehended immediately. At the defendant's trial, the co-defendant testified that he committed the crime alone and that he did not know the defendant. He was impeached on cross-examination with a statement he had made to police prior to the events in question, apparently in connection with a separate investigation, acknowledging a connection to the defendant. The statement had not been produced in discovery, and the defendant claimed a discovery violation. The trial judge disagreed, but the court of appeals remanded for further consideration, instructing the judge to determine whether the state "should have reasonably known that the statement related to the charges against defendant yet failed to disclose it." *Id* at 773.

222. G.S. 15A-904(a).

need only be produced in written or recorded form if the statements contain "significantly new or different information" compared to the witness's prior statements.[223] When a witness's statement is reduced to writing, the statement need not contain every detail reported by the witness. However, it must contain the "substance" of the witness's statement and must be detailed enough to prevent unfair surprise during trial.[224] Similarly, whether a statement made by a witness to a prosecutor alone contains "significantly new or different information" depends on whether nondisclosure of the additional information would result in unfair surprise.[225]

The state's obligation to provide discovery is a continuing one.[226] However, the state may seek a protective order limiting or denying discovery if it believes that there is a "substantial risk to any person of physical harm, intimidation," or other danger.[227] When requesting a protective order, the state must file a written motion and may proceed ex parte.[228]

Scope of Statutory Discovery for the State

If the state is ordered to provide discovery, or if it voluntarily provides discovery upon request, it is entitled to limited reciprocal discovery. Generally, the state is entitled to the following:]

- To inspect and copy any documents, photographs, and tangible objects in the defendant's custody that the defendant intends to introduce at trial and to test any physical evidence in the defendant's custody that the defendant intends to introduce.[229]
- To inspect and copy any "results or reports of physical or mental examinations" or other tests that the defendant intends to introduce or that were prepared by a witness that the defendant intends to call.[230]
- To advance notice if the defendant intends to raise "a defense of alibi, duress, entrapment, insanity, mental infirmity, diminished capacity, self-defense, accident, automatism, involuntary intoxication, or voluntary intoxication."[231]

223. G.S. 15A-903(a)(1)c.

224. State v. Rainey, 198 N.C. App. 427, 439 (2009) (a witness testified that the defendant used a racial slur to describe the victim, a Mexican; the version of the witness's statement produced in discovery adverted to the defendant's prejudice against Mexicans but did not refer to the slur; no discovery violation). *See also* State v. Zamora-Ramos, 190 N.C. App. 420, 424 (2008) (rejecting the defendant's argument that the state was required to produce detailed witness statements rather than the "summaries" it actually provided; the summaries contained the "substance" of the witness's statements, and the defendant suffered no prejudice or unfair surprise).

225. State v. Small, 201 N.C. App. 331, 336 (2009) (a shooting victim told a prosecutor the same version of events he had told police, but also told the prosecutor that he did not remember speaking with police; the prosecutor's failure to disclose the latter fact did not amount to a discovery violation, as the victim's "account of the actual incident remained consistent").

226. G.S. 15A-907.

227. G.S. 15A-908(a).

228. *Id.*

229. G.S. 15A-905(a) (generally); 15A-905(b) (right to test physical evidence).

230. G.S. 15A-905(b). This provision may be redundant. If the defendant intends to introduce the results or reports, they are discoverable under the preceding provision, while if the results or reports were prepared by a witness the defendant intends to call, they are likely discoverable under the provisions for expert discovery, discussed below.

231. G.S. 15A-905(c)(1). Such notice "must be given within 20 working days after the date the case is set for trial pursuant to G.S. 7A-49.4, or such other later time as set by the court." *Id.* For some of the listed defenses, the defendant may be required to provide additional information. G.S. 15A-905(c)(1)a.–b.

- To certain discovery in connection with any expert witnesses that the defendant reasonably expects to call, as discussed below.[232]
- To a witness list at the beginning of jury selection.[233]

Statutory Discovery Regarding Expert Witnesses

Capital cases often involve expert witnesses. The discovery statutes impose identical obligations on the state and on the defense regarding their experts. Each side must give notice to the other of any expert witnesses that it "reasonably expects to call."[234] The witness must prepare, and the party must disclose, a "report of the results of any examinations or tests conducted by the expert."[235] The party must also disclose "the expert's curriculum vitae, the expert's opinion, and the underlying basis for that opinion."[236] This must be done "within a reasonable time prior to trial, as specified by the court."[237]

Several issues may arise regarding expert discovery. The first concerns timing. Often, a judge will enter a scheduling order mandating the exchange of expert discovery by a certain date. Absent such an order, what is a "reasonable time prior to trial"? The leading case is *State v. Cook*,[238] a second-degree murder case arising out of an impaired driving accident. The state retained an expert to perform a retrograde analysis of the defendant's blood alcohol content. The witness completed his report five weeks prior to trial, but the state only identified the expert and provided his curriculum vita five days (three working days) before trial and did not provide his report until three days (one working day) prior to trial. The defendant sought a continuance based on the late disclosure, but the trial court denied the motion. The state supreme court eventually reviewed the case and held that the trial court had erred, though it found that the error was harmless. The court found that the defendant was unfairly surprised by the timing of the disclosure because he "had just a weekend to find his own expert in this field and to decide whether to call such a witness to counter the State's evidence."[239] Thus, *Cook* suggests that disclosure just a few days before trial may be inadequate and that the adequacy of discovery should be measured by whether the discovery provides sufficient notice to prevent surprise and to allow the opposing party to prepare to meet the evidence in question.[240]

The second issue that arises frequently with respect to experts is how much detail a party must provide when describing the expert's opinion and its basis. Few, if any, North Carolina cases speak directly to this issue. However, the courts' emphasis on preventing unfair surprise suggests that the disclosure must provide enough detail to allow the opposing party to prepare to meet the expert's testimony, whether by cross-examination or by presenting an expert of its own. A related issue is the

---

232. G.S. 15A-905(c)(2).

233. G.S. 15A-905(c)(3).

234. G.S. 15A-903(a)(2) (state); 15A-905(c)(2) (defense). The discovery statutes do not require disclosure of information concerning nontestifying experts. *See generally* State v. White, 331 N.C. 604 (1992) (error to order the defendant's experts to prepare written reports regardless of whether the defendant intended to call them as witnesses at trial).

235. G.S. 15A-903(a)(2) (state); 15A-905(c)(2) (defense) (using the language "report of the results of the examinations or tests conducted by the expert").

236. G.S. 15A-903(a)(2) (state); 15A-905(c)(2) (defense).

237. G.S. 15A-903(a)(2) (state); 15A-905(c)(2) (defense).

238. 362 N.C. 285 (2008).

239. *Id.* at 292.

240. *See also generally* State v. Greene, 206 N.C. App. 763 (2010) (unpublished) (state's disclosure of expert witnesses during jury selection was untimely, but two-day continuance to allow defendant to prepare was sufficient remedy).

extent to which a party is entitled to access the notes and raw data of the opposing party's expert. Generally, the discovery statutes provide for robust access to such information, as do the relevant cases.[241]

Finally, issues may arise concerning the proper remedy for a violation of the expert discovery statutes. Several options are available under G.S. 15A-910, including granting a continuance to allow the surprised party additional time to prepare; prohibiting the introduction of the evidence in question; or granting a mistrial or even a dismissal.[242] However, when the violation is due to the conduct of an expert—rather than a party—the court's options may be limited by *State v. Gillespie*.[243] In *Gillespie*, the trial judge ordered the parties to exchange reports from their mental health experts two weeks before trial. The defendant's experts failed to produce their reports in a timely fashion, so the trial judge sanctioned the defendant by prohibiting him from calling the experts. On review, the state supreme court ordered a new trial, ruling that G.S. 15A-910 only allows the court to sanction parties for their own discovery violations, not for violations committed by third parties, which is how it viewed the defendants' experts. Yet *Gillespie* was followed by *State v. Lane*,[244] a case in which the supreme court found no abuse of discretion in the trial court's exclusion of testimony from the defendant's expert witness as a sanction for discovery violations where, despite the state's repeated requests for a report, the witness never provided more than an email that purported to be a "preliminary" report. The tension between *Gillespie* and *Lane* leaves the law in this area rather unsettled.

Constitutional Discovery Rights

There are several constitutional issues connected to what the Supreme Court has said "might loosely be called the area of constitutionally guaranteed access to evidence."[245] These issues are not unique to capital cases but arise regularly in such cases, so a short summary of the relevant law is provided here.

241. G.S. 15A-903(a)(1)a. (defendant is entitled to all "results of tests" and "data" in the sta te's file, as well as various other information concerning evidence "submitted for testing or examination"); G.S. 15A-905(b) (state is normally entitled to "results or reports of . . . examinations or . . . tests" performed or conducted by defense witnesses); State v. Davis, 353 N.C. 1, 45 (2000) (the "defendant contend[ed] that the trial court erred in ordering defendant's mental health expert . . . to prepare and disclose to the State a written report of his findings and a copy of his handwritten notes of interviews with defendant," but the supreme court disagreed, holding that the order was proper under G.S. 15A-905(b); the court also rejected the defendant's argument that the interviews were protected by the attorney-client privilege, holding that the privilege was lost when the expert testified and that it must give way in any event in the interest of justice); State v. Atkins, 349 N.C. 62, 93 (1998) (trial court did not err in ordering defense expert to produce "all of his notes" to the state, including notes from interviews with the defendant) (internal quotation marks omitted).

242. Some discovery violations may be so harmless that no remedy is required. *See, e.g.*, State v. Moncree, 188 N.C. App. 221 (2008) (state produced SBI laboratory reports in discovery but failed to give required notice that SBI agent would testify as an expert that the substance found in the defendant's shoe was marijuana; given that other officers properly testified to the identity of the substance, the discovery violation was harmless).

243. 362 N.C. 150 (2008).

244. 365 N.C. 7 (2011).

245. United States v. Valenzuela-Bernal, 458 U.S. 858, 867 (1982).

Right to Material Evidence That Is Exculpatory or Mitigating

Although a defendant does not have a general constitutional right to discovery of the state's evidence,[246] in *Brady v. Maryland*,[247] the United States Supreme Court held that "the suppression by the prosecution of evidence favorable to an accused upon request violates due process where the evidence is material either to guilt or to punishment, irrespective of the good faith or bad faith of the prosecution."[248] Subsequent cases have clarified the following points about the state's obligation to disclose favorable evidence to the defense:

- The obligation exists whether or not the defense requests disclosure.[249]
- The obligation extends to evidence in the possession of law enforcement agencies, even if the prosecutor is not aware of the evidence.[250]
- The obligation extends to evidence that may be used to impeach the state's witnesses as well as evidence that the defendant may wish to introduce as part of his or her case.[251]
- The obligation is limited to material evidence. Evidence is material if there is a reasonable probability that disclosure of the evidence would change the outcome of the trial.[252]
- Disclosure must occur in time for the defendant to make effective use of the evidence at trial, though that does not necessarily mean that disclosure must take place prior to trial.[253]

State's Obligation Not to Use False Evidence

As a matter of professional ethics, no lawyer may knowingly present false evidence.[254] If a prosecutor presents false evidence, he or she also violates the defendant's due process rights.[255] Even if the prosecutor did not intentionally elicit the false evidence, he or she is required to correct it.[256] If there

---

246. United States v. Agurs, 427 U.S. 97, 111 (1976) (rejecting the idea that a "prosecutor has a constitutional duty routinely to deliver his entire file to defense counsel"); Moore v. Illinois, 408 U.S. 786, 795 (1972) ("We know of no constitutional requirement that the prosecution make a complete and detailed accounting to the defense of all police investigatory work on a case").

247. 373 U.S. 83 (1963).

248. *Id.* at 87.

249. Strickler v. Greene, 527 U.S. 263, 280 (1999) ("We have since held that the duty to disclose such evidence is applicable even though there has been no request by the accused.").

250. Kyles v. Whitley, 514 U.S. 419, 438 (1995) (stating that the obligation extends to evidence "known only to police investigators and not to the prosecutor") (footnote omitted).

251. United States v. Bagley, 473 U.S. 667, 676 (1985) ("Impeachment evidence . . . as well as exculpatory evidence, falls within the *Brady* rule.").

252. *Id.* at 682 (stating the evidence is material "if there is a reasonable probability that, had the evidence been disclosed to the defense, the result of the proceeding would have been different").

253. State v. Taylor, 344 N.C. 31, 50 (1996) ("[D]ue process and *Brady* are satisfied by the disclosure of the evidence at trial, so long as disclosure is made in time for the defendants to make effective use of the evidence.").

254. N.C. R. Prof'l Conduct 3.3(a)(3) (stating that a lawyer may not "offer evidence that the lawyer knows to be false").

255. Napue v. Illinois, 360 U.S. 264 (1959) (reversing conviction because cooperating co-defendant falsely testified that he had not been promised anything in exchange for his cooperation, and prosecutor failed to correct the testimony).

256. *Id.* at 269 ("The same result obtains when the State, although not soliciting false evidence, allows it to go uncorrected when it appears."); State v. Boykin, 298 N.C. 687, 694 (1979) (noting that the use of false testimony is improper "even though the State did not solicit the false evidence but allowed it to go uncorrected when it appeared"). This may be so even if the prosecutor did not know that the evidence was false. For example, in *Giglio v. United States*, 405 U.S. 150 (1972), one of the defendant's associates testified for the government and claimed that he had not been promised that he would not be prosecuted if he testified. In fact, although the trial prosecutor did not know it, another prosecutor had made such a promise. The Supreme Court reversed the defendant's conviction, citing *Napue* as well as *Brady*.

is a reasonable likelihood that the prosecutor's knowing use of, or knowing failure to correct, false evidence affected the verdict in a case, the defendant is entitled to a new trial.[257]

Lost or Destroyed Evidence

Sometimes the police lose or destroy evidence before trial. The framework for addressing such arguments is set out in *Arizona v. Youngblood*.[258] Under *Youngblood*, if "no more can be said than that [the evidence] could have been subjected to tests, the results of which might have exonerated the defendant," the defendant must show that the police acted in bad faith in order to establish a due process violation.[259]

L. Discrimination in Selecting Grand Jury Foreperson

When a grand jury is impaneled, "the presiding judge must appoint one of the grand jurors as foreman."[260] A defendant may move to quash, or dismiss, the indictment against him or her on the basis that the judge selected the foreperson in a racially discriminatory manner. Any such motion is considered a "challenge to the array" within the meaning of G.S. 15A-955(1), and it therefore must normally be filed within the time limits set forth in G.S. 15A-952.[261]

The seminal case in this area is *State v. Cofield*.[262] The defendant in *Cofield* was black. He was indicted for rape and other crimes in Northampton County, the population of which was 61 percent black and 39 percent white. The available evidence suggested that the racial composition of the grand jury, over time, generally reflected that of the county. However, just one black person had served as foreperson in the past twenty-eight years, and the foreperson of the grand jury that had indicted the defendant was white. The defendant moved to dismiss the indictment, alleging racial discrimination in the selection of the foreperson. The trial court denied the motion and the defendant was convicted. On appeal, the state supreme court ruled that racial discrimination in the appointment of a foreperson violates Article I, Section 26, of the state constitution[263] and that "a bl ack defendant may make

257. United States v. Agurs, 427 U.S. 97, 103 (1976) (holding that a defendant's conviction "must be set aside if there is any reasonable likelihood that the false testimony [knowingly used by a prosecutor] could have affected the judgment of the jury" (footnote omitted)).

258. 488 U.S. 51 (1988).

259. *Id.* at 57, 58. North Carolina cases decided under *Youngblood* include *State v. Taylor*, 362 N.C. 514 (2008) (no due process violation because, although the police lost photos of bullets and spent shells found at crime scene, there was no evidence of bad faith and it was speculative whether the evidence would have been helpful to the defendant); *State v. Robinson*, 346 N.C. 586 (1997) (similar ruling, where police released murder victim's car and its contents to a finance company before trial); *State v. Hunt*, 345 N.C. 720, 725 (1997) (similar ruling, where the evidence in question consisted of "articles of evidence seized at defendant's home," including a knife, a bottle of alcohol, and the clothes worn by the defendant's accomplice on the night of the murder); and *State v. Mlo*, 335 N.C. 353 (1994) (similar ruling, where the victim's car was released to the victim's estate). *See also* State v. Graham, 200 N.C. App. 204 (2009) (evidence about the defendant's car and soil samples taken from it were properly admitted, even though the police lost the car prior to trial; there was no evidence of bad faith, and the defendant had access to the soil samples).

260. G.S. 15A-622(e).

261. State v. Miller, 339 N.C. 663 (1995); State v. Robinson, 327 N.C. 346 (1990); *see also* State v. Green, 329 N.C. 686 (1991) (holding that by pleading guilty to the two charges of first-degree murder, the defendant waived his right to challenge the indictment based on alleged discrimination in the selection of the foreperson).

262. 320 N.C. 297 (1987) (referred to as *Cofield I*).

263. Article I, Section 26, provides that "[n]o person shall be excluded from jury service on account of sex, race, color, religion, or national origin." The court also found a violation of the equal protection guarantee of

out a prima facie case of racial discrimination in the foreman's selection by showing either (1) that the selection procedure itself was not racially neutral, or (2) that for a substantial period in the past relatively few blacks have served in the position of foreman even though a substantial number have been selected to serve as members of grand juries."[264] It ruled that the defendant had established a prima facie case under the second prong of the test, and so it remanded the case to the trial court "in order to afford the state an opportunity to rebut defendant's prima facie showing."[265]

On remand, the state's evidence established that the presiding judge asked the district attorney, the clerk, and the sheriff for recommendations regarding who should be appointed as foreperson; that the district attorney suggested a black person while the sheriff, with the assent of the clerk, suggested a white person whom the sheriff knew personally, who had a background in management, and whom the sheriff viewed as "dependable" and "mature"; and that the trial judge appointed the white person on the basis of his leadership abilities, not his race.[266] The trial court ruled that this evidence rebutted the defendant's prima facie case. The defendant appealed again, and the supreme court reversed.[267] Although the court professed to be "satisfied that there was not the slightest hint of racial motivation" in the trial judge's actions, it nonetheless found that the process used to select the foreman was discriminatory "because it excluded from consideration as foreman all of the black grand jury members."[268] The court indicated that only the person ultimately appointed received genuine consideration, apparently because he was the only person recommended to the judge based on personal knowledge of his attributes. Based on this conclusion, the supreme court ordered that the indictment be dismissed.[269] However, it stated that the defendant could be reindicted by a grand jury with a properly appointed foreperson and retried.[270]

In the years immediately following the *Cofield* decisions, there was a significant amount of litigation regarding the selection of grand jury forepersons.[271] There are few recent cases in this area, however, perhaps because of changes in the way judges typically select forepersons. For example,

---

the United States Constitution but emphasized the state constitutional violation, as it did in its later opinion in the same case, described below.

264. *Cofield I*, 320 N.C. at 308–09. Presumably the court's reasoning would apply to any race.

265. *Id.* at 309.

266. State v. Cofield (*Cofield II*), 324 N.C. 452, 455 (1989) (referencing trial court testimony).

267. *Cofield II*, 324 N.C. 452.

268. *Id.* at 459, 460.

269. The court had ruled previously in *Cofield I* that "[t]he effect of racial discrimination on the outcome of the proceedings is immaterial," i.e., that a discriminatory appointment requires dismissal regardless of whether the defendant can establish that the discriminatory appointment of the foreperson had any effect on the indictment against the defendant. 320 N.C. at 304. Courts nationally are split on that issue. *See generally* 4 Wayne R. LaFave et al., Criminal Procedure § 15.4(e) (3d ed. 2007).

270. *Cofield II*, 324 N.C. at 464–65.

271. *See, e.g.*, State v. Jefferies, 333 N.C. 501 (1993) (holding that the defendant established a prima facie case of discrimination by showing that for the past nineteen years, 3.8 percent of grand jury forepersons in a particular county were black while 19.7 percent of members of grand juries were black, but that the state rebutted the defendant's prima facie case by showing that the superior court judge appointed the relevant grand jury foreperson in a racially neutral manner, based on the recommendation of the foreperson of the prior grand jury and the fact that the foreperson volunteered; note that this case was decided solely under the ruling in *Cofield I*, not *Cofield II*); State v. Moore, 329 N.C. 245 (1991) (holding that a black defendant has standing to object to the removal of a white foreperson and ruling that a black foreperson was unconstitutionally appointed solely on the basis of race when the district attorney specifically requested that the superior court judge remove the current white grand jury foreperson and replace him with a black person and the judge did so); State v. Phillips, 328 N.C. 1 (1991) (finding no discrimination when the presiding judge instructed the grand jurors to nominate as foreperson any one of their members, including the present foreperson).

some judges now ask all grand jurors to complete a written questionnaire, which the judges then use to select a foreperson without ever knowing the race of the grand jurors in question.[272]

M. Discrimination in Selecting the Jury Panel and the Fair Cross Section Requirement

The Sixth Amendment to the United States Constitution guarantees the right to trial by jury. "[T]he American concept of the jury trial contemplates a jury drawn from a fair cross section of the community."[273] If a defendant can show that a "distinctive" group is significantly underrepresented in a jury pool as a result of "systematic exclusion," he or she has made a prima facie case that his or her fair cross section rights have been violated.[274] Unless the state is able to rebut the prima facie case,[275] a new jury pool must be drawn or other appropriate relief provided.

At one time, the names of prospective jurors were taken principally from voter registration records, a source which may not reflect the racial composition of the community. Since 1983, G.S. 9-2(b) has required the inclusion of licensed drivers as a source of names used in preparing the list of prospective jurors.[276] This has reduced the likelihood of a successful fair cross section challenge.

Case Summaries: Discrimination in Selecting the Jury Panel

Berghuis v. Smith, 559 U.S. 314 (2010).[277] African Americans made up 7.28 percent of the local jury-eligible population, but over the six months leading up to the defendant's trial comprised only 6 percent of the jury pool in the felony court where the defendant was tried. The "absolute disparity" was therefore 1.28 percent (7.28 percent – 6 percent = 1.28 percent), while in relative terms, African Americans were 18 percent underrepresented (1.28 percent/7.28 percent = 18 percent). The defendant's fair cross section claim was rejected by the trial judge and ultimately by the state supreme court; was granted by the Sixth Circuit; and then was denied again by the United States Supreme Court. The Court found both absolute and relative disparity to be "imperfect" measures of representation, and declined to specify the proper method for determining underrepresentation. Applying the deferential standard of review mandated by the Antiterrorism and Effective Death Penalty Act, the Court found insufficient evidence that any underrepresentation was the result of systematic exclusion.

---

272. Sample questionnaires may be found at www.sog.unc.edu/sites/www.sog.unc.edu/files/Grand JuryForepersonQuestionnaires.pdf, and a sample order appointing a foreperson and sample questionnaire on foreperson selection may be found at www.sog.unc.edu/sites/www.sog.unc.edu/files/Grand%20Jury%20 Foreperson_June%202012.pdf. Both documents are part of the School of Government's online publication THE SURVIVAL GUIDE: SUPERIOR COURT JUDGES' BENCHBOOK (known informally as the benchbook for superior court judges), www.sog.unc.edu/node/1092.

273. Taylor v. Louisiana, 419 U.S. 522, 527 (1975).

274. Duren v. Missouri, 439 U.S. 357, 364 (1979) (internal quotation marks omitted).

275. The state may so rebut by showing that the disparity is the result of qualification criteria that "manifestly and primarily advance[]" significant state interests and that the disparity is not so great that the jury pool no longer represents the community. *Duren*, 439 U.S. at 367. It is difficult to imagine that the systematic exclusion of, for example, a racial group could ever be justified, but the exclusion of, for example, the mentally retarded from jury service would seem to be permissible under *Duren*.

276. *See* S.L. 1981-720. Although originally in subsection (c) of G.S. 9-2, the provision requiring the inclusion of licensed drivers is in subsection (b) as a result of S.L. 2003-226.

277. For a fuller discussion of *Smith*, see Jeff Welty, *Fair Cross Section*, N.C. CRIM. L., UNC SCH. OF GOV'T BLOG (Mar. 31, 2010), http://sogweb.sog.unc.edu/blogs/ncclaw/?p=1175.

State v. Rogers, 355 N.C. 420 (2002). Excusing jurors over age 65 upon their request under G.S. 9-6.1 did not deprive the defendant of his right to a jury pool that was a fair cross section of the community. People over 65 are not a distinctive group subject to fair cross section analysis because there is no evidence that the values and attitudes of such people are cohesive, consistent, or different from those of other community members.

State v. Williams, 355 N.C. 501 (2002). Although Wake County's population was 20.8 percent black while only 8.7 percent of the defendant's jury pool was black, a 12.1 percent absolute disparity was insufficient to show an unreasonable underrepresentation of African Americans in the jury pool. Further, because the defendant's only evidence was "statistics," he failed to establish "that the alleged deficiency of African-Americans on the jury was because of the systematic exclusion of this group."

State v. Golphin, 352 N.C. 364 (2000). Although the defendants' trial was held in Cumberland County, a special venire was drawn from Johnston County. Cumberland County was 31.8 percent black, while Johnston County was 17.5 percent black. The defendants argued that this created a fair cross section violation. The court ruled that the 14.3 percent absolute disparity was not inherently unfair or unreasonable; that "defendants are not entitled to a special venire from the population of a county which exactly mirrors the population of Cumberland County"; and that statistics from a single jury pool were insufficient to show systematic exclusion of a cognizable group.

State v. McNeill, 326 N.C. 712 (1990). The defendant's evidence, which showed that only 5 percent of the jury panel was black but 23 percent of the county's population was black, failed to show that the procedure in establishing the jury panel was not racially neutral or that there was a history of relatively few African Americans serving on the county's juries.

State v. McLaughlin, 323 N.C. 68 (1988). The defendant failed to establish a prima facie case of racial discrimination by showing that 34 percent of the county's population was black and 24 percent of the jury panel was black. The defendant failed to show what portion of the county's black population was actually eligible to serve as jurors, that the jury selection procedure was not racially neutral, or that there was a history of relatively few African Americans on the county's juries.

State v. McCoy, 320 N.C. 581 (1987). The defendant's evidence was insufficient to show that African Americans had been systematically excluded by the method used to select jurors in Rutherford County, which tended to exclude the urban population. There was no evidence of the precise number of African Americans excluded, and a defense witness's testimony on this issue was not persuasive.

State v. Johnson, 317 N.C. 343 (1986). The defendant failed to establish a prima facie case of racial discrimination merely by showing that 25.4 percent of the county's population was black and only 14.6 percent of the jury panel was black. (At the time of the trial of this case, the jury panel was drawn only from the county's voter registration list.) The defendant also failed to show that the jury commissioners systematically excluded African Americans from the jury process.

State v. Avery, 315 N.C. 1 (1985). There was no systematic exclusion of non-whites from the jury pool when non-whites constituted 35.9 percent of the county population eligible for jury service and the actual jury panel was 26.3 percent non-white. The jury pool was drawn from the voter registration list.

N. Statutory Violations in Selecting the Jury Panel

Chapter 9 of the General Statutes sets out procedures by which a county jury commission prepares the jury list from which prospective jurors are selected, the procedure for selecting jury panels for each session, the rules regarding excusal of prospective jurors by a district court judge before sessions of superior or district court, and other related matters. The North Carolina Supreme Court has ruled that statutory irregularities in performing these functions are not grounds for challenging an indictment or dismissing a jury panel unless the defendant presents evidence of corrupt intent, systematic discrimination, or irregularities that affected the actions of the jurors actually drawn and summoned.[278]

O. Motions for Change of Venue and Special Venire

Generally, a criminal trial should be held in the county in which the charged offense was committed.[279] However, G.S. 15A-957 provides that if, on the defendant's motion, a judge determines that the defendant cannot obtain a fair and impartial trial in the county where the case is pending, the judge must either (1) transfer the trial to another county within the prosecutorial district or to another county in an adjoining prosecutorial district or (2) order a special venire under G.S. 15A-958—essentially, a pool of jurors drawn from another county. This section appears to be intended to effectuate a defendant's constitutional right to a fair and impartial jury.[280]

A defendant seeking a change of venue or a special venire has the burden of proof in showing that there is a reasonable likelihood that pretrial publicity will prejudice his or her right to a fair and

---

278. In *State v. Vaughn*, 296 N.C. 167 (1978), the defendant moved to quash the indictment against him, alleging that the jury commission followed improper procedure in compiling the final jury list from which members of his grand jury were selected. The court ruled that the motion was properly denied because there was no "showing of corrupt intent or systematic discrimination in the compilation of the list, or a showing of the presence upon the grand jury itself of a member not qualified to serve," which is the standard for indictment dismissal. *Id.* at 175. The *Vaughn* standard has since been applied to alleged statutory violations concerning petit jurors. *See, e.g.*, State v. Murdock, 325 N.C. 522, 525 (1989) (the defendant challenged the way in which the district court judge excused jurors from the jury panel for the week of superior court in which the defendant was tried; the judge apparently "granted all requests regardless of the reason," and in some cases allowed his wife to sign the excuses on his behalf; the supreme court stated that while the district court judge failed to comply strictly with G.S. 9-6, which states that excuses should be granted only in cases of "compelling personal hardship" or in the public interest, the defendant was not entitled to a new trial because the evidence tended to negate any corrupt intent, discrimination, or irregularities that affected the actions of the jurors actually drawn and summoned); State v. Johnson, 317 N.C. 343 (1986) (the jury list was compiled by two jury commissioners after the death of a third commissioner and prior to the appointment of a replacement; further, because of computer problems, the list was compiled without including licensed drivers; although this procedure did not comply with G.S. 9-1, which requires three jury commissioners, and G.S. 9-2, requiring the inclusion of licensed drivers on the jury list, these statutory irregularities did not require reversal absent a showing of corrupt intent, systematic discrimination in the compilation of the list, or irregularities that affected the actions of the jurors actually drawn and summoned, a showing that the defendant failed to make); State v. Massey, 316 N.C. 558, 567, 570 (1986) (the defendant alleged that the jury commission "failed to prepare the jury list at least thirty days prior to [January 1, as required by G.S. 9-5] . . . failed to follow the procedure set forth in [G.S.] 9-2(d) in selecting the jurors, and failed to put in writing a procedure whereby the data processing department was to maintain and effectively preserve public access to the list of prospective jurors . . . in violation of [G.S.] 9-2.1"; but these "technical and insubstantial" violations failed to meet the *Vaughn* standard).

279. *See generally* G.S. 15A-131; State v. Yelverton, 334 N.C. 532, 539 (1993) (stating that a "trial should be held in a county different from the one in which a crime was allegedly committed only in rare cases . . . because of the significant interest of county residents in seeing criminals who commit local crimes being brought to justice").

280. *See, e.g.*, Sheppard v. Maxwell, 384 U.S. 333 (1966).

impartial trial in the county where the case is pending.[281] To state it another way: "A defendant's motion for a change of venue should be granted when he [or she] establishes that it is reasonably likely that prospective jurors would base their decision in the case upon pretrial information rather than the evidence presented at trial and would be unable to remove from their minds any preconceived impressions they might have formed."[282] The defendant need not show that it would be "virtually impossible or at least highly unlikely" for him or her to receive a fair trial.[283]

The decision about where to move the trial belongs to the court, not the defendant. That is, a defendant may not condition a motion to change venue on the trial court's agreeing to transfer the trial to a particular county that the defendant specifies.[284] Furthermore, although G.S. 15A-957 limits the counties to which the trial may be transferred, a judge has the inherent authority to order a trial transferred to anywhere in the state.[285]

Likewise, although G.S. 15A-957 provides only for a "motion of the defendant," a judge has the inherent authority to order a change of venue on the state's motion.[286] A judge may also transfer a case in the interest of justice even if a transfer is not legally required.[287]

Motions for change of venue and motions for a special venire are subject to the timing rules in G.S. 15A-952, meaning that they normally must be filed within twenty-one days of indictment if no request for arraignment is made at or before arraignment as specified in the statute if an arraignment is requested. A defendant whose pretrial motion for a change of venue has been denied may renew that motion if jury selection indicates that the defendant cannot receive a fair trial.[288]

When venue is transferred to a different prosecutorial district, "the prosecutor of the prosecutorial district where the case originated must prosecute the case unless the prosecutor of the district to which venue has been changed consents to conduct the prosecution."[289]

Generally, to succeed in obtaining a new trial on appeal, a defendant must identify prejudice among the trial jurors who actually sat on the case and show that the defendant exhausted his or her peremptory challenges in unsuccessfully seeking to remove them.[290]

---

281. *See, e.g.*, State v. Ward, 338 N.C. 64 (1994).

282. State v. Wallace, 351 N.C. 481, 510 (2000) (quoting State v. Jerrett, 309 N.C. 239, 254–55 (1983)).

283. State v. Moore, 319 N.C. 645, 649–50 (1987) (emphasis omitted).

284. State v. Prevatte, 356 N.C. 178 (2002).

285. State v. Barfield, 298 N.C. 306 (1979). See the discussion of *Barfield* in *State v. Chandler*, 324 N.C. 172 (1989). Even if a defendant fails to make a sufficient showing of prejudice to change venue, the trial court has the inherent authority to change venue. *Prevatte*, 356 N.C. 178.

286. *Chandler*, 324 N.C. 172; *Barfield*, 298 N.C. 306; State v. Griffin, 136 N.C. App. 531 (2000) (ruling that the trial judge did not abuse his discretion in granting the state's motion to change the venue of the trial based on the physical limitations of the county courthouse and the number of pending murder cases in the county and recommending that a trial judge make findings in support of such an order).

287. *Prevatte*, 356 N.C. at 211 (although "defendant failed to present a sufficient showing of prejudice to change venue," the trial court "used its sound discretion and evoked its inherent authority to change venue in the interest of and furtherance of justice," moving the trial to a nearby county where there was less publicity about the case, jury selection would proceed faster, and the dockets were not crowded).

288. A supplemental motion was made by the defendant in *State v. Moseley*, 338 N.C. 1 (1994).

289. G.S. 15A-133(d).

290. State v. Wallace, 351 N.C. 481, 510 (2000); State v. King, 326 N.C. 662 (1990). However, the court in *State v. Jerrett*, 309 N.C. 239 (1983), based on the particular circumstances of that case, ordered a new trial without requiring the defendant to show identifiable prejudice.

Case Summaries: Denial of Defendant's Motion for Change of Venue Was Error

State v. Jerrett, 309 N.C. 239 (1983). The court ruled that the trial judge erred in denying the defendant's motion for a change of venue. The case was tried in a rural county that had a population of less than 10,000 people and "was, in effect, a neighborhood." A third of the jury pool knew the victim or a member of his family, and many knew the state's witnesses. All of the witnesses presented at the pretrial hearing on the motion for change of venue, including a deputy sheriff and a magistrate, testified that it would be difficult or impossible to select a jury who had not heard about the case and that potential jurors had likely formed preconceived opinions about the defendant's guilt. Several witnesses opined that the defendant would not receive a fair trial by an impartial jury. The evidence revealed, according to the court, a reasonable likelihood that the defendant could not receive a fair trial in this county. The court stated that, although a showing of identifiable prejudice is normally required for a defendant to win a new trial, under the particular circumstances of this case, no such showing was needed.

Case Summaries: Denial of Defendant's Motion for Change of Venue Was Proper

State v. Ridgeway, 185 N.C. App. 423 (2007). The defendant's motion for a change of venue or a special venire was properly denied. Although "there had been six news articles in area newspapers about the case and a local lawyer had been involved in a discussion about the case with some of her church members who felt defendant was obviously guilty," the "jury selection process effectively screened out any jurors who might have been influenced by pretrial publicity." All the jurors who sat on the case "either indicated that they had no prior knowledge of the case or . . . expressly stated that they could decide the case solely on the evidence presented at trial."

State v. Wallace, 351 N.C. 481 (2000). The defendant's motion for a change of venue was properly denied. The defendant presented "evidence of pretrial publicity, including numerous television and newspaper reports and two press conferences held by [the police]," plus two telephone surveys of public opinion. This showing was insufficient to necessitate a change of venue. "[F]actual news accounts of the crimes and pretrial proceedings are not sufficient to establish prejudice against a defendant." Further, while the surveys showed that many area residents were "aware of the crimes and defendant's identity[,] . . . the surveys did not measure the prejudicial effect of the media coverage," nor did they assess "potential jurors' attitudes toward the presumption of innocence or their ability to confine their determinations as jurors to the evidence presented in court." The passage of time since the defendant's arrest and the large size of the county in which the trial was to take place also weighed against the need for a change of venue.

State v. Soyars, 332 N.C. 47 (1992). Although there was extensive pretrial publicity and some of it was inflammatory, the trial judge did not err in denying the defendant's motion for a change of venue or, in the alternative, for a special venire. The defendant's jury was composed of eight people who had prior knowledge of the case and four who did not. When questioned during voir dire, the jurors with prior knowledge stated that they had not formed an opinion, could set aside what they had heard or read, and could base their verdict on the evidence presented in court. The court ruled that the trial judge did not abuse his discretion in concluding that the jurors' prior knowledge of the case failed to establish a reasonable likelihood that they would base their decisions on pretrial information. The court held that a defendant is not necessarily entitled to a new trial simply because he or she can show (1) that jurors had prior knowledge of the case; (2) that the defendant exhausted his or her peremptory challenges; and (3) that a juror objectionable to the defendant served on the jury. These factors may be necessary but they are not sufficient.

State v. Ward, 338 N.C. 64 (1994). The defendant failed to meet his burden of proof to show reasonable likelihood that pretrial publicity (a newspaper article appearing on the day after mailing of notices for jury duty) might have affected the fairness of the trial; the trial judge properly denied a motion for a continuance. No prospective jurors had read the article, and jury voir dire did not reveal any problems with pretrial publicity.

State v. Moseley, 338 N.C. 1 (1994). The defendant's pretrial motion and supplemental motion (filed after jury selection) for change of venue because of prejudicial pretrial publicity were properly denied. Media coverage was not inflammatory. Prospective jurors were thoroughly questioned on their exposure to pretrial publicity. Each juror who served stated unequivocally that he or she could put aside anything read, seen, or heard about the defendant and would decide the case solely on the evidence presented in the courtroom. The defendant did not satisfy his burden of proof that there was a reasonable likelihood that pretrial publicity prevented him from receiving a fair trial in the county.

Additional cases in which the court ruled that a motion for a change of venue was properly denied are *State v. Trull*, 349 N.C. 428 (1998) (judge properly denied defendant's motion based on pretrial publicity); *State v. Hill*, 347 N.C. 275 (1997) (judge properly denied defendant's motion based on pretrial publicity); *State v. Rose*, 339 N.C. 172 (1994) (judge initially screened out from panel those who had formed an opinion); *State v. King*, 326 N.C. 662 (1990) (court noted that new trial should be granted only if defendant specifically identifies prejudice among jurors selected and exhausts peremptory challenges); *State v. Vereen*, 312 N.C. 499 (1985) (court noted that primary focus in motion for change of venue is on jurors who were ultimately selected to determine defendant's guilt or innocence; court distinguished *State v. Jerrett*, 309 N.C. 239 (1983)); *State v. Watson*, 310 N.C. 384 (1984) (judge properly denied defendant's motion based on pretrial publicity because news reports were factual and there were few close in time to the trial; the court also ruled that the defendant could not show prejudice as he did not attempt to peremptorily challenge any jurors after exhausting his allotted strikes, and so failed to show "that an objectionable person sat on the jury").

Case Summaries: Defendant's Motion for a Special Venire

State v. Golphin, 352 N.C. 364 (2000). The defendants were charged with several offenses committed in Cumberland County, including the murders of two law enforcement officers. The trial judge ordered a special venire from Johnston County for the trial in Cumberland County. The court ruled that the trial judge had the inherent authority to change venue to conduct the jury selection in Johnston County.

State v. Duvall, 304 N.C. 557 (1981). A superior court judge denied the state's motion for a special venire from another county to try this case. Six months later, the state made an identical motion, without new supporting evidence, before a different superior court judge. This judge granted the motion. The court here ruled that the second judge erred because the state did not make a sufficient showing of a substantial change of circumstances from when the first motion was denied.

State v. Geddie, 345 N.C. 73 (1996). The court ruled that excuses heard by district court judges for a special venire did not violate the defendant's state constitutional right to be present at all stages of a capital trial when all the excuses were heard before the case was called for trial.

P. Defendant's Motion for a Continuance

A defendant may seek a continuance on a variety of grounds, including

- the need for additional time to investigate, prepare, and present a defense;
- the lateness of discovery provided by the state and the concomitant need for additional time to prepare a defense;
- the need for additional time to locate witnesses who have failed to respond to subpoenas;
- a defense expert's need for additional time to conduct tests and evaluations; and
- prejudicial pretrial publicity that prevents the defendant from receiving a fair trial.

By statute, a judge must consider certain factors in deciding whether to allow a continuance, including (1) whether the failure to grant a continuance would likely result in a miscarriage of justice and (2) whether the case is so unusual and complex that more time is needed for adequate preparation.[291] Often, a defendant requesting a continuance will also cite constitutional grounds in support of his or her motion. Constitutional provisions that may be implicated in a motion for a continuance include the right to effective assistance of counsel under the Sixth Amendment; the right to have compulsory process for obtaining witnesses for the defense under the Sixth Amendment; the right to a reasonable amount of time to investigate, prepare, and present a defense under the Due Process Clause of the Fourteenth Amendment; and the right to confront and cross-examine adverse witnesses under the Sixth Amendment.[292] There are also state constitutional provisions comparable to each of the foregoing.

When a motion to continue is not based on constitutional grounds, it is addressed to the discretion of the trial judge, and denial of the motion is reviewed for abuse of discretion. However, when a defendant cites constitutional considerations in support of a motion to continue, the denial of the motion is "fully reviewable" on appeal.[293] Even when a constitutional violation is alleged, the defendant is not entitled to relief on appeal unless he or she was prejudiced by the denial of a continuance,[294] but "prejudice is presumed . . . when the likelihood that any lawyer, even a fully competent one, could provide effective assistance [without the continuance] is remote."[295]

---

291. G.S. 15A-952(g).

292. For a discussion of these constitutional provisions, see *State v. Tunstall*, 334 N.C. 320 (1993), and the other cases summarized below.

293. State v. Mitchell, 194 N.C. App. 705, 708 (2009).

294. State v. Williams, 355 N.C. 501, 540, 541 (2002) (holding that the trial court did not err in denying the defendant's motion for a continuance, which sought more time for a mitigation investigator to "look into possible additional information" and more time to investigate similar offenses for which the defendant had not been tried; the defendant was unable to show "that the lack of additional time prejudiced his case" or that he would have been better prepared with more time). Although the state supreme court has not always been clear about the matter, it is likely the state's burden to establish a lack of prejudice when constitutional considerations are claimed to have supported a continuance. G.S. 15A-1443(b) ("A violation of the defendant's rights under the Constitution of the United States is prejudicial unless the appellate court finds that it was harmless beyond a reasonable doubt. The burden is upon the State to demonstrate, beyond a reasonable doubt, that the error was harmless."); State v. Cook, 362 N.C. 285 (2008) (citing G.S. 15A-1443(b) in connection with the denial of a motion to continue).

295. *Tunstall*, 334 N.C. at 329 (citations, internal quotation marks omitted). The presumption of prejudice in such circumstances is based on *United States v. Cronic*, 466 U.S. 648, 658, 661 (1984) (footnote omitted) (holding that ineffective assistance of counsel claimants must normally establish prejudice, but that "[t]here are . . . circumstances that are so likely to prejudice the accused that the cost of litigating their effect in a particular case is unjustified," including the complete denial of counsel and cases in which "the surrounding circumstances made it . . . unlikely that any lawyer could provide effective assistance").

G.S. 15A-952 sets out procedures for filing pretrial motions in superior court. G.S. 15A-952(b) provides that a motion for a continuance, as well as certain other motions, must be made within the time limitations set out in G.S. 15A-952(c) unless a judge permits filing the motion at a later time. Generally, G.S. 15A-952(c) provides that a motion for a continuance must be made at or before the time of arraignment if a written request is filed for arraignment and arraignment is held before the session of court for which the trial is calendared. If arraignment is to be held at the session for which the trial is calendared, the motion must be filed by the Wednesday before the session during which the trial of the case will begin. If a written request for arraignment is not filed, then a motion for a continuance must be filed not later than twenty-one days from the date of the return of the bill of indictment.

Case Summaries: Denial of Defendant's Motion for Continuance Was Proper

State v. Mitchell, 194 N.C. App. 705 (2009). The state provided supplemental discovery materials to the defendant on the Tuesday and Wednesday before Thanksgiving, with trial scheduled to start the following Monday. The materials included notes from re-interviews of previously identified witnesses and from interviews of new witnesses and also might have included ballistic reports. Defense counsel requested a one-day continuance to review the materials. The state opposed the continuance, arguing that its first three witnesses were officers for whom there was no supplemental discovery. After a brief recess, "defense counsel requested fifteen minutes to finish reading the material and to confer with defendant," but the trial judge denied counsel's request. Counsel later "suggested that he and defendant could examine the supplemental discovery during the State's opening statement" and made other comments indicating that the discovery problem had been "solve[d]." The court of appeals ruled that the denial of a continuance was not error, noting that most of the state's discovery materials had been produced earlier; that the defendant offered only a "vague description" on appeal of the supplemental material; and that the supplemental discovery was not relevant to the first portion of the trial.

State v. Jones, 339 N.C. 114 (1994). The trial judge did not err in denying the defendant's motion for a one-week continuance of the capital sentencing hearing (the judge had offered a one-day continuance). The motion was based on the defendant's assertion that he was surprised by and unprepared for live testimony about his prior violent felony convictions offered as evidence of an aggravating circumstance. The court noted that, based on its review of the facts in this case, the defendant had sufficient advance notice of testimony of the victims. Although the defendant argued on appeal that a defense investigation of the prior felony convictions may have revealed grounds for their exclusion from evidence, the defendant failed to explain why the investigation was not conducted before trial. The court ruled that the defendant failed to show how he was prejudiced by the denial of the motion.

State v. Tunstall, 334 N.C. 320 (1993). The defendant's counsel made a motion for a continuance based on the defendant's unavailability (he was at Central Prison) until the day before trial and the lateness of discovery provided by the state. The trial judge denied the motion. The court noted that there was no evidence demonstrating that the defendant and his counsel were unable to consult with each other during the seven months between the appointment of counsel and the defendant's later removal to Central Prison. Reviewing the facts surrounding the state's compliance with discovery, the court noted that it was impossible, based on the appellate record, to determine whether additional time to review the state-provided materials would have benefited the defendant. The court also noted that the defendant effectively used the discovery material in cross-examination at trial. The court concluded that the defendant failed to offer evidence to establish a violation of his constitutional right to a reasonable period of time to investigate, prepare, and present his defense. Thus, the trial judge did not err in denying the defendant's motion for a continuance. *See also* State v. Stager, 329 N.C. 278 (1991) (trial judge's denial of a continuance to the defendant to investigate a tape recording offered by the state was not error; the defendant had ample time to conduct an investigation); State v. Bearthes, 329 N.C. 149 (1991) (trial judge did not err in denying defendant's motion to continue because the defendant failed to show that the content of the discovery provided to him two days before trial required additional time to prepare a defense); State v. Horner, 310 N.C. 274 (1984) (similar ruling); State v. Parton, 303 N.C. 55 (1981) (trial judge did not err in denying the defendant's motion to continue, despite the fact that the defendant was confined at Dorothea Dix Hospital for fifty-eight of the 135 days from the time of arrest to trial; the defendant failed to show why this amount of time was insufficient to prepare a defense).

State v. Roper, 328 N.C. 337 (1991). A witness for the defendant failed to appear in response to a properly served subpoena. The state's extensive good faith efforts to locate him were unsuccessful. Evidence indicated that the witness was able to live in the woods for an extended period of time. The trial judge admitted as defense evidence the statements of this witness to law enforcement officers and to defense counsel. Based on these and other facts, the court ruled that the trial judge properly denied the defendant's motions for a recess or continuance after this witness could not be located. The defendant's federal constitutional rights (Sixth Amendment right to compulsory process and due process rights) and comparable state constitutional rights were not violated. *See also* State v. Kuplen, 316 N.C. 387 (1986) (trial judge did not err in denying a motion for a continuance when the defendant could not show how an absent defense witness's testimony would be helpful to him; the defendant waited until four days before trial to issue a subpoena, even though he was aware for several weeks of the trial date); State v. Perkins, 57 N.C. App. 516 (1982) (trial judge did not err in denying a motion for a continuance when defense witnesses had not been located when subpoenaed a week before trial; there was no evidence that the witnesses could ever be located, and the defendant could not show how their testimony would be helpful to him).

State v. Schneider, 306 N.C. 351 (1982). The trial judge did not err in denying the defendant's motion for a continuance after the jury had been selected but before it had been impaneled. The defense counsel wanted the defendant to undergo a neurological examination. However, the court noted that the defendant had already been found competent to stand trial by a psychiatric evaluation, and defense counsel neither disputed this determination nor asserted that the defendant's capacity to proceed would be improved if a continuance was granted. *See also* State v. Massey, 316 N.C. 558 (1986) (trial judge did not err in denying a continuance so that a recently hired defense psychologist could evaluate the defendant's mental condition; court noted that this expert eventually evaluated the defendant and testified favorably for him); State v. Vereen, 312 N.C. 499 (1985) (trial judge did not err in denying a continuance so that a defense expert could have additional time to prepare for a hearing on a change of venue; the court noted that defense counsel had six weeks to prepare for the hearing); State v. Smith, 310 N.C. 108 (1984) (trial judge did not err in denying a continuance so that defense counsel could have additional time to employ a private psychiatrist with state funds; counsel had already had five weeks to do so, which was a reasonable amount of time).

State v. Branch, 306 N.C. 101 (1982). The court noted that the defendant had failed to timely make his motion for a continuance under G.S. 15A-952(c). The court then ruled that the trial judge did not abuse his discretion by failing to exercise the authority under G.S. 15A-952(e) to grant the defendant relief from the waiver of his right to move for a continuance. The defendant made an oral motion to continue his trial until certain witnesses could be contacted. (The court stated that it encourages counsel to offer affidavits or other evidence when making a motion for a continuance under G.S. 15A-952.) The court noted that the defendant did not inform the trial judge of a single witness that he wanted for his trial. Also, the defendant did not offer any evidence of what he sought to prove through these witnesses or any proof of the likelihood that they could ever be located or be available for trial if they, in fact, existed. The defendant also failed to show why the four-month period between formal charges and his trial date was insufficient to locate necessary witnesses and have them present for trial. *See also* State v. McCullers, 341 N.C. 19 (1995) (motion to continue made on day of trial was properly denied; defendant failed to show how potential witnesses—whom the defendant wanted time to locate and interview—would be helpful to the defense); State v. Searles, 304 N.C. 149 (1981) (trial judge did not err, based on facts in this case, in not granting more than a two-day continuance to locate potential alibi witness); State v. Jones, 342 N.C. 523 (1996) (court, in upholding denial of motion for a continuance, noted that the motion was not supported by an affidavit).

Case Summaries: Denial of Defendant's Motion for Continuance Was Error

State v. Cook, 362 N.C. 285 (2008). The defendant drank alcohol and used drugs then drove, causing a fatal accident. His second-degree murder trial was scheduled to start on a Monday. The Wednesday before trial, the state disclosed that it would be calling an expert witness to testify about retrograde extrapolation of the defendant's blood alcohol content. The state disclosed the expert's report on the Friday before trial. The defendant moved for a continuance based on surprise and on a need to retain a defense expert to meet the state's evidence. The trial court denied a continuance. The supreme court ruled that this was an abuse of discretion, though it found the error harmless in light of the other evidence of the defendant's impairment.

State v. Barlowe, 157 N.C. App. 249 (2003). The court ruled that the trial judge erred in denying the defendant's motion for a continuance because the defendant needed additional time to hire a blood-spatter expert to respond to the report of the state's blood-spatter expert. (See the court's detailed discussion of the facts in its opinion.) The blood-spatter evidence was critical to the state's case because it was the only physical evidence potentially placing the defendant at the murder scene. It also contradicted the defendant's testimony. In addition, the defendant was provided with the state's report shortly before trial and had contacted blood-spatter experts but none of them could be available to testify at trial on such short notice.

State v. Rogers, 352 N.C. 119 (2000). The court ruled that the trial judge erred in not granting defense counsel's motion for a continuance in a capital trial. Two lawyers were appointed to the case, which involved multiple incidents in multiple locations over a two-day period, for which the lawyers had only thirty-four days to prepare. (See the opinion for additional facts, including another lawyer's prior involvement in representing the defendant.) The court stated that it was unreasonable to expect that any lawyer, no matter what his or her level of experience, could have adequately prepared to conduct a bifurcated capital trial for a case that was complex and involved many witnesses. The court concluded, citing *State v. Maher*, 305 N.C. 544 (1982), and other cases, that prejudice to the defendant was presumed because one cannot be certain how trial counsel might have been able to perform if they had had adequate time to prepare for trial.

State v. Sanders, __ N.C. __, 410 S.E.2d 66 (N.C. 1991).[296] Upon petitions for certiorari by the defendant and a psychiatric expert, the North Carolina Supreme Court reversed a trial judge's orders declining to continue the proceedings in this criminal case. The court directed the trial judge to consult with counsel for the defendant and counsel for the psychiatric expert to determine if the expert would be able to serve as the defendant's expert if the proceeding was rescheduled to a later date. If the trial judge and counsel were unable to schedule the proceeding to afford the expert a reasonable period within which to perform the services reasonably necessary to ensure the defendant's rights under *Ake v. Oklahoma*, 470 U.S. 68 (1985), the court directed the trial judge to enter such other orders as necessary to ensure the protection of these rights.

State v. Maher, 305 N.C. 544 (1982). The defendant's attorney withdrew from representing the defendant four days before trial, and on the same day a new attorney was hired. The new attorney, through an associate, moved to continue the case on that day. The motion was denied. The new attorney renewed the motion on the day of trial. The trial judge denied the motion and gave the attorney fifteen minutes to confer with the defendant before the trial would begin. The attorney represented the defendant at trial, and the defendant was convicted. Based on these and other facts, the court ruled that the defendant was deprived of his constitutional right to effective assistance of counsel when the trial judge denied the motion to continue. The court also ruled that prejudice was properly presumed on these facts and that the state failed to show that the error was harmless beyond a reasonable doubt. *See also* State v. Moore, 39 N.C. App. 643 (1979) (trial judge erred in denying a motion for a continuance when defense counsel had only seventeen days to prepare a defense).

State v. McFadden, 292 N.C. 609 (1977). The defendant had retained counsel who was engaged in a federal trial, the trial judge's denial of a continuance motion caused a junior associate of the defendant's retained counsel to try the case, and the junior associate did not have a reasonable time to prepare and to present a defense. The court ruled that the trial judge's denial of the defendant's motion for a continuance violated his constitutional rights to counsel of his own choice and to the effective assistance of counsel.

State v. Smathers, 287 N.C. 226 (1975). The defendant was arrested for first-degree burglary on June 30, 1974. The case was placed on the calendar for the week of November 11, 1974. The defendant was indicted on November 14, 1974, and the case was called for trial that same day. The defendant made a motion to continue the case because of the absence of material witnesses who would testify on behalf of his alibi defense. Defense counsel explained that the witnesses (who were from South Carolina) were in court earlier in the week and had indicated that they would voluntarily appear when the trial began, but the continuance motion was denied. Based on these and other facts, the court here ruled that the trial judge erred in not granting the motion to continue because the defendant did not have an opportunity to prepare and present his defense.

296. There is no citation for this case in *North Carolina Reports*. In addition, this was a brief, unsigned order of the court, and therefore few facts were provided in the order other than what is discussed below. Another brief order granting a continuance upon certiorari review was entered by the court in *State v. Stuart*, 359 N.C. 279 (2004).

Q. Defendant's Motion to Withdraw Guilty Plea

Sometimes a defendant may plead guilty then move to withdraw his or her guilty plea. Typically, such a motion is made prior to sentencing, and in such a case, the motion should be granted if the defendant can show "any fair and just reason,"[297] that is, it should be "granted with liberality"[298] absent any "evidence of concrete prejudice to [the state's] case."[299]

Among the factors a court should consider in deciding whether a defendant's motion to withdraw a guilty plea should be granted are whether the defendant has asserted legal innocence, the strength of the state's proffer of evidence, the length of time between the entry of the guilty plea and the motion to withdraw it, whether the defendant had competent counsel at all relevant times, whether the defendant misunderstood the consequences of the guilty plea, and whether the defendant was rushed, confused, or coerced into pleading guilty.[300] The length of time between the defendant's plea and his or her motion to withdraw it is a factor on which the appellate courts have placed especially "heavy reliance."[301]

Despite the liberality with which pre-sentencing motions to withdraw a guilty plea are granted, the appellate courts have affirmed the denial of such motions in a number of cases. Several such cases are summarized in the margin.[302]

---

297. State v. Handy, 326 N.C. 532, 536 (1990).

298. *Id.* at 537.

299. *Id.* at 539. Such prejudice might include, for example, the destruction of physical evidence after the defendant's guilty plea.

300. *Id.* The court in *Handy* ruled that the defendant's motion to withdraw his guilty plea should be granted because the defendant sought to withdraw his plea within twenty-four hours after he entered it, he asserted his innocence of the armed robbery that was necessary to support his plea to first-degree felony murder, and he felt pressured by his attorneys in entering the plea. The court also noted that the state had not yet assembled its witnesses when the defendant had initially entered his guilty plea and the state did not argue that it would be substantially prejudiced by the plea withdrawal.

301. State v. Robinson, 177 N.C. App. 225, 229 (2006) (trial judge did not err in denying the defendant's motion to withdraw his guilty plea where the motion came over three months after the plea was entered and the defendant did not assert his innocence).

302. State v. Meyer, 330 N.C. 738, 743 (1992) (the defendant pled guilty, and a jury was impaneled for a capital sentencing hearing; during the hearing, the defendant escaped from the county jail and the judge declared a mistrial; after the defendant was apprehended but before a new sentencing hearing began, the defendant moved to withdraw his guilty pleas on the sole ground of a "change of circumstances," citing the extensive media coverage of the case and his escape from jail; the trial judge properly denied the motion; the defendant did not assert his legal innocence and there was no evidence that he was confused or coerced regarding his plea; the court rejected the defendant's argument that a motion to withdraw a guilty plea must be granted unless the state can show concrete prejudice to its case, holding instead that the state need not address this issue until the defendant has asserted a fair and just reason for withdrawing the guilty plea, which was not done in this case) (internal quotation marks omitted); State v. Chery, 203 N.C. App. 310, 318 (2010) (the defendant pled guilty to conspiracy to commit armed robbery but moved to withdraw his plea when his co-defendant was acquitted; the trial court properly denied the motion, inter alia because the state's proffer of evidence at the time the plea was entered was strong, and the strength of the proffer must be assessed at the time it was made, not in light of what happened at the co-defendant's trial; the court of appeals noted that although the defendant sought to withdraw his plea only nine days after he entered it, this was not evidence of a "swift change of heart" in light of the fact that he executed his transcript of plea several months earlier) (internal quotation marks omitted); State v. Watkins, 195 N.C. App. 215, 226 (2009) (defendant's statement that "I ain't completely innocent, but I ain't completely guilty" was an equivocal assertion of innocence at best; in light of that, and the fact that he had competent counsel and did not promptly move to withdraw his guilty plea, the defendant's motion was properly denied) (internal quotation marks omitted); State v. Villatoro, 193 N.C. App. 65 (2008) (similar).

Less often, a defendant may seek to withdraw his or her plea after sentencing. The defendant must do so by filing a motion for appropriate relief, which should be granted only to "avoid manifest injustice."[303]

303. *Handy*, 326 N.C. at 536. *See also* State v. Salvetti, 202 N.C. App. 18, 25 (2010) ("A post-sentencing motion to withdraw a plea is a motion for appropriate relief.").

Chapter 3

Selected Trial Issues

Chapter 3

Selected Trial Issues

This chapter discusses legal issues that frequently arise at the guilt-innocence stage of a capital trial. Although not all of the issues considered in this chapter are unique to capital cases, the emphasis is on such issues. Other reference works exist for issues common to all criminal trials.

A. Jurisdiction

Generally, a defendant may be prosecuted in North Carolina's courts only for crimes committed in North Carolina.[1] To be more precise, "North Carolina courts have jurisdiction over a crime if any of the essential acts forming the offense occurred in this State."[2] Thus, *jurisdiction* refers to the authority of the state of North Carolina to try a defendant for a criminal offense committed in the state. By contrast, *venue* refers to the place of a trial within the state of North Carolina; venue is discussed in Chapter 2.

If the defendant does not raise the issue of jurisdiction, it need not be considered by the court or submitted to the jury.[3]

If the issue is raised, there are three possible scenarios. First, if the trial judge determines that the offense did not take place in North Carolina, the judge must rule that jurisdiction is lacking and must dismiss the case.[4]

Second, if the trial judge determines that jurisdiction is reasonably disputed, the issue must be submitted to the jury. In other words, if "the trial court makes a preliminary determination that

---

1. *See, e.g.,* State v. Tickle, 238 N.C. 206, 209 (1953) ("An act to be punishable as a crime in this state must be an act committed here and against this sovereignty.").

2. State v. White, 134 N.C. App. 338, 339–40 (1999). *See also* Section 15A-134 of the North Carolina General Statutes (hereinafter G.S.) (permitting the trial of a defendant in North Carolina if the alleged crime took place partly in North Carolina and partly elsewhere, so long as the defendant "has not been placed in jeopardy for the identical offense in another state").

3. *Cf.* State v. Darroch, 305 N.C. 196, 212 (1982) ("Because the locus of the principal offense was not challenged, no instruction on the burden of proof on that issue was required."); State v. Batdorf, 293 N.C. 486, 493 (1977) (stating that "when jurisdiction is challenged," the burden of establishing it is on the state); WAYNE R. LAFAVE ET AL., 4 CRIMINAL PROCEDURE § 16.4(d) (3d ed. 2007) ("[W]here the prosecution evidence pointing to jurisdiction . . . is not disputed, the court ordinarily has no obligation to charge the jury on the issue of the locus of the crime.").

4. G.S. 15A-954(a)(8).

sufficient evidence exists upon which a jury could conclude beyond a reasonable doubt that the murder occurred in North Carolina, the trial court must also instruct the jury that unless the State has satisfied it beyond a reasonable doubt that the murder occurred in North Carolina, a verdict of not guilty should be returned."[5] The trial judge should instruct the jury to return a special verdict on the jurisdiction issue.[6] There is a pattern jury instruction (hereinafter referred to as N.C.P.I) and a special verdict form on point.[7] If the jury finds that the state has jurisdiction to try the offense, then it must continue its deliberations on the charged offense and return the special verdict on jurisdiction along with its verdict on the charged offense. If the jury finds that the state does not have jurisdiction to try the offense, then it must report the special verdict to the trial judge without any further deliberations on the charged offense.

Third, the judge may determine that all the evidence shows that the offense took place in North Carolina and that there is no factual support for the defendant's claim that jurisdiction is lacking. May the judge rule that jurisdiction is proper and decline to submit the issue to the jury? At least one case suggests that the answer is yes,[8] and such a procedure would be consistent with how requests for other kinds of jury instructions are handled. However, a judge wishing to err on the side of caution may prefer to submit the issue to the jury whenever it is raised by the defense.

When the victim's body, the murder weapon, and materials used to conceal the body are found in North Carolina, this constitutes a prima facie showing of jurisdiction sufficient to take the matter to the jury.[9] If the issue of jurisdiction has been determined at a prior trial, it may not be relitigated at a subsequent trial.[10] A leading treatise contains an extended discussion of jurisdiction.[11]

B. Defendant's Right to Be Present at Trial

Article I, Section 23, of the North Carolina Constitution provides that "every person charged with crime has the right . . . to confront the accusers and witnesses with other testimony." This language has been interpreted to accord a capital defendant[12] an unwaiveable right to be present at all stages of his or her trial:

---

5. State v. Rick, 342 N.C. 91, 100–01 (1995) (victim's body was found in South Carolina; nonetheless, there was sufficient evidence of jurisdiction to submit the case to a North Carolina jury; but because the trial judge failed to submit the issue of jurisdiction to the jury, the defendant's conviction was vacated).

6. *Batdorf*, 293 N.C. at 494.

7. N.C.P.I. Crim.—311.10.

8. State v. Drakeford, 104 N.C. App. 298, 301 (1991) (state's evidence of jurisdiction was "sufficient to carry [the case] to the jury without need of a special jury instruction").

9. *Batdorf*, 293 N.C. at 494–95.

10. State v. Dial, 122 N.C. App. 298 (1996). In *Dial*, the trial judge at the defendant's first murder trial, before declaring a mistrial, accepted the jury's special verdict that the state had jurisdiction to try the defendant for murder. The court of appeals ruled that the defendant could not litigate the jurisdiction issue at his second trial based on principles of res judicata and collateral estoppel.

11. LaFave et al., *supra* note 3, at § 16.4. *See also* Jessica Smith, North Carolina Crimes 1617 (UNC School of Government, 7th ed. 2012) (shorter discussion, but specific to North Carolina).

12. The right belongs to a defendant in a capital trial even if the outcome of the proceeding is not a death sentence. State v. Johnston, 331 N.C. 680 (1992) (the trial judge's private unrecorded bench conferences with prospective jurors violated the defendant's right to be present and required a new trial for a defendant who was tried capitally but received a sentence of life imprisonment). *See also* State v. Moss, 332 N.C. 65 (1992) (court reaffirmed prior rulings that when a new trial is ordered for a capital offense because the defendant's right to be present was violated, the defendant also will receive a new trial for the noncapital offenses that were tried with the capital offense).

> Although the United States Supreme Court has stated that the confrontation clause of the federal constitution guarantees each criminal defendant the fundamental right to personal presence at *all critical stages* of the trial, . . . our state constitutional right of confrontation has been interpreted as being broader in scope, guaranteeing the right of every accused to be present at *every stage* of his trial . . . providing that defendant's right to be present cannot be waived, and imposing on the trial court the duty to insure defendant's presence at trial.[13]

By contrast, a defendant in a noncapital case, including a noncapital first-degree murder case, may waive his or her right to be present at trial.[14]

When a capital defendant is denied his or her right to be present at trial, a new trial is required unless the state is able to prove that the error was harmless beyond a reasonable doubt.[15] If the proceedings held in the defendant's absence were recorded, the record may reveal whether the error was harmless.[16] If the proceedings were not recorded, reconstructing the proceedings on the record may be helpful.[17] However, any reconstruction of the record must take place at trial, not on appeal.[18]

One important issue is the extent to which the right applies at pretrial stages of a capital case. The appellate courts have not comprehensively analyzed this issue. It is clear that the right does not extend

---

13. State v. Huff, 325 N.C. 1, 29 (1989) (emphases in original) (citations omitted), *vacated on other grounds*, 497 U.S. 1021 (1990).

14. State v. Pittman, 332 N.C. 244 (1992); State v. Forrest, 168 N.C. App. 614, 622 (2005) ("[I]n a non-capital trial, the defendant's right to be present is personal and may be waived.").

15. *Huff*, 325 N.C. at 33 ("[W]e hold that the proper standard of reversal in reviewing violations under article I, section 23, of defendant's right to be present at all stages of his capital trial is the rigorous standard prescribed for review of violations of defendant's right to be present at trial under the federal constitution. . . . We will order a new trial unless the State proves, and we find, that the error was harmless beyond a reasonable doubt . . .") (citations omitted), *vacated on other grounds*, 497 U.S. 1021 (1990).

16. State v. Payne, 328 N.C. 377 (1991) (the trial judge asked prospective jurors some questions while the court reporter and defense counsel were present but the defendant had not yet been brought into the courtroom; based on the transcribed questions and answers, the error was ruled harmless beyond a reasonable doubt).

17. *Compare, e.g.*, State v. Bacon, 337 N.C. 66 (1994) (no prejudicial error where the trial judge had an unrecorded communication at the bench with a prospective juror about her fitness to serve, in part because the judge reconstructed the substance of the communication); State v. Lee, 335 N.C. 244 (1994) (the trial judge excused several prospective jurors for medical reasons outside the defendant's presence; the judge's interactions with the jurors were not recorded, but the judge described the nature of the interactions briefly on the record; the judge also reconstructed an unrecorded conversation with a seated juror during trial; the record showed that the violation of the defendant's right to presence was harmless beyond a reasonable doubt); State v. Williams, 339 N.C. 1 (1994) (judge reconstructed communications with prospective jurors; harmless error also existed with communications with other prospective jurors that were not reconstructed); State v. Willis, 332 N.C. 151 (1992) (communication with juror during trial was error, but harmless beyond a reasonable doubt; judge reconstructed communication for the record); State v. Davis, 325 N.C. 607 (1989) (the trial judge had two telephone conversations with a prospective juror in the presence of the prosecutor and defense attorneys but not the defendant; the judge repeated for the record the content of the calls; any error was harmless); *and* State v. Hudson, 331 N.C. 122 (1992) (assuming that the trial judge's conversations with jurors in the hallway during a break violated the defendant's right to presence, the error was harmless beyond a reasonable doubt when the reconstructed conversations showed that their content was not significant), *with, e.g.*, State v. Smith, 326 N.C. 792 (1990) (judge's private unrecorded bench conferences with prospective jurors violated the defendant's right to be present; since no record was made of these conferences, the state supreme court ruled that the errors were not harmless beyond a reasonable doubt); *and* State v. Payne, 320 N.C. 138 (1987) (no harmless error because record did not show the content of the judge's admonitions to the jury; for ruling of harmless error, as to questioning of jurors in defendant's absence, in later proceeding, see *Payne*, 328 N.C. 377).

18. State v. Boyd, 332 N.C. 101 (1992) (rejecting affidavits from the trial judge and deputy clerk, offered by the state four days before oral argument in the supreme court, that purported to reconstruct the content of the judge's private conversation with a prospective juror; reconstruction of conversations must occur at trial to be part of the record on appeal). *See also* State v. McCarver, 329 N.C. 259 (1991) (similar).

to the Rule 24 hearing,[19] to pretrial conferences and similar proceedings,[20] to hearings at which a judge announces a ruling on a pretrial motion,[21] and to administrative proceedings involving jurors—such as the hearing of jury excuses—that are conducted before the defendant's case is called.[22] The question of whether the right attaches to hearings on pretrial motions is unsettled.[23]

Once the state calls a capital case for trial and jury selection begins, it is clear that the defendant has a right to be present. Communications between the judge and jurors, whether prospective or seated, have been a fertile ground for litigation about this right. Once a defendant's case is called, a judge may not hear jury excuses in the absence of the defendant.[24] Nor should the judge engage in private communications with jurors during jury selection[25] or during the evidentiary stage of the trial.[26] However, brief unrecorded bench conferences with prospective jurors *and counsel for the state*

19. State v. Chapman, 342 N.C. 330 (1995).

20. State v. Locklear, 349 N.C. 118 (1998) (no right to be present when the prosecutor communicated with the judge about scheduling a hearing on arraigning the defendant); State v. Buckner, 342 N.C. 198 (1995) (no right to be present at a pretrial conference held four days before the trial began; the defendant's attorney was present).

21. State v. Rich, 346 N.C. 50 (1997) (judge announced ruling on state's motion to obtain the defendant's prison records in open court; neither the defendant nor defense counsel was present).

22. State v. McCarver, 341 N.C. 364 (1995) (a district court judge, acting under G.S. 9-6(b), excused some prospective jurors and deferred others while screening a special venire for a capital trial; neither the defendant nor his attorney was present; the state supreme court ruled that the defendant did not have a constitutional right to be present during pretrial jury selection matters, even when the proceedings involved a jury venire that was picked specifically for the defendant's trial); State v. Geddie, 345 N.C. 73 (1996) (similar); State v. Rannels, 333 N.C. 644 (1993) (a superior court judge announced the commencement of the criminal session, welcomed the pool of potential jurors, then had unrecorded bench conferences with five potential jurors who had requested to speak with the judge, excusing three of them; the defendant's case was subsequently called for trial; the defendant's right to presence was not violated because the defendant's trial had not begun when the unrecorded bench conferences with prospective jurors took place); State v. Cole, 331 N.C. 272 (1992) (a jury panel was present at the beginning of a week of court; a superior court judge considered excuses without the defendant or his counsel being present; the next day, the defendant's case was called for trial and jury selection began; the following day, a second pool of prospective jurors reported for jury duty and the judge again considered excuses at the bench and off the record without the presence of the defendant and his attorney; the supreme court ruled that the trial judge erred only with respect to considering excuses from the second group of jurors, as the defendant's trial had not yet begun when the judge considered excuses from the first group).

23. *Compare* State v. Zuniga, 320 N.C. 233 (1987) (assuming, without deciding, that the defendant's absence from a pretrial change-of-venue hearing was constitutional error), *and* State v. Hayes, 130 N.C. App. 154, 176 (1998) (stating that the right to presence extends to "motions *in limine* related to [the defendant's] trial") (italics in original), *with* State v. Golphin, 352 N.C. 364, 388–90 (2000) (no violation of the defendants' right to presence where they were not present at a pretrial "meeting" between the prosecutor, judge, and defense counsel regarding possible change of venue or special venire; defendants were present at subsequent in-court hearing), *Chapman*, 342 N.C. at 338 (right "does not arise prior to the commencement of trial," and so doesn't extend to Rule 24 hearings), *and* State v. Davis, 290 N.C. 511 (1976) (holding that the defendant's right to be present did not apply to a pretrial hearing on a discovery motion when his counsel was present at the hearing).

24. *Cole*, 331 N.C. 272 (a jury panel was present at the beginning of a week of court; a superior court judge considered excuses without the defendant or his counsel being present; the next day, the defendant's case was called for trial and jury selection began; the following day, a second pool of prospective jurors reported for jury duty and the judge again considered excuses at the bench and off the record without the presence of the defendant and his attorney; the state supreme court ruled that the trial judge erred only with respect to considering excuses from the second group of jurors, as the defendant's trial had not yet begun when the judge considered excuses from the first group).

25. State v. Moss, 332 N.C. 65 (1992) (holding that the trial judge's private unrecorded conferences with prospective jurors violated the defendant's right to be present; the trial judge did not reconstruct for the record the content of the conferences; new trial ordered). For similar rulings, see *State v. Boyd,* 332 N.C. 101 (1992); *State v. Monroe,* 330 N.C. 846 (1992); *State v. McCarver,* 329 N.C. 259 (1991); and *State v. Smith,* 326 N.C. 792 (1990).

26. State v. Jones, 346 N.C. 704 (1997) (during trial, the judge passed a note to an alternate juror without revealing its contents to the defendant or his counsel; this violated the defendant's right to be present; but the violation was harmless beyond a reasonable doubt because the record indicated that the note involved a personal matter unrelated to the trial).

and the defendant may be permissible.[27] It is also permissible for the judge to communicate with the jury through the bailiff on administrative matters and to remind the jury to abide by the court's instructions.[28] A defendant has no right to be present for certain purely administrative tasks, such as dividing a jury pool among several cases to be tried during a single week of court.[29] However, if the jury submits a question to the judge, the defendant has a right to review the question.[30]

Communications between the judge and the lawyers, in the absence of the defendant, have also been challenged. Brief unrecorded bench conferences during the evidentiary stage of trial have generally been held to be permissible.[31] In-chambers conferences conducted without the defendant, by

---

27. State v. Lee, 335 N.C. 244 (1994) (the trial judge conducted an unrecorded bench conference with a prospective juror and counsel for the state and the defendant; defense counsel then excused the juror; the defendant was present in the courtroom and was able to observe the context in which the bench conference arose and to ask his counsel about its substance; this bench conference did not violate the defendant's right to be present).

28. State v. Bacon, 337 N.C. 66 (1994) (the trial judge's communications through the bailiff involved administrative matters—for example, having the jurors fill out a questionnaire and directing the jury to take a break—and therefore no constitutional violation occurred); State v. May, 334 N.C. 609 (1993) (the trial judge instructed the bailiff to tell the jury to leave the jury room for a fifteen-minute recess; no error; proper to assume that the bailiff followed the judge's instructions absent contrary evidence); State v. Gay, 334 N.C. 467 (1993) (the bailiff's communication to the jury, made at the trial judge's direction, informing the jurors to take a break and abide by the judge's earlier instructions, did not violate the defendant's right to be present); State v. Coleman, 161 N.C. App. 224, 230 (2003) (during deliberations, apparently at lunchtime, a juror "informed the trial court that, due to a personal problem, she would be unable to return to the courtroom" until the late afternoon; the trial judge admonished the remaining jurors not to discuss the case in the interim and sent the bailiff to convey the same message to the absent juror; the court of appeals assumed that the bailiff followed the court's directions; having the bailiff remind the jury to follow the court's instructions is not the type of interaction at which the defendant has a right to be present). *Cf.* State v. Thompson, 359 N.C. 77 (2004) (during deliberations at the penalty phase of the defendant's trial, the judge announced that he was going to release the jury for the day; a few minutes later, before the jury was released but after the bailiff and the judge conferred at the bench, the bailiff announced that the jury had a verdict; the defendant argued that the interaction between the bailiff and the judge, and the judge's decision not to release the jury, suggested that there was an interaction between the bailiff and the jury; the defendant asserted that he was denied his right to presence because he was present for neither interaction; the state supreme court ruled that the defendant could only speculate, not show, that improper communications took place).

29. State v. Williams, 363 N.C. 689, 710 (2009) (after the defendant's case was called for trial, the jury clerk, acting on the trial judge's instructions and with the parties' consent, divided the pool of prospective jurors, assigning some to the defendant's case and others to other trials; the assignment of particular prospective jurors to particular matters was a purely administrative matter at which the defendant had no right to be present; "defendant's right to be present at all proceedings does not extend to the jury assembly room"). *Cf.* State v. Badgett, 361 N.C. 234, 249 (2007) (defendant failed to establish a violation of his right to presence where he alleged that the clerk may have selected prospective jurors from the pool outside the courtroom; the record suggested that the clerk drew the prospective jurors' names "in here," i.e., in the courtroom, and the fact that she did not call out the names aloud did not establish otherwise; any violation would be harmless given that the prospective jurors would still be selected at random as required by statute).

30. State v. Smith, 188 N.C. App. 207, 214 (2008) (the trial judge received questions from the jury but did not allow the defendant to review them before responding; this violated the defendant's right to presence; such violations require a new trial unless the state can prove harmlessness beyond a reasonable doubt; here, "the questions indicated that the jury had already agreed unanimously on second-degree murder, and was confused as to whether [its] rejection of first-degree murder had to be unanimous"; the court's reiteration of its original instructions on that issue was legally correct and did not contribute to the verdict against the defendant, who was convicted of second-degree murder; therefore, the error was harmless).

31. *Lee,* 335 N.C. at 264 (noting that "generally, a defendant's right to be present is not violated if defense counsel is present at the bench conference and the defendant is actually in the courtroom," unless the defendant's Confrontation Clause rights are implicated or there is a particular need for his or her participation); State v. Cummings, 332 N.C. 487 (1992) (noting that G.S. 15A-1241 does not require recordation of bench conferences between a trial judge and the attorneys for the state and the defendant, but that if either party requests that the subject matter of a private bench conference be placed in the record for possible appellate review, the trial judge should accurately reconstruct the matter discussed); State v. Buchanan, 330 N.C. 202 (1991) (bench

contrast, are generally improper, though if the subject matter of the conference is reconstructed and reexamined in the courtroom with the defendant present, the error may be harmless.[32]

Other issues that have been litigated include the defendant's right to be present during a jury view of a crime scene;[33] the defendant's absence, at his own request, during a portion of the state's case;[34] the defendant's absence due to disruptive behavior;[35] and the defendant's absence from a pretrial deposition.[36]

---

conferences took place during jury selection and during the guilt-innocence phase of the defendant's trial; none of the conferences were recorded; they apparently dealt with legal issues such as the scope of questions during voir dire of prospective jurors, excusal of certain jurors for cause, timing of recesses during proceedings, and evidentiary questions; the defendant's absence from these conferences did not prejudice him and did not violate his right to presence; however, if the subject matter of a conference implicates the defendant's confrontation rights or if the defendant's presence would have a reasonably substantial relation to the opportunity to defend himself or herself, then the defendant would have a constitutional right to be present). *See also Bacon,* 337 N.C. 66 (defendant failed to satisfy burden of proof to show need for his presence at bench conferences).

32. State v. Meyer, 345 N.C. 619 (1997) (in-chambers conference during jury selection for a capital sentencing hearing violated the defendant's right to be present; because there was no record of what occurred during the conference, the court could not determine whether the constitutional error was harmless beyond a reasonable doubt; new sentencing hearing ordered); State v. Exum, 343 N.C. 291 (1996) (at the conclusion of testimony by a defense witness, the trial judge conducted an unrecorded in-chambers conference without the defendant; this violated the defendant's right to be present; there was no record of what occurred at this conference, so the court was unable to determine harmlessness; new trial ordered); State v. Call, 349 N.C. 382 (1998) (holding that part of the jury charge conference in chambers violated the defendant's right to be present); State v. Williams, 339 N.C. 1 (1994) (any error in excluding the defendant from an in-chambers conference during a hearing on the defendant's motion to represent himself was harmless beyond a reasonable doubt; the trial judge did not decide the motion at the in-chambers conference but fully explored the issue with the defendant in open court before ruling on the motion); State v. Brogden, 329 N.C. 534 (1991) (similar; defendant apparently was absent from in-chambers jury charge conference but was present when formal jury charge conference was held in the courtroom); State v. Ferguson, 145 N.C. App. 302 (2001) (in-chambers conference reconstructed and summarized when defendant was present in the courtroom; harmless error found).

33. State v. Harris, 333 N.C. 543 (1993) (during a jury view of the home where the homicide being tried was committed, jurors were permitted to roam independently and were not held together as a body to inspect the home; this did not violate the defendant's right to be present, as there is no constitutional or statutory requirement that the defendant in a capital case must be in the presence of all members of the jury, composed as a single body, throughout a jury view).

34. State v. Huff, 325 N.C. 1 (1989) (the trial judge violated the defendant's unwaiveable right to be present when the judge allowed the defendant, at his and his attorney's request, to be excused from the courtroom during the investigating detective's testimony about the defendant's confession to killing his son and the medical examiner's testimony about the son's autopsy, but the error was harmless beyond a reasonable doubt because the proceedings were transcribed, both attorneys were present, and the judge allowed attorneys to confer with the defendant about his returning to the courtroom at any time), *vacated on other grounds,* 497 U.S. 1021 (1990).

35. State v. Cunningham, 344 N.C. 341 (1996) (the trial judge ordered the defendant removed from trial for short periods of time for disruptive behavior; the defendant was able to observe all the court proceedings by an audio-video hookup, and when he returned, he was allowed to object to anything that occurred during his absence; error, but harmless beyond a reasonable doubt). The court in *Cunningham* stated that "when a defendant in a capital case is removed from the courtroom for disruptive behavior, his constitutional right to be present at every stage of the trial is violated if the trial is continued in his absence." *Id.* at 354. As support for that conclusion, the court cited *Huff,* 325 N.C. 1. However, in *Huff,* "[w]hile defendant's conduct . . . could be characterized as disruptive, the trial court did not excuse defendant from the courtroom based on his disruptive conduct but did so in response to the request of defendant and his attorneys." 325 N.C. at 28 n.2. The *Huff* court expressly declined to address whether a capital defendant could be removed based on disruptive conduct or could be deemed constructively present after removal. Thus, the ruling in *Cunningham* is not well supported by *Huff.* Still, a judge dealing with a disruptive capital defendant likely should err on the side of restraining the defendant, *see generally* G.S. 15A-1031, rather than removing him or her on the theory that he or she has forfeited the unwaiveable right to be present, *see generally* G.S. 15A-1032.

36. State v. McCollum, 334 N.C. 208 (1993) (any error when the defendant was absent during videotaped depositions regarding mitigating circumstances, conducted in New Jersey by defense counsel and the state, was harmless beyond a reasonable doubt).

C. Jury Selection

Generally

Very generally, jury selection in a capital case follows the same process as in any other criminal case. That process is established by statute, with the relevant statutes located principally in Article 72 of G.S. Chapter 15A.[37] In a capital case, jury selection must be recorded.[38]

First, the presiding judge must "identify the parties and their counsel and briefly inform the prospective jurors" about the case.[39] The clerk must randomly select prospective jurors from the panel and call them into the jury box.[40] The judge may question the prospective jurors[41] and may excuse any jurors who are not qualified to sit or as to whom a challenge for cause would be allowed.[42]

The prosecutor next questions the prospective jurors. He or she is not prohibited from asking a question simply because the judge also asked that question.[43] The prosecutor then makes any challenges for cause and exercises any peremptory challenges.[44] In a capital case, the state has fourteen peremptory challenges per defendant, and each defendant has fourteen peremptory challenges.[45] It is not error for the prosecutor to identify members of the victim's family during the process of questioning prospective jurors.[46]

Replacements must immediately be called for any excused jurors, and the prosecutor continues questioning and challenging jurors until he or she is satisfied with the twelve prospective jurors in the jury box. At that point, "defense counsel, or the defendant if not represented by counsel," questions the prospective jurors and makes any challenges for cause and exercises any peremptory challenges.[47]

Once the defense has finished with the prospective jurors, the jurors who have satisfied both parties are seated, and new prospective jurors are called by the clerk to fill the remaining seats in the box. The process then repeats, with the court, then the prosecutor, and then the defendant examining the jurors. Deviation from this statutory procedure is error, though only reversible if prejudicial.[48]

---

37. G.S. 15A-1211 *et seq.* Chapter 9 of the General Statutes contains some additional relevant provisions.
38. G.S. 15A-1241.
39. G.S. 15A-1213.
40. G.S. 15A-1214(a).
41. G.S. 15A-1214(b). *See generally* State v. Bearthes, 329 N.C. 149 (1991) (trial judge did not err in questioning prospective juror; judge expressed no opinion about the case and did not demonstrate an alliance with the prosecutor).
42. The required qualifications are set forth in G.S. 9-3. Grounds for challenges for cause are set forth in G.S. 15A-1212. The judge's authority to excuse jurors at this stage was implicitly established by *State v. Quick*, 329 N.C. 1 (1991) (prospective jurors properly excused by court due to inability to impose a death sentence under any circumstances; defendant was given an opportunity to question the jurors or to object to their removal).
43. G.S. 15A-1214(c); State v. Conner, 335 N.C. 618 (1994); State v. Jones, 336 N.C. 490 (1994). The right of the parties to question prospective jurors is also guaranteed by G.S. 9-15.
44. G.S. 15A-1214(d).
45. G.S. 15A-1217(a). In noncapital cases, the number is six rather than fourteen. G.S. 15A-1217(b). A first-degree murder case in which the state is not seeking the death penalty is a noncapital case for this purpose. State v. Jackson, 317 N.C. 1 (1986).
46. State v. Reeves, 337 N.C. 700, 724 (1994).
47. G.S. 15A-1214(c), (e). A defendant who is represented by counsel does not have a right to question prospective jurors personally. State v. Bell, 338 N.C. 363 (1994).
48. *See, e.g.,* State v. Garcia, 358 N.C. 382 (2004) (on two occasions, prosecutor passed a panel of fewer than twelve jurors to the defense; this was done without objection and for the convenience of the jurors; although the procedure did not comply with the statutes, the defendant was unable to show prejudice).

In limited circumstances, voir dire as to a seated juror may be reopened before the impanelment of the jury.[49] In such a case, either party or the court may challenge the prospective juror for cause, and either party may exercise any remaining peremptory challenges with respect to the juror.[50]

At least two alternate jurors must be selected in a capital case, and they must be treated in the manner provided by statute.[51] "Each party is entitled to one peremptory challenge for each alternate juror in addition to any unused challenges."[52]

The trial judge has considerable discretion to regulate the process of jury selection. For example, the judge apparently may require a single defense attorney to conduct the process on the defendant's behalf.[53] Likewise, the judge may generally require the attorneys to pose questions to the entire group of prospective jurors under consideration, rather than addressing the prospective jurors one at a time.[54] It is also within the judge's discretion whether to grant a party's request that the prospective jurors fill out a questionnaire as a part of the jury selection process.[55]

An important issue that often arises is whether to conduct jury selection individually, that is, with only a single prospective juror present in the courtroom. The judge may order individual voir dire "for good cause shown."[56] The decision is discretionary.[57] When individual voir dire is allowed, the state passes prospective jurors one at a time to the defense; the state need not pass twelve prospective jurors individually before the defense questions the jurors.[58] The judge also may order that jury selection be done in the usual manner but may allow individual voir dire on particular issues. Some form of individualized questioning may be useful when one prospective juror's answer to a question has the potential to taint other prospective jurors, such as when inquiring about a juror's exposure

---

49. G.S. 15A-1214(g) (allowing the reopening of voir dire when "it is discovered that the juror has made an incorrect statement during voir dire or . . . some other good reason exists"); State v. Goss, 361 N.C. 610, 619 (2007) (trial judge properly reopened voir dire when two prospective jurors did not respond when the prosecutor asked whether any prospective jurors had any "close friends or relatives who have either been a witness, a defendant, or a victim in a criminal case," but the state later learned that both jurors had relatives who had been convicted of murder). In some cases, it may be proper to reopen voir dire even after impanelment. State v. Brady, 299 N.C. 547, 553 (1980) (proper to reopen voir dire after trial began when a juror revealed that he was "employed by and worked closely with defendant's brother").

50. G.S. 15A-1214(g). *See also* State v. Freeman, 314 N.C. 432 (1985) (once trial judge allows reopening of voir dire, parties' right to exercise remaining peremptory challenges is absolute); State v. Locklear, 145 N.C. App. 447 (2001) (where voir dire on a seated regular juror was reopened during the selection of alternate jurors, a defendant who had used eleven peremptory challenges on the twelve regular jurors, then three more during the selection of alternates, still had challenges available for use on the seated regular juror; the three challenges used during the selection of the alternate jurors were not necessarily the three unused challenges from the selection of the regular jurors).

51. G.S. 15A-1215(b).

52. G.S. 15A-1217(c).

53. State v. Fullwood, 343 N.C. 725, 732, 733 (1996) (given judge's "broad discretion to regulate jury *voir dire*," it did not violate the defendant's right to two attorneys to require that a single lawyer conduct voir dire, where the lawyers were able to communicate with one another and there was no discernable impact upon the jurors actually selected; however, the court noted that the defendant did not preserve an argument that this procedure deprived him of his right to the effective assistance of counsel) (italics in original).

54. State v. Campbell, 340 N.C. 612 (1995) (no abuse of discretion where trial judge required questions to be posed to all prospective jurors as a group; the defendant was nonetheless allowed to question jurors individually at several points during jury selection, and the jurors responded individually to group questions if the questions required a response based on their personal views). *See also* State v. Allen, 322 N.C. 176 (1988).

55. State v. Lyons, 340 N.C. 646 (1995) (no error in denying the defendant's motion for a questionnaire); State v. Fisher, 336 N.C. 684 (1994) (similar).

56. G.S. 15A-1214(j). *See also* State v. Wilson, 313 N.C. 516 (1985).

57. *See, e.g.*, State v. Jones, 358 N.C. 330, 359 (2004) (whether to allow individual voir dire is "within the trial court's discretion"); State v. Burke, 342 N.C. 113, 121–22 (1995) (similar); State v. Holden, 321 N.C. 125 (1987).

58. State v. Roache, 358 N.C. 243 (2004).

to pretrial publicity, personal knowledge about a case, or, in a resentencing proceeding, knowledge of a defendant's prior death sentence.[59]

Prospective Jurors' Views about the Death Penalty

Jurors Who Are Biased Against the Death Penalty

Under *Wainwright v. Witt*,[60] a prospective juror in a capital case is subject to a challenge for cause if his or her views about capital punishment would "prevent or substantially impair the performance of his [or her] duties as a juror in accordance with his [or her] instructions and . . . oath."[61] Similarly, under G.S. 15A-1212(8), a juror may be challenged for cause if he or she "[a]s a matter of conscience, regardless of the facts and circumstances, would be unable to render a verdict with respect to the charge in accordance with the law of North Carolina." The process of removing prospective jurors whose opposition to capital punishment meets this standard is sometimes called the "death qualification" of the jury.

The mere fact that a prospective juror is opposed to capital punishment is not enough to satisfy the *Witt* test.[62] However, when a juror's personal beliefs about the death penalty would substantially limit his or her ability to follow the court's instructions during a capital sentencing hearing or would prevent the juror from fairly considering the imposition of a death sentence, the juror must be excused. Furthermore, the juror's bias need not be "unmistakably clear" to justify removal; it is enough that the trial judge is left with the "definite impression" that the juror would not be impartial.[63]

Defendants sometimes argue that a death-qualified jury will be more inclined to convict than a jury that has not been death qualified. The state supreme court has rejected this argument.[64] The United States Supreme Court has ruled that even if this were so, death qualification would not violate a defendant's Sixth Amendment right to a fair and impartial jury.[65] Therefore, a defendant is not entitled to two different juries—one that has not been death qualified to consider guilt or innocence

---

59. *See, e.g., Roache*, 358 N.C. at 274 (emphasizing "the trial court's inherent authority to permit individual *voir dire* as to specific sensitive issues in any given case") (italics in original); State v. Gregory, 340 N.C. 365, 385 (1995) (noting that "to assure a fair and impartial trial, the trial court allowed individual *voir dire* on the issue of pretrial publicity") (italics in original); State v. Moseley, 338 N.C. 1, 17 (1994) ("During jury selection, the trial court permitted the individual *voir dire* of prospective jurors on the media exposure issue.") (italics in original); State v. Simpson, 331 N.C. 267, 271 (1992) (during jury selection at a resentencing, "[t]he parties uncovered the jurors' prior knowledge [including about the defendant's previous death sentence] and opinions during individual, sequestered *voir dire*"; note that the court declined to impose a *per se* rule against service by jurors with knowledge of a defendant's previous death sentence so long as the jurors could agree to make a decision based on the facts of the case and without regard to the previous sentence) (italics in original).

60. 469 U.S. 412 (1985).

61. *Id.* at 424 (footnote, internal quotation marks omitted).

62. *Id.* at 421 (noting the trial court's responsibility to "distinguish[] between prospective jurors whose opposition to capital punishment will not allow them to apply the law or view the facts impartially and jurors who, though opposed to capital punishment, will nevertheless conscientiously apply the law to the facts adduced at trial").

63. *Id.* at 425–26.

64. *See, e.g.*, State v. Taylor, 332 N.C. 372, 390 (1992) ("[W]e have often rejected the argument that a 'death qualified' jury is more likely to convict the defendant.").

65. Lockhart v. McCree, 476 U.S. 162 (1986).

and a second that has been death qualified to consider punishment.[66] Likewise, it is proper to death qualify a jury for a joint trial that is capital as to one defendant but noncapital as to another.[67]

The state has a right to ask prospective jurors questions that are designed to determine whether the jurors are subject to a *Witt* challenge. Thus, a prosecutor may ask prospective jurors whether their views about the death penalty would substantially impair their ability to sit on the jury[68] and whether they would have the "intestinal fortitude" to vote for a sentence of death if satisfied that the legal requirements for such a sentence had been met.[69]

When the state challenges a prospective juror under *Witt*, the defense may ask the judge for the opportunity to question the juror. This request is commonly known as the opportunity to rehabilitate, since the defendant wants to show that the juror's purported opposition to capital punishment would not substantially impair his or her performance of duties as juror and that the state's challenge for cause should therefore be denied. A trial judge may not automatically deny the defendant's request but instead must exercise his or her discretion in deciding whether to allow a defendant to rehabilitate a prospective juror.[70] If a juror's responses are clear and unequivocal and the defendant fails to show that defense questioning would likely produce different responses, then the judge may grant the state's challenge for cause without allowing the opportunity to rehabilitate the juror.[71]

Consistent with the general principles governing the reopening of voir dire, discussed above, there are limited circumstances in which it is permissible to revisit the death qualification of a seated juror. For example, it was proper to reopen voir dire of a juror who reported that after she was seated, she became so agitated and emotional when contemplating the prospect of deciding whether to impose the death penalty that she sought medical attention, then stated emphatically that she would never be able to vote for the death penalty.[72] It was also proper for the court to reopen voir dire immediately prior to the sentencing phase of a capital case when the court learned that a juror had expressed to a third party her inability to follow the law and to consider returning a sentence of death.[73]

---

66. State v. Berry, 356 N.C. 490 (2002); State v. Holden, 321 N.C. 125 (1987); State v. Bondurant, 309 N.C. 674, 682 (1983) (holding that G.S. 15A-2000 "contemplates that the same jury which determines guilt will recommend the sentence").

67. Buchanan v. Kentucky, 483 U.S. 402 (1987).

68. State v. Price, 326 N.C. 56, 67 (1990) (citing State v. Quesinberry, 325 N.C. 125 (1989)).

69. State v. Murrell, 362 N.C. 375, 390–91 (2008) (holding that the trial judge properly permitted the prosecutor to ask prospective jurors whether they had the "intestinal fortitude" to vote for the death penalty; the question addressed the jurors' ability to follow the law during a capital sentencing proceeding).

70. State v. Brogden, 334 N.C. 39 (1993) (ordering a new sentencing hearing where the trial judge denied the defendant the opportunity to rehabilitate a prospective juror whose responses supported a challenge for cause but were not completely unequivocal; the judge acted under an apparent misapprehension of law that a defendant's attempt to rehabilitate is never permitted).

71. *See, e.g.*, State v. Kemmerlin, 356 N.C. 446, 469 (2002) (the trial judge properly denied the defendant an opportunity to rehabilitate two prospective jurors whose statements during voir dire showed "an unmistakable commitment to automatically vote against the death penalty, regardless of the facts and circumstances which might be presented"); State v. Nicholson, 355 N.C. 1 (2002) (stating that denying the defendant an opportunity to rehabilitate a prospective juror may be an abuse of discretion unless the juror's prior statements were unequivocal but finding no abuse of discretion where the juror had candidly and consistently explained the basis for his views); State v. Davis, 340 N.C. 1 (1995); State v. Reeves, 337 N.C. 700 (1994) (the defendant's request to rehabilitate was properly denied where a prospective juror had unequivocally answered questions from both the prosecutor and the trial judge in such a way as to demonstrate her bias).

72. State v. Barts, 316 N.C. 666 (1986). *See also* State v. Parton, 303 N.C. 55 (1981) (similar, where seated juror discussed his opposition to the death penalty with other jurors prior to impanelment).

73. State v. Holden, 321 N.C. 125 (1987).

Of course, if a prospective juror expresses reservations about the death penalty that are not serious enough to justify a *Witt* challenge, the state may use a peremptory strike to remove the juror.[74]

If the trial court wrongly excuses a juror under *Witt*, when in fact the juror's reservations about the death penalty do not rise to the requisite level, any resulting death sentence must be vacated.[75] However, the defendant's conviction of first-degree murder remains intact.[76]

Case Summaries: Jurors Who Are Biased Against the Death Penalty

Uttecht v. Brown, 551 U.S. 1 (2007). The trial judge granted the state's challenge for cause of a potential juror who, despite repeated explanations of the law by the judge and the lawyers, appeared to be "confused about the conditions under which [a] death [sentence] could be imposed and seemed to believe it only appropriate when there was a risk of release and recidivism," even though state law provided for life without parole for first-degree murderers not sentenced to death. Although the juror said "six times that he could consider the death penalty or follow the law[,] . . . these responses were interspersed with more equivocal statements." The United States Supreme Court held that the defendant was not entitled to federal habeas relief. Applying AEDPA deference,[77] the Court emphasized that the trial judge was in the best position to judge the juror's demeanor, noted that the defendant did not object when the juror was removed (though an objection is not required for a defendant to seek relief under *Witt*, the Court viewed the lack of one as a relevant factor), and concluded that the juror was substantially impaired in his ability to impose a death sentence in this case, as there was no possibility that the defendant would be released if convicted, and that appeared to be the only circumstance under which the juror would consider endorsing a death sentence.

Adams v. Texas, 448 U.S. 38 (1980). A Texas statute provided that a prospective juror was disqualified from serving as a juror unless he or she stated under oath that the mandatory penalty of death or life imprisonment would not affect his or her deliberations on any issue of fact. The court ruled that the application of this statute in this case impermissibly excluded prospective jurors who stated that they would be "affected" by the possibility of the death penalty but who apparently only meant that the potentially lethal consequences of their decision would invest their deliberations with greater seriousness and gravity or would involve them emotionally.

Greene v. Georgia, 519 U.S. 145 (1996). The United States Supreme Court ruled that *Witt* is not controlling authority as to the standard of review to be applied by state appellate courts reviewing trial judges' rulings on jury selection because *Witt* involved federal habeas review, when deference to state court findings is mandated by federal statute. Thus, a state appellate court need not necessarily accord a presumption of correctness to state trial judges' findings of juror bias, but it may choose to do so if it wishes. [*Author's note*: The North Carolina Supreme

---

74. *See, e.g.*, State v. Fullwood, 323 N.C. 371 (1988); State v. Allen, 323 N.C. 208 (1988).

75. Gray v. Mississippi, 481 U.S. 648 (1987) (rejecting the applicability of harmless error analysis).

76. *See, e.g.*, State v. Rannels, 333 N.C. 644 (1993) (the defendant was convicted of first-degree murder but sentenced to life imprisonment; any *Witt* error did not justify a new trial).

77. AEDPA refers to the Anti-Terrorism and Effective Death Penalty Act of 1996, Pub. L. No. 104-132, 110 Stat. 1214 (codified as amended at 28 U.S.C. §§ 2241 *et seq.*). Under AEDPA, the federal courts review habeas claims by state inmates under a deferential standard. A federal court may grant relief only if the state court's adjudication of a prisoner's claims was "contrary to, or involved an unreasonable application of, clearly established Federal law, as determined by the Supreme Court of the United States; or . . . was based on an unreasonable determination of the facts in light of the evidence presented in the State court proceeding." 28 U.S.C. §§ 2254(d)(1)–(2).

Court has repeatedly accorded deference to trial judges' rulings in this area. *See, e.g.,* State v. Waring, 364 N.C. 443 (2010) (below); State v. Garcell, 363 N.C. 10 (2009) (also below).]

State v. Waring, 364 N.C. 443 (2010). The state challenged for cause a prospective juror who said he had "two answers" about whether he was opposed to the death penalty. His head understood that "the law is the law," while his heart was "not for capital punishment." At one point, he agreed with the prosecutor that this conflict would prevent him from being able to vote for a sentence of death, but he later told defense counsel that he might be able to do so under some circumstances. Overall, the juror's responses were "hairsplitting and unilluminating." The trial judge excused the juror, concluding that his views on the death penalty would substantially impair his ability to serve, and the state supreme court affirmed, emphasizing that "[t]he trial court was in the best position to observe and evaluate [the prospective juror's] responses."

State v. Garcell, 363 N.C. 10 (2009). The trial court properly excused three prospective jurors based on their opposition to the death penalty. One had "a moral objection to the death penalty and stated he did not believe he could vote [for it]." A second stated that he would consider voting for the death penalty only if the victim were a child. The third said that she would never vote for a death sentence because of her religious beliefs.

State v. Rouse, 339 N.C. 59 (1994). Considering all the prospective juror's responses, including "I don't believe I could vote for the death penalty" and "I think I would [automatically vote against the death penalty]," the trial judge did not abuse his discretion in determining that the juror's views would prevent or substantially impair her from performing her duties as a juror.

State v. Ward, 338 N.C. 64 (1994). When prospective jurors ambiguously stated that they could not or would not vote for (1) first-degree murder, knowing that the death penalty was one of the punishments, or (2) the death penalty, even though they were satisfied that legal standards called for the death penalty, the trial judge properly excused the jurors for cause and properly denied the defendant the opportunity to question the jurors, as additional questioning would not likely have produced different answers.

State v. Skipper, 337 N.C. 1 (1994). The prosecutor and trial judge questioned a prospective juror extensively about her ability to follow the law on capital punishment. Although the juror stated that she could impose the death penalty under some circumstances, she also affirmatively responded three times that she would be substantially impaired in following the law because of her scruples and Christian beliefs. The judge excused the juror for cause and also in his discretion denied the defendant an opportunity to rehabilitate her. The court upheld both rulings. While the juror's answers were somewhat equivocal, they were sufficiently revealing to justify excusal for cause in the trial judge's discretion. And defense questioning of the juror would have made the situation more confusing.

State v. Jennings, 333 N.C. 579 (1993). The trial judge properly excused a prospective juror for cause when the juror was unable to agree affirmatively to follow the law and recommend a sentence based on the law and evidence. Rather, she felt that she would be trying to find ways she could vote against the death penalty and would be predisposed or biased in some respect against the death penalty.

State v. Syriani, 333 N.C. 350 (1993). The trial judge properly excused a prospective juror for cause based on all of the juror's answers (including his response, "I could possibly say yes" to the prosecutor's question as to whether his beliefs would prevent or substantially impair the performance of his duties in accordance with the court's instructions and his oath), which revealed that he did not believe in the death penalty and that his views on the death penalty would interfere with the performance of his duties at both the guilt and sentencing phases. The court noted that a prospective juror's biases may not always be provable with unmistakable clarity, and an appellate court must defer to the trial judge's judgment as to whether the prospective juror would be able to follow the law impartially.

State v. Cummings, 326 N.C. 298 (1990). Prospective jurors who had been instructed about the nature of their responsibilities in a capital case and who gave an affirmative response to a question by the trial judge based on *Witt*—"Is your view of the death penalty such that it would prevent or substantially impair your performing your sworn duties as a juror?"—were properly excused by challenges for cause by the prosecutor.

State v. Davis, 325 N.C. 607 (1989). The trial judge properly granted the prosecutor's challenges for cause of two prospective jurors whose conflicting answers about the death penalty showed that bias, in some instances, may not be provable with unmistakable clarity. (For example, one juror said that if the state satisfied its burden at sentencing, he would "have to follow the law but I wouldn't like it at all" and later expressed uncertainty about his ability to ever vote for a death sentence.) In such cases, reviewing courts must defer to the trial judge's judgment as to whether the prospective juror would be able to follow the law impartially.

State v. Brown, 320 N.C. 179 (1987). A prospective juror who admitted to having "mixed feelings" about the death penalty was properly excused for cause since her responses demonstrated that she would be unable to render a verdict according to law. She said, in essence, that she "might not" be able to find the defendant guilty because of her death penalty views. *See also* State v. Burr, 341 N.C. 263 (1995) (although a juror gave conflicting responses about her views on the death penalty, the trial judge properly excused her for cause); State v. Johnson, 317 N.C. 343 (1986) (although there was some equivocation on her inability to vote for the death penalty, a prospective juror was properly removed for cause); State v. Kirkley, 308 N.C. 196 (1983) (it was proper to remove for cause a prospective juror who, when asked whether she would vote for the death penalty under appropriate circumstances, answered that she didn't feel she could and didn't feel she would); State v. Williams, 305 N.C. 656 (1982) (prospective jurors' responses about their returning a death penalty verdict, "I'm not sure I could" and "I'm not positive I could," were sufficient, considering all their responses, to justify their excusal for cause); State v. Avery, 299 N.C. 126 (1990) (similar ruling).

Jurors Who Are Biased in Favor of the Death Penalty

In *Morgan v. Illinois*,[78] the United States Supreme Court held that

> A juror who will automatically vote for the death penalty in every case will fail in good faith to consider the evidence of aggravating and mitigating circumstances as the instructions require him to do. Indeed, because such a juror has already formed an opinion on the merits, the presence or absence of either aggravating or mitigating circumstances is entirely irrelevant to such a juror. Therefore, based on the requirement of impartiality embodied in the Due Process Clause of the Fourteenth Amendment, a capital defendant may challenge for cause any prospective juror who maintains such

78. 504 U.S. 719 (1992).

views. If even one such juror is empaneled and the death sentence is imposed, the State is disentitled to execute the sentence.[79]

In order to challenge "automatic death" jurors, the defendant must be allowed an opportunity to question prospective jurors about their ability to consider a sentence other than death for first-degree murder.[80] Because the defendant's rights under *Morgan* are the counterpart to the state's rights under *Witt,* it appears that the state should have the same opportunity to rehabilitate prospective jurors challenged for cause by the defendant as the defendant has to rehabilitate prospective jurors challenged for cause by the state.

Case Summaries: Jurors Who Are Biased in Favor of the Death Penalty

Ross v. Oklahoma, 487 U.S. 81 (1988). The trial judge erroneously refused to excuse for cause, on the defendant's motion, a prospective juror who said he would automatically vote to impose the death penalty if the defendant was convicted of first-degree murder. The defendant then exercised a peremptory challenge to remove the juror. None of the twelve jurors who served on the case was challenged for cause by the defendant. The United States Supreme Court ruled that the loss of a peremptory challenge did not violate the defendant's constitutional rights.

State v. Garcell, 363 N.C. 10 (2009). Citing *State v. Simpson,* 341 N.C. 316 (1995), the court ruled that the trial judge properly prevented the defense from asking a prospective juror what the juror thought about the sentence of life in prison without parole and whether the juror had "a feeling whether the death penalty is more or less harsh than life in prison without parole[.]"

State v. Cummings, 361 N.C. 438 (2007). The trial court properly denied the defendant's challenge for cause of a prospective juror. The juror expressed strong support for the death penalty, stated that if "you've taken a life, you don't deserve to live," and responded affirmatively to defense counsel's question, "if a person were to be convicted of cold-blooded, first degree murder, is it your view that you would vote for the death penalty every time?" On the other hand, the juror stated that he could follow the law, hold the state to its burden of proof at each stage of the capital sentencing process, and fairly consider life without parole. The trial judge viewed some of the juror's initial responses as reflecting his confusion about the sentencing process and, based in part on the juror's demeanor, determined that his views on the death penalty would not substantially impair his ability to serve.

State v. Campbell, 359 N.C. 644 (2005). A prospective juror "initially . . . stated she did not think that life without parole was a severe enough punishment for murder," but later stated that she could consider it, would set aside her predispositions, and would give both possible punishments "equal weight." Her "unequivocal statements that she could set aside her predispositions and follow the law show[ed] her excusal was not mandatory."

State v. Roache, 358 N.C. 243 (2004). The prosecutor asked a series of questions during voir dire that the defendant viewed as designed to coach prospective jurors about how to avoid dismissal under *Morgan v. Illinois,* 504 U.S. 719 (1992) (discussed in the text above). For example, the prosecutor emphasized jurors' "obligation . . . to consider both possibilities [life imprisonment and the death penalty]" before asking a prospective juror whether she could do so, and

79. *Id.* at 729.

80. *Id.* at 729–34. Cases discussing the extent of this right, as well as when it may be constrained by the rule against so-called stakeout questions, are summarized in the following pages.

cautioned the juror that "the jury is not supposed to do anything running on automatic or . . . knee jerk." The defendant objected to this line of inquiry, the trial judge overruled the objection, and the state supreme court found no abuse of discretion, noting that the prosecutor's remarks "were a correct statement of the law [and] . . . served to ensure that the impaneled jury would consider both punishment alternatives."

State v. Robinson, 339 N.C. 263 (1994). The defendant was conducting jury voir dire during a death penalty resentencing hearing for three first-degree murder convictions. The trial judge prevented the defendant from asking this question of two jurors that ultimately sat on the case: "[I]f you were to also find during the sentencing hearing that the defendant had a previous first[-] degree murder conviction prior to the murders for which he is being sentenced this week, could you still follow the Court's instructions and weigh the aggravating and mitigating circumstances and consider life imprisonment as a sentencing option[?]" The court ruled that this question was improper because it was an attempt to stake out the prospective jurors—to determine if, under a given state of facts, the jurors would automatically vote against a life sentence. The court noted that the defendant was properly allowed under *Morgan* to ask these jurors if they would automatically vote for the death penalty based solely on one or more convictions of first-degree murder. *See also* State v. Lynch, 340 N.C. 435 (1995) (similar ruling regarding questions about whether prospective jurors would "automatically tend to feel that the death penalty should be imposed" when a child was the victim).

State v. Sexton, 336 N.C. 321 (1994). The trial judge did not err in denying the defendant's challenge for cause. Although a prospective juror initially stated that he could not consider life imprisonment, he later indicated that he could do so. *See also* State v. Quesinberry, 319 N.C. 228 (1987) (similar ruling); State v. Kandies, 342 N.C. 419 (1996) (similar ruling).

State v. Robinson, 336 N.C. 78 (1994). The defendant was afforded a fair opportunity in this case to make the inquiries authorized under *Morgan*. *See also* State v. Simpson, 341 N.C. 316 (1995) (similar ruling).

State v. Conner, 335 N.C. 618 (1994). The court ruled that the trial judge in a capital case erred, under *Morgan*, in not permitting defense counsel to ask the following questions of prospective jurors: (1) "Is your support for the death penalty such that you would find it difficult to consider voting for life imprisonment for a person convicted of first degree murder?" (2) "Would your belief in the death penalty make it difficult for you to follow the law and consider life imprisonment for first degree murder?" The court noted that even though defense counsel did not use the words "automatically" or "always," the gist of the questions was to determine whether a juror was willing to consider a life sentence in appropriate circumstances or would automatically vote for the death penalty. The court, however, upheld the trial judge's refusal to allow the following question: "Do you feel that the death penalty is the appropriate penalty for someone convicted of first degree murder?" The court noted that this question was overly broad and asked about a legislative policy. The court also ruled that in light of *Morgan* and the ruling in this case, the first three questions considered inappropriate in *State v. Taylor*, 304 N.C. 249 (1981), are now proper questions because they ask, in effect, whether a prospective juror would automatically impose the death penalty if the defendant was convicted of a capital offense. The questions from *Taylor* are (1) "[I]f the State convinced you beyond a reasonable doubt that the defendant was guilty of premeditated murder and you had returned that verdict guilty, do you think then that you would feel that the death penalty was the only appropriate punishment?" (2) "[I]f you had sat on the jury and had returned a verdict of guilty of first degree murder, would you then presume that the penalty should be death?" (3) "At the first stage of the trial and because of that you voted guilty for first degree murder, then do you think that you could at that time consider a life sentence or would your feelings about the death penalty be so strong that you couldn't consider a life sentence?"

State v. Lane, 334 N.C. 148 (1993). A prospective juror told the prosecutor that she would be able to return a verdict of life imprisonment. However, when questioned by the defendant, she indicated that the only time that the death penalty was not appropriate was when a defendant was acting in self-defense. The trial judge rejected the defendant's challenge for cause and allowed the prosecutor the opportunity to rehabilitate the juror. After the prosecutor explained the role of mitigating circumstances to the juror, she stated that she would be able to consider every mitigating circumstance that she was instructed to consider. The juror assured the trial judge that she would be able to return a sentence of life imprisonment. The court ruled that the trial judge did not err in rejecting the defendant's renewed challenge for cause.

Proper and Improper Voir Dire Questions

There are a large number of reported decisions concerning proper and improper voir dire questions. Because the courts' rulings defy easy summary, the decisions are simply organized into general categories below. Part of the explanation for the apparent inconsistency of the cases may be the appellate courts' emphasis on trial judges' broad discretion in controlling jury selection. If one judge allows a question in one trial, while a different judge disallows a similar question in another trial, both judges' rulings may properly be affirmed. Of course, there are some limits to trial courts' discretion, as reflected in the cases.

Case Summaries: Questions about the Death Penalty's Cost, Deterrent Value, and Similar Matters

State v. Garcell, 363 N.C. 10 (2009). Citing *State v. Simpson*, 341 N.C. 316 (1995), the court ruled that the trial judge properly prevented the defense from asking a prospective juror what the juror thought about the sentence of life in prison without parole and whether the juror had "a feeling whether the death penalty is more or less harsh than life in prison without parole[.]"

State v. Elliott, 360 N.C. 400 (2006). It was not an abuse of discretion for the trial judge to prohibit defense counsel from asking prospective jurors the following: "Do you have any preconceived notions about the cost of executing someone compared to the cost of keeping [him] in prison for the rest of [his] life?" The defendant was given a sufficient opportunity to determine jurors' ability to follow the law regarding capital sentencing.

State v. Willis, 332 N.C. 151 (1992). The court ruled that the prosecutor was properly permitted to ask this question: "[Juror's name], how do you feel about the death penalty, sir, are you opposed to it or you feel like it's a necessary law?"

State v. Ali, 329 N.C. 394 (1991). The trial judge did not err in prohibiting the defendant from asking prospective jurors whether they believed that capital punishment was a deterrent to crime. The court stated that this issue was irrelevant to the jury's sentencing determination.

State v. Price, 326 N.C. 56 (1990). The trial judge properly sustained the state's objection to the defendant's question of whether a prospective juror believed it should be necessary that the state show additional aggravating circumstances before the juror would vote to impose the death penalty. Although questioning may properly focus on the juror's ability to follow the law, it is improper to ask questions designed to gauge a juror's approval of the law or to test a juror's comprehension of the law.

State v. Weeks, 322 N.C. 152 (1988). The trial judge properly prohibited defense counsel from asking prospective jurors whether they believed the death penalty was imposed too often or whether it should be imposed for crimes other than first-degree murder. These questions involved legislative policy and therefore were not relevant.

Case Summaries: Questions about Parole Eligibility

[*Author's note*: G.S. 15A-2002 states that "[t]he judge shall instruct the jury, in words substantially equivalent to those of this section, that a sentence of life imprisonment means a sentence of life without parole." The pattern voir dire instruction for capital cases, N.C.P.I.—Crim. 106.10, provides that the trial judge should inform the jury that if the case reaches the sentencing phase, the choice will be between death and "life imprisonment without parole."]

State v. Haselden, 357 N.C. 1 (2003). The trial court properly denied defense counsel's request "to *voir dire* jurors regarding their opinions and beliefs concerning parole and parole eligibility." The jurors had been instructed in keeping with G.S. 15A-2002, and during deliberations "the jurors neither indicated any confusion regarding the meaning of life without parole nor requested any additional instruction from the trial court."

State v. Neal, 346 N.C. 608 (1997). Distinguishing *Simmons v. South Carolina*, 512 U.S. 154 (1994) (holding that where a defendant's future dangerousness is at issue, and state law does not allow parole, the sentencing jury be informed that the defendant will not be released on parole), the court ruled that the trial judge did not err in prohibiting defense counsel during jury voir dire from questioning prospective jurors about their understanding of a sentence of life without parole. *See also* State v. Page, 346 N.C. 689 (1997) (similar ruling).

State v. Payne, 337 N.C. 505 (1994). Distinguishing *Simmons v. South Carolina*, 512 U.S. 154 (1994), the court ruled that the defendant was properly denied permission to question prospective jurors about their beliefs about parole eligibility. [*Author's note*: This case was decided under the parole eligibility law that was effective for offenses of first-degree murder committed before October 1, 1994.]

State v. Jones, 336 N.C. 229 (1994). One prospective juror had stated that he would have difficulty following the court's instruction to "consider a life sentence to mean that defendant would be imprisoned for life and . . . not take the possibility of parole into account in reaching a verdict." Another prospective juror echoed that sentiment, and both were excused for cause. At least where "a prospective juror has raised the question," the defendant "has a right to inquire as to whether a prospective juror will follow the court's instruction" to treat a life sentence as such.

Case Summaries: "Stakeout" Questions about Particular Facts

State v. Cummings, 361 N.C. 438 (2007). The state supreme court rejected the defendant's argument that "the trial court abused its discretion in not allowing him to question prospective jurors on what they might view as harm experienced by a child exposed to domestic violence, the effects on children who had been exposed to physical abuse[,] . . . how a particular family was affected by alcohol abuse, why a juror thought people would abuse hard drugs, and whether, in a prospective juror's personal experience, the effects of drug abuse were negative," among other matters. "[I]t was within the trial court's authority to limit questioning on these matters and not permit the hypothetical and speculative questions that the trial court could have determined were being used to try defendant's mitigation evidence during *voir dire*."

State v. Chapman, 359 N.C. 328 (2005). The trial judge properly permitted the prosecutor to ask prospective jurors, "Would you feel sympathy towards the defendant simply because you would see him here in court each day of the trial?" The question was not an improper attempt to stake out jurors.

State v. Richmond, 347 N.C. 412 (1998). The trial judge did not allow the defendant to ask prospective jurors whether, if they knew that the defendant had previously been convicted of first-degree murder, they would still be able to consider mitigating circumstances and impose a life sentence. The court, relying on *State v. Robinson*, 339 N.C. 263 (1994), ruled that the question was an impermissible stakeout question; that is, the question sought to discover in advance what a prospective juror's decision would be under a certain state of evidence. The court also stated that a stakeout question is not made proper simply because it is predicated on a set of facts that is cast as uncontroverted rather than hypothetical. The court distinguished *State v. Bond*, 345 N.C. 1 (1996) (the state was properly allowed to ask a prospective juror if he could follow the law by considering the death penalty for an accessory who did not actually pull the trigger), by noting that the court in that case concluded that the trial judge did not abuse his discretion by allowing the state to inquire about the prospective jurors' ability to follow the law, when that inquiry neither indoctrinated the jurors about unproven facts nor committed them to a decision before they were instructed on the law. The court also distinguished *Morgan v. Illinois*, 504 U.S. 719 (1992) (defendant is entitled to ask prospective jurors if they would impose the death penalty automatically without regard to mitigating circumstances), by noting that *Morgan* does not entitle a defendant to ask stakeout questions.

State v. Walls, 342 N.C. 1 (1995). The court ruled, relying on a similar ruling in *State v. Smith*, 328 N.C. 99 (1991), that the trial judge did not err in allowing the prosecutor to ask prospective jurors whether they would feel sympathy toward the defendant because they would be able to see him each day of the trial but would not be able to see the murder victim. The question was not designed to suggest to jurors that they should disregard any sympathy they felt for the defendant; rather, the question was to determine whether the jurors would feel sympathy for the defendant based solely on his presence in court. The court also ruled that the question was not an improper attempt to stake out the jurors, that is, elicit in advance what the juror's decision will be under a certain state of evidence or on a given state of facts.

State v. Miller, 339 N.C. 663 (1995). The trial judge properly sustained the state's objection when the defendant sought to ask prospective jurors whether, because of the defendant's drug abuse, the jurors could consider a particular mitigating circumstance. General questions, such as whether the juror could follow instructions about considering mitigating circumstances, are permissible. This inquiry was an improper attempt to stake out the jurors. *See also* State v. Skipper, 337 N.C. 1 (1994) (similar ruling); State v. Walls, 342 N.C. 1 (1995) (similar ruling). For an extensive discussion of hypothetical questions, see *State v. Vinson*, 287 N.C. 326 (1975).

State v. Robinson, 339 N.C. 263 (1994). The trial judge prevented the defendant from asking this question of two prospective jurors: "[I]f you were to also find during the sentencing hearing that the defendant had a previous first[-]degree murder conviction prior to the murders for which he is being sentenced this week, could you still follow the Court's instructions and weigh the aggravating and mitigating circumstances and consider life imprisonment as a sentencing option[?]" The court ruled that this question was improper because it was an attempt to stake out the prospective jurors—to determine if, under a given state of facts, the jurors would automatically vote against a life sentence. The court noted that the defendant was properly allowed under *Morgan v. Illinois,* 504 U.S. 719 (1992), to ask jurors if they would automatically vote for the death penalty based solely on one or more convictions of first-degree murder. *See also* State v. Lynch, 340 N.C. 435 (1995) (similar ruling); State v. Kandies, 342 N.C. 419 (1996) (similar ruling).

State v. Hill, 331 N.C. 387 (1992). The court ruled that the trial judge properly refused to allow the defendant to ask prospective jurors, before they had been instructed on the applicable legal principles, what type of crimes they felt were deserving of the death penalty and whether they believed that any type of premeditated murder was deserving of the death penalty.

State v. Leroux, 326 N.C. 368 (1990). The trial judge properly barred the defendant's questioning of a prospective juror, including inquiries such as "Would your theories about the overindulgence of alcohol tend to color your thinking about [defendant] if you find that he is an alcoholic from the evidence?" and "Do you have such strong feelings about the use of alcohol that you couldn't be fair to someone that you believe to be an alcoholic?" Counsel may not "fish" for legal conclusions or argue its case during jury voir dire, the court held.

State v. Davis, 325 N.C. 607 (1989). The trial judge properly sustained the state's objection to this question by the defendant of a prospective juror: "Would the fact that the defendant had no significant history of any criminal record, would that be something that you would consider important in determining whether or not to impose the death penalty?" The question was hypothetical and an impermissible attempt to indoctrinate a juror concerning the existence of a mitigating circumstance.

State v. Laws, 325 N.C. 81 (1989). The following prosecutor's question was found not to be an improper stakeout of prospective jurors: "If the State satisfied you beyond a reasonable doubt . . . that the aggravating circumstances were sufficiently substantial to call for the imposition of the death penalty, then I take it you could give the defendant the death penalty for beating two human beings to death with a hammer, is that correct?"

State v. Parks, 324 N.C. 420 (1989). The trial judge properly barred defense counsel from asking prospective jurors whether there was anyone among them "who feels that because the Defendant had a gun in his hand, no matter what the circumstances might be, that if that—if he pulled the trigger to that gun and that person met their death as a result of that, that simply on those facts alone that he must be guilty of something[.]" Jurors may not be asked what kind of verdict they would render under specific named circumstances.

State v. McKoy, 323 N.C. 1 (1988). The trial judge did not err in allowing the prosecutor to ask prospective jurors whether they would be sympathetic toward a defendant who was intoxicated at the time of the offense being tried and allow that sympathy to affect their verdict. The question did not "stake out" the jurors to disregard the trial judge's instructions on the effect of intoxication in determining the defendant's guilt or innocence or the appropriate sentence. It did not inquire about the jurors' potential verdict or how they would vote under a given state of facts.

State v. Clark, 319 N.C. 215 (1987). The prosecutor informed prospective jurors that the state would rely on circumstantial evidence and then defined circumstantial evidence and asked jurors whether the lack of eyewitnesses would cause them any problems. The court ruled that this question was not an improper hypothetical.

State v. Johnson, 317 N.C. 343 (1986). The trial judge properly barred the defendant from asking prospective jurors whether, if the evidence showed that the defendant was an abused and neglected child, they could consider that evidence in the sentencing phase of the trial. That question was an impermissible hypothetical designed to elicit in advance what a juror's decision would be under a certain state of the evidence.

State v. Avery, 315 N.C. 1 (1985). The trial judge properly barred the defendant's question of a prospective juror asking if she was thinking, "well, if [the defendant] says he has [post-traumatic stress disorder], for that reason alone I would vote that he is guilty." Such a question was an impermissible hypothetical.

Case Summaries: Questions about the Defendant's Failure to Testify or to Put on a Defense

State v. Campbell, 359 N.C. 644 (2005). It was not an abuse of discretion for the trial judge to "refus[e] to allow defendant to ask prospective jurors whether, given that defendant had made a confession, defendant's election not to testify would adversely influence their decision." The question was an attempt to stake out jurors' opinions about a specific set of facts. The defendant "was allowed to ask prospective jurors whether his decision not to testify would affect their impartiality" and the prospective jurors "were properly instructed that defendant had a right not to testify."

State v. Blankenship, 337 N.C. 543 (1994). The trial judge properly sustained the state's objection to the defendant's question of a prospective juror whether the juror would hold it against the defendant if he chose not to put on a defense; it is improper because it asks a juror an abstract question that cannot be answered before hearing the evidence against the defendant. Only after hearing the case against the defendant can a juror reasonably determine how to view the defendant's failure to offer a defense. The court noted that this kind of question is distinguishable from a question concerning a defendant's failure to testify in his or her own defense. *See also* State v. Phillips, 300 N.C. 678 (1980) (similar ruling).

State v. Hill, 331 N.C. 387 (1992). The court ruled that the trial judge properly refused to allow the defendant to ask prospective jurors, before they had been instructed on the applicable legal principles, whether they would "feel the need to hear from" the defendant to find him not guilty.

State v. Rogers, 316 N.C. 203 (1986). The trial judge properly barred the defendant from asking prospective jurors whether the fact that the defense called fewer witnesses than the state would make a difference in their verdict. It was an improper hypothetical question that attempted to stake out each juror's future decision.

State v. Phillips, 300 N.C. 678 (1980). The trial judge properly barred the defendant from asking a prospective juror if the defendant would have to prove anything to her before he would be entitled to a verdict of not guilty. The court stated that jurors should not be asked what kind of verdict they would render under certain named circumstances.

Case Summaries: Questions about Whether Jurors Have the Personal Strength to Return a Sentence of Death

State v. Murrell, 362 N.C. 375 (2008). It was proper for a trial judge to allow a prosecutor to ask prospective jurors whether they had the "intestinal fortitude" to vote for a sentence of death. The question served to determine whether the jurors would be able to follow the law regarding capital punishment.

State v. Call, 349 N.C. 382 (1998). The prosecutor asked prospective jurors during voir dire if they could write the word "death" on the recommendation form and if they could announce their verdict of death in open court. The court ruled that the prosecutor's question properly sought to determine the jurors' ability to carry out their duties. The court cited *State v. White*, 343 N.C. 378 (1996) (proper to ask prospective juror whether he could stand up and tell the defendant, "I sentence you to be executed"; this question "was fairly aimed at determining the extent of [the juror's] reservations about imposing the death penalty").

State v. Willis, 332 N.C. 151 (1992). The court ruled that the prosecutor was properly permitted to ask, "Do you feel that you could be part of the legal machinery which might bring [the death penalty] about in this particular case?"

State v. Smith, 328 N.C. 99 (1991). The following prosecutor's question of prospective jurors was ruled proper: Are you "strong enough to recommend the death penalty?" Such an inquiry did not effectively stake out the juror to a position that the juror felt obligated to return a sentence of death once the trial reached the sentencing phase. *See also* State v. Hinson, 310 N.C. 245 (1984) (prosecutor's question as to whether a prospective juror had the "backbone" to impose the death penalty was proper); State v. Oliver, 302 N.C. 28 (1981) (similar ruling).

Case Summaries: Questions about Jurors' Ability to Withstand Pressure during Deliberations

State v. Maness, 363 N.C. 261 (2009). The trial court properly prohibited defense counsel from asking prospective jurors "about their ability (1) to not surrender their honest convictions for the purpose of returning a sentencing recommendation and (2) to recommend a life sentence even if other jurors disagreed." Questions designed to determine how well a prospective juror would withstand pressure to change his or her mind during deliberations are impermissible stakeouts.

State v. Syriani, 333 N.C. 350 (1993). The defendant's question of a prospective juror, "Are you a person who has pretty strong opinions and pretty well stick[s] to your opinions when you make them, or are you easily swayed?" was an impermissible stakeout question if the defendant had wanted to determine how well the juror could stand up to other jurors in the event of a split decision. The defendant was properly permitted by the trial judge to ask the juror whether she could deliberate with other people "pretty regularly." In addition, the defendant had accepted the juror and had not exhausted his peremptory challenges.

State v. Bracey, 303 N.C. 112 (1981). The trial judge properly barred the defendant from asking prospective jurors whether, if they held an opinion that the defendant was not guilty, they would change that opinion simply because eleven other jurors held a different opinion. Such a question was an impermissible hypothetical.

Case Summaries: Questions about Jurors' Personal Lives, Experiences, and Beliefs

State v. Anderson, 350 N.C. 152 (1999). The court ruled that the trial judge did not err in sustaining the state's objection to the defendant's questions about prospective jurors' religious beliefs. The impermissible questions concerned jurors' church memberships and whether their churches' members ever expressed opinions about the death penalty. The court noted that instead of questions relating to the jurors' religious beliefs, the impermissible questions concerned their affiliations and beliefs espoused by others in their churches.

State v. Mash, 328 N.C. 61 (1991). The trial judge properly prohibited the defendant from questioning prospective jurors about their "difficulty" in considering expert mental health testimony and the jurors' personal experiences with alcohol. The court stated that neither the state nor defense counsel has the right to delve without restraint into matters concerning prospective jurors' private lives. The court noted that the trial judge allowed sufficient inquiry in this case about the jurors' inability to be fair, to consider the evidence, and to follow the law.

State v. Laws, 325 N.C. 81 (1989). The trial judge properly barred the defendant's question as to whether a prospective juror believed in a literal interpretation of the Bible; the court stated that counsel's right to inquire about jurors' beliefs to determine their biases and attitudes does not extend to all aspects of their private lives or religious beliefs. The judge had allowed the defendant to inquire about other aspects of the jurors' religious activities. *See also* State v. Lloyd, 321 N.C. 301 (1988) (trial judge properly barred defendant's inquiry into prospective jurors' religious denominations and extent of their participation in church activities); State v. Huffstetler, 312 N.C. 92 (1984) (trial judge properly barred defendant's inquiry of the prospective jurors concerning the death penalty positions held by the leaders of their churches).

Case Summaries: Questions about Race and Sex

Turner v. Murray, 476 U.S. 28 (1986). The defendant, who was black, was tried for the murder of a storeowner, who was white. The trial judge refused to allow the defendant to question prospective jurors about their racial biases. The defendant was convicted and sentenced to death. The United States Supreme Court ruled that a defendant who is charged with an interracial capital crime is constitutionally entitled to inform prospective jurors of the victim's race and question them about their racial biases. The Court ordered that the defendant's death sentence be vacated, but not the murder conviction. It stated that its ruling in this case was based on an unacceptable risk of racial prejudice adversely affecting the capital sentencing hearing, but not the guilt-innocence phase.

State v. Anderson, 350 N.C. 152 (1999). The court ruled that the trial judge did not err in allowing the state to ask prospective jurors, "[W]ould the fact that the Defendant is a female[] in any way affect your deliberations with regard to the death penalty?" The question was not an impermissible hypothetical or stakeout question. The court stated that an inquiry into the possible sensitivities of prospective jurors toward a female defendant facing the death penalty is not an inappropriate effort to ferret out any prejudice arising from the defendant's gender.

State v. Robinson, 330 N.C. 1 (1991). The court ruled that the trial judge in this case complied with the ruling in *Turner v. Murray*, 476 U.S. 28 (1986), discussed above, by permitting the defendant to ask prospective jurors about their racial biases.

Case Summaries: Other Proper and Improper Questions

State v. Payne, 328 N.C. 377 (1991). To the extent that a prosecutor's statements during jury voir dire about aggravating circumstances are allowed at all, a prosecutor may properly state briefly what he or she anticipates the evidence may show if such statements are made in good faith and are reasonably based on the available evidence. Thus, a prosecutor should not refer to aggravating circumstances on which the prosecutor will not offer evidence (for example, improperly referring to all the underlying felonies in G.S. 15A-2000(e)(5)).

State v. Allen, 322 N.C. 176 (1988). The trial judge properly barred the defendant from asking repetitious questions of prospective jurors. The trial judge did not err in requiring the defendant initially to ask questions of the entire panel since the judge allowed individual questioning when appropriate. *See also* State v. Brown, 315 N.C. 40 (1985) (trial judge properly barred repetitious questioning of juror); State v. Huffstetler, 312 N.C. 92 (1984) (similar ruling) (discussed below).

State v. Huffstetler, 312 N.C. 92 (1984). The trial judge properly barred defense counsel from discussing with prospective jurors the legal meaning of a bill of indictment. The court stated that it was within the trial judge's discretion to prohibit an attempt by counsel to give instructions on the law to prospective jurors during voir dire.

State v. Denny, 294 N.C. 294 (1978). The trial judge properly barred the defendant from asking prospective jurors, "Would you be willing to be tried by one in your present state of mind if you were on trial in this case?" This was an impermissible hypothetical question.

Batson and Discrimination

Under the United States Supreme Court's landmark ruling in *Batson v. Kentucky*,[81] it is a violation of the Equal Protection Clause for the state or the defendant to exercise a peremptory challenge on the basis of a prospective juror's race or sex.[82] The state constitution also prohibits discrimination in jury selection.[83] The defendant need not be of the same race or sex as the prospective juror who was excused in order to claim that the state challenged the juror improperly.[84]

---

81. 476 U.S. 79 (1986).

82. Although *Batson* concerned only racial discrimination, its principles were extended to sex discrimination in *J.E.B. v. Alabama*, 511 U.S. 127 (1994).

83. Section 26 of Article I of the Constitution of North Carolina provides that "[n]o person shall be excluded from jury service on account of sex, race, color, religion, or national origin." Section 19 of Article I provides in part that "[n]o person shall be denied the equal protection of the laws; nor shall any person be subjected to discrimination by the State because of race, color, religion, or national origin." The precise scope of these provisions remains to be resolved by court rulings. The inclusion of religion and national origin in these antidiscrimination provisions suggests that they may be more extensive than *Batson.* State v. Montgomery, 331 N.C. 559 (1992) (concurring opinion stated that prosecutor's peremptory challenge, based on prospective juror's African heritage, violated Article I, Section 26, of North Carolina Constitution—discrimination based on national origin). However, the North Carolina Supreme Court has ruled that the *Batson* process, discussed below, is the same process to be used under the North Carolina Constitution when a party claims that the other party has engaged in race- or sex-based discrimination in exercising peremptory challenges. State v. Waring, 364 N.C. 443, 474 (2010) ("Our review of race-based or gender-based discrimination during petit jury selection has been the same under both the Fourteenth Amendment to the United States Constitution and Article 1, Section 26 of the North Carolina Constitution."); State v. Maness, 363 N.C. 261, 271–72 (2009) (similar); State v. Nicholson, 355 N.C. 1, 21 (2002) ("Our courts have adopted the *Batson* test for reviewing the validity of peremptory challenges under the North Carolina Constitution."); State v. Floyd, 343 N.C. 101 (1996).

84. Powers v. Ohio, 499 U.S. 400 (1991); State v. Locklear, 349 N.C. 118 (1998).

Statements of counsel based on a prospective juror's appearance are not sufficient to establish the race of a prospective juror, nor are the subjective impressions of the court reporter. Instead, the prospective juror should be asked to state his or her race.[85] Presumably the juror may do so in a questionnaire or in open court.

When a party contends that the other party has exercised a peremptory challenge in a discriminatory manner—that is, when a party makes a *Batson* claim—the trial judge must follow a three-step process to resolve the issue:

1. *Prima facie showing.* The party making the *Batson* claim must make a prima facie showing that the other party exercised a peremptory challenge on the basis of race or sex.
2. *Neutral justification.* If a prima facie showing has been made, the other party must offer a justification for its use of its peremptory challenge that is not based on race or sex.
3. *Pretext for purposeful discrimination.* The party making the *Batson* claim may then attempt to show that the nondiscriminatory justification is pretextual and that the other party in fact engaged in purposeful discrimination.[86]

Each of these steps will be discussed further below.

Prima Facie Showing

The *Batson* requirement of a prima facie showing "is not intended to be a high hurdle for defendants to cross."[87] Indeed, the Supreme Court ruled in *Johnson v. California*[88] that establishing a prima facie case does not require a litigant to show that it is more likely than not that the opposing party has engaged in discrimination. Nonetheless, the showing must be a strong enough to permit an inference of discrimination and to require a response. As reflected in the case summaries below, more than a few *Batson* challenges fail at this stage. Among the factors that a court may consider in assessing whether such a showing has been made by a defendant alleging racial discrimination are

> the defendant's race, the victim's race, the race of the key witnesses, questions and statements of the prosecutor which tend to support or refute an inference of discrimination, repeated use of peremptory challenges against blacks such that it tends to establish a pattern of strikes against blacks in the venire, the prosecution's use of a disproportionate number of peremptory challenges to strike black jurors in a single case, and the State's acceptance rate of potential black jurors.[89]

Presumably, similar factors would be relevant when considering a defendant's claim of sex discrimination or a claim by the state that the defendant exercised a peremptory challenge in a discriminatory manner.

If the trial judge finds that the party making a *Batson* claim has failed to make a prima facie showing, the judge may terminate the inquiry at that stage. (The judge also has the option of proceeding

85. State v. Brogden, 329 N.C. 534 (1991) (holding that the defendant failed to preserve a *Batson* claim by defense counsel's subjective impressions of jurors' race and notations made by the court reporter of her subjective impressions); State v. Payne, 327 N.C. 194 (1990) (defense lawyer's affidavit was insufficient to establish jurors' race); State v. Mitchell, 321 N.C. 650 (1988) (if there is any question about a prospective juror's race, it must be resolved by the trial judge's questioning of the juror or other proper evidence; statements of counsel alone or a court reporter's notations are insufficient).

86. *See generally* Snyder v. Louisiana, 552 U.S. 472, 476–77 (2008).

87. State v. Hoffman, 348 N.C. 548, 553 (1998).

88. 545 U.S. 162 (2005).

89. State v. Quick, 341 N.C. 141, 145 (1995).

to the second and third steps in the *Batson* process, a procedure that may facilitate appellate review if the judge's ruling on the adequacy of the prima facie case is rejected on appeal.[90]) If the judge rules that the party has made a prima facie showing, the remaining steps in the three-step process must be completed. If a party offers, or the trial judge requests, a neutral justification before the trial judge has ruled on the sufficiency of the prima facie case, the sufficiency of the prima facie case becomes moot, and the issue becomes the validity of the neutral justification.[91]

Case Summaries: Prima Facie Showing

Johnson v. California, 545 U.S. 162 (2005). The defendant, who was black, was charged with murder. Out of a pool of forty-three prospective jurors for his trial, three were black. The prosecutor used three of his twelve peremptory strikes to remove the African-American jurors. The defendant objected under *Batson*, but the trial judge ruled that the defendant had failed to establish a prima facie case of discrimination. Under California law, a defendant was required to present "strong evidence" of discrimination to make a prima facie case; the state supreme court indicated that this required evidence that it was "*more likely than not*" that the prosecutor had acted in a discriminatory manner. The United States Supreme Court reversed, holding that the California courts used "an inappropriate yardstick by which to measure the sufficiency of a prima facie case" and that a defendant need only present "evidence sufficient to permit the trial judge to draw an inference that discrimination has occurred," apparently a lower threshold than the preponderance standard employed below.

State v. Waring, 364 N.C. 443 (2010). The trial court correctly ruled that the defendant failed to make a prima facie showing where the state successfully challenged for cause the first three black prospective jurors then peremptorily challenged the fourth; the fourth juror expressed personal opposition to the death penalty, even though she ultimately stated that she could follow the law and consider capital punishment if seated.

State v. Maness, 363 N.C. 261 (2009). At the time the prosecutor struck prospective juror A, who was black, the prosecutor had used five of eight peremptory challenges to remove black jurors and had accepted only three of eight black prospective jurors. Nonetheless, the trial court correctly rejected the defendant's *Batson* claim for lack of a prima facie case. Numerical analysis, "while often useful, is not necessarily dispositive," and the court noted that race was not a factor in the trial and that the state had questioned prospective jurors in a consistent manner regardless of race.

---

90. State v. Cofield, 129 N.C. App. 268, 278 n.2 (1998) ("The procedure utilized by the trial court in this case, although not required, facilitates appellate review. In the event it is determined on appeal, as in this case, that the trial court erred in finding that race-neutral explanations were not offered by the challenging attorney, this Court can, on the record before it, review whether the explanations are pretextual without remanding for a new *Batson* hearing.").

91. Hernandez v. New York, 500 U.S. 352 (1991); State v. Williams, 343 N.C. 345, 359 (1996) ("If the prosecutor volunteers his reasons for the peremptory challenges in question before the trial court rules whether the defendant has made a *prima facie* showing or if the trial court requires the prosecutor to give his reasons without ruling on the question of a *prima facie* showing, the question of whether the defendant has made a *prima facie* showing becomes moot, and it becomes the responsibility of the trial court to make appropriate findings on whether the stated reasons are a credible, nondiscriminatory basis for the challenges or simply pretext.") (italics in original). If the judge rules that no prima facie case has been established and subsequently asks for a neutral justification, the judge's ruling on the prima facie case is not moot. *Hoffman*, 348 N.C. 548; State v. Smith, 347 N.C. 453 (1998).

State v. Taylor, 362 N.C. 514 (2008). When the state exercised a third peremptory challenge on a black prospective juror, the defendant made a *Batson* claim. The trial court properly found no prima facie case. The state had also used seven challenges on white jurors and had accepted two black jurors. The fact that "the state had accepted two out of five, or forty percent, of eligible African–American jurors" tended to show a lack of discrimination. Furthermore, "the prosecutor's statements and questions during voir dire appear[ed] evenhanded and not racially motivated," and the prospective juror expressed hesitation about her ability to vote for the death penalty.

State v. Barden, 356 N.C. 316 (2002), *remanded in light of* Snyder v. Louisiana, 552 U.S. 472 (2008), Rice v. Collins, 546 U.S. 333 (2006), *and* Miller-El v. Dretke, 545 U.S. 231 (2005) (all discussed in this chapter), 362 N.C. 277 (2008). The trial judge erred in ruling that the defendant had not made a prima facie showing of racial discrimination under *Batson.* When the defendant asserted the *Batson* claim, the prosecutor had accepted only 28.6 percent of the African-American prospective jurors (peremptorily challenging five of seven eligible jurors) but had accepted 95 percent of the white jurors (peremptorily challenging only one of twenty eligible white jurors). The court stated that although a numerical analysis is not necessarily dispositive, it can be useful in determining whether a prima facie case has been made. The court also stated that the issue was a close one and noted that it had ruled in *State v. Gregory,* 340 N.C. 365 (1995), that a 37.5 percent acceptance rate of minority jurors had not established a prima facie case.

State v. Smith, 351 N.C. 251 (2000). The defendant failed to establish a prima facie case under *Batson.* The defendant noted that the state exercised six of its eight peremptory challenges to excuse African Americans and that number was disproportionate to the population of Halifax County, which was 50 to 60 percent black. The court noted that the state had accepted the first black prospective juror to enter the jury box and also had struck whites before striking the prospective black juror in issue. The court also noted that the defendant, the victim, and the state's key witnesses were all black. The court also concluded that the prosecutor did not make any racially motivated statements or ask any racially motivated questions of prospective African-American jurors.

State v. Hoffman, 348 N.C. 548 (1998). A black defendant was tried for the murder of a white person. The state successfully challenged the first black prospective juror for cause based on her death penalty views. The state exercised a peremptory challenge to the second black prospective juror. The trial judge ruled that the defendant had not yet established a prima facie showing. The state initially accepted the third black prospective juror but was allowed the next day to excuse this juror for cause based on her death penalty views that had been revealed that next day. The state exercised a peremptory challenge on the fourth black prospective juror, who twice had been represented by defendant's trial counsel. The state supreme court ruled that the trial judge did not err in ruling that the defendant had not yet established a prima facie case. Eleven white jurors had been seated when the state then exercised a peremptory challenge against another prospective African-American juror. The trial judge again ruled that the defendant had not yet established a prima facie case. The supreme court determined that this ruling was error. It noted that the state had peremptorily challenged every black prospective juror who was not excused for cause. Later, during the selection of the alternate jurors, the state peremptorily challenged the next prospective black juror. The court ruled that the trial judge again erred in his ruling that the defendant had not yet established a prima facie case.

State v. Ross, 338 N.C. 280 (1994). The defendant failed to make a prima facie showing of discrimination. The prosecutor accepted two black jurors who sat on the trial jury, and there was no other evidence showing discrimination by the prosecutor. (The court's opinion has a useful discussion of what constitutes a prima facie case.)

State v. McCord, 140 N.C. App. 634 (2000). The defendant was convicted of first-degree murder and other offenses. The defendant was black and the victim was white. The initial panel of prospective jurors consisted of ten white jurors and two black jurors, A and B. The defendant objected on *Batson* grounds to the state's use of peremptory challenges of A and B. Before ruling on whether the defendant had established a prima facie case to require the state to give reasons for the challenges, the trial judge allowed the state to offer reasons. The judge considered the reasons and ruled that they were nondiscriminatory. (The court upheld the trial judge's ruling concerning jurors A and B.) Later during the voir dire, the state exercised peremptory challenges of two additional African-American jurors, C and D, and the defendant again objected on *Batson* grounds. The trial judge ruled that the defendant had failed to establish a prima facie case, but the court of appeals ruled, relying on *State v. Hoffman*, 348 N.C. 548 (1998), discussed in detail above, that the defendant had established a prima facie case concerning jurors C and D. The court noted that the defendant was black and the victim was white, that the state used its peremptory challenges to excuse four of the six black jurors in the jury pool, and that the composition of the jury panel was eleven white jurors and one black juror.

State v. Locklear, 349 N.C. 118 (1998). The court ruled that under *Powers v. Ohio*, 499 U.S. 400 (1991), the defendant, a Native American, had standing to contest the state's peremptory challenges of prospective black jurors. The court rejected the defendant's argument that it was a violation of the Equal Protection Clause for the trial judge to consider his *Batson* motion separately as to challenged Native American and black prospective jurors. The court noted that racial identity between the defendant and some of the challenged jurors in this case was a legitimate factor that the trial judge could consider in ruling on the defendant's motion. Likewise, the fact that the defendant and the challenged black jurors were of different races was also a relevant circumstance that the trial judge could consider.

State v. Cofield, 129 N.C. App. 268 (1998). During jury selection the state accepted a jury of six black and six white jurors and passed them to the defendant. The defendant peremptorily challenged four white prospective jurors on behalf of the defendant, who was black. The state challenged the exercise of these challenges as racially discriminatory under *Batson*. The trial judge correctly ruled that a prima facie case had been established.

Neutral Justification

If the party making a *Batson* claim presents a prima facie case, the other party must come forward with a neutral justification for its use of its peremptory strikes. The justification must be "comprehensible"[92] and "clear[,] and reasonably specific,"[93] but it "need not rise to the level of a challenge for cause."[94] Indeed, at this stage, the explanation need not be "persuasive, or even plausible."[95] Because it will

92. State v. Maness, 363 N.C. 261, 272 (2009).

93. *Batson*, 476 U.S. at 98 n.20.

94. *Maness*, 363 N.C. at 272.

95. Purkett v. Elem, 514 U.S. 765, 766, 768 (1995) (per curiam) (prosecutor's statement that he struck a prospective juror because he didn't like the juror's "long . . . curly, unkempt hair" and because the juror's mustache and goatee looked "suspicious" provided a race-neutral justification for striking the juror; the Court stated that

rarely, if ever, be the case that a party admits purposeful discrimination at this stage, the second step in the process is not normally dispositive. (It can be, however, if a party fails to present a neutral justification for the dismissal of each prospective juror when several are at issue[96] or if "a discriminatory intent is inherent in the explanation" offered by a party.[97]) Rather, the second step is typically a prelude to the third step, when the judge assesses the validity of the proffered justification.

Pretext for Purposeful Discrimination

In the final step of the process, the court must determine whether the party whose conduct is at issue engaged in purposeful discrimination, i.e., whether the party's neutral justification is a mere pretext. The burden of showing discrimination rests with the party making a *Batson* claim.[98] However, the party making the claim need not show that the other party used its peremptory challenge based solely or exclusively on the race or sex of the prospective juror. It is sufficient to show that the juror's race or sex was a "significant"[99] or motivating[100] factor in striking the juror.[101]

Determining whether a party has engaged in intentional discrimination requires consideration of all relevant circumstances.[102] The factors that are relevant at the prima facie case stage are also relevant here. For example, if the party accepted some jurors of the same race or sex as the juror that the party excused, that is a factor that weighs against a finding of intentional discrimination.[103] Whether the party accepted an unusually high or low percentage of prospective jurors from a particular group would also be relevant.

Recently, appellate courts considering *Batson* claims have often focused on whether the reason given by the party using the peremptory challenge applied equally to prospective jurors of a different race or sex who were not challenged by the party. For example, "[i]f a prosecutor's proffered reason for striking a black panelist applies just as well to an otherwise-similar nonblack who is permitted to serve, that is evidence tending to prove purposeful discrimination to be considered at *Batson's*

---

whether a justification is "implausible or fantastic" may properly be considered as part of the *third* step of the *Batson* process, but not the second).

96. State v. Wright, 189 N.C. App. 346, 352 (2008) (defendant raised a *Batson* claim, asserting that every prospective juror struck by the state was black; the claim was improperly denied because "[a]t most the prosecutor offered a race-neutral explanation for five of the seven . . . jurors" excused by the state).

97. State v. Fletcher, 348 N.C. 292, 313 (1998). The trial judge in *Fletcher* ruled that a prospective juror's membership in the NAACP—an organization that the prosecutor characterized as opposed to the death penalty—was not a race-neutral justification for excusing the juror. However, the state supreme court questioned this ruling in dicta. *Id.* at 315–17 (referencing and quoting trial court).

98. Rice v. Collins, 546 U.S. 333, 338 (2006). Accordingly, the party making the claim must be given an opportunity to rebut the neutral justification offered by the other party. State v. Green, 324 N.C. 238 (1989). This opportunity does not include cross-examining the prosecutor about his or her use of peremptory challenges. State v. Jackson, 322 N.C. 251, 258 (1988) ("We hold that a defendant who makes a *Batson* challenge does not have the right to examine the prosecuting attorney. . . . The presiding judges are capable of passing on the credibility of prosecuting attorneys without the benefit of cross-examination.").

99. Miller-El v. Dretke, 545 U.S. 231, 252 (2005).

100. State v. Waring, 364 N.C. 443, 480–81 (2010).

101. Whether the party that acted with discriminatory intent should then be given an opportunity to argue that although "a discriminatory intent was a substantial or motivating factor[,] . . . this factor was not determinative" in that the prospective juror would have been removed on other grounds has not been decided by the United States Supreme Court. Snyder v. Louisiana, 552 U.S. 472, 485 (2008).

102. *Id.* at 478 ("[I]n considering a *Batson* objection, or in reviewing a ruling claimed to be *Batson* error, all of the circumstances that bear upon the issue of racial animosity must be consulted.").

103. State v. Bell, 359 N.C. 1, 12 (2004) ("This Court has held that the State may use several general factors to rebut charges of discrimination in the jury selection process, including evidence that the State accepted some jurors of the challenged minority race and that the State did not use all of its peremptory challenges.").

third step."[104] In *Snyder v. Louisiana*,[105] the prosecutor struck a juror because "[h]e's a student teacher . . . [and] might, to go home quickly, come back with guilty of a lesser verdict so there wouldn't be a penalty phase."[106] However, the United States Supreme Court found this explanation to be pretextual, in part because of "the prosecutor's acceptance of white jurors who disclosed conflicting obligations that appear to have been at least as serious as" the excused juror's student teaching.[107]

Such juror comparisons have sometimes been characterized as "[m]ore powerful than . . . bare statistics."[108] Yet courts have also noted the difficulty of finding appropriate comparisons, given the many factors a party may consider when assessing the suitability of a juror.[109]

Case Summaries: Pretext for Purposeful Discrimination

Miller-El v. Dretke, 545 U.S. 231 (2005). The United States Supreme Court granted habeas relief to a capital defendant based on racial discrimination by the prosecution during jury selection. The state struck ten of eleven eligible black prospective jurors; explained some of its strikes with reasons that applied equally to white jurors who were not removed; questioned black and white prospective jurors differently about the death penalty; used a Texas procedure called the "jury shuffle" to minimize the number of African Americans likely to sit on the jury; and apparently relied on a training manual that expressly encouraged prosecutors to remove minorities from the jury. In light of this evidence, the Court determined that the state's race-neutral reasons for its strikes were pretexts for purposeful discrimination.

State v. Waring, 364 N.C. 443 (2010). The trial court correctly found no purposeful discrimination in the state's decision to excuse a black prospective juror. The prosecutor's race-neutral reasons were (1) the fact that the juror had never formed a personal view about the death penalty; (2) the fact that she did not keep up with the news; and (3) the fact that she had been charged with a felony. The state supreme court noted that only two of the nine peremptory challenges exercised by the prosecutor were used on black jurors and that two black jurors were passed by the state, an acceptance rate of 50 percent. Further, the court compared the prospective juror at issue with white jurors accepted by the state and found that the reasons given by the prosecutor were genuine distinctions.

---

104. *Miller-El*, 545 U.S. at 241. *See also* Rice v. Collins, 546 U.S. 333, 341 (2006) (a prosecutor struck a black prospective juror and explained that she did so because the juror was young, with few community ties, and so might be tolerant of crime; applying AEDPA deference (see *supra* note 77 for an explanation of this term), the United States Supreme Court found nothing unreasonable about the trial court's decision to credit the prosecutor's neutral explanation, in part because "she used a peremptory strike on a white male juror . . . with the same characteristics"); State v. Barden, 362 N.C. 277, 279 (2008) (remanding for further consideration of a *Batson* challenge and instructing the trial court to "consider the voir dire responses of prospective juror Baggett and those of Teresa Birch, a white woman seated on defendant's jury" and to give "[t]he State . . . an opportunity to offer race-neutral reasons for striking juror Baggett while seating juror Birch").

105. 552 U.S. 472 (2008).

106. *Id.* at 478.

107. *Id.* at 483. The state also used peremptory challenges on all five black prospective jurors who were not removed for cause.

108. *Miller-El*, 545 U.S. at 241.

109. State v. Porter, 326 N.C. 489, 501 (1990) ("Choosing jurors, more art than science, involves a complex weighing of factors. Rarely will a single factor control the decision-making process. Defendant's approach in this appeal involves finding a single factor among the several articulated by the prosecutor as to each challenged prospective juror and matching it to a passed juror who exhibited that same factor. This approach fails to address the factors as a totality which when considered together provide an image of a juror . . . .").

State v. Maness, 363 N.C. 261 (2009). The trial court did not clearly err in accepting the prosecutor's race-neutral justification for removing an African-American prospective juror. The prosecutor noted that the juror had a history of mental illness and had worked with substance abusers and so might "overly identify with defense evidence pertaining to defendant's cannabis dependence and attention deficit disorder."

State v. Spruill, 338 N.C. 612 (1994). The court found no *Batson* error after considering the following factors: (1) the race of the defendant, victims, and key witnesses; (2) the prosecutor's questions and statements during voir dire; (3) the prosecutor's use of a disproportionate number of peremptory challenges to strike black jurors in a single case; and (4) the prosecutor's acceptance rate of black jurors.

State v. Jackson, 322 N.C. 251 (1988). The criteria prosecutors used in selecting jurors were valid: they wanted a jury that was "stable, conservative, mature, government oriented, sympathetic to the plight of the victim, and sympathetic to law enforcement crime solving problems and pressures." The court upheld the trial judge's conclusion that the state did not discriminate in exercising its peremptory challenges based on such criteria used in this case.

State v. Porter, 326 N.C. 489 (1990). Disparate treatment or questioning of prospective jurors does not necessarily show discrimination in selecting jurors. *See also* State v. Williams, 339 N.C. 1 (1994); State v. Lyons, 343 N.C. 1 (1996).

State v. Rouse, 339 N.C. 59 (1994). Evidence supported the contention that the reason for the prosecutor's peremptory challenge of a black juror was the juror's reservations about the death penalty and not her race.

State v. Cofield, 129 N.C. App. 268 (1998). During jury selection the state accepted a jury of six black and six white jurors and passed them to the defendant. The defendant peremptorily challenged four white prospective jurors on behalf of the defendant, who was black. The state challenged the exercise of these challenges as racially discriminatory under *Batson*. The court ruled that the trial judge did not err in finding, based on the evidence before the judge, that the defendant's explanations for the challenges were merely pretextual excuses for purposeful racial discrimination.

Remedies

In *Batson*, the United States Supreme Court stated the following:

> [W]e express no view on whether it is more appropriate in a particular case, upon a finding of discrimination against black jurors, for the trial court to discharge the venire and select a new jury from a panel not previously associated with the case . . . or to disallow the discriminatory challenges and resume selection with the improperly challenged jurors reinstated on the venire.[110]

In *State v. McCollum*,[111] the court stated that when a trial judge determines that a party has committed a *Batson* violation, it is the "better practice" and "clearly fairer" to order that jury selection start over with a new panel of prospective jurors.[112] According to the court, asking "jurors who have

110. 476 U.S. 79, 99 n.24 (1986) (citations omitted).
111. 334 N.C. 208 (1993).
112. *Id.* at 236.

been improperly excluded from a jury because of their race to then return to the jury[,] to remain unaffected by that recent discrimination, and to render an impartial verdict without prejudice toward either the State or the defendant, would . . . require near superhuman effort."[113] Nonetheless, the court of appeals affirmed a case in which the trial judge found a *Batson* violation by the defendant and required the improperly challenged jurors to sit.[114]

Appellate courts review trial judges' *Batson* rulings deferentially.[115] If an appellate court nonetheless determines that a trial judge erred in finding no prima facie case, the usual remedy is a remand for a retrospective *Batson* hearing.[116] If an appellate court rules that a trial judge erred in finding no purposeful discrimination, *Batson* itself demands that the defendant's "conviction be reversed."[117] No North Carolina case explains how an appellate court should proceed if it rules that a trial court erred in finding a *Batson* violation by a defendant and therefore incorrectly forced the defendant to accept a juror that the defendant wished to remove.[118]

D. Jury Administration

Capital cases involve many of the same jury administration issues as other jury trials. However, because capital trials often attract considerable attention from the media and others, certain jury administration issues are more likely to arise in such cases. Three such issues are discussed below: the use of anonymous juries, jury sequestration, and juror misconduct and jury tampering.

First, if a capital case is likely to receive an extreme amount of media attention, or if it involves a defendant who is likely to attempt to intimidate or otherwise improperly influence jurors, the trial judge may consider using an anonymous jury. No North Carolina case directly addresses the propriety of such a procedure, though the jury in *State v. Garcell*[119] asked that individual jurors be addressed by number rather than by name. Cases from other jurisdictions generally hold that an anonymous jury may be used if there is a specific and compelling justification for the procedure and if it is implemented in a way that does not send a message to the jurors that the defendant is a danger to them.[120] When the principal concern is undue media scrutiny of jurors, an alternative may be to

---

113. *Id.* As a practical matter, it may be possible to ameliorate this concern somewhat by hearing *Batson* challenges outside the presence of the jury.

114. State v. Cofield, 129 N.C. App. 268 (1998). *Cf.* State v. Fletcher, 348 N.C. 292, 316 (1998) (the trial judge found a *Batson* violation, and the state "elected to withdraw its challenge of [the prospective juror in question], and so accepted him as a juror"; the trial court found this to be a sufficient remedy; that ruling was not directly discussed by the majority on appeal).

115. "On appeal, a trial court's ruling on the issue of discriminatory intent must be sustained unless it is clearly erroneous." Snyder v. Louisiana, 552 U.S. 472, 477 (2008).

116. *See, e.g.*, State v. Barden, 356 N.C. 316 (2002); State v. Hoffman, 348 N.C. 548 (1998); State v. McCord, 140 N.C. App. 634 (2000).

117. *Batson*, 476 U.S. at 100.

118. In *Rivera v. Illinois*, 556 U.S. 148 (2009), the United States Supreme Court held that the proper remedy for depriving a defendant of a peremptory challenge through an incorrect *Batson* ruling is a matter of state law. "If a defendant is tried before a qualified jury composed of individuals not challengeable for cause, the loss of a peremptory challenge due to a state court's good-faith error is not a matter of federal constitutional concern. Rather, it is a matter for the State to address under its own laws." *Id.* at 157.

119. 363 N.C. 10 (2009). Here, the jurors, after being polled regarding their verdict at the conclusion of the guilt phase of a capital trial, asked to be referred to by number rather than by name. The reviewing court held that the request itself was not evidence of juror misconduct.

120. *See, e.g.*, United States v. Stewart, 590 F.3d 93, 124 (2d Cir. 2009) (internal quotation marks omitted) (proper to empanel an anonymous jury in a terrorism case; such a jury may be used when there is a "strong

allow the jurors' names to be known to the parties but not released to the public or the media until the conclusion of the trial.[121]

Second, one or both parties in capital cases sometimes move for the sequestration of the jury. Under G.S. 15A-1236(b), "[t]he judge in his discretion may direct that the jurors be sequestered."[122] Only a few North Carolina cases address sequestration; they are collected in the margin.[123] If a judge decides to order sequestration, it should be handled carefully, as it is difficult and unpleasant for jurors and for court staff.[124] Partial sequestration—allowing the jurors to sleep at their own homes but keeping them together and isolated during the trial day—is also possible.[125]

---

reason to believe the jury needs protection," and when care is taken to protect the defendant's rights, including through a thorough voir dire and by giving the jury a plausible, non-prejudicial reason for not disclosing the jurors' identities); United States v. Deitz, 577 F.3d 672, 685 (6th Cir. 2009) (proper to empanel an anonymous jury in a drug case in which the defendant was a member of a motorcycle gang with a history of violence and obstruction of justice; anonymity was "appropriate as a safety precaution and to avoid interference with the jury's ability to function"; an anonymous jury should be given a neutral explanation for anonymity, such as the desire to protect the jurors from unwanted media contact); United States v. Wecht, 537 F.3d 222 (3d Cir. 2008) (trial judge improperly ordered an anonymous jury in a public corruption case; the media has a presumptive First Amendment right of access to jurors' names, the appeals court noted, and the generalized concerns about jury tampering and publicity relied upon by the trial judge are present in nearly every case and were not specific enough to support the order); State v. Ross, 174 P.3d 628, 637 (Utah 2007) (trial judge did not commit plain error in empaneling an anonymous jury in a capital case; judge's decision was supported by "compelling reasons" and was effectuated in a way designed to minimize prejudice, appellate court found; compelling reasons may include "the defendant's involvement in organized crime [or with other dangerous groups]; . . . the defendant's past attempts to interfere with the judicial process; . . . the potential that, if convicted, the defendant will [receive a severe sentence]; and . . . extensive publicity that [risks] intimidation or harassment [of jurors]") (citations omitted). *See also generally* Timothy R. Murphy, Nat'l Ctr. for State Courts, Managing Notorious Trials 83–85 (2d ed. 1998) (noting that the use of anonymous juries may be permitted and discussing management concerns).

121. *See, e.g.*, United States v. Blagojevich, 612 F.3d 558, 559, 561 (7th Cir. 2010) (trial judge ordered that "the names of jurors selected for the trial would not be released until the trial has ended," due to overwhelming media interest in the case; appellate court noted that anonymous juries may be used under certain circumstances, such as "when the jurors' safety would be jeopardized by public knowledge[] or the defendant has attempted to bribe or intimidate witnesses or jurors," and that delayed disclosure of jurors' identity is less drastic than the use of an anonymous jury; on remand, the federal district court ordered the release of the jurors' names "at 9 a.m. on the morning of the first calendar day after the verdict is read and at least twelve hours after the reading of the verdict." No. 08 CR 888-1, 2011 WL 812116, at *3 (N.D. Ill. Feb. 28, 2011)).

122. *See also* G.S. 9-17 (providing for sequestration and requiring the state to pay expenses associated therewith); G.S. 15A-1214(j) (providing for sequestration of jurors during jury selection in a capital case).

123. State v. King, 326 N.C. 662, 672 (1990) (the defendant filed a motion to "prohibit jury dispersal," which effectively sought sequestration of the jury; the motion does not appear to have been heard, and so it may be deemed waived; if it was heard and denied, the denial was proper given the defendant's failure to do more than speculate about the possibility of prejudicial media exposure); State v. McLaughlin, 323 N.C. 68, 87 (1988) (denial of the defendant's motion to sequester was proper where "the jury was selected from citizens of another county[, t]he trial court quite frequently admonished the jury against discussing the case or gaining information about it from outside sources[, and the d]efendant presented no evidence that the jury did anything other than follow the trial court's orders"); State v. Wilson, 322 N.C. 117, 127 (1988) (the trial judge properly denied, in his discretion, a joint motion by the state and the defense to sequester the jury in a capital case; the motion was based on publicity near the time of trial regarding the execution of another defendant from the same county; it was "pure speculation to suggest whether such publicity would tend to favor the State or defendant," and the defendant had made no showing that it would contaminate the jury); State v. Stokes, 308 N.C. 634, 643 (1983) (defendant moved to sequester the jury; trial court denied motion; affirmed on appeal without extensive discussion; court emphasized the trial court's discretion and noted the defendant's failure to show any "inflammatory, nonfactual reporting by the news media or that any seated juror was affected by pretrial publicity").

124. *See generally* Murphy, *supra* note 120, at 90–92; Jeff Welty, *Jury Sequestration*, N.C. Crim. L., UNC Sch. of Gov't Blog (Sept. 20, 2011), http://nccriminallaw.sog.unc.edu/?tag=jury-sequestration.

125. Official Commentary to G.S. 15A-1236.

A third and final issue concerning jury management is what to do when there is an indication of juror misconduct or jury tampering. Juror misconduct refers to case-related misbehavior by a juror, such as failure to follow the court's instructions, and it may take many forms. Recent cases have involved jurors alleged to have fallen asleep during trial,[126] to have left the jury room and entered the courtroom during a non-jury hearing,[127] to have sought advice about the case from an attorney not involved in the matter,[128] to have discussed the case with other jurors[129] or with family members[130] prior to the conclusion of the trial, and to have engaged in inappropriate conversation in the jury room.[131] Generally, the cases provide that if the trial judge is presented with reliable evidence of misconduct by a juror and the alleged misconduct is potentially prejudicial, the judge should make an appropriate inquiry into the allegations. The inquiry often includes questioning the juror or jurors reportedly involved. If the inquiry establishes prejudicial misconduct, the trial judge should take appropriate remedial action, which may include steps such as dismissing one or more jurors or declaring a mistrial.

Jury tampering, by contrast, involves allegations of wrongdoing by someone else in connection with a juror. Recent cases have involved allegations of courtroom spectators following jurors after court[132] or talking to jurors about the case in public areas of the courthouse,[133] allegations of similar

---

126. State v. Cox, 190 N.C. App. 714, 718 (2008) (defense counsel moved for a mistrial based on an allegedly sleeping juror; the trial judge questioned the juror, who did not rule out the possibility of having dozed off briefly but claimed that he had generally "heard everything" (quoting from court's questioning of juror); mistrial properly denied).

127. State v. Murillo, 349 N.C. 573 (1998) (the trial court did not err in failing to dismiss a juror ex mero motu where the juror, on several occasions, briefly entered the courtroom during non-jury hearings; the juror's misconduct did not create a risk of prejudice and the trial judge was not required to investigate further).

128. State v. Gladden, 168 N.C. App. 548, 553, 554 (2005) (during a recess in deliberations, a juror "asked an attorney unrelated to the case to provide her with the legal definition of premeditation"; the attorney refused "and the juror did not communicate her question to any other member of the jury"; the trial court inquired into the incident and determined that the defendant had not been prejudiced; the defendant's motion for a mistrial was properly denied).

129. State v. Wood, 168 N.C. App. 581 (2005) (an attorney not involved in a trial reported that, while eating lunch at a restaurant, he overheard several jurors discussing witnesses; the trial judge questioned all jurors about whether they had expressed an opinion regarding the defendant's guilt, heard such an opinion from another juror, and were able to decide the case based on the evidence presented; all jurors answered in the affirmative, with one stating that the lunch conversation involved joking about certain witnesses' facial expressions; because the defendant was not prejudiced by the misconduct, his motion for a mistrial was properly denied).

130. State v. Aldridge, 139 N.C. App. 706, 712, 713 (2000) (a defense attorney's secretary received a phone call from a person who claimed that a seated juror was discussing an ongoing trial with a relative and had told the relative that she initially thought the defendant was guilty based on his appearance; the trial judge declined to make inquiry of the juror, concluding that the evidence of misconduct was not "credible, reliable, substantive or believable"; the court of appeals affirmed, noting that "[a]n examination of the juror involved in alleged misconduct is not always required, especially where the allegation is nebulous or where the witness did not overhear the juror or third party talk about the case") (quoting trial court findings).

131. State v. Womble, 343 N.C. 667, 694 (1996) (trial judge determined that two jurors had engaged in "inappropriate conversation in the jury room" and dismissed them; this was a sufficient remedy and a mistrial was not required).

132. State v. Taylor, 362 N.C. 514 (2008) (a person who was seated near the defendant's family in the courtroom allegedly followed a juror for a period of time after court one evening; the trial judge questioned the person, who denied the allegation, and questioned the juror who claimed to have been followed and another who claimed to have witnessed the event, and both stated that they could remain fair and impartial; mistrial properly denied).

133. State v. Bethea, 173 N.C. App. 43 (2006) (courtroom spectators told several jurors while in a courthouse elevator that certain witnesses were lying; the trial judge asked the jurors if they could set that contact aside, and they said that they could; the trial judge also instructed the entire jury to base its decision on the evidence presented in court; this was an appropriate inquiry and no further action by the court was required).

conduct by witnesses,[134] and allegations of court personnel making improper remarks to jurors about a case.[135] Again, if presented with credible evidence of jury tampering, the trial judge should make inquiry and take appropriate remedial measures.

E. Presence and Conduct of Spectators

Emotions often run high during capital cases, and spectators and witnesses may engage in conduct that is not often encountered in other criminal trials. As the Supreme Court of North Carolina has explained, "[t]he unfortunate reality of a capital trial includes both the grief and anguish of those the victim has left behind and the awesome uncertainty as to the accused's fate. It is the trial court's responsibility to keep these powerful emotions in check in order to assure an impartial jury and a fair trial."[136] Trial judges have several tools at their disposal, including their authority to limit access to the courtroom,[137] their authority to remove disruptive persons as needed to maintain order,[138] and in extreme cases, their contempt powers.[139]

A specific issue that sometimes arises is spectators' wearing of badges, ribbons, or other mementos in remembrance of the victim. Out-of-state cases suggest that, under some circumstances, such behavior may be sufficiently prejudicial to require a mistrial.[140] The leading North Carolina case on this topic is *State v. Braxton*,[141] where the court found, on a limited record, that spectators' wearing of badges that may have contained a photograph of a murder victim did not require a mistrial.[142]

---

134. State v. Childers, 80 N.C. App. 236, 244, 244–45 (1986) (one of the state's witnesses talked to several jurors during the trial; the trial judge investigated and determined that "the contact was casual and not related to the case"; the court of appeals stated that "[w]here juror misconduct is alleged, it is the duty of the trial judge to investigate the matter and to make such inquiry as is appropriate under the circumstances," then found that this duty was satisfied here and that the defendant was not prejudiced; mistrial properly denied).

135. State v. Johnson, 295 N.C. 227, 235 (1978) (jury officer's pro-prosecution comment to the jury "appears to have been calculated to result in harm to the defendant," and concerned a contested issue in the case, found the court, thus requiring a new trial); State v. Lippard, 152 N.C. App. 564, 573 (2002) (although a deputy sheriff serving as jury officer made disparaging remarks about the defendant's witnesses, the jurors who heard the comments "stated they were not influenced by [them] and could make a fair and impartial decision after the presentation of all the evidence"; mistrial properly denied for lack of prejudice).

136. State v. Turner, 330 N.C. 249, 266 (1991).

137. G.S. 15A-1034(a).

138. G.S. 15A-1033.

139. *See generally* G.S. 5A-11(a) (stating that it is criminal contempt of court willfully to interrupt a court's proceedings, disrespect a court, and so forth).

140. *See, e.g.*, Norris v. Risley, 918 F.2d 828 (9th Cir. 1990) (spectators wore large buttons reading "women against rape"; the court found that this deprived the rape defendant of a fair trial); State v. Franklin, 327 S.E.2d 449 (W. Va. 1985) (spectators, including the sheriff, wore MADD (Mothers Against Drunk Driving) lapel buttons during the defendant's trial for DWI resulting in death; this deprived the defendant of a fair trial, concluded the court).

141. 344 N.C. 702 (1996).

142. The defendant in *Braxton* was tried capitally for two murders. He moved for a mistrial "on the grounds that members of the audience were wearing badges that appeared to be photographs of one of the victims." 344 N.C. at 709–10. The trial judge denied the motion and the state supreme court affirmed, noting that there were "no facts in the record showing the number and identity of the spectators wearing the buttons, the identity of the person shown in the photograph, and whether the jury even noticed the buttons." *Id.* at 710.

Emotional displays, often by the victim's friends and relatives, also may take place during capital cases. Trial judges have very broad discretion to respond to and manage such outbursts, which will necessitate a mistrial "[o]nly in rare and obvious instances of unmitigated and unfair prejudice."[143]

Especially when the victim is a law enforcement officer, the presence and conduct of officers who attend the trial may raise concerns.[144] A leading federal case is *Woods v. Dugger*,[145] where the court granted a new trial to a defendant charged with killing a prison guard when uniformed prison guards, in a show of solidarity with the victim, constituted approximately half the spectators filling the courtroom. The leading North Carolina case may be *State v. Maness*.[146] In *Maness*, the defendant was charged with killing a police officer. When autopsy photographs of the officer were circulated to the jury, three uniformed officers stepped up to between 1.5 and 3 feet from the jury box. The judge immediately instructed the officers to sit down. At a bench conference, the state explained that the officers wanted to screen the victim's mother from the images. Defense counsel argued that the officers' actions could have intimidated or influenced the jurors and moved for a mistrial. The trial judge denied the mistrial, finding that few jurors noticed the officers and characterizing their conduct as "peculiar," not intimidating.[147] The state supreme court found no abuse of discretion.[148]

F. Evidence

The law of evidence is the same in capital trials as it is in criminal trials generally. Therefore, it is beyond the scope of this book. However, one issue arises so frequently in capital trials that it is worth addressing here: the admissibility of post-mortem photographs of the victim, either at the crime scene or during an autopsy.

This issue is discussed in somewhat greater detail elsewhere,[149] but the general rule is that such images are admissible even if "gory, gruesome, horrible or revolting, so long as an excessive number

---

143. State v. Turner, 330 N.C. 249, 266 (1991) (a murder victim's friends and family engaged in emotional displays throughout the defendant's trial, prompting the trial judge to ask the prosecutor to speak with them and to move them into a less prominent position in the courtroom; new trial not required). *See also* State v. Powell, 340 N.C. 674, 692 (1995) (there was an "outburst" by spectators at the defendant's trial when the jury found him guilty of first-degree murder; the defendant moved for a mistrial of the sentencing phase so that a different jury, untainted by the spectators' reaction, could determine his sentence; the motion was properly denied because the court admonished the spectators and confirmed that each juror would be able to be fair and impartial despite the outburst); State v. Revels, 153 N.C. App. 163, 169 (2002) (mistrial properly denied in murder case where "the trial judge had to caution the audience several times regarding audible emotions" and "a member of [the victim's] family began sobbing and . . . rose and attempted to leave the courtroom"; in addition to admonishing the spectators, the trial judge also instructed the jury not to consider the outbursts).

144. In *Holbrook v. Flynn*, 475 U.S. 560 (1986), the United States Supreme Court rejected a claim that the presence of four officers, in addition to normal court security personnel, at a six-defendant trial deprived one defendant of a fair trial; however, the Court stated that it did "not minimize the threat that a roomful of uniformed and armed policemen might pose to a defendant's chances of receiving a fair trial." *Id.* at 570–71.

145. 923 F.2d 1454 (11th Cir. 1991).

146. 363 N.C. 261 (2009).

147. *Id.* at 281 (quoting from trial judge's ruling).

148. *See also* State v. Larry, 345 N.C. 497, 512 (1997) (the defendant was charged with killing an officer; the trial court did not abuse its discretion in denying the defendant's motion to exclude uniformed officers from the trial; the trial court stated that it would consider the motion further if there were a "concerted demonstration or show of force" by officers).

149. Jessica Smith, *Photographs of Homicide Victims*, N.C. Crim. L., UNC Sch. of Gov't Blog (Apr. 19, 2010), http://nccriminallaw.sog.unc.edu/?p=1216.

of photographs are not used solely to arouse the passions of the jury."[150] A few cases have found error in the admission of multiple, graphic, and inflammatory pictures.[151] More have upheld the admission of such photographs.[152]

Among the factors that are relevant in balancing the probative value and prejudicial effect of such pictures under Rule 403 of the North Carolina Rules of Evidence are the number of pictures, their size, the extent to which they duplicate one another, the extent to which they are relevant to a disputed issue, and how graphic their subject matter.

G. Closing Argument

Many issues regarding jury arguments are not unique to capital trials. For example, lawyers may violate the rule against vouching for their witnesses in all types of cases. Those common issues are not addressed here.[153] What follows is a discussion of issues that are unique to, or unusually likely to arise in, capital cases. Closing arguments at the penalty phase are discussed in Chapter 4.

---

150. State v. Rogers, 323 N.C. 658, 665 (1989).

151. *See, e.g.*, State v. Hennis, 323 N.C. 279 (1988) (abuse of discretion to admit thirty-five autopsy and crime scene photographs of murdered mother and children for illustrative purposes, even with a limiting instruction; photographs were displayed on a large screen and were distributed to jurors one at a time for an hour); State v. Mercer, 275 N.C. 108, 121 (1969) (case featured photographs of victim's dead body, with projecting probes indicating entry and exit points of bullet; evidence was uncontradicted as to cause of death and showed that victim was lying on a bed when shot; photographs were called "poignant and inflammatory"), *overruled on other grounds by* State v. Caddell, 287 N.C. 266 (1975); State v. Johnson, 298 N.C. 355 (1979) (prejudicial error in sentencing phase of capital trial to admit photographs of the murder victim's body, two months after his death, in advanced stages of decomposition); State v. Temple, 302 N.C. 1 (1981) (criticizing admission of photographs of victim's exhumed body lying in a casket).

152. *See, e.g.*, State v. Walters, 357 N.C. 68 (2003) (close-up of murder victim's face, showing blood on her face and a fly on her eyelid); State v. Haselden, 357 N.C. 1 (2003) (one close-up of the murder victim's head and two of her body; defendant's stipulation as to cause of death did not preclude use of the photographs); State v. Early, 194 N.C. App. 594 (2009) (eight autopsy photographs, displayed by monitor and showing location of wounds and whether they were entrance or exit wounds, were found to have illustrated the manner of the killing and to have had probative value as to the defendant's claim of self-defense); State v. Bare, 194 N.C. App. 359 (2008) (photographs of the murder victim's partially decomposed body included (1) three photos of the victim's trunk and lower body, depicting the remains of a fire, mummification and decay of flesh, branches placed over the body, and the victim's pants and shoes; (2) two shots of a skull and jawbone; (3) four pictures of other bones, all largely devoid of flesh; (4) one image of a partially decayed hand; and (5) two photographs of the underbrush where the victim was found; photographs illustrated officer's testimony regarding the condition of the body when it was discovered, including that body had been partially eaten by animals and was missing part of an arm, fingers, and a hand); State v. Snider, 168 N.C. App. 701 (2005) (three autopsy photographs used to illustrate the testimony of the medical examiner who testified as to location of knife and gunshot wounds and that gunshot wound was the cause of death; photographs were projected onto a screen in the courtroom); State v. Gladden, 168 N.C. App. 548 (2005) (ten autopsy photographs used to illustrate the testimony of pathologist; seven were of the victim's body wrapped in plastic and three were of the victim's head, with one showing the face; number of photographs was not excessive).

153. For a general discussion of proper and improper argument, see Jessica Smith, "Jury Argument: Content of Opening and Closing Statements," *in* THE SURVIVAL GUIDE: SUPERIOR COURT JUDGES' BENCHBOOK (UNC School of Government, Apr. 2012), www.sog.unc.edu/sites/www.sog.unc.edu/files/Content%20of%20Opening%20and%20Closing%20Statements_cite%20checked_April%202012.pdf.

Number of Arguments and Time Limitations

In the guilt-innocence phase of a capital trial, just as in any noncapital trial, the state has the opening and closing jury arguments when the defendant presents evidence during the trial.[154] The defense has the jury argument between the state's opening and closing jury arguments. If the defendant does not present evidence, the defense has the opening and closing jury arguments and the state has the jury argument between the defendant's opening and closing arguments.[155] Sometimes attorneys will waive the opening jury argument for tactical or other reasons.

In a capital trial, the judge may limit the number of lawyers who may address the jury to three attorneys per side.[156] The judge may not limit argument to a single attorney.[157] Furthermore, during the defense portion of jury argument, defense counsel may address the jury as many times as they want and as long as they want,[158] as may the prosecutors during the state's portion of jury argument. For example, one defense lawyer may argue for as long as she wants. When she has finished, a second defense lawyer, and then a third defense lawyer, may do the same. They may continue to follow one another without limitation. If the defendant presents evidence, all the defense attorneys' jury arguments must occur before the state's closing argument, but the number and duration of addresses still may not be limited.[159]

Defense Lawyer's Admission of Defendant's Guilt of Lesser-Included Offenses

Sometimes defense attorneys may want to admit, in arguing that the defendant is not guilty of first-degree murder, that the defendant is guilty of a lesser-included offense of first-degree murder, such as second-degree murder, voluntary manslaughter, or involuntary manslaughter. However, defense counsel likely must receive the defendant's authorization before doing so. The North Carolina Supreme Court ruled in *State v. Harbison*[160] that a defense lawyer who makes such an admission without the defendant's authorization renders ineffective assistance of counsel, automatically providing the defendant with a new trial. The court reasoned that the attorney, in admitting the defendant's guilt, was not functioning as a defense attorney and instead was effectively entering a guilty plea on behalf of the defendant without the defendant's consent. The court has instructed trial judges and attorneys to make a record of the defendant's authorization if this issue arises at trial.[161]

---

154. Gen. R. Prac. Super. & Dist. Cts. 10. A defendant presents evidence under this rule even if he or she introduces evidence during cross-examination of a state's witness without calling witnesses him or herself. State v. Skipper, 337 N.C. 1 (1994); State v. Macon, 346 N.C. 109 (1999). However, simply conducting cross-examination does not itself constitute the introduction of evidence. *See, e.g.,* State v. Matthews, __ N.C. App. __, 720 S.E.2d 829 (2012). If there are multiple defendants, the state has the opening and closing jury arguments if any defendant presents evidence. Gen. R. Prac. Super. & Dist. Cts. 10.

155. Gen. R. Prac. Super. & Dist. Cts. 10.

156. G.S. 7A-97. *See also* State v. Eury, 317 N.C. 511 (1986); State v. Campbell, 332 N.C. 116 (1992).

157. State v. Barrow, 350 N.C. 640 (1999). If the trial judge errs in not permitting more than one counsel to make a closing jury argument, the defendant automatically receives a new trial. Harmless error analysis is not conducted. State v. Mitchell, 321 N.C. 650 (1988).

158. G.S. 7A-97. *See also Eury*, 317 N.C. 511; *Campbell*, 332 N.C. 116.

159. State v. Gladden, 315 N.C. 398 (1986).

160. 315 N.C. 175 (1985).

161. *See* State v. House, 340 N.C. 187, 197 (1995) ("[W]e take this opportunity to urge both the bar and the trial bench to be diligent in making a full record of a defendant's consent when a *Harbison* issue arises at trial."). For cases in which the court ruled that the defendant authorized defense counsel's jury argument, see *State v. Wiley*, 355 N.C. 592 (2002); *State v. Strickland*, 346 N.C. 443 (1997); *State v. McNeill*, 346 N.C. 233 (1997); *State v. Greene*, 332 N.C. 565 (1992); *State v. Thomas*, 329 N.C. 423 (1991); *State v. McDowell*, 329 N.C. 363 (1991).

The continuing vitality of *Harbison* was called into question when the United States Supreme Court decided *Florida v. Nixon*.[162] *Nixon* was a capital case in which defense counsel wanted to admit that the defendant was guilty of first-degree murder, thereby preserving counsel's credibility for what he viewed as an inevitable penalty phase. Several times, he discussed his plan with the defendant, but the defendant was nonresponsive, neither approving nor disapproving of the strategy. At trial, the lawyer conceded the defendant's guilt, and the defendant was convicted and sentenced to death. The Florida courts, applying a rule similar to *Harbison*, ordered a new trial, but the Supreme Court reversed. It held that an attorney's decision to admit his or her client's guilt was not *per se* ineffective assistance, but rather should be evaluated under the two-part standard established in *Strickland v. Washington*,[163] which asks whether the attorney performed deficiently and whether the defendant was prejudiced as a result. The Court strongly suggested that the conduct of the defense lawyer in *Nixon* was a reasonable effort to maintain candor with the jury and to preserve his credibility for the penalty phase.

Although the reasoning of *Nixon* is somewhat at odds with that of *Harbison*, the court of appeals has ruled that *Harbison* remains the law. However, its status in capital cases is unclear. In *State v. Maready*,[164] the court distinguished *Nixon* based on "the unique nature of death penalty cases,"[165] suggesting that *Harbison* may remain the law in noncapital cases but that *Nixon* might apply in capital proceedings. But the *Maready* court also stated that "subsequent to *Nixon*, the North Carolina Supreme Court has continued to apply the analysis set forth in *Harbison*, even in death penalty cases,"[166] and also suggested that *Harbison* might be grounded in the state constitution and so might be more protective of defendants' rights than the federal standard enunciated in *Nixon*. Thus, it remains advisable for judges in capital cases to determine whether defense counsel plans to admit the defendant's guilt, and if so, whether the defendant consents to the admission.

Finally, it should be noted that in *State v. Walls*,[167] the court stated that *Harbison* applied only to the guilt-innocence phase and rejected its application to the sentencing phase.[168]

Defense Lawyer's Statement of Punishment Severity

The defendant's lawyer may properly inform the jury during jury argument of the maximum punishment for first-degree murder to encourage the jury to consider the case carefully. However, the argument may not suggest to the jury that they should return a verdict of not guilty simply because of the severity of the punishment.[169]

162. 543 U.S. 175 (2004).
163. 466 U.S. 668 (1984).
164. 205 N.C. App. 1 (2010).
165. *Id.* at 8.
166. *Id.* at 9–10.
167. 342 N.C. 1 (1995).
168. *See also* State v. Fletcher, 354 N.C. 455 (2001) (not ineffective assistance of counsel when defense counsel admitted existence of aggravating circumstance in jury argument in capital sentencing hearing).
169. Among the relevant cases in this area are the following: *State v. Chapman*, 342 N.C. 330 (1995) (the trial judge erred in instructing the jury that defense counsel's argument discussing the possible punishment should be disregarded, but the error was not prejudicial); *State v. Buckner*, 342 N.C. 198 (1995) (similar); *State v. Smith*, 335 N.C. 539 (1994) (new trial ordered because the trial judge improperly barred defense counsel from stating to the jury the maximum punishment for first-degree murder, in the context of an argument about the gravity of the case and the possibility of the defendant's innocence); and *State v. McMorris*, 290 N.C. 286 (1976) (delineating proper and improper purposes for informing the jury of the possible punishment). *See also* G.S. 15-176.5 ("When a case will be submitted to the jury on a charge for which the penalty is a sentence of death, either party in its argument to the jury may indicate the consequences of a verdict of guilty of that charge.").

H. Jury Instructions and Verdicts

Jury Instructions

At the guilt-innocence phase, the law governing jury instructions is not different in capital trials than in other trials. There are several pattern jury instructions available, depending on the state's theory of first-degree murder; which lesser-included offenses are to be submitted, if any; and the defenses presented, if any.[170]

A common issue is whether to submit second-degree murder or other lesser-included offenses to the jury. The general rule is that a lesser-included offense must be submitted if "the evidence would permit a jury rationally to find [the defendant] guilty of the lesser offense and acquit him [or her] of the greater."[171] On the other hand, if the state's evidence is positive as to every element of first-degree murder and there is no conflicting evidence, then an instruction on lesser-included offenses is not appropriate.[172] A defendant is not automatically entitled to an instruction on lesser-included offenses.[173]

A judge should instruct on a lesser-included offense if the facts support the instruction, even if the defendant does not request the instruction,[174] or indeed, objects to it.[175] However, if the defendant expressly objects to such an instruction, the erroneous failure to give the instruction will be unreviewable invited error.[176]

The theory or theories of first-degree murder at issue may influence whether it is appropriate to submit lesser-included offenses. The North Carolina Supreme Court explained in *State v. Millsaps*[177] that

> the following principles have evolved in our first-degree felony murder jurisprudence: (i) If the evidence of the underlying felony supporting felony murder is in conflict and the evidence would support a lesser-included offense of first-degree murder, the trial court must instruct on all lesser-included offenses supported by the evidence whether the State tries the case on both premeditation and deliberation and felony murder or only on felony murder. . . . (ii) If the State tries the case on both premeditation and

170. The instructions begin with N.C.P.I.—Crim. 206.00 and continue through N.C.P.I.—Crim. 206.20.

171. State v. Leazer, 353 N.C. 234, 237 (2000) (internal quotation marks omitted).

172. State v. Millsaps, 356 N.C. 556, 562 (2002). *See also, e.g.,* State v. Locklear, 363 N.C. 438, 455 (2009) (trial judge properly declined to submit second-degree murder where state presented ample evidence of premeditation and deliberation and the only evidence to the contrary was the defendant's self-serving statement to law enforcement that he had beaten the victim to death in a rage; the defendant "failed to show that his rage was of such magnitude that it rendered him incapable of deliberate thought and ability to reason"); State v. Taylor, 362 N.C. 514, 532 (2008) (trial judge properly declined to submit second-degree murder where defendant entered a store, armed and planning to rob it, and subsequently engaged in a gun battle with the proprietors, killing one; even if he did not enter the store planning to kill and did not shoot first, "[n]either absence of evidence of a plan to commit murder nor existence of evidence that one was not the first to fire in a gunfight negates premeditation and deliberation").

173. State v. Strickland, 307 N.C. 274 (1983).

174. State v. Lowe, 150 N.C. App. 682, 686 (2002) (stating that a judge should instruct on a lesser included offense "even in the absence of a request by the defendant, where sufficient evidence of the lesser offense is presented at trial") (internal quotation marks omitted).

175. *See* Jeff Welty, *Jury Instructions on Lesser Included Offenses*, N.C. Crim. L., UNC Sch. of Gov't Blog (July 27, 2011), http://nccriminallaw.sog.unc.edu/?p=2732.

176. State v. Williams, 333 N.C. 719, 727, 728 (1993) (defendant was charged with first-degree murder and indicated to the judge that he did not want the jury instructed on second-degree murder; "any error in not instructing on the lesser-included offense was invited by defendant," so defendant was "not entitled to any relief and will not be heard to complain on appeal"); State v. Sierra, 335 N.C. 753 (1994) (similar); G.S. 15A-1443(c) ("A defendant is not prejudiced by the granting of relief which he has sought or by error resulting from his own conduct.").

177. 356 N.C. 556 (2002).

> deliberation and felony murder and the evidence supports not only first-degree premeditated and deliberate murder but also second-degree murder, or another lesser offense included within premeditated and deliberate murder, the trial court must submit the lesser-included offenses within premeditated and deliberate murder irrespective of whether all the evidence would support felony murder.... (iii) If the evidence as to the underlying felony supporting felony murder is not in conflict and all the evidence supports felony murder, the trial court is not required to instruct on the lesser offenses included within premeditated and deliberate murder if the case is submitted on felony murder only.[178]

There are also cases addressing the submission of lesser-included offenses when the theory of first-degree murder is lying in wait[179] or poisoning.[180]

Issues may also arise regarding whether to instruct the jury on certain defenses. For example, a defendant may claim that, because of diminished capacity, he or she was unable to premeditate, deliberate, or form a specific intent to kill.[181] In some circumstances, diminished capacity may also provide a defense to felony murder.[182] Generally, the defendant bears the burden of producing sufficient evidence to require a jury instruction on diminished capacity.[183] However, the state then bears the ultimate burden of proving each element of first-degree murder beyond a reasonable doubt. There is a pattern jury instruction on diminished capacity.[184]

Voluntary intoxication is a defense that is closely related to diminished capacity, in that a defendant may claim that voluntary intoxication rendered him or her unable to premeditate, deliberate, or form a specific intent to kill.[185] The applicability of this defense to other theories of first-degree murder is

---

178. *Id.* at 565. *See also* State v. Gwynn, 362 N.C. 334 (2008) (state proceeded on felony murder only; evidence of underlying felony was not in doubt; trial judge properly denied defendant's request for an instruction on second-degree murder).

179. State v. Camacho, 337 N.C. 224 (1994) (sole theory of first-degree murder was lying in wait; defendant's evidence showed that he did not lie in wait; trial judge should have submitted second-degree murder); State v. Leroux, 326 N.C. 368 (1990) (evidence of lying in wait was not conflicting, so defendant not entitled to lesser-included offense instructions).

180. State v. Moore, 335 N.C. 567 (1994) (trial judge properly declined to instruct on lesser-included offenses); State v. Johnson, 317 N.C. 193 (1986) (similar).

181. *See, e.g.,* State v. Clark, 324 N.C. 146 (1989) (trial judge did not err in refusing to instruct on diminished capacity; defendant's evidence was insufficient to create a reasonable doubt about the defendant's inability to premeditate and deliberate); State v. Rose, 323 N.C. 455 (1988) (defendant was entitled to instruction).

182. Felony murder does not require premeditation, deliberation, or a specific intent to kill, so diminished capacity is not directly relevant. State v. Carroll, 356 N.C. 526 (2002). However, if the underlying felony requires specific intent, and the defendant's diminished capacity prevented him or her from forming such an intent, diminished capacity would provide a defense to the underlying felony and so to felony murder, too. *Cf.* State v. Roache, 358 N.C. 243, 305–06 (2004) (stating that "the trial court informed the jury that diminished capacity applied to armed robbery, which was the underlying felony.... With this instruction the jurors would have understood that diminished capacity could be considered as a defense for ... felony murder.").

183. *Cf.* State v. Skipper, 337 N.C. 1 (1994) (constitutional to place burden of production on defendant regarding instruction on voluntary intoxication).

184. N.C.P.I.—CRIM. 305.11. The sufficiency of the pattern was generally upheld in *Roache,* 358 N.C. 243.

185. *See generally* Jeff Welty, *Voluntary Intoxication,* N.C. CRIM. L., UNC SCH. OF GOV'T BLOG (June 8, 2011), http://nccriminallaw.sog.unc.edu/?p=2538; State v. Long, 354 N.C. 534 (2001) (evidence of impairment several hours after the murder did not require an instruction on voluntary intoxication); State v. Morganherring, 350 N.C. 701 (1999) (evidence that defendant drank two 40-ounce beers and smoked a large quantity of crack cocaine in the time surrounding the murders being tried required an instruction); State v. Herring, 338 N.C. 271 (1994) (evidence that defendant consumed alcohol and marijuana did not require an instruction where defendant had a detailed memory of events and was in control of his actions); State v. Mash, 323 N.C. 339, 341 (1988) (evidence

discussed in the margin.[186] As with diminished capacity, the initial burden of production is on the defendant,[187] but if the defendant satisfies that burden and the jury is instructed on voluntary intoxication, the burden then rests with the state to prove each element of first-degree murder beyond a reasonable doubt. There is a pattern jury instruction on voluntary intoxication.[188]

A final common defense is self-defense. Several of the pattern jury instructions for first-degree murder include self-defense.[189] Self-defense is also addressed comprehensively in another School of Government publication,[190] though readers should be aware of recent statutory changes to the law in this area.[191]

Verdicts

When a case is submitted on more than one theory of first-degree murder, it is a good practice for the jury to indicate the theory or theories on which it based its verdict.[192] For example, when a case is submitted on both felony murder and premeditation and deliberation, if the jury returns a general verdict of guilty, the court must treat the conviction as a conviction of felony murder; that is, it must arrest judgment on the felony and may not use it to support certain aggravating circumstances.[193] By contrast, if the jury returns a verdict specifying that it found the defendant guilty under both theories, the court may treat the conviction as a conviction for premeditated murder. Having the jury specify the theory or theories on which it based its verdict may also be helpful if, for example, an appellate court finds fault with a particular theory.[194] If there is evidence that supports the defendant's guilt on a theory of accessory before the fact, additional findings by the jury may be required, as discussed in the margin.[195]

When the case is submitted to the jury on the theory of felony murder, and when there is more than one possible predicate felony, questions sometimes arise regarding unanimity. The appellate courts have ruled that the jury need not be unanimous regarding which felony serves as a predicate

---

that the defendant drank heavily, was drunk, "changed," and was "out of control" required an instruction on voluntary intoxication) (quoting from witness testimony).

186. Because specific intent is not an element of first-degree murder by lying in wait, voluntary intoxication is not a defense to that theory of first-degree murder. State v. Baldwin, 330 N.C. 446 (1992). Like diminished capacity, voluntary intoxication would be relevant to felony murder only if it provided a defense to an underlying specific intent felony. State v. Kyle, 333 N.C. 687 (1993) (error, though harmless on the facts of this case, for the trial judge to refuse to instruct on voluntary intoxication regarding burglary and kidnapping); State v. Golden, 143 N.C. App. 426 (2001) (error for the trial judge to refuse to instruct on voluntary intoxication for robbery where that was the predicate for felony murder).

187. *Skipper*, 337 N.C. 1 (constitutional to place burden of production on the defendant).

188. N.C.P.I.—Crim. 305.10.

189. N.C.P.I.—Crim. 206.10 (deadly weapon used); N.C.P.I.—Crim. 206.11 (no deadly weapon).

190. John Rubin, The Law of Self-Defense in North Carolina (UNC School of Government, 1996). (Readers should note that a second edition of this publication is forthcoming in 2013.)

191. John Rubin, *The New Law of Self-Defense?* N.C. Crim. L., UNC Sch. of Gov't Blog (Apr. 17, 2011), http://nccriminallaw.sog.unc.edu/?p=2798.

192. State v. Stokes, 308 N.C. 634 (1983).

193. *See, e.g.,* State v. Silhan, 302 N.C. 223 (1981).

194. *See, e.g.,* State v. Lynch, 327 N.C. 210 (1990) (case submitted on premeditation and deliberation and lying in wait; general verdict of guilty; reviewing court found insufficient evidence to support lying in wait; because it was impossible to determine the theory upon which the jury based its verdict, new trial required).

195. Under G.S. 14-5.2, a person who is convicted on the theory of accessory before the fact normally is punishable as a principal to the felony. However, if the conviction is based solely on the uncorroborated testimony of one or more persons involved in the crime, an accessory before the fact to a first-degree murder is punishable as a Class B2 felon. N.C.P.I.—Crim. 206.10A instructs the jury to indicate whether the conviction was based solely on accomplice testimony.

for felony murder. For example, in *State v. Coleman*,[196] the reviewing court "[could] not determine if the jury was unanimous in which felony served as the underlying felony for purposes of the felony murder verdict,"[197] but nonetheless affirmed the verdict because the various possible predicates were simply "alternative means" of committing a "single wrong."[198] Of course, in some circumstances, it may be desirable to have the jury make a finding regarding whether it agreed unanimously on a particular predicate felony or felonies, such as when there are several possible predicates and the state is concerned that one or more may be vulnerable on appeal.

If a defendant is convicted of felony murder, the judge must ultimately arrest judgment on the predicate felony, which is said to "merge" into the murder conviction.[199] However, if a defendant is convicted of multiple predicates, the trial judge should not arrest judgment on all of the predicates. Instead, he or she should choose one of the predicates on which to arrest judgment and should impose a sentence for the others.[200]

---

196. 161 N.C. App. 224 (2003).

197. *Id.* at 234–35.

198. *Id.* at 235 (internal quotation marks omitted). *See also* State v. Taylor, 362 N.C. 514 (2008).

199. State v. Barlowe, 337 N.C. 371 (1994); State v. Gardner, 315 N.C. 444, 460 (1986) ("[A] defendant may not be punished both for felony murder and for the underlying, 'predicate' felony, even in a single prosecution.").

200. *Barlowe*, 337 N.C. 371; State v. Ridgeway, 185 N.C. App. 423, 437 (2007) ("Where the trial court's jury instructions did not specify which of the multiple felonies were to be considered as the underlying felony for purposes of the felony murder conviction, it was within the trial court's discretion to select which felony conviction would serve as the underlying felony.").

Chapter 4

The Capital Sentencing Hearing

Chapter 4

The Capital Sentencing Hearing

This chapter discusses selected issues that commonly arise in the capital sentencing hearing, except that aggravating and mitigating circumstances are discussed in Chapters 5 and 6, respectively.

A. Overview

If a defendant in a capital trial is convicted by a jury of first-degree murder, a capital sentencing hearing must be held before the same jury, unless the trial jury is unable to reconvene for the hearing.[1] Alternate jurors selected for the trial remain as alternate jurors for the capital sentencing hearing, unless they are needed to replace one of the trial jurors.[2] If a defendant pleads guilty to first-degree murder and there is evidence of at least one aggravating circumstance, a jury must be selected for the capital sentencing hearing.[3]

The parties do not have a right to give opening statements in a capital sentencing hearing,[4] though some judges may allow such statements as a matter of discretion.[5] Evidence presented during the trial is automatically admissible during the hearing; it need not be resubmitted.[6] The state may present evidence at the hearing or rely on evidence introduced at the trial to prove one or more aggravating

1. Section 15A-2000(a)(2) of the North Carolina General Statutes (hereinafter G.S.) provides that if the trial jury is unable to reconvene for a sentencing hearing, then the trial judge must impanel a new jury for that purpose. Otherwise, the same jury is used for both the guilt and sentencing phases of a capital trial. In *State v. Berry*, 356 N.C. 490 (2002), the court reiterated its prior ruling in *State v. Bondurant*, 309 N.C. 674 (1983), that a trial judge has no authority to order a non-death-qualified jury to try the guilt-innocence phase of a first-degree capital murder trial and then to order a death-qualified jury to hear the capital sentencing hearing if the defendant is convicted of first-degree murder. The *Bondurant* court reasoned that such a proposed procedure "contravenes G.S. 15A-2000(a)(2), which contemplates that the same jury which determines guilt will recommend the sentence." 309 N.C. at 682.

2. G.S. 15A-2000(a)(2).

3. *Id.*

4. State v. Call, 349 N.C. 382 (1998).

5. *See, e.g.*, State v. Waring, 364 N.C. 443, 504 (2010) (referring to "opening statement[s] in the sentencing proceeding").

6. G.S. 15A-2000(a)(3); State v. McLaughlin, 341 N.C. 426 (1995) (evidence from guilt-innocence stage of trial was competent and admissible as a matter of law at capital resentencing hearing).

circumstances; the defendant then may present evidence of mitigating circumstances.[7] The state may then present rebuttal evidence.[8]

The state may present jury argument and then the defendant may present jury argument. The defendant has the right to the last jury argument.[9] The judge then instructs the jury, and the jury deliberates and delivers its sentence recommendation (death or life imprisonment), which must be unanimous.[10] If the jury unanimously agrees on a sentence recommendation, the judge must poll the jury to make sure that each juror agrees to that recommendation.[11] The judge is required to sentence the defendant according to the jury's recommendation.[12]

State law provides that if the jury is unable to agree on a sentence recommendation within a "reasonable time," the judge must impose a sentence of life imprisonment.[13] An additional general description of the penalty phase of a capital trial is provided in Chapter 1.

B. General Constitutional Issues

The United States Supreme Court has generally affirmed the constitutionality of the death penalty,[14] subject to the categorical limits described in Chapter 1, such as the prohibition against the imposition of capital punishment on juveniles and the mentally retarded. Likewise, the North Carolina Supreme Court has repeatedly rejected broad-based attacks on the constitutionality of capital punishment.[15] Rejected arguments include (1) that North Carolina's statutory framework for capital cases fails to guide a jury's discretion with objective standards, and therefore invites arbitrariness and caprice;[16] and (2) that the death penalty is unconstitutional due to racial bias.[17]

---

7. G.S. 15A-2000(a)(3).

8. As to the right to present rebuttal evidence generally, see, e.g., *State v. Silhan*, 302 N.C. 223, 273 (1981) (where the defendant presented evidence of his good character in mitigation, "the state was entitled to show in rebuttal that defendant's reputation among others familiar with it was not good," and generally "[b]oth the state and defendant are entitled to a fair sentencing hearing, and the jury is entitled to have as full a picture of a defendant's character as our capital sentencing statute and constitutional limitations will permit"). Presumably the defendant would have the right to present surrebuttal evidence in an appropriate case.

9. G.S. 15A-2000(a)(4).

10. G.S. 15A-2000(b).

11. *Id.*

12. G.S. 15A-2002.

13. G.S. 15A-2000(b).

14. *See, e.g.*, Gregg v. Georgia, 428 U.S. 153 (1976).

15. *See, e.g.*, State v. Elliott, 360 N.C. 400, 423–24 (2006) ("The constitutionality of North Carolina's capital punishment statute has been affirmed numerous times by this Court, and we find no reason to overrule our precedent.").

16. State v. Keel, 337 N.C. 469 (1994).

17. State v. Green, 329 N.C. 686, 689 (1991) (rejecting the defendant's argument that the death penalty violates the Equal Protection Clause, the Eighth Amendment, and the state constitution; although the defendant cited studies that "show that a person is more likely to be executed if the murder victim is white and the chance is more likely yet if the defendant is black," the court, based on *McCleskey v. Kemp*, 481 U.S. 279 (1987), ruled that general studies that are not specific to North Carolina or to a particular district within the state are insufficient to establish a constitutional violation). For a further discussion of race and the death penalty, see Chapter 7.

C. Selected Evidence Issues

Rules of Evidence at Sentencing Hearing

The North Carolina Supreme Court has ruled that trial evidence rules do not apply to the sentencing hearing.[18] Instead, as provided in G.S. 15A-2000(a)(3), "[a]ny evidence which the court deems to have probative value may be received." In particular, a defendant may have a due process right to introduce relevant evidence, even if it does not meet the requirements for admissibility under state evidence rules.[19] However, those rules "do provide [the courts] guidance" in resolving evidentiary disputes.[20]

In keeping with the foregoing, hearsay evidence offered by the state or defendant that may be inadmissible at trial may be admitted at the sentencing hearing if it is relevant to the issues involved in the hearing.[21] However, evidence offered by the state must not violate a defendant's rights under the Confrontation Clause.[22] Because of the dramatic change in Confrontation Clause jurisprudence wrought by *Crawford v. Washington*,[23] some of the pre-*Crawford* cases in this area include Confrontation Clause rulings that are not correct under current law.[24]

---

18. *See, e.g.*, State v. Raines, 362 N.C. 1, 17 (2007) ("[T]he Rules of Evidence are not controlling in a capital penalty proceeding."); State v. Campbell, 359 N.C. 644, 683 (2005) (to rebut the state's evidence that the victim was non-violent, the defendant sought to call witnesses "who would have stated that one night an unknown man knocked on their doors, claiming that the victim attempted to rape him"; although the rules of evidence do not apply at capital sentencings, the proffered evidence was not reliable and relevant enough to be admissible); State v. Anderson, 350 N.C. 152, 181 (1999) (ruling admissible a psychiatric expert's testimony at the capital sentencing hearing to the effect that the defendant's disorder would not relieve her of responsibility; noting that the rules of evidence do not apply at a capital sentencing hearing; and stating that the term "responsibility," in the context of the expert's testimony, was a medical term used appropriately to describe the effect of the defendant's mental conditions on her actions); State v. Rose, 339 N.C. 172 (1994).

19. Green v. Georgia, 442 U.S. 95 (1979) (notwithstanding state evidence rules, the defendant had a due process right to introduce seemingly reliable hearsay evidence tending to show that he was not the triggerman and that his accomplice was much more culpable than he); State v. Jones, 339 N.C. 114 (1994) (when evidence is relevant to a critical issue in the sentencing hearing, it must be admitted, despite contrary state evidence rules; the trial judge erred in prohibiting a witness from testifying that the defendant told him that he was sorry for what he had done, which prevented the defendant from offering evidence of his remorse as a mitigating circumstance); State v. Barts, 321 N.C. 170 (1987) (holding that the defendant's due process right to a fair capital sentencing hearing was violated when the trial judge excluded a witness's testimony and written statement in which an accomplice to the murder described the accomplice's role in the murder and did not mention the defendant's role; the declarations were sufficiently reliable and were highly relevant, since they showed that the defendant had not personally administered the fatal beating; the court noted that evidence rules that normally apply to the guilt-innocence stage do not necessarily apply to the sentencing hearing). *But see* State v. Walls, 342 N.C. 1 (1995) (distinguishing *Green*, the court ruled that proposed defense testimony was irrelevant and lacked indicia of reliability).

20. State v. Williams, 363 N.C. 689, 711 (2009) (defendant argued that evidence relating to conduct of which he was acquitted was wrongly introduced at his capital sentencing proceeding; court disagreed, citing non-capital evidence case). *See also Raines*, 362 N.C. at 19 (stating that the rules of evidence "serve as guidelines" during the penalty phase).

21. G.S. 15A-2000(a)(3) ("Any evidence which the court deems to have probative value may be received.").

22. *See, e.g.*, State v. Nobles, 357 N.C. 433 (2003) (holding that the trial court erred in allowing the state to introduce, as evidence of a prior violent felony by the defendant, the transcript of the victim's testimony at the defendant's trial on the previous charges; the state failed to establish the victim's unavailability, creating a Confrontation Clause problem); State v. Holmes, 355 N.C. 719 (2002); State v. McLaughlin, 341 N.C. 426 (1995). For a detailed discussion of the Confrontation Clause, see Jessica Smith, *Understanding the New Confrontation Clause Analysis:* Crawford, Davis, *and* Melendez-Diaz , Admin. of Just. Bull. No. 2010/02 (UNC School of Government, 2010), http://sogpubs.unc.edu/electronicversions/pdfs/aojb1002.pdf.

23. 541 U.S. 36 (2004).

24. *See, e.g.*, State v. Robinson, 339 N.C. 263 (1994) (deeming properly admitted hearsay evidence from an affidavit for a search warrant; the evidence was used to prove circumstances surrounding a prior Colorado murder conviction).

Victim Impact Evidence

In *Booth v. Maryland*,[25] the United States Supreme Court held that victim impact evidence is "irrelevant to a capital sentencing decision, and that its admission creates a constitutionally unacceptable risk that the jury may impose the death penalty in an arbitrary and capricious manner." Four years later, in *Payne v. Tennessee*,[26] the Court reconsidered the issue and concluded that the prosecution in a capital trial may properly use victim impact evidence to humanize the victim and to illustrate "the specific harm caused by the defendant." As shown by the case summaries below, since *Payne*, the North Carolina Supreme Court has ruled consistently that the state may offer victim impact evidence. The General Assembly likewise has given its imprimatur to the use of victim impact evidence by enacting G.S. 15A-833, a portion of the Crime Victims' Rights Act that broadly endorses the use of such evidence.[27]

The use of victim impact evidence remains subject to some limitations, however. It is "usually irrelevant during the guilt-innocence portion of a capital trial,"[28] and so normally must be introduced only during the penalty phase. Furthermore, *Payne* left intact the holding in *Booth* that prohibits the introduction of evidence about the victim's "family members' opinions and characterizations of the crimes and the defendant."[29] Thus, victim impact witnesses should not be allowed to describe the murder as horrific or the defendant as a monster. Finally, while the state "should be given some latitude in fleshing out the humanity of the victim," it may not "go too far," for example, by asking that the defendant be given the death penalty because the victim was a good person.[30]

Case Summaries: Victim Impact Evidence

Payne v. Tennessee, 501 U.S. 808 (1991). The defendant was convicted and sentenced to death for murdering a woman and her 2-year-old daughter and convicted of feloniously stabbing the woman's 3-year-old son. The state presented the mother of the murdered woman, who testified how the woman's son had been affected by the murders of his mother and sister. He cried for his sister and asked his grandmother if she missed his sister. The prosecutor, in arguing for the death penalty in closing and rebuttal arguments, commented on the continuing effects of the son's experience, including that the son knew what had happened to his mother and sister, and stated that when the son grew up, he would want to know "what type of justice was done." The prosecutor also spoke about what the murdered sister's life might have been like, how the murdered mother would never kiss her son at night again, and he also talked about the effect of the deaths on the surviving relatives of the victims. Partially overruling *Booth v. Maryland*, 482 U.S. 496 (1987), discussed immediately below, the United States Supreme Court ruled that both the testimony of the murdered woman's mother and the argument by the prosecutor were proper. The Eighth Amendment does not by itself bar evidence about the victim and the impact of the murder on the victim's family. The Court noted that a due process violation may occur if victim impact evidence is so unduly prejudicial as to render the sentencing hearing fundamen-

---

25. 482 U.S. 496, 503 (1987). *See also* South Carolina v. Gaithers, 490 U.S. 805 (1989) (similar holding as to prosecutor's comments during closing argument about the victim's personal characteristics).

26. 501 U.S. 808, 825 (1991).

27. The statute, which is not specific to capital cases, provides in part that "[a] victim has the right to offer admissible evidence of the impact of the crime" and describes certain types of evidence that the victim may offer. G.S. 15A-833(a).

28. State v. Maske, 358 N.C. 40, 50 (2004).

29. *Booth*, 482 U.S. at 502. The North Carolina Supreme Court noted that this portion of *Booth* remains good law in *State v. Thompson*, 359 N.C. 77, 90–91 (2004).

30. State v. Reeves, 337 N.C. 700, 723 (1994).

tally unfair. Because this case did not involve family members' characterizations and opinions about the crime, the defendant, or the appropriate sentence—evidence ruled unconstitutional in *Booth*—the Court's overruling of *Booth* did not apply to this kind of evidence.

Booth v. Maryland, 482 U.S. 496 (1987). The defendant murdered an elderly couple. Consistent with Maryland law, a victim impact statement was prepared and read to the jury. Generally, it "described the personal characteristics of the victims and the emotional impact of the crimes on the family" and "set forth the family members' opinions and characterizations of the crimes and the defendant." The Supreme Court ruled that both types of evidence were "irrelevant to a capital sentencing decision, and that [their] admission creates a constitutionally unacceptable risk that the jury may impose the death penalty in an arbitrary and capricious manner." The Court was also concerned that the introduction of victim impact evidence would result in minitrials about the victims' character. As noted above, the Court's holding as to evidence of "the personal characteristics of the victims and the emotional impact of the crimes on the family" was later overruled in *Payne*.

State v. Allen, 360 N.C. 297 (2006). The trial judge did not commit plain error in allowing the victim's sister to testify that she suffered panic attacks after the victim's death; that she "sought help"; that she was devastated; that her brother was her "sidekick" and made her complete; and that his death destroyed her children's lives as well.

State v. Thompson, 359 N.C. 77 (2004). A social worker testified on behalf of the defendant at the penalty phase. On cross-examination, the social worker stated that she had attempted to contact the victim's family but that, understandably, they had refused to speak with her. The state supreme court agreed with the defendant that evidence of the victim's family's "opinions and characterizations of the crimes" and of the defendant remain inadmissible under *Booth* even after *Payne* but held that the social worker's testimony on cross-examination did not constitute such evidence.

State v. Roache, 358 N.C. 243 (2004). The defendant killed five members of a family. The state presented victim impact evidence from one victim's brother and from three children of two of the victims. Generally, the witnesses "testified as to the physical, psychological, and emotional effect the [victims'] deaths had on themselves and others in the family and community." Such testimony was proper victim impact evidence.

State v. Maske, 358 N.C. 40 (2004). The victim's sister testified during the guilt phase that the victim was a good person, that her relationship with the victim was close, and that the victim's death had affected her and her children deeply. The court noted that victim impact evidence is "usually irrelevant during the guilt-innocence portion of a capital trial" but held that any error in admitting the evidence was not prejudicial given the overwhelming evidence of the defendant's guilt.

State v. White, 355 N.C. 696 (2002). The court ruled that a cookbook dedicated to the murder victim was properly admitted as victim impact evidence. The evidence reflected the high regard in which the victim was held among her family and throughout the community.

State v. Nicholson, 355 N.C. 1 (2002). The defendant shot and killed his wife. The court ruled that the trial judge properly admitted victim impact testimony by the mother of the defendant's wife. She described the effect of the death on the victim's children, her brother, and on herself and her husband. She related how her granddaughter now lacked the mother figure on whom she had always relied. She also described the murder's effect on the victim's brother, who was an eyewitness to the murder—he cried constantly, could not bear to turn the lights off, and began to do poorly in school.

State v. Hooks, 353 N.C. 629 (2001). The court ruled that the trial judge did not err in admitting victim impact evidence offered by the victim's brother. He testified that the victim was easygoing; gave everything "110 percent"; wanted to make something of himself; and was loving, kind, and respectful. He also testified that the victim had accepted Jesus Christ after a neighbor died of a heart attack and that the victim left a favorable impression on everyone he met. The court stated that the comment concerning the victim's acceptance of Jesus Christ briefly addressed the religious facet of the victim's life and did not inflame the jury to sentence the defendant to death because the victim was a Christian.

State v. Davis, 353 N.C. 1 (2000). The court ruled, citing *State v. Reeves,* 337 N.C. 700 (1994), that victim impact evidence by a longtime friend of the victim was properly admitted at the sentencing hearing. The friend testified about the impact of the victim's death on him at his workplace and when he was at home—the victim was constantly on his mind.

State v. Smith, 352 N.C. 531 (2000). The court ruled that the following victim impact testimony of the murder victim's brother was properly admitted at the capital sentencing hearing: "The impact has been, No. 1, that I've lost a confidant[e]. No. 2, that I feel like she was taken from me at a stage in our lives where we needed each other and we were still learning about life, as if a predator had come and taken one of two sibling birds out of the nest." The court ruled that this testimony was restrained, described the emotional or psychological effect of his sister's death on him, was well within the parameters of G.S. 15A-833, and was constitutional under *Payne* and other cases.

State v. Williams, 350 N.C. 1 (1999). The court ruled, relying on *State v. Harden,* 344 N.C. 542 (1996), that it is not error in a capital sentencing hearing to admit a photograph of the murder victim as she appeared when she was alive. The state may use such photographs of the victim to emphasize to the jury that she was once alive, that she is now dead, and that the defendant was the person responsible for her death.

State v. Flippen, 349 N.C. 264 (1998). The defendant was sentenced to death for the first-degree murder of his 2-year-old stepdaughter. The court ruled that the trial judge did not err in allowing the state to show a videotape of the murder victim that had been taken forty-nine days before her death to show the victim's vulnerability and to show why it would be especially heinous, atrocious, and cruel for a man as large and powerful as the defendant to murder her with his hands while she was in his care.

State v. Conaway, 339 N.C. 487 (1995). The prosecutor's jury argument that attempted to inform the jury of the unique losses suffered by the parents and siblings of the two victims, and especially by the 3-year-old son of one of the victims, was proper argument to enable the jury to assess meaningfully the defendant's moral culpability and blameworthiness.

State v. Reeves, 337 N.C. 700 (1994). The defendant was convicted of first-degree murder and sentenced to death. The state offered evidence at the sentencing hearing that the victim "was a very good person. She always went to church. She loved her children. She was a good wife and mother. And she was just a very good person, would do anything for anybody, and she died not knowing what happened to her two-and-a-half-year-old child." The court ruled that the admission of this evidence was constitutional under *Payne* and was relevant. The court stated that "[w]hile evidence of a victim's character may not by the strictest interpretation be relevant to any given issue, the State should be given some latitude in fleshing out the humanity of the victim so long as it does not go too far. The State should not be permitted to ask for the death sentence because the victim is a 'good person,' any more than a defendant should be entitled to seek life imprisonment because the victim was someone of 'bad character.' The State did not do so in this case."

State's Offer of Rebuttal Evidence of Defendant's Bad Character

The North Carolina Supreme Court has ruled that the state may offer evidence of the defendant's bad character only in response to the defendant's introduction of evidence of his or her good character; this is because a defendant's bad character is not an aggravating circumstance under G.S. 15A-2000.[31] Thus, the state may not offer this kind of evidence during its case-in-chief at a capital sentencing hearing. However, a defendant may present evidence of his or her good character in mitigation, and if he or she does so, the state is entitled to present evidence of the defendant's bad character in rebuttal.[32]

In some cases, evidence that is relevant to an aggravating circumstance—such as evidence that the defendant has a prior violent felony conviction under G.S. 15A-2000(e)(3)—will also reflect poorly on the defendant's character. Of course, the state properly may offer such evidence in its case-in-chief, notwithstanding its incidental relevance to the defendant's character.

Case Summaries: State's Offer of Rebuttal Evidence of Defendant's Bad Character

State v. Duke, 360 N.C. 110 (2005). The defendant beat two men to death. During the penalty phase of his capital trial, he called his sister as a witness. She testified that "he's not an animal. He really is a decent, kind human being if you knew him." On cross-examination, she admitted that he had "threatened the lives of [the witness], her child, and her husband after an argument." The testimony was properly admitted because it impeached her testimony that they were "a big happy family," undercut her testimony about the defendant's character, and tended to rebut the defendant's proposed mitigating circumstance that he had a "deep emotional bond" with his sister.

State v. Hedgepeth, 350 N.C. 776 (1999). At a capital sentencing hearing, the defendant offered a witness's testimony about the defendant being a good father and stepfather and a devoted husband who worked hard, got along with his co-workers, and provided for his family. The defendant also offered the testimony of mental health experts that included evidence of prior antisocial behavior in the context of explaining that his ability to appreciate the criminality and consequences of his actions was impaired. The state was permitted on rebuttal to offer evidence of his prior violent acts toward his first wife, former girlfriends, and others. The court ruled that this evidence was properly admitted to rebut the defendant's mitigating evidence.

State v. Williams, 339 N.C. 1 (1994). When the defendant elicited testimony from his mother "regarding his character for nonviolence," it opened the door for rebuttal testimony from the state about this character trait, even if such evidence would have been inadmissible in the state's case-in-chief at the sentencing hearing. Therefore, it was not error to allow rebuttal evidence about the defendant's criminal conduct, including evidence that, when he was a juvenile, he

---

31. State v. Carter, 338 N.C. 569 (1994).

32. *Id.*

brandished a knife at an officer and evidence that he had a reputation for violence. North Carolina Rule of Evidence 609, which generally disallows the use of juvenile adjudications to impeach witnesses, did not prohibit this evidence, since it was not offered to impeach the credibility of a witness. It was offered to rebut the defendant's evidence that he was not a violent person.

State v. Carter, 338 N.C. 569 (1994). The court reaffirmed its ruling in *State v. Silhan,* 302 N.C. 223 (1981), that the state in a capital sentencing hearing may offer evidence of the defendant's bad character only in rebuttal to the defendant's offer of good character evidence. The court ruled that the state's evidence (prior criminal behavior) offered in rebuttal in this case was properly admitted. The court noted that while the defendant did not offer "good character" evidence *per se,* his adoptive mother testified that she felt that the defendant was the "normal Marcus," kind, giving, and helping. *Cf.* State v. Oliver, 309 N.C. 326 (1983) (error when state offered evidence of the defendant's bad reputation before defendant offered good character evidence).

State v. Ward, 338 N.C. 64 (1994). When the defendant offers evidence during the sentencing phase of his or her good character (in this case, evidence by the defendant that he had been a good son, sibling, and father), the state on cross-examination of a defense witness (in this case, the defendant's mother) may ask about the defendant's prior convictions and crimes, including the circumstances of those convictions and crimes. *See also* State v. Roper, 328 N.C. 337 (1991).

State v. Porter, 326 N.C. 489 (1990). The trial judge erred during the sentencing hearing in permitting the state to cross-examine the defendant about convictions over ten years old without qualifying them under North Carolina Rule of Evidence 609(b) (which requires advance notice and a balancing of the convictions' probative value versus their prejudicial effect). In addition, the convictions would have been inadmissible even if they had been offered in rebuttal, since there was no evidence of the statutory mitigating circumstance under G.S. 15A-2000(f)(1) (no significant prior criminal history) and the defendant did not offer evidence of his good character during the sentencing hearing.

State v. Brown, 320 N.C. 179 (1987). The state was properly permitted to introduce evidence of the defendant's prior convictions in rebuttal to the defendant's good character evidence at the sentencing hearing. It was admissible evidence even though the defendant had not offered evidence of the statutory mitigating circumstance under G.S. 15A-2000(f)(1) (no significant prior criminal history).

D. Jury Argument

After evidence has been presented, the state and the defense present jury arguments. Defense counsel have the statutory right to present the last argument whether or not the defendant presents evidence at the sentencing hearing but, in contrast to the rule at the guilt phase, they do not have the right to make the first argument as well.[33] As with jury argument at the guilt phase, defense counsel may make as many addresses to the jury as they want and may do so without any time limitations. The trial judge may limit to three the number of defense counsel who may make the last argument.[34]

33. G.S. 15A-2000(a)(4); State v. Jones, 339 N.C. 114 (1994); State v. Wilson, 313 N.C. 516 (1985).

34. G.S. 7A-97; State v. Barton, 335 N.C. 696 (1994) (trial judge erred in allowing only one defense counsel to make last argument at capital sentencing hearing).

What follows is a discussion of rulings on jury argument that are especially likely to arise in capital sentencing hearings. The section generally does not include cases on issues that are relevant to all trials.[35]

Parole Eligibility

For first-degree murder offenses committed on or after October 1, 1994, G.S. 15A-2002 requires a judge to instruct the jury that a sentence of life imprisonment means a sentence of life imprisonment without parole. This provision generally ensures compliance with the ruling of the United States Supreme Court in *Simmons v. South Carolina*,[36] which held that when the defendant's future dangerousness is in issue at a capital sentencing hearing[37] and state law prohibits the defendant's release on parole if sentenced to life in prison, due process requires that the sentencing jury must be informed that the defendant is ineligible for parole.[38]

For first-degree murder offenses committed before October 1, 1994,[39] it is improper to mention[40] the parole eligibility of a defendant who is convicted of first-degree murder and sentenced to life imprisonment. If the jury asks the judge about parole eligibility, the judge must instruct the jury that parole is not a proper matter in considering the appropriate punishment for the defendant and must inform the panel that it should consider that life imprisonment means imprisonment in the state's prison for life.[41]

Applicable only to a first-degree murder committed on or after October 1, 1994, and before December 1, 1998, after a defendant has served twenty-five years imprisonment of a life sentence without parole, G.S. 15A-1380.5 requires a review of the sentence by a superior court judge and a recommendation to the governor or designated executive agency whether or not the sentence should be altered

35. For a discussion of jury argument generally, see Jessica Smith, "Jury Argument: Content of Opening and Closing Statements," *in* THE SURVIVAL GUIDE: SUPERIOR COURT JUDGES' BENCHBOOK (UNC School of Government, Apr. 2012), www.sog.unc.edu/sites/www.sog.unc.edu/files/Content%20of%20Opening%20and%20Closing%20Statements_cite%20checked_April%202012.pdf.

36. 512 U.S. 154 (1994).

37. The Court adopted a relatively expansive view of when dangerousness is in issue in *Kelly v. South Carolina*, 534 U.S. 246, 254 (2002), where it held that any "evidence with a tendency to prove dangerousness in the future" raises the issue, even if the evidence is relevant to other issues in the case or is limited to a defendant's violence in prison or propensity to escape from prison.

38. Before G.S. 15A-2002 came into effect, the North Carolina Supreme Court had consistently held that the *Simmons* ruling did not require the parole ineligibility instruction on the grounds that defendants sentenced to life imprisonment would, in fact, eventually be eligible for parole. *See, e.g.*, State v. Skipper, 337 N.C. 1 (1994).

39. The legislative amendment requiring the judge to instruct the jury on the parole eligibility of a defendant sentenced to life imprisonment is applicable only to offenses committed on or after October 1, 1994, as explained in footnote 4 of *State v. Price*, 337 N.C. 756 (1994) (distinguishing *Simmons* and ruling that the trial judge properly denied the defendant's request to argue to the jury that the defendant had already received a life sentence in Virginia and the judge could make a life sentence in North Carolina run consecutively to the Virginia sentence; the court noted that the defendant would have been eligible for parole if he had received a life sentence in North Carolina and stated that the *Simmons* ruling was limited to cases in which the alternative to a death sentence was life imprisonment without the possibility of parole). *See also* State v. Green, 336 N.C. 142 (1994).

40. In *State v. Hill*, 331 N.C. 387 (1992), the prosecutor during jury argument asked whether, if the jury did not recommend the death penalty, the jury could guarantee that the defendant would not get a firearm in the future and kill again. The court rejected the defendant's argument that this improperly prompted the jury to consider the possibility of parole. The court noted that the prosecutor never mentioned the term "parole" and never argued the consequences of a life sentence.

41. State v. Robbins, 319 N.C. 465 (1987).

or commuted.[42] Absent legislative authorization to do so, it appears to be improper to mention the provisions of G.S. 15A-1380.5.

Other Issues

Case Summaries: Addressing Jurors Individually

State v. Gell, 351 N.C. 192 (2000). The court ruled, relying on *State v. Wynne,* 329 N.C. 507 (1991), and distinguishing *State v. Holden,* 321 N.C. 125 (1987), summarized immediately below, that a prosecutor's jury argument at a capital sentencing hearing was not improper when the prosecutor called each juror by name and informed the juror that it was time to impose the death penalty. The court stated that the argument merely sought to remind the jurors that they had affirmed during jury voir dire that they could follow the law if the state proved what was required to impose the death penalty.

State v. Holden, 321 N.C. 125 (1987). The defendant was properly barred during jury argument from asking each juror individually to spare the defendant's life. Such an argument was improper because it asked each juror to decide the sentence recommendation on an emotional basis without following the procedures set out in G.S. 15A-2000 and in disregard of the jurors' duty to deliberate with each other in attempting to reach a unanimous verdict. *But cf.* State v. Wynne, 329 N.C. 507 (1991) (not error to allow prosecutor—during jury argument at guilt-innocence phase—to address each juror by name and ask each to have no doubt and not to disregard the duty to deliberate together to reach a unanimous verdict; *Holden* distinguished).

Case Summaries: References and Comparisons to People and Events Not in Evidence

State v. Taylor, 362 N.C. 514 (2008). The trial judge properly sustained the state's objection to the defendant's references to Eric Rudolph (the "Olympic Park Bomber"), serial killers, and those who kill children when discussing whether the defendant's murder was heinous, atrocious, and cruel. These references were improper comparisons to matters not in the record.

State v. Jones, 355 N.C. 117 (2002). The defendant was convicted of first-degree murder and sentenced to death. The court ruled that the prosecutor's jury argument during the capital sentencing hearing was improper and prejudicial to the defendant and ordered a new sentencing hearing. The prosecutor's jury argument was improper in part because he referred to the Columbine school shootings and the Oklahoma City federal building bombing in a thinly veiled attempt to appeal to the jury's emotions by comparing the defendant's crime with these two heinous acts. This argument (1) referred to events and circumstances outside the record, (2) by implication, urged jurors to compare the defendant's acts with the infamous acts of others, and (3) attempted to divert jurors from the evidence by appealing instead to passion and prejudice. *See also* State v. Walters, 357 N.C. 68 (2003) (court stated that, despite comment in *Jones* that jury arguments based on matters outside trial record are inappropriate, court does not restrict jury arguments to matters that are only within trial record to exclusion of any historical references; however, such arguments may not inflame jury by making inappropriate comparisons or analogies—for example, the prosecutor's inappropriate reference to Adolph Hitler).

42. G.S. 15A-1380.5 was repealed by S.L. 1998-212, effective for first-degree murders committed on or after December 1, 1998.

State v. Anthony, 354 N.C. 372 (2001). The court ruled, relying on *State v. Gardner*, 316 N.C. 605 (1986), and other cases, that defense counsel was properly prohibited from reading facts from a North Carolina Supreme Court case on the aggravating circumstance of especially heinous, atrocious, or cruel for the purpose of urging the jury not to find this aggravating circumstance.

Case Summaries: Prosecutor's Reference to Victim and Victim's Family

Readers interested in this topic may also wish to see the section in this chapter on the related topic of victim impact evidence.

State v. Waring, 364 N.C. 443 (2010). The prosecutor's description of an imaginary conversation with the victim's father about the details of the murder was a "permissible reminder from a different perspective of how the victim had suffered and the nature of defendant's actions."

State v. Conaway, 339 N.C. 487 (1995). The prosecutor's attempt to inform the jury of the unique losses suffered by the parents and siblings of the two victims, and especially by the 3-year-old son of one of the victims, was proper argument to enable the jury to assess meaningfully the defendant's moral culpability and blameworthiness. *See also* State v. Gregory, 340 N.C. 365 (1995) (similar ruling).

Case Summaries: Prosecutor's Reference to Deterrence

State v. Garcell, 363 N.C. 10 (2009). The prosecutor told the jury that a death verdict "would be a verdict which says that in this community we're not going to put up with this." Although arguably an improper appeal to general deterrence, this argument also could be viewed as asking the jury to act as the conscience of the community; therefore, it was not so grossly improper as to require intervention by the trial judge.

State v. Steen, 352 N.C. 227 (2000). The court ruled, relying on *State v. Richmond,* 347 N.C. 412 (1998), and *State v. Williams,* 350 N.C. 1 (1999), that the prosecutor's jury argument at the capital sentencing hearing about the defendant's future dangerousness to prison personnel was proper. A prosecutor may argue that the death penalty would specifically deter the defendant from committing future crimes. However, the court clearly indicated that a prosecutor may not, in an argument on future dangerousness, point out that a defendant may escape from prison when serving a life sentence without parole.

State v. Ward, 338 N.C. 64 (1994). A prosecutor may properly argue for the death penalty based on specific deterrence; that is, he or she may argue that the death penalty will prevent the particular defendant from killing again. For similar rulings, see *State v. Alston,* 341 N.C. 198 (1995); *State v. Basden,* 339 N.C. 288 (1994); *State v. Syriani,* 333 N.C. 350 (1993); and *State v. Zuniga,* 320 N.C. 233 (1987).

State v. Hill, 331 N.C. 387 (1992). The prosecutor during jury argument asked whether, if the jury did not recommend the death penalty, the jury could guarantee that the defendant would not get a firearm in the future and kill again. The court rejected the defendant's argument that this improperly prompted the jury to consider the possibility of parole. The court noted that the prosecutor never mentioned the term "parole" and never argued the consequences of a life sentence.

State v. Kirkley, 308 N.C. 196 (1983). A prosecutor may not argue for the death penalty as a general deterrent; thus, the argument that "I'm asking you to impose the death penalty as a deterrent, to set a standard of conduct" was ruled improper.

Case Summaries: Prosecutor's Reference to Quality of Life in Prison

State v. Taylor, 362 N.C. 514 (2008). While the prosecutor improperly argued facts outside the record in listing "various prison amenities defendant would enjoy if sentenced to life imprisonment," the prosecutor's argument was not so grossly improper as to require judicial intervention absent a defense objection.

State v. Holden, 346 N.C. 404 (1997). A prison guard testified during the resentencing rehearing that the defendant was permitted, during his incarceration, to watch television, play cards, lift weights, play basketball, go to the music room, and eat lunch with other inmates. The court ruled, relying on *State v. Alston,* 341 N.C. 198 (1995), that the prosecutor was properly permitted to comment during jury argument on the quality of life the defendant would have in prison. The court noted that it was reasonable to infer that the defendant would continue to enjoy these privileges if sentenced to life imprisonment.

State v. Smith, 347 N.C. 453 (1998). The prosecutor argued to the jury in a capital sentencing hearing that if the defendant was sentenced to life in prison, he would spend his time comfortably doing things such as playing basketball, lifting weights, and watching television. The court upheld this argument, citing *State v. Alston,* 341 N.C. 198 (1995), noting that the state's argument emphasized the state's position that the defendant deserved the death penalty rather than a comfortable life in prison.

Case Summaries: Prosecutor's Reference to Mercy or Sympathy

State v. Cummings, 361 N.C. 438 (2007). The prosecutor made the following statement: "They want to talk about compassion, mercy. That's not the law. That's not the standard. If it was, you wouldn't forget about the compassion and mercy that he showed for her. No, don't base it on any of that." This was a proper argument designed to encourage the jury to decide the case based on the law rather than on feelings of sympathy.

State v. Price, 326 N.C. 56 (1990). A prosecutor may properly argue that the jurors' feelings of sympathy and forgiveness that are rooted in their hearts but are not based on the evidence may not be permitted to affect their recommendation on the death penalty. The court noted that the prosecutor did not refer to the evidence offered by the defendant in mitigation, about which a sympathetic appraisal by the jurors may be appropriate. The court stated that its ruling was in accord with *California v. Brown,* 479 U.S. 538 (1987) (holding that instruction to jury that it must "not be swayed by 'mere sentiment, conjecture, sympathy, passion, prejudice, public opinion or public feeling' " was not improper and in fact served the useful purpose of preventing the jury from relying on extraneous emotional factors).

State v. Artis, 325 N.C. 278 (1989). The prosecutor argued to the jury during the sentencing hearing that the jurors should "try this case without . . . prejudice and sympathy; strictly on the facts" of the case. The court upheld this argument, noting that the import of the prosecutor's argument was that mitigating circumstances are to be supported by the evidence, not by emotion.

Case Summaries: Prosecutor's Reference to Mitigating Circumstances

State v. Raines, 362 N.C. 1 (2007). When discussing several of the defendant's proposed mitigating circumstances, the prosecutor argued "Where is the connection? Why does it make what he did to [the victims] less deserving of the ultimate penalty? We are here to talk about and deal with what happened on [the date of the murders]." In context, this was not an improper argument that every mitigating circumstance must have a nexus to the crime—a position rejected in *Tennard v. Dretke*, 542 U.S. 274 (2004)—but rather was a proper argument that the proposed circumstances had no mitigating value.

State v. Basden, 339 N.C. 288 (1994). The prosecutor's jury argument that some of the defendant's nonstatutory mitigating circumstances "border[ed] on the ridiculous" was a legitimate attempt to deprecate or belittle the significance of mitigating circumstances. It was a proper comment on the weight of the defendant's evidence.

State v. Robinson, 336 N.C. 78 (1994). The prosecutor's characterization of the defendant's evidence in mitigation as an "evasion of responsibility" was properly directed to the weight that the jury should give to the defendant's evidence.

State v. Huff, 325 N.C. 1 (1989). The prosecutor's description of a mitigating circumstance during jury argument as evidence that lessens or reduces the severity of the crime was proper.

Case Summaries: Prosecutor's Reference to Aggravating Circumstance Not Submitted

State v. Cummings, 361 N.C. 438 (2007). The defendant stabbed his neighbor to death and stole her ATM card; he was convicted of robbery and murder. The trial judge decided to submit only the (e)(5) aggravator (murder during a specified felony), not the (e)(6) aggravator (murder for pecuniary gain), because the same evidence supported both. The prosecutor emphasized during closing that the defendant "did it for money." The defendant argued on appeal "that this left the impression that the jury could consider defendant's desire for pecuniary gain although a pecuniary gain aggravating circumstance was not submitted," but the court ruled that the jury could properly consider the defendant's motive in connection with the (e)(5) aggravator and the robbery.

State v. Sanderson, 336 N.C. 1 (1994). At the close of evidence during the capital sentencing hearing, the trial judge specifically refused the prosecutor's request that the judge submit the aggravating circumstance that the murder was committed during the perpetration of rape. Despite this ruling, the prosecutor asserted during argument that the defendant deserved to die, at least in part because he had raped the victim. This argument was improper since there was a lack of forensic evidence to support it; together with other misconduct, it necessitated a new sentencing hearing.

Case Summaries: Prosecutor's Reference to Defendant's Demeanor and Lack of Remorse

State v. Taylor, 362 N.C. 514 (2008). The prosecutor stated that "[n]owhere in any of the testimony during the sentencing phase has remorse been mentioned about the defendant's remorse for [the victim's] death." This properly called the jury's attention to the defendant's lack of remorse without suggesting that lack of remorse is an aggravating circumstance, found the court.

State v. Call, 349 N.C. 382 (1998). The court ruled that the trial judge erred in allowing the state to argue that the defendant should be sentenced to death based on improperly elicited testimony that the defendant had not confessed or expressed remorse to his jailers; this violated the defendant's right to due process and his privilege against self-incrimination. The court noted that the defendant had been informed of his constitutional right to silence at his first appearance in district court. He never waived that privilege. He never made a statement to law enforcement officers, and he did not testify at his trial or sentencing hearing. The defense never presented evidence or argument concerning statements made by the defendant concerning the alleged crimes or his feelings or attitudes toward the victims. At the capital sentencing hearing, the defendant called four jailers to testify that he had been a model prisoner during his pretrial incarceration. The state then elicited testimony, over the defendant's objection, that the defendant had neither confessed nor shown remorse for the crimes he was accused of committing. The court ruled that this testimony was improperly allowed under *State v. Hoyle*, 325 N.C. 232 (1989) (due process violation when using silence against defendant who has been advised of right to remain silent under *Miranda*). The court concluded that the state may alert the jury of the defendant's lack of remorse as long as it does not urge the jury to consider the lack of remorse as an aggravating circumstance. However, the state's questions in this case clearly emphasized to the jury that the defendant had not denied the accusations and encouraged the jury to use the exercise of his right to silence when considering whether to recommend life or death.

State v. Price, 326 N.C. 56 (1990). While lack of remorse is not a statutory aggravating circumstance, a prosecutor's comment on a defendant's lack of remorse is proper argument, as long as the prosecutor does not cite this characteristic as an aggravating circumstance. *See also* State v. Gell, 351 N.C. 192 (2000); State v. McNatt, 342 N.C. 173 (1995); State v. Robinson, 336 N.C. 78 (1994); State v. Artis, 325 N.C. 278 (1989).

State v. Brown, 320 N.C. 179 (1987). A prosecutor may properly refer to the defendant's lack of contrition based on the defendant's demeanor in the courtroom. Such an argument does not improperly comment on the defendant's privilege not to testify.

Case Summaries: Prosecutor's Request That Jurors Put Themselves in Victim's Place

State v. Garcell, 363 N.C. 10 (2009). Referring to the death of the victim by strangulation, the prosecutor stated the following: "Think about that instant when you hold your breath too long. What does that feel like? Imagine that." The court held that this remark properly "asked the jury to appreciate the circumstances of the crime," which is especially appropriate when the state is arguing for the aggravating circumstance that the murder was heinous, atrocious, and cruel.

State v. Perkins, 345 N.C. 254 (1997). Relying on *State v. McCollum*, 334 N.C. 208 (1993), discussed immediately below, the court ruled that a prosecutor's jury argument at a capital sentencing hearing that asked jurors to imagine themselves in the victim's position was improper. Specifically, the argument asked jurors to put themselves in the position of the victim as she was raped and murdered. However, the impropriety was not so great as to require a new sentencing hearing.

State v. McCollum, 334 N.C. 208 (1993). The court, quoting from *United States v. Pichnarcik*, 427 F.2d 1290 (9th Cir. 1970), stated that asking jurors to put themselves in the place of victims will not be condoned. In *McCollum*, the prosecutor repeatedly asked the jurors to imagine the murder victim as their own child. The court, assuming without deciding that the argument was improper, ruled that it did not deny the defendant due process. *See also* State v. Garner, 340 N.C. 573 (1995) (similar ruling). *But see* State v. Green, 336 N.C. 142 (1994) (prosecutor's argument that murder victims were in the "same place you and I might be at 6:00" was not an argument that asked the jurors to place themselves in the place of the victims; the argument was merely pointing out that the victims were engaging in activity common to all people).

State v. Artis, 325 N.C. 278 (1989). The victim was strangled to death. During closing argument at the defendant's sentencing hearing, the prosecutor asked the jurors to hold their breath for as long as they could over a four-minute period so they could understand the dynamics of manual strangulation. The argument was proper in that it urged jurors to appreciate the circumstances of the crime. The court noted that an argument that might be prejudicially improper in the guilt-innocence phase may be proper in the sentencing phase. *See also* State v. Gregory, 340 N.C. 365 (1995) (similar ruling; prosecutor did not ask jurors to put themselves in the place of the victims when describing how they died); State v. Alston, 341 N.C. 198 (1995) (similar ruling; prosecutor took three-minute pause that was intended to show the period of time it took for the victim to die of asphyxiation); State v. Walls, 342 N.C. 1 (1995) (similar ruling; prosecutor took four-minute pause that was intended to show the period of time it took for the victim to die from drowning); State v. Warren, 348 N.C. 80 (1998) (proper for prosecutor during jury argument in trial stage to ask jury to imagine the fear and emotions of the victim as she was being murdered).

Case Summaries: Prosecutor's Reference to Community Sentiment

State v. Artis, 325 N.C. 278 (1989). The court stated that it is not improper for a prosecutor to tell the jury during argument in the sentencing hearing that its verdict will "send a message to the community" about what may befall a person convicted of first-degree murder. However, it is improper to intimate to the jury community preferences about capital punishment, which are not evidence or proper considerations for the sentencing jury. For example, a prosecutor may not ask the jury "to lend an ear to the community rather than a voice." On the other hand, it is not improper to remind the jury that its voice is the conscience of the community.

Case Summaries: Prosecutor's Biblical References

State v. Haselden, 357 N.C. 1 (2003). The prosecutor's jury argument made several biblical references in arguing for the death penalty. Defense counsel did not object to this argument. The court ruled that the prosecutor's use of biblical references was not so grossly improper that the trial judge erred in failing to intervene ex mero motu, although the court strongly encouraged counsel to base their jury arguments solely on secular law and facts. Jury arguments based on any of the world's religions inevitably pose a danger of distracting the jury from its sole and exclusive duty of applying secular law and unnecessarily risk reversal of otherwise error-free trials and sentencing hearings.

State v. Lloyd, 354 N.C. 76 (2001). The prosecutor recited a poem referred to by the court as "Dance, Death" during closing argument of the capital sentencing hearing and added the following words: "Let the Judge set the date. The death penalty is the only appropriate punishment in this case for what [the defendant] did to [the victim]." The court noted that it had reluctantly ruled in this case that the prosecutor's recitation of this poem (without the additional language) during jury argument in the guilt-innocence phase did not require the trial judge's intervention ex mero motu, although the court disapproved of and cautioned prosecutors against using such an argument. The court then stated the following: "This additional language, however, crosses the line into impropriety by linking the law enforcement powers of the State, and specifically the judge, to divine powers of God. We admonish the State against making such arguments at defendant's new sentencing proceeding."

State v. Williams, 350 N.C. 1 (1999). The court made the following statements (with citations deleted) about biblical jury arguments:

> We continue to hold that it is not so grossly improper for a prosecutor to argue that the Bible does not prohibit the death penalty as to require intervention *ex mero motu* by the trial court, *but we discourage such arguments* [italics supplied by court]. . . . We caution all counsel that they should base their jury arguments solely upon the secular law and the facts. Jury arguments based on any of the religions of the world inevitably pose a danger of distracting the jury from its sole and exclusive duty of applying secular law and unnecessarily risk reversal of otherwise error-free trials. . . . Although we may believe that parts of our law are divinely inspired, it is the secular law of North Carolina which is to be applied in our courtrooms. Our trial courts must vigilantly ensure that counsel for the State and for defendant do not distract the jury from their sole and exclusive duty to apply secular law.

State v. Moose, 310 N.C. 482 (1984). The prosecutor's argument was improper when he cited biblical passages and argued, in effect, that the powers of public officials, including police, prosecutors, and judges, are ordained by God, as said officials are God's representatives on earth, and that to resist these powers is to resist God.

Case Summaries: Prosecutor's Reference to Defendant's Exercise of Rights

State v. Garcell, 363 N.C. 10 (2009). The prosecutor noted that the victim had a right to life, then said of the defendant: "He is big on rights now. He wants his right to a trial, his right to two very good lawyers, his right to due process, to the presumption of innocence, to reasonable doubt. Yes, he wants all of his rights now. But what about [the victim]? What about her rights?" This remark did not require the trial judge to intervene ex mero motu because the prosecutor's focus was on the defendant's violation of the victim's rights; the prosecutor "never disparaged [the] defendant for exercising his rights."

Case Summaries: Prosecutor's Disparagement of Defendant

State v. Matthews, 358 N.C. 102 (2004). The court found that the prosecutor made an improper jury argument when the prosecutor engaged in name-calling and used scatological language in referring to the defendant's theory of the case. The prosecutor characterized the defendant as a "monster," "demon," "devil," "a man without morals," and as having a "monster mind." The court stated that these improper characterizations constituted improper name-calling; the prosecutor was not arguing the evidence or conclusions that can be inferred from the evidence. In addition, the prosecutor improperly used scatological language by stating "That's bull crap" in an attack on the defendant's theory of the case. *See also* State v. Maske, 358 N.C. 40 (2004) (prosecutor improperly referred to defendant as an "SOB").

State v. Roache, 358 N.C. 243 (2004). The defendant, acting with an accomplice, killed five people and was convicted of five counts of first-degree murder. The court ruled that the prosecutor's jury argument was improper when it characterized the defendant and his accomplice as wild dogs high on the taste of blood and power over their victims.

State v. Jones, 355 N.C. 117 (2002). The court ordered a new sentencing hearing, in part because the prosecutor engaged in improper name-calling, as evidenced by the following remark: "You got this quitter, this loser, this worthless piece of . . . who's mean . . . . He's as mean as they come. He's lower than the dirt on a snake's belly."

Case Summaries: Prosecutor's Disparagement of Witnesses

State v. Waring, 364 N.C. 443 (2010). The prosecutor's use of the phrase "laugh, laugh," in the course of discussing what he contended were the inconsistent opinions of two defense experts, "may well have been meant to ridicule the defense experts" but was so "ambiguous and confusing in context," according to the court, that it did not require the trial judge to intervene ex mero motu.

State v. Taylor, 362 N.C. 514 (2008). The prosecutor referred to the defendant's mental health expert as a "professional witness." This was not so improper as to require the trial judge to intervene ex mero motu.

State v. Rogers, 355 N.C. 420 (2002). The court ruled that the prosecutor's improper cross-examination of a defense expert psychiatrist and improper jury argument in a capital sentencing hearing sufficiently prejudiced the defendant to require a new capital sentencing hearing. The court stated that the prosecutor ascribed the basest of motives to the defendant's expert. He also indulged in ad hominem attacks, disparaged the expert's field of expertise, and distorted his testimony, all of which prompted the court to state the following: "We admonish counsel to refrain from arguing that a witness is lying solely on the basis that the witness has been or will be compensated for his or her services. We also instruct trial judges to be prepared to intervene *ex mero motu* if such arguments continue to be made."

State v. Smith, 352 N.C. 531 (2000). The court found parts of the prosecutor's jury argument to be improper. The prosecutor improperly maligned a mental health expert's profession, the court concluded, and her scatological references to a witness's testimony were similarly improper.

Case Summaries: Prosecutor's Reference to Appellate Review

State v. Jones, 296 N.C. 495 (1979). It was improper for the prosecutor during jury argument to read the provisions in G.S. 15A-2000 about the North Carolina Supreme Court's review of a judgment of conviction and death sentence (and to read the parole statute). A reference to appellate review is irrelevant in the jury's deliberations in making its sentencing recommendation. *See also* Caldwell v. Mississippi, 472 U.S. 320 (1985) (prosecutor's argument during capital sentencing urging jury not to view itself as finally determining whether defendant would die because death sentence would be reviewed by state supreme court was improper under Eighth Amendment, based on facts in this case).

Case Summaries: Defendant's Reference to Life Sentence if Jury Does Not Agree

State v. Johnson, 317 N.C. 343 (1986). The defendant was properly barred during jury argument from reading the provision in G.S. 15A-2000(b) that requires that a life sentence be imposed if the jury cannot unanimously agree to its sentence recommendation within a reasonable time.

Case Summaries: Defendant's Description of Execution Procedure

State v. Holden, 321 N.C. 125 (1987). The defendant was properly barred during jury argument from describing the execution procedure. *See also* State v. Boyd, 311 N.C. 408 n.1 (1984) (court stated that defense argument describing execution procedure was improper).

Case Summaries: Defendant's Reference to Absence of Aggravating Circumstances

State v. Buckner, 342 N.C. 198 (1995). Relying on *State v. Brown*, 306 N.C. 151 (1982) (absence of a particular aggravating circumstance is not a mitigating circumstance), the court ruled that the trial judge did not err in prohibiting defense counsel from telling the jury during jury argument of the aggravating circumstances that the state did not present.

Case Summaries: Defense Counsel's Admission That Defendant Committed Prior Crimes

State v. Al-Bayyinah, 359 N.C. 741 (2005). The defendant was convicted of first-degree murder and sentenced to death. During jury argument at the capital sentencing hearing, defense counsel appeared to admit, without the defendant's consent, that the defendant had committed the crimes for which he had been previously convicted. The defendant was willing to allow defense counsel to admit that the defendant had been convicted, but not to admit he had committed the crimes. The court ruled that the defendant failed to show that the jury argument prejudiced his defense; he thus was not provided with ineffective assistance of counsel. The court found that the state had the necessary proof of the convictions at issue to support the aggravating circumstance of prior violent felony convictions. The court noted that the United States Supreme Court in *Florida v. Nixon*, 543 U.S. 175 (2004), ruled that whether or not a defendant expressly consented to counsel's argument was not dispositive in finding ineffective assistance of counsel. In addition, the court noted, citing *State v. Walls*, 342 N.C. 1 (1995), that the ruling in *State v. Harbison*, 315 N.C. 175 (1985) (counsel's admission of defendant's guilt is *per se* ineffective assistance of counsel), does not apply to sentencing proceedings.

Case Summaries: Defendant's Reference to Residual Doubt

State v. Fletcher, 354 N.C. 455 (2001). The court ruled that defense counsel was properly prohibited from arguing residual doubt as mitigating evidence in a capital resentencing hearing. The court stated that just as defense counsel may not argue residual doubt about the first-degree murder conviction during a capital sentencing or resentencing hearing, counsel may not argue residual doubt about the basis underlying a first-degree murder conviction, such as premeditation and deliberation.

E. Defendant's Lack of Right of Allocution

A defendant who is represented by defense counsel has no right to make an unsworn statement in his or her behalf to the jury during the sentencing hearing—a right commonly known as the right of allocution.[43] Of course, the defendant has the right to testify under oath at a capital sentencing hearing and be subject to cross-examination.

---

43. Although a defendant in a noncapital case has a statutory right to allocution, G.S. 15A-1334(b), the right has been held inapplicable in capital proceedings. State v. Green, 336 N.C. 142 (1994). The *Green* court ruled that the only remnant of the common law right of allocution in capital cases is the defendant's right to present legal arguments to the trial judge as to why a judgment should not be entered. *See also* State v. Ray, 137 N.C. App. 326 (2000) (trial judge properly denied defendant's motion for allocution that requested that (1) defendant be permitted to make unsworn statement to jury without being subject to cross-examination and (2) defendant's counsel be permitted to read written statement from defendant to jury).

F. Replacement of Juror or Entire Jury

After a jury has returned a verdict of guilty of first-degree murder and before the jury has begun deliberations in the capital sentencing hearing, a judge may replace a juror with an alternate juror for a sufficient reason. For example, the North Carolina Supreme Court has ruled that a judge did not err in removing a juror after a verdict of first-degree murder and substituting an alternate juror before the capital sentencing hearing had begun when the judge learned that the juror had changed her mind and could not vote for the death penalty under any circumstances.[44] On the other hand, a judge may not replace a juror with an alternate juror once the jury has begun deliberations in a capital sentencing hearing.[45]

Although G.S. 15A-2000(a)(2) provides that the sentencing hearing must be conducted "before the trial jury," it also allows a new jury to be used if the trial jury is "unable to reconvene." An example of the proper use of a new jury is *State v. Williams*.[46] In that case, after the defendant was found guilty of first-degree murder but before the commencement of the penalty phase of his capital trial, the defendant physically attacked one of his attorneys. The judge allowed both of the defendants' attorneys to withdraw and declared a mistrial of the penalty phase. Three years later, a new jury was summoned and a penalty phase was held. The defendant was sentenced to death. Citing G.S. 15A-2002(a)(2), the defendant argued that the new jury "lacked jurisdiction to recommend a sentence of death."[47] The state supreme court disagreed, ruling that convening the original jury a second time would have been a "practical impossibility"[48] and noting that the use of a new jury was directly attributable to the defendant's own conduct in attacking his lawyer.[49]

G. *Enmund* Issue: When May the Death Penalty Be Imposed on a Defendant Who Is an Accomplice to Felony Murder?

In *Enmund v. Florida*,[50] the United States Supreme Court held that the Eighth Amendment prohibits the imposition of the death penalty on a defendant who "aids and abets a felony in the course of which a murder is committed by others but who does not himself kill, attempt to kill, or intend that a killing take place or that lethal force will be employed."[51] It therefore vacated the death sentence imposed upon the defendant in that case, a man who had been the getaway driver for an armed robbery that went awry and resulted in a double murder. The Court reasoned that the death penalty is rarely sought for, and rarely imposed upon, defendants who are guilty as accomplices to felony murder but whose culpability is reduced by their lack of direct involvement in the victim's death.

---

44. State v. Holden, 321 N.C. 125 (1987).

45. State v. Bunning, 346 N.C. 253 (1997) (trial court replaced ill juror during deliberations; state supreme court ordered new capital sentencing hearing and rejected state's argument that court should undertake harmless error analysis).

46. 363 N.C. 689 (2009).

47. *Id.* at 708.

48. *Id.*

49. *Id.* at 708–09 (quoting G.S. 15A-1443(c) ("A defendant is not prejudiced . . . by error resulting from his own conduct.").

50. 458 U.S. 782 (1982).

51. *Id.* at 797.

In *Tison v. Arizona*,[52] the Court added to the *Enmund* rule another category of defendants upon whom the death penalty may be imposed: those who do not themselves kill, attempt to kill, or intend death or the use of lethal force but "whose participation [in the underlying felony] is major and whose mental state is one of reckless indifference to the value of human life."[53] Accordingly, the Court affirmed the death sentences imposed upon two men who arranged to break their father out of prison, knowing that he had killed a guard in a previous escape, and who stood by and watched as their father killed a family from whom the two sons, the father, and another escapee had stolen a car. The Court distinguished *Enmund* based on both the extent of the defendants' participation in the underlying felony (a getaway driver not on the scene in *Enmund* versus active participants in *Tison*) and on the risk posed by that felony (only the "possibility of bloodshed . . . inherent in the commission of any violent felony"[54] in *Enmund*, as opposed to a series of crimes "likely to result in the loss of innocent human life"[55] in *Tison*).

The *Tison* Court did not explain clearly what it means to be a major participant in a felony or what is required to show a defendant's reckless indifference to human life. Two North Carolina cases have held that defendants who are present for and who participate actively in robberies that result in murder satisfy the *Tison* standard.[56] The cases do not state that presence at the scene of the crime is required under *Tison*, though at least one commentator has suggested that actual presence may be mandatory.[57]

There is no *Enmund* issue when the defendant committed the murder alone because, in such a case, he or she must have committed the killing personally. There is also no *Enmund* issue when the defendant is convicted on a theory of premeditation and deliberation because intent to kill is required for such a conviction.[58] Our supreme court has held that this is so even if the defendant is convicted of acting in concert to commit a premeditated murder.[59] Thus, the *Enmund* issue generally arises only

---

52. 481 U.S. 137 (1987).

53. *Id.* at 152.

54. *Id.* at 151.

55. *Id.* at 154.

56. State v. Howell, 335 N.C. 457 (1994); State v. Leary, 344 N.C. 109 (1996).

57. David McCord, *State Death Sentencing for Felony Murder Accomplices Under the* Enmund *and* Tison *Standards*, 32 Ariz. St. L.J. 843, 874–75 (2000).

58. State v. Fletcher, 354 N.C. 455 (2001); State v. Robinson, 342 N.C. 74 (1995).

59. Under the law of acting in concert, a defendant who joins with another to commit a crime is guilty not only of that crime, but also of any other crimes committed by the other person that are in furtherance of, or are natural and probable consequences of, the original crime, so long as the defendant is actually or constructively present. State v. Barnes, 345 N.C. 184 (1997). This is so even if the defendant did not intend that the other person commit the additional crimes. Therefore, there may be cases in which a defendant is responsible, under the acting in concert doctrine, for a premeditated murder committed by another which the defendant did not commit, attempt to commit, or intend be committed. Existing North Carolina precedent suggests that no *Enmund* issue would exist in such circumstances. State v. Watts, 357 N.C. 366, 375 (2003) (italics omitted) (the defendant was convicted of premeditated murder but argued that the *Enmund* issue should have been submitted because he could have been convicted on the theory of acting in concert and could have lacked the intent to kill; because the acting in concert instruction actually given by the trial court required the jury to find that "the defendant intended to kill the victim," the state supreme court held that the issue need not have been submitted); State v. Golphin, 352 N.C. 364 (2000) (stating that the *Enmund* issue need not be submitted where the defendant is convicted of premeditated murder, even if the conviction may be based on the theory of acting in concert). However, it is not completely clear that the United States Supreme Court would agree that a defendant convicted of premeditated murder under North Carolina's expansive theory of acting in concert who did not him or herself kill, attempt to kill, or intend death or the use of deadly force would be death-eligible even if his or her participation in the agreed-upon felony was relatively minor. If the *Enmund* case itself had arisen in North Carolina, and if the triggermen had been convicted of premeditated murder, it appears that defendant Enmund would have been guilty of premeditated murder under the theory of acting in concert instead of felony murder

in felony murder cases[60] and only when more than one person is involved in the crime. The mere fact that a defendant was acquitted of premeditated murder does not mean that the defendant is ineligible for the death penalty under *Enmund*.[61]

Under North Carolina law, *Enmund* issues are decided by the jury.[62] The burden is on the state to prove beyond a reasonable doubt[63] that the defendant killed, attempted to kill, intended death or the use of deadly force, or was a major participant in the underlying felony and thereby showed a reckless indifference to human life. The basic capital pattern jury instruction, N.C.P.I.—CRIM. 150.10, contains a section that addresses the *Enmund* issue. The jury is asked to consider the *Enmund* issue prior to considering and weighing aggravating and mitigating circumstances, because if it finds the defendant to be ineligible for the death penalty under *Enmund*, that obviates the need for further deliberation. Issue One-A on the pattern verdict form correspondingly addresses the *Enmund* issue.

As a final note, the *Enmund* issue has no application to noncapital cases. The Eighth Amendment does not forbid a sentence of life without parole for a defendant properly convicted of felony murder, regardless of the degree of his or her involvement in the murder.[64]

H. Mental Retardation

Both the Eighth Amendment and North Carolina statutory law prohibit the imposition of the death penalty on a defendant who is mentally retarded.[65] For purposes of the statutory prohibition, mental retardation is defined in G.S. 15A-2005(a). In summary, the definition requires "significantly subaverage . . . intellectual functioning" (i.e., an IQ below 70) and "significant limitations in adaptive functioning" (i.e., deficits in certain statutorily-enumerated life skills), both manifesting before the age of 18. The constitutional prohibition comes from *Atkins v. Virginia*,[66] in which the United States Supreme Court held that evolving standards of decency, combined with the diminished culpability of mentally

---

only. (He was not actually present during the murders, but a plausible argument can be made that he was present constructively.) However, that would not have changed his culpability, and so arguably should not change his eligibility for the death penalty. The applicability of the *Enmund* issue in vicarious premeditated murders was discussed briefly, but not decided, in *Fletcher*, 354 N.C. 455.

60. No cases discuss whether the doctrine could apply to murder committed by specified means, such as murder by torture or murder by poisoning. The fact patterns under which these theories of first-degree murder are used rarely involve defendants with attenuated connections to the murder, so it is not surprising that the appellate courts have not been asked to consider applying *Enmund* to these theories.

61. State v. Mann, 355 N.C. 294 (2002).

62. The United States Supreme Court held in *Cabana v. Bullock*, 474 U.S. 376 (1986), that *Enmund* issues may be addressed by a trial or appellate court rather than by a jury. Whether *Cabana* survives *Ring v. Arizona*, 536 U.S. 584 (2002) (holding that the Sixth Amendment requires any aggravating circumstances necessary to the imposition of the death penalty to be found by a jury), is debatable. *Compare, e.g.*, Hall v. Quarterman, 534 F.3d 365, 386 (5th Cir. 2008) ("Little remains of *Cabana* after *Ring*."), *with, e.g.*, State v. Galindo, 774 N.W.2d 190, 236 (Neb. 2009) ("*Cabana* remain[s] good law [after *Ring*]. *Enmund/Tison* 'findings' are not elements of the offense of felony murder, even when the death penalty is imposed."). It is not necessary to resolve the matter, however, because the *Enmund* issue is decided by the jury under North Carolina law.

63. State v. Stokes, 319 N.C. 1 (1987). *See also* N.C.P.I.—CRIM. 150.10 (requiring the jury to find the defendant death-eligible beyond a reasonable doubt).

64. State v. Hightower, 168 N.C. App. 661 (2005).

65. Atkins v. Virginia, 536 U.S. 304 (2002); G.S. 15A-2005(b). North Carolina's statutory prohibition took effect October 1, 2001, and so predated *Atkins*. S.L. 2001-346. [*Author's note*: Although some mental health experts now prefer terms like "intellectually disabled," the term "mentally retarded" is used here because that is the term used in the case law and the statutes.]

66. 536 U.S. 304 (2002).

retarded offenders, rendered the imposition of the death penalty on the mentally retarded cruel and unusual punishment. The Court noted in footnote 3 of its opinion the definitions of mental retardation adopted by the American Association of Mental Retardation[67] and the American Psychiatric Association, but it did not adopt either one of them as a constitutional standard. Both definitions are generally similar to North Carolina's statutory definition.

As noted in Chapter 2, a defendant may move for a pretrial determination on mental retardation by submitting a motion "supported by appropriate affidavits."[68] The trial judge "may" order a hearing on the matter; the judge "shall" hold a hearing if the state consents.[69] At such a hearing, the burden is on the defendant to show that he or she is mentally retarded by clear and convincing evidence. If the defendant meets this burden, "the court shall declare the case noncapital."[70] The law provides for a pretrial determination because it "avoids the needless burden of capital proceedings for those defendants whose mental retardation is clearly and convincingly evident."[71]

If a judge conducts a pretrial hearing under G.S. 15A-2005(c) and does not find the defendant mentally retarded, the defendant is entitled to present the issue to the jury at the capital sentencing hearing. Although not stated expressly in the statute, presumably the defendant may also seek a jury determination on the issue if he or she did not request a pretrial determination or if his or her request for a pretrial hearing was denied. The defendant must prove to the jury[72] by a preponderance of the evidence[73] that he or she is mentally retarded.

The statute provides that "the court shall submit a special issue to the jury as to whether the defendant is mentally retarded . . . . This special issue shall be considered and answered by the jury prior to the consideration of aggravating or mitigating factors and the determination of sentence."[74] There are at least three possible ways in which a court might try to follow this mandate:

- The sentencing proceeding could be *bifurcated*, with a mental retardation phase preceding an aggravation/mitigation phase.
- The sentencing proceeding could be *unitary*, with the evidence of mental retardation and aggravation/mitigation presented together, followed by the parties' arguments on both issues, followed by instructions on both issues, with both issues submitted to the jury at the same time (though the jury would be instructed to consider mental retardation first and to stop deliberating if it were to resolve the retardation issue in the defendant's favor).
- The sentencing proceeding could be *semi-unitary*, with the evidence of mental retardation and aggravation/mitigation presented together, but with the argument, instruction, and

67. Now the American Association on Intellectual and Developmental Disabilities.

68. G.S. 15A-2005(c).

69. *Id.* The Supreme Court of North Carolina erroneously paraphrased the statute in *State v. Locklear*, 363 N.C. 438 (2009), where it indicated that "[t]he State must consent to such a [pretrial] hearing." *Id.* at 462.

70. *Locklear*, 363 N.C. at 463 (quoting G.S. 15A-2005(e)).

71. *Id.* at 462–63.

72. For a discussion of possible outcomes if a jury does not unanimously agree on the issue of mental retardation, see John Rubin, *2001 Legislation Affecting Criminal Law and Procedure*, ADMIN. OF JUST. BULL. No. 2002/02 (UNC Institute of Government, Jan. 2002).

73. No North Carolina case addresses the constitutionality of placing the burden of proving mental retardation on the defendant. *See generally* Stripling v. State, 711 S.E.2d 665 (Ga. 2011) (holding that it is constitutional to require a defendant to prove that he or she is mentally retarded beyond a reasonable doubt); Pruitt v. State, 834 N.E.2d 90 (Ind. 2005) (holding that the burden of proving mental retardation may constitutionally be placed on the defendant, though the defendant may not be required to establish his or her retardation by clear and convincing evidence).

74. G.S. 15A-2005(e).

verdict concerning mental retardation taking place prior to any argument, instruction, and verdict concerning aggravation/mitigation.

The pattern jury instruction on this issue[75] envisions a bifurcated or semi-unitary proceeding. That is, it "is written in a manner which contemplates that the jury will return to court with its answer to the mental retardation question before hearing arguments and being instructed [on the aggravation/mitigation issues covered by N.C.P.I.—Crim. 150.10]."[76] In *State v. Ward*,[77] the Supreme Court of North Carolina ruled that a trial judge has discretion on the matter of whether to hold a bifurcated capital sentencing proceeding; the court did not distinguish between what is described above as a "unitary" and a "semi-unitary" proceeding.

At least if the defendant requests such an instruction, the jury must be told that if it finds that the defendant is mentally retarded, the defendant will be sentenced to life in prison without parole.[78] Such an instruction is now part of the pattern jury instruction.[79]

If the jury finds that the defendant is mentally retarded, the death penalty may not be imposed and the judge must sentence the defendant to life imprisonment without parole.[80] Even if the jury determines that the defendant is not mentally retarded, it may consider any evidence of mental retardation presented during the capital sentencing hearing when determining aggravating and mitigating circumstances and the defendant's sentence.[81]

I. Jury Deliberations and Related Issues

Requirement of Unanimity and "Reasonable Time" to Reach Unanimous Recommendation

Except for Issue Two on the issues and recommendation form, discussed further in Chapter 6, which asks each juror to make an individual determination regarding the existence of any mitigating circumstances, the jury's decision on the issues presented at the penalty phase of a capital trial must be unanimous.[82]

G.S. 15A-2000(b) provides that the judge must impose a sentence of life imprisonment if the jury cannot unanimously agree on its sentence recommendation within a "reasonable time." The North Carolina Supreme Court has ruled that a judge's determination of what is a reasonable time is left to his or her discretion, subject to appellate review for abuse of that discretion.[83]

However, it is improper for a judge to inform the jury that the judge must impose a sentence of life imprisonment if the jury does not unanimously agree on its sentence recommendation within a

75. N.C.P.I.—Crim. 150.05.

76. *Id.*

77. 364 N.C. 157, 160 (2010) (finding the statute "inherently ambiguous" and arguing that in some cases considerations of judicial economy and avoidance of undue prejudice may warrant consideration of a bifurcated proceeding).

78. State v. Locklear, 363 N.C. 438 (2009).

79. N.C.P.I.—Crim. 150.05.

80. G.S. 15A-2005(e).

81. G.S. 15A-2005(g).

82. State v. McLaughlin, 341 N.C. 426 (1995); State v. McCarver, 341 N.C. 364, 392 (1995) (requiring unanimity "ensures that the jury *properly* fulfills its duty to deliberate *genuinely* for a *reasonable* period of time") (emphases in original).

83. State v. Kirkley, 308 N.C. 196 (1983).

reasonable time.[84] This is so even if the jury inquires about what will happen if it is unable to agree unanimously on its sentence recommendation. In such a case, the trial judge should inform the jurors that their inability to reach a unanimous verdict should not be their concern but should simply be reported to the court.[85]

If the jury is having difficulty reaching a unanimous verdict, a judge may give an instruction set out in G.S. 15A-1235(b).[86]

Case Summaries: "Reasonable Time" to Reach Unanimous Recommendation

State v. Maness, 363 N.C. 261 (2009). After approximately an hour and a half of deliberations, the jury signaled that it had reached a unanimous verdict. The verdict sheet, and the jurors when asked as a group, indicated that the verdict was for a life sentence. During polling, however, many jurors said that they did not agree with the verdict. The judge determined that there was not a unanimous verdict and instructed the jury to continue deliberations, denying the defendant's motions to impose a life sentence and for a mistrial. The jury subsequently returned a unanimous verdict for the death penalty. The state supreme court, noting G.S. 15A-1238 (providing, for criminal trials in superior court generally, that "[i]f upon the poll there is not unanimous concurrence, the jury must be directed to retire for further deliberations"), held that the trial judge properly ordered further deliberations. The court stated that "[e]ven when . . . an inconsistency arises between the verdict and the responses of jurors during the polling process, the trial court must nevertheless allow the jury a reasonable opportunity to attempt to reach a unanimous sentence recommendation. . . . A nonunanimous poll does not necessarily indicate that a jury cannot agree to a unanimous sentencing recommendation within a reasonable time, nor does such a poll automatically give the trial court authority to impose a life sentence." Here, given the short duration of deliberations, there was no evidence that the jury would not be able to agree within a reasonable time. The defendant's motion for a mistrial—based on the fact that the jurors saw the courtroom reaction to the nonunanimous verdict for a life sentence—was properly denied in the trial judge's discretion.

State v. Jones, 339 N.C. 114 (1994). After several hours of deliberations, the jury returned to the courtroom and reported, in response to the trial judge's inquiry, that it had not reached a unanimous decision. The trial judge then gave an instruction according to G.S. 15A-1235(b). Distinguishing *State v. Smith*, 320 N.C. 404 (1987), discussed below, and relying on *State v. Price*, 326 N.C. 56 (1990), also below, the court ruled that the instruction was proper.

State v. Price, 326 N.C. 56 (1990). After the jury had deliberated for about four hours, it reported that it was "hung." The trial judge then gave an instruction according to G.S. 15A-1235(b). The jury resumed its deliberations for an hour and returned with a unanimous recommendation for the death penalty. The court ruled that the trial court did not err in its instructions and in requesting the jury to resume its deliberations.

---

84. *McCarver*, 341 N.C. 364; State v. Smith, 305 N.C. 691 (1982); State v. Johnson, 298 N.C. 355 (1979).

85. State v. Smith, 320 N.C. 404 (1987). In *Jones v. United States*, 527 U.S. 373 (1999), the United States Supreme Court ruled that the Eighth Amendment does not require a jury instruction about the consequences of a capital sentencing jury's failure to agree on a verdict.

86. State v. Jones, 339 N.C. 114 (1994); State v. Green, 336 N.C. 142 (1994). The statute generally provides for an instruction that jurors should "consult with one another . . . with a view to reaching an agreement" if possible and that they should be willing to reexamine their own views and opinions, but that each juror should decide the case for him or herself and should not surrender his or her own honest opinion based on the opinion of other jurors. G.S. 15A-1235(b). *See* N.C.P.I.—Crim. 101.40 (pattern instruction incorporating the provisions of the statute).

State v. Huff, 325 N.C. 1 (1989). This case involved two first-degree murder convictions. The judge submitted two aggravating circumstances and twenty-four mitigating circumstances. The jury deliberated on Friday for less than two hours when it returned a nonunanimous verdict that was not accepted by the judge. The judge informed the jury that its recommendation must be unanimous. The following Monday the jury deliberated for less than two hours and forty-five minutes before reaching a unanimous recommendation. Under these circumstances, the trial court did not abuse its discretion in refusing to impose a life sentence.

State v. McLaughlin, 323 N.C. 68 (1988). The trial judge did not err in denying the defendant's motion to impose a life sentence after the jury had deliberated for seven hours. The jury was considering three murder convictions, each with multiple aggravating and mitigating circumstances.

State v. Smith, 320 N.C. 404 (1987). After deliberating for three hours, the sentencing jury asked the judge what the result would be if it failed to reach a unanimous verdict. The judge responded by stating that the jury's decision must be unanimous. The state supreme court ruled that the judge's statement to the jury, in light of the inquiry from the apparently divided panel, probably was misleading and probably resulted in coerced unanimity. The supreme court stated that if a jury makes an inquiry like the jury did in this case, then the judge should inform the jurors that their inability to reach a unanimous verdict should not be their concern but should simply be reported to the judge.

State v. Kirkley, 308 N.C. 196 (1983). What constitutes a "reasonable time" for jury deliberation in the sentencing hearing is left to the trial judge's discretion, subject to appellate review for an abuse of discretion. In this case, a jury's deliberation for seven and one-half hours was reasonable when there were two murder convictions, each with one aggravating circumstance and fourteen mitigating circumstances.

State v. Johnson, 298 N.C. 355 (1979). The trial judge did not give a jury instruction requested by the defendant stating that if the jury cannot within a reasonable time unanimously agree to its sentence recommendation, the judge must impose a sentence of life imprisonment. The failure to give the instruction was not error. Such an instruction is improper because it would not assist the jury in making its recommendation and would allow the jury to escape the difficult task of recommending a sentence. *See also* State v. Hutchins, 303 N.C. 321 (1981); State v. Williams, 308 N.C. 47 (1983).

Verdict Form

A sample verdict form is provided at the end of N.C.P.I.—Crim. 150.10. A proper verdict form must be submitted to the jury. In *State v. Coffey*,[87] the judge properly instructed the jury but inadvertently submitted a verdict form that omitted Issue Three and instead repeated Issue Four twice. The state supreme court ruled that the verdict form was insufficient to support the recommended death sentence because it did not establish that the mitigating circumstances were insufficient to outweigh the aggravating circumstances, as required by G.S. 15A-2000(c)(3).

In *State v. Hunt*, 323 N.C. 407 (1988), the court ruled that Issue Three on the issues and recommendation form is not unconstitutional in requiring the jury to answer the following question: "Do you

87. 326 N.C. 268 (1990).

find beyond a reasonable doubt that the mitigating circumstance or circumstances you have found is, or are, insufficient to outweigh the aggravating circumstance you have found?" The defendant argued that this question improperly required the jury to answer "yes" if it found that the aggravating and mitigating circumstances were evenly balanced. The court rejected this argument. It stated that if the jury must be satisfied beyond a reasonable doubt before finding that the mitigating circumstances are insufficient to outweigh the aggravating circumstances, and the jury is in a state of equipoise on the issue, it must answer the issue "no."

Juror Misconduct

"Juror misconduct" generally refers to jurors' failure to follow the law or the court's instructions. For example, jurors may make contact with people involved in the trial; may conduct independent research into the facts; or may discuss the case before all the evidence has been received or in groups of fewer than all the jurors. Juror misconduct is not an issue unique to capital cases, though because such cases typically last longer than, and are more closely scrutinized than, other criminal trials, allegations of juror misconduct may arise more frequently in capital cases. Appellate decisions concerning juror misconduct in capital cases are summarized below.

State v. Taylor, 362 N.C. 514 (2008). The trial judge did not err in denying the defendant's motion for a mistrial during a capital sentencing hearing, where the evidence showed only fleeting, nonverbal contact outside of court between jurors who had suffered a flat tire and state's witnesses who offered a can of Fix-a-Flat to the jurors.

State v. Elliott, 360 N.C. 400 (2006). Evidence that two jurors prayed together outside the jury room did not show that the jurors had deliberated together and outside the presence of the remaining jurors. Therefore, the evidence did not support the defendant's motion for appropriate relief.

State v. Sanders, 347 N.C. 587 (1998). The court ruled that the trial judge did not err during a capital sentencing hearing in granting the state's motion for a mistrial over the defendant's objection, when manifest necessity supported the mistrial based on juror misconduct during deliberations. The following, among other facts, supported the mistrial: twice after being sent out to deliberate, the jurors sent back a statement that revealed they were not deliberating as the judge had instructed but were discussing improper matters such as parole eligibility, a juror's investigation outside the jury room, evidence at a previous trial, and whether one juror believed in the death penalty.

State v. Hester, __ N.C. App. __, 715 S.E.2d 905 (2011). Evidence that a juror engaged in misconduct during the penalty phase of a capital trial did not require a mistrial of the guilt phase, as the misconduct could not have affected the jury's verdict at that stage.

Polling Jury about Its Recommendation

G.S. 15A-2000(b) requires that, upon the delivery by the jury's foreperson of the jury's sentence recommendation, the jurors must be individually polled to determine whether each juror concurs and agrees to the sentence recommendation returned (whether it is death or life imprisonment). The North Carolina Supreme Court has ruled that the jury must be polled only about its recommendation of death or life imprisonment; there is no polling requirement regarding the jurors' answers to individual issues addressed during their sentencing deliberations (for example, the finding of aggravating and mitigating circumstances).[88]

Case Summaries: Polling Jury about Its Recommendation

State v. Maness, 363 N.C. 261 (2009). After approximately an hour and a half of deliberations, the jury signaled that it had reached a unanimous verdict. The verdict sheet, and the jurors when asked as a group, indicated that the verdict was for a life sentence. During polling, however, many jurors said that they did not agree with the verdict. The judge determined that there was not a unanimous verdict and instructed the jury to continue deliberations, denying the defendant's motions to impose a life sentence and for a mistrial. The jury subsequently returned a unanimous verdict for the death penalty. The state supreme court, noting G.S. 15A-1238 (providing, for criminal trials in superior court generally, that "[i]f upon the poll there is not unanimous concurrence, the jury must be directed to retire for further deliberations"), held that the trial judge properly ordered further deliberations. The court stated that "[e]ven when . . . an inconsistency arises between the verdict and the responses of jurors during the polling process, the trial court must nevertheless allow the jury a reasonable opportunity to attempt to reach a unanimous sentence recommendation. . . . A nonunanimous poll does not necessarily indicate that a jury cannot agree to a unanimous sentencing recommendation within a reasonable time, nor does such a poll automatically give the trial court authority to impose a life sentence." Here, given the short duration of deliberations, there was no evidence that the jury would not be able to agree within a reasonable time. The defendant's motion for a mistrial—based on the fact that the jurors saw the courtroom reaction to the nonunanimous verdict for a life sentence—was properly denied in the trial judge's discretion.

State v. Richmond, 347 N.C. 412 (1998). In polling the jurors on their recommendations of three death sentences, the clerk asked each juror if each death sentence was his or her recommendation. Following each juror's affirmative responses for each of the three death sentences, the clerk then failed to ask some of the jurors the additional question, "Do you still assent thereto?" The court ruled that the polling of the jury was properly done because the first question satisfies the requirements of G.S. 15A-2000(b).

State v. Lee, 335 N.C. 244 (1994). The court ruled that the jury must be polled under G.S. 15A-2000(b) only about its final recommendation (death or life imprisonment). Jurors need not be polled about their individual answers to the individual issues addressed during their deliberations.

State v. Buchanan, 330 N.C. 202 (1991). The trial judge failed to conduct individual polling of capital sentencing jurors as required by G.S. 15A-2000(b). Instead, the judge polled the jurors collectively. The court ruled that the defendant was entitled to a new sentencing hearing. The judge's failure to follow the statutory mandate was not waived by the defendant's failure to object to how the judge conducted the polling of the jury in this case.

State v. McLaughlin, 323 N.C. 68 (1988). The sentencing jury originally returned with a recommendation to impose a death sentence in all three murder cases (A, B, and C). During the jury poll for murder A, all jurors recommended the death penalty, but one juror recanted her decision to recommend the death penalty for murder B and murder C. When asked if she

88. State v. Lee, 335 N.C. 244 (1994).

wanted to reconsider the death sentence for murder A, the juror reaffirmed her death sentence recommendation in that case. The court ruled that the trial judge did not err in not conducting another poll of the juror or in refusing to permit the jury to deliberate further in that case.

State v. Spruill, 320 N.C. 688 (1987). A juror sufficiently concurred and agreed with the death penalty recommendation when she, while under some emotional distress, nodded her head affirmatively to the questions whether the death penalty recommendation was her verdict and whether she still assented to it.

State v. Martin, 315 N.C. 667 (1986). The jury was properly polled after its verdict for first-degree murder and other offenses. After a mistake was discovered in one of the verdicts, the judge questioned the jury, received the verdict, and the defendant declined the judge's offer to poll the jury again. During the capital sentencing hearing, a juror approached the judge and attempted to change her verdict from first-degree murder to second-degree murder. The defendant requested that the judge poll the jury again, and the judge refused. The court ruled that the trial judge acted properly. A juror may not impeach the jury's verdict after it has been rendered and received in open court.

J. Issues Pertinent to Second or Subsequent Capital Sentencing Hearings

A second or subsequent capital sentencing hearing may be held only for a defendant who was sentenced to death in his or her prior trial or trials but who subsequently won a new trial or new sentencing hearing. The Double Jeopardy Clause of the United States Constitution prohibits the state from seeking the death penalty against a defendant who was sentenced to life in prison upon the recommendation of a previous jury and later obtained a new trial.[89] The North Carolina Supreme Court has considered several issues that are pertinent to second or subsequent capital sentencing hearings, resulting in the following holdings:

- The Double Jeopardy Clause does not bar the submission of an aggravating circumstance at a second or subsequent capital sentencing hearing even though it was not submitted or found at a prior capital sentencing hearing.[90]
- The state at a second or subsequent capital sentencing hearing is not bound by a stipulation made at a prior capital sentencing hearing that an aggravating circumstance did not exist when evidence supports its submission at the later sentencing hearing.[91]
- The defendant at a second or subsequent capital sentencing hearing is not entitled to a peremptory jury instruction for a statutory mitigating circumstance simply because the state had stipulated to its existence at a prior capital sentencing hearing.[92]
- The defendant at a second or subsequent capital sentencing hearing is not entitled under the collateral estoppel doctrine to a jury instruction that a mitigating circumstance was

89. Bullington v. Missouri, 451 U.S. 430 (1981).
90. State v. Duke, 360 N.C. 110 (2005); State v. Sanderson, 346 N.C. 669 (1997).
91. State v. Adams, 347 N.C. 48 (1997).
92. State v. Flippen, 349 N.C. 264 (1998).

established as a matter of law because the jury unanimously found it to exist at a prior capital sentencing hearing.[93]

Case Summaries: Issues Pertinent to Capital Resentencing Hearings

Bobby v. Bies, 556 U.S. 825 (2009). The defendant was convicted of murder. His trial took place before the United States Supreme Court issued its decision in *Atkins v. Virginia*, 536 U.S. 304 (2002), so although he presented evidence of mental retardation at sentencing, the jury considered retardation only in the context of mitigating circumstances generally, and the defendant was sentenced to death. The state appellate courts that reviewed the defendant's case stated that his retardation merited "some weight" in mitigation, but they affirmed his death sentence nonetheless. After *Atkins*, the defendant sought relief from his sentence and argued that the state was collaterally estopped from contesting his retardation based on the state courts' previous consideration of the issue. The Supreme Court disagreed, because it was not clear that the state courts had truly determined that the defendant was retarded, and even if they had, the determination was not essential to the courts' final judgment, which was a sentence of death. Therefore, the state was free to oppose the defendant's request for *Atkins* relief. [*Author's note*: Although not directly involving a capital resentencing hearing, the analysis in this case supports the conclusion that a jury finding of a mitigating circumstance, or the lack of an aggravating circumstance, in an earlier capital sentencing proceeding does not bar the state from relitigating the issue in a subsequent proceeding.]

State v. Duke, 360 N.C. 110 (2005). The court ruled, relying on *State v. Sanderson*, 346 N.C. 669 (1997), and distinguishing *Ring v. Arizona*, 536 U.S. 584 (2002), that there is no double jeopardy violation in submitting an aggravating circumstance in a capital resentencing hearing that had not been submitted in the first capital sentencing hearing in which the defendant had received a death sentence.

State v. Sanderson, 346 N.C. 669 (1997). At the defendant's first capital sentencing hearing, aggravating circumstance G.S. 15A-2000(e)(5) (murder committed during rape) was not submitted; the trial judge had excluded portions of the defendant's confession when he confessed to raping the victim. At the defendant's second capital sentencing hearing, the defendant's brother testified that the defendant admitted he raped the victim before killing her, and the defense mental health expert testified that the defendant told her he had raped the victim. The prosecutor requested that this aggravating circumstance be submitted, but the trial judge refused to submit it. At the defendant's third capital sentencing hearing, the trial judge submitted this circumstance after the state presented evidence that the defendant raped the victim before he killed her. The defendant argued that the submission of this aggravating circumstance at the third capital sentencing hearing violated double jeopardy principles. The court, disavowing statements in *State v. Silhan*, 302 N.C. 223 (1981), that were contrary to the ruling in the later case of *Poland v. Arizona*, 476 U.S. 147 (1986) (failure to find aggravating circumstance is not equivalent to acquittal under double jeopardy principles), ruled that jeopardy attaches in a capital sentencing hearing only after there has been a finding that no aggravating circumstance is present (that is, when life imprisonment must be imposed). The court noted that each of the juries in the first and second capital sentencing hearings found at least one aggravating circumstance to exist and recommended the death sentence. Thus, double jeopardy principles did not bar the

93. *Adams*, 347 N.C. 48. *Cf.* Bobby v. Bies, 556 U.S. 825 (2009) (summarized in the text, above).

trial judge from submitting aggravating circumstances at the third capital sentencing hearing that were supported by the evidence. What occurred at the first and second hearings was irrelevant. The trial judge thus did not violate the defendant's double jeopardy rights by submitting G.S. 15A-2000(e)(5) at the third capital sentencing hearing.

State v. Adams, 347 N.C. 48 (1997). The defendant was sentenced to death at a second capital sentencing. (1) At the first capital sentencing hearing, the state had stipulated that there was insufficient evidence of aggravating circumstance G.S. 15A-2000(e)(5) (murder committed during rape). At the second capital sentencing hearing, the state advised the judge that it had sufficient evidence of this aggravating circumstance. The judge allowed the evidence of the circumstance to be submitted to the jury under *State v. Case*, 330 N.C. 161 (1991) (state cannot agree with defendant not to submit aggravating circumstance supported by sufficient evidence). The court ruled that the trial judge's ruling was correct—the state was not bound by its prior stipulation. The court also ruled, relying on *State v. Sanderson*, 346 N.C. 669 (1997), that the trial judge's ruling did not violate double jeopardy principles. (2) The court ruled, relying on *Poland v. Arizona*, 476 U.S. 147 (1986) (failure to find aggravating circumstance is not equivalent to acquittal under double jeopardy principles), that the defendant was not entitled, under the collateral estoppel doctrine, to a jury instruction at the second capital sentencing hearing that a mitigating circumstance unanimously found by the jury at the first capital sentencing hearing was established as matter of law. Double jeopardy principles do not preclude the relitigation of the existence of mitigating circumstances.

State v. Flippen, 349 N.C. 264 (1998). At a capital resentencing hearing, the defendant was sentenced to death for the first-degree murder of his 2-year-old stepdaughter. At the prior capital sentencing hearing, the state had stipulated to the existence of statutory mitigating circumstance G.S. 15A-2000(f)(1) (no significant prior criminal history). At this capital sentencing hearing, the state offered evidence that the defendant had twice assaulted his wife. Relying on *State v. Adams*, 347 N.C. 48 (1997), the court ruled that the prior stipulation did not foreclose the state at a later capital sentencing hearing from offering evidence to rebut the existence of the mitigating circumstance. Thus, the trial judge did not err in failing to give a peremptory instruction on this mitigating circumstance; the existence of the circumstance was not uncontroverted.

State v. Adams, 347 N.C. 48 (1997). During the state's cross-examination of a defense witness at the second capital sentencing hearing, the witness inadvertently revealed that the defendant had been on death row. The court ruled that the trial judge correctly denied the defendant's motion for a mistrial because the state did not elicit this fact from the witness and the remark did not result in substantial and irreparable prejudice to the defendant. *See also* State v. Spruill, 338 N.C. 612 (1994) (prosecutor's inadvertent reference to defendant's presence on death row did not require new capital sentencing hearing). *But see* State v. Britt, 288 N.C. 699 (1975) (court ordered new capital sentencing hearing when prosecutor improperly questioned defendant in manner that elicited testimony that defendant had previously been sentenced to death).

Chapter 5

Aggravating Circumstances

Chapter 5

Aggravating Circumstances

This chapter discusses the eleven statutory aggravating circumstances and the case law interpreting them. These aggravating circumstances are listed in subdivisions (1) through (11) of North Carolina General Statutes (hereinafter G.S.) Section 15A-2000(e). The eleven aggravating circumstances are as follows:

- (e)(1) The murder was committed by an incarcerated defendant.
- (e)(2) The defendant was previously convicted of a capital felony.
- (e)(3) The defendant was previously convicted of a violent felony.
- (e)(4) The murder was committed to prevent arrest or to effect an escape.
- (e)(5) The murder was committed during the commission of a specified felony.
- (e)(6) The murder was committed for pecuniary gain.
- (e)(7) The murder was committed to hinder a governmental function or the enforcement of law.
- (e)(8) The murder was committed against a law enforcement officer or specified others.
- (e)(9) The murder was especially heinous, atrocious, or cruel.
- (e)(10) The defendant created a great risk of death to more than one person by a hazardous weapon.
- (e)(11) The murder was part of the defendant's course of violent conduct toward another person or persons.

A. General Rules Concerning Aggravating Circumstances

The aggravating circumstances that may be found by the jury are limited to those listed in G.S. 15A-2000(e).[1] A first-degree murder indictment need not allege the aggravating circumstances on which the state will rely.[2] Nor is a defendant entitled to a bill of particulars setting forth these

1. The statute provides that "[a]ggravating circumstances . . . shall be limited to" those listed therein. *See also* State v. Brown, 320 N.C. 179 (1987) (noting that because bad reputation is not an enumerated aggravating circumstance, the state may not present evidence thereof in its case-in-chief).

2. State v. Hunt, 357 N.C. 257 (2003).

aggravating circumstances.[3] (For a discussion of the Rule 24 (General Rules of Practice for the Superior and District Courts) mandatory pretrial conference and notification of aggravating circumstances by the state, see Chapter 2.)

When deciding whether to submit an aggravating circumstance to the jury, the court must view the evidence in the light most favorable to the state and must give the state the benefit of all reasonable inferences from the evidence.[4] However, the state supreme court has also stated that "[w]here it is doubtful whether a particular aggravating circumstance should be submitted, the doubt should be resolved in favor of [the] defendant."[5]

The jury must find the existence of an aggravating circumstance unanimously and beyond a reasonable doubt before it may consider the circumstance during its deliberations.[6] The jury must give some weight to any aggravating circumstance that it finds, but how much weight to give a particular aggravating circumstance is for the jury to decide.[7]

The Double Jeopardy Clause of the United States Constitution does not bar the submission of an aggravating circumstance at a capital resentencing hearing even when that circumstance was not submitted or found at a prior capital sentencing hearing.[8] The state at a capital resentencing hearing is not bound by a stipulation at a prior capital sentencing hearing that an aggravating circumstance did not exist when evidence supports its submission at the resentencing hearing.[9] However, the state may not appeal a jury's recommendation of a life sentence,[10] nor may the state seek the death penalty if a defendant who had received a life sentence is awarded a new trial.[11]

---

3. State v. Holden, 321 N.C. 125 (1987). The state is also not required to give notice of prior convictions that it will use to prove an aggravating circumstance, such as (e)(3) (previous conviction of violent felony). State v. Roper, 328 N.C. 337 (1991).

4. *See, e.g.,* State v. Allen, 360 N.C. 297 (2006).

5. State v. Oliver, 302 N.C. 28, 61 (1981).

6. As to unanimity, see *State v. Kirkley*, 308 N.C. 196, 218 (1983) (holding that "the jury must unanimously find that an aggravating circumstance exists before that circumstance may be considered by the jury in determining its sentence recommendation"). As to beyond a reasonable doubt, see G.S. 15A-2000(c)(1) (referring to "[t]he statutory aggravating circumstance or circumstances which the jury finds beyond a reasonable doubt"). In *Ring v. Arizona*, 536 U.S. 584 (2002), the United States Supreme Court ruled that allowing a judge—without a jury—to find an aggravating circumstance necessary to impose a death sentence violates the federal Constitution's Sixth Amendment right to a jury trial.

7. State v. Laws, 325 N.C. 81, 117 (1989) ("[B]y enacting specific aggravating circumstances to be considered in capital sentencing, the legislature intended that a jury having found one of those statutory aggravating circumstances to exist must give it weight in aggravation when determining the appropriate sentence to recommend. . . . The amount of weight to be given such statutory aggravating circumstances is, however, left to the determination of the jury.") (citations omitted); *Holden*, 321 N.C. 125 (jury decides how much weight to give aggravating and mitigating circumstances).

8. State v. Duke, 360 N.C. 110 (2005); State v. Sanderson, 346 N.C. 669 (1997) (disavowing prior contrary statements in *State v. Silhan*, 302 N.C. 223 (1981)).

9. State v. Adams, 347 N.C. 48 (1997).

10. *Silhan*, 302 N.C. 223 (so holding, on double jeopardy grounds); *see also* Arizona v. Rumsey, 467 U.S. 203 (1984) (similar ruling).

11. Bullington v. Missouri, 451 U.S. 430 (1981) (holding that the jury's decision to impose a life sentence at the defendant's first trial amounted to an acquittal of the death penalty, meaning that double jeopardy precludes trying the defendant capitally a second time). *Bullington* does not apply in cases in which a life sentence is imposed as a result of a jury deadlock rather than a unanimous life verdict. Sattazahn v. Pennsylvania, 537 U.S. 101 (2003) (holding that a life sentence in such an instance is not a de facto acquittal of the death penalty and thereby distinguishing *Bullington*). However, in North Carolina, G.S. 15A-1335, which prohibits a more severe sentence after a successful appeal, bars retrying a defendant capitally after a life sentence is imposed, even if by deadlock.

The North Carolina Supreme Court has held that the *corpus delecti* rule, which generally provides that a defendant's confession alone is insufficient evidence to support a criminal conviction,[12] does not apply to proving aggravating circumstances.[13]

The North Carolina Supreme Court has decided several cases concerning the relationship between elements of first-degree murder and aggravating circumstances. In *State v. Cherry*,[14] the court held that when a defendant is convicted of first-degree murder based solely on the felony murder theory, the underlying felony may not be used to support the (e)(5) aggravating circumstance (murder during the commission of a specified felony). The court reasoned that allowing an element of felony murder, namely, the underlying felony, to support an aggravating circumstance would result in an aggravating circumstance being added to every felony murder case. This, the court concluded, would unfairly increase the chance that a felony murder defendant would be sentenced to death when compared to a defendant convicted solely of premeditated murder. The reasoning of *Cherry* might also apply, for example, to a case in which a defendant was convicted of first-degree murder by means of a nuclear, chemical, or biological weapon of mass destruction. In such a case, it might be improper to use the fact that the defendant employed such a weapon to support the (e)(10) aggravating circumstance (use of hazardous weapon to endanger multiple others).

It is reasonable to ask whether *Cherry* stands for the broader proposition that evidence necessary to support an element of first-degree murder cannot be used to support an aggravating circumstance. In *State v. Quesinberry*,[15] the state supreme court noted that such a rule exists by statute for noncapital cases[16] and adopted a related rule—the rule against using the same evidence to support multiple aggravating circumstances—as a matter of equity in capital cases. But the court has never expressly broadened *Cherry* beyond the bounds of felony murder, and several cases suggest that even if there is a general rule against using an element of first-degree murder to establish an aggravating circumstance, there is no general rule against using *evidence that supports* an element of first-degree murder also to support an aggravating circumstance. For example, in *State v. Oliver*,[17] the supreme court held that it was proper to submit the (e)(6) aggra vating circumstance (murder for pecuniary gain) based on evidence that the defendant had killed the victim during a robbery, notwithstanding the fact that the robbery formed the basis for the defendant's conviction of felony murder. The court stated that acting for pecuniary gain is not an element of robbery and that the aggravating circumstance instead addresses the separate consideration of the defendant's motive; the evidence in the case established both the robbery and the motive. Likewise, in *State v. Moore*,[18] the court ruled that evidence that the defendant slowly poisoned the victim, causing protracted suffering followed by death, was properly used to support both a conviction of first-degree murder by poisoning and the (e)(9) aggravating circumstance (especially heinous, atrocious, or cruel). The court noted that poisoning may be fast or

---

12. *See generally* State v. Trexler, 316 N.C. 528 (1986).

13. State v. Lee, 335 N.C. 244 (1994) (holding that the defendant's description of how the victim had died a slow and painful death was sufficient by itself to prove the (e)(9) aggravating circumstance (especially heinous, atrocious, or cruel)).

14. 298 N.C. 86 (1979).

15. 319 N.C. 228 (1987).

16. Although *Quesinberry* was decided during the lifespan of the Fair Sentencing Act, a similar provision exists today under Structured Sentencing. *See* G.S. 15A-1340.16(d) ("Evidence necessary to prove an element of the offense shall not be used to prove any factor in aggravation, and the same item of evidence shall not be used to prove more than one factor in aggravation.").

17. 302 N.C. 28 (1981).

18. 335 N.C. 567 (1994).

slow, i.e., that the protracted suffering inflicted by the defendant was not inherent to the commission of murder by poisoning, thereby distinguishing *Cherry.*

The Use of the Same Evidence to Support Multiple Aggravating Circumstances

A somewhat related issue concerns the use of the same evidence to support multiple aggravating circumstances. Generally, the state supreme court has ruled that the submission of two or more aggravating circumstances based on the same evidence is prohibited.[19] The court has reasoned that this is an unnecessary duplication of aggravating circumstances that unfairly tips the balance of aggravating circumstances versus mitigating circumstances against the defendant.[20] For example, it is improper to submit both (e)(5) (murder during a specified felony, namely, robbery) and (e)(6) (murder for pecuniary gain) when the motive for the robbery was pecuniary gain.[21] This prohibition, however, does not apply when there is some separate evidence to support each aggravating circumstance, even though the evidence supporting each may overlap.[22]

There is an exception to the general rule against using the same evidence to support multiple aggravating circumstances: the same evidence may be used when the several aggravating circumstances are directed at different aspects of the defendant's character or the murder for which the defendant is to be punished. For example, the North Carolina Supreme Court has ruled that it was not error to submit, on the same evidence, both (e)(4) (murder to prevent arrest or effect escape) and (e)(8) (murder of law enforcement officer or specified others performing duties) because (e)(4) focuses on the defendant's motivation in committing the murder and (e)(8) focuses on the factual circumstances of the murder.[23]

The North Carolina Supreme Court has stated that a trial judge should instruct the jury that it may not use the same evidence to find more than one aggravating circumstance.[24] Such an instruction is located after the instruction for aggravating circumstance (e)(11) (course of violent conduct) in the relevant North Carolina Pattern Jury Instruction (referred to hereinafter as N.C.P.I.).[25] However, the judge need not instruct the jury which specific pieces of evidence it may use to support which aggravating circumstances, so long as he or she makes clear that the same evidence cannot support multiple aggravators.[26]

Note the following summaries of cases on the submission of multiple aggravating circumstances on the same or similar evidence. Many of the cases are also summarized under the particular aggravating circumstances that are discussed later in this chapter.

---

19. *See, e.g.,* State v. Goodman, 298 N.C. 1 (1979).

20. *Id.*

21. *Quesinberry,* 319 N.C. 228. *But cf.* State v. East, 345 N.C. 535 (1997) (proper to submit aggra vating circumstances (e)(5) (murder during the commission of a specified felony, in this case, robbery) and (e)(6) (murder for pecuniary gain) because these circumstances were supported by separate evidence on the facts of this case).

22. *See, e.g.,* State v. Jennings, 333 N.C. 579 (1993).

23. State v. Hutchins, 303 N.C. 321 (1981).

24. State v. Gay, 334 N.C. 467 (1993). *But cf.* State v. Rouse, 339 N.C. 59 (1994) (failure to request such an instruction limited appellate review to plain error analysis, and court did not find plain error in this case).

25. N.C.P.I.—CRIM. 150.10. So long as he or she conveys the relevant principle about not using the same evidence, a judge is not required to use the pattern instruction. State v. Smith, 359 N.C. 199, 214 (2005) (the trial judge submitted aggravating circumstance (e)(5) (murder during the commission of a specified felony) twice, once for kidnapping the victim and once for robbing him; although the trial court did not expressly instruct the jury not to use the same evidence to support more than one aggravating circumstance, it achieved the same result by stating that the state was required to prove that the "restraint was a separate complete act independent of and apart from the robbery").

26. State v. Tirado, 358 N.C. 551 (2004).

Case Summaries: Multiple Aggravating Circumstances Properly Submitted—Separate Evidence

State v. Waring, 364 N.C. 443 (2010). The defendant and an accomplice stole the victim's wallet, raped her, and murdered her by stabbing her repeatedly. The trial judge submitted aggravating circumstances (e)(5) (murder during a specified felony, in this case, rape), (e)(6) (murder for pecuniary gain), and (e)(9) (especially heinous, atrocious, or cruel). Separate evidence supported each, and the prosecutor's argument did not ask the jury to find more than one aggravating circumstance based on the same evidence.

State v. Smith, 359 N.C. 199 (2005). The defendant entered the victim's home, choked him into unconsciousness, bound him, and taped over his nose and mouth, leaving him to die of asphyxiation. He then ransacked the residence, stealing several items. The trial judge submitted aggravating circumstance (e)(5) (murder during a specified felony) twice, once for kidnapping and once for robbery. This was proper, as the "binding and taping was not an inherent, inevitable part of the robbery" and therefore provided separate evidence to support the aggravating circumstance regarding the kidnapping. Further, although the trial court did not expressly instruct the jury not to use the same evidence to support more than one aggravating circumstance, it achieved the same result by stating that the state was required to prove that the "restraint was a separate complete act independent of and apart from the robbery."

State v. Tirado, 358 N.C. 551 (2004). The defendant and others trapped a car in a dead-end street and forced the two occupants of the vehicle into its trunk. The defendant and his accomplices drove the vehicle around, then stopped and robbed the occupants of their jewelry. Later, they shot and killed the occupants. The trial judge submitted aggravating circumstances (e)(5) (murder during a specified felony, in this case, kidnapping), (e)(6) (murder for pecuniary gain), and (e)(11) (course of violent conduct). This was proper as separate evidence supported each: the carjacking supported (e)(5), the jewelry theft supported (e)(6), and the multiple killings supported (e)(11). Further, the trial court was not required to instruct the jury which specific pieces of evidence it could use to support which aggravating circumstances, so long as it made clear that the same evidence could not support multiple aggravators.

State v. Jones, 358 N.C. 330 (2004). The defendant shot and killed his wife and his 14-year-old stepson. The trial court submitted aggravating circumstance (e)(11) (course of violent conduct) for each murder and aggravating circumstance (e)(9) (especially heinous, atrocious, or cruel) for the child's murder. The killing of each victim supported the submission of (e)(11) for the other, and the fact that the defendant was a father figure to the child supported the submission of (e)(9).

State v. White, 355 N.C. 696 (2002). The court ruled that separate evidence supported the submission of both (e)(5) (murder during a specified felony, here, robbery) and (e)(6) (murder for pecuniary gain). The theft of the victim's keys and car supported (e)(5). The defendant stole the car for transportation, not to sell it. The defendant's theft of the victim's money supported (e)(6). Thus, separate, independent evidence supported submission of these aggravating circumstances. The court noted that the jury instructions properly limited the jury's consideration of the evidence supporting each circumstance. *See also* State v. East, 345 N.C. 535 (1997) (similar ruling).

State v. DeCastro, 342 N.C. 667 (1996). The court ruled that separate evidence supported the submission of (e)(9) (especially heinous, atrocious, or cruel) and (e)(11) (course of violent conduct; in this case the defendant killed the murder victim's husband). Evidence supporting (e)(9) included the defendant's infliction of twenty-three stab wounds on the victim. The victim did not die a quick, painless death but remained conscious during the five to ten minutes that elapsed before she died. In addition, her jeans and panties had been pulled to her ankles, her shirt torn open, and her bra pulled above her breasts, exposing her breasts, torso, and lower body. The evidence supporting (e)(11) was entirely different from the evidence supporting (e)(9): before killing the victim, the defendant robbed, beat, and murdered the victim's husband.

State v. Daughtry, 340 N.C. 488 (1995). The court ruled that separate evidence supported the submission of (e)(5) (murder during a specified felony, here, a sex offense) and (e)(9) (especially heinous, atrocious, or cruel). Evidence supporting (e)(5) showed that some object had been inserted into the victim's rectum or vagina. Evidence supporting (e)(9) showed severe blunt trauma wounds to the victim's head and many abrasions about her body. *See also* State v. Kandies, 342 N.C. 419 (1996) (similar ruling).

State v. Conaway, 339 N.C. 487 (1995). The court reviewed the evidence at the sentencing hearing and ruled that separate substantial evidence supported each of the following three aggravating circumstances in a double murder case: (e)(5) (murder during a specified felony, in this case, kidnapping); (e)(6) (murder for pecuniary gain, in this case, by taking money from cash register during armed robbery); and (e)(11) (course of violent conduct; in this case, the defendant killed a second person). The court stated that when there is separate substantial evidence to support each aggravating circumstance, it is proper for each circumstance to be submitted even though evidence supporting each may overlap. *See also* State v. Rose, 339 N.C. 172 (1994) (separate evidence supported submission of both (e)(3) (previous conviction of violent felony) and (e)(11) (course of violent conduct)).

State v. Rouse, 339 N.C. 59 (1994). Separate evidence supported the submission of both (e)(5) (murder during a specified felony, in this case, attempted rape and attempted armed robbery) and (e)(9) (especially heinous, atrocious, or cruel). The victim was stabbed seventeen times and suffered for fifteen minutes as she lost half of her blood. The court noted that evidence supporting each aggravating circumstance may overlap as long as the same evidence doesn't support more than one aggravating circumstance.

State v. Moseley, 338 N.C. 1 (1994). The court ruled that the jury properly found two statutory aggravating circumstances under (e)(5) (murder during a specified felony) because the murder was committed while the defendant was engaged in the commission of (1) first-degree sexual offense and (2) first-degree rape. Both aggravating circumstances were supported by distinct and separate evidence, even though they involved the same victim.

State v. Sanderson, 336 N.C. 1 (1994). Distinguishing *State v. Quesinberry*, 319 N.C. 228 (1987), discussed below, the court ruled that the trial judge properly submitted both (e)(4) (murder to prevent arrest or effect escape) and (e)(5) (murder during a specified felony, here, while the defendant was engaged in a kidnapping) because these aggravating circumstances were supported by different evidence.

State v. Gibbs, 335 N.C. 1 (1993). The trial judge did not err in submitting both (e)(5) (murder during a specified felony, in this instance, burglary) and (e)(11) (course of violent conduct). These aggravating circumstances were not supported by the same evidence. Proof that the defendant committed a murder during the burglary did not also require proof of the commission of violence toward the other victims (two other people were murdered). And the defendant need not have engaged in a violent course of conduct to have committed a murder in the course of the burglary. *See also* State v. Gay, 334 N.C. 467 (1993).

State v. Jennings, 333 N.C. 579 (1993). The trial judge properly submitted aggravating circumstances (e)(5) (murder during a specified felony, in this case, a sex offense) and (e)(9) (especially heinous, atrocious, or cruel) because they were not based on the same evidence. There was substantial evidence of the especially heinous, atrocious, or cruel nature of the murder (the savage beating of the victim) apart from the evidence that the murder was committed while attempting to penetrate the victim's anus with an object.

State v. Jones, 327 N.C. 439 (1990). Distinguishing *State v. Quesinberry*, 319 N.C. 228 (1987), discussed below, the court ruled that the submission of both (e)(6) (murder for pecuniary gain) and (e)(11) (course of violent conduct) was proper. The aggravating circumstances were not supported by the same evidence. Evidence of the robbery of a convenience store supported (e)(6). Evidence that the defendant killed the victim, wounded another, and fired shots endangering others supported (e)(11).

State v. McLaughlin, 323 N.C. 68 (1988). Aggravating circumstance (e)(11) (course of violent conduct) was properly submitted for each of two murders committed by the defendant during the same night.

Case Summaries: Multiple Aggravating Circumstances Properly Submitted—Different Aspects

State v. Berry, 356 N.C. 490 (2002). The defendant killed a woman "to keep her from talking about a murder he had previously committed" and about which he had told her. The trial court submitted the (e)(4) (murder to prevent arrest or effect escape) and (e)(11) (course of violent conduct) aggravating circumstances. Citing *State v. Hutchins*, 303 N.C. 321 (1981), discussed below, the state supreme court affirmed, stating that (e)(4) focused on the defendant's motive, while (e)(11) concerned the "objective facts of the two murders."

State v. Smith, 347 N.C. 453 (1998). The defendant was convicted of first-degree murder after he set fire to an apartment building by lighting kerosene, killing one person and seriously injuring others. Distinguishing *State v. Quesinberry*, 319 N.C. 228 (1987), discussed below, the court ruled that aggravating circumstances (e)(5) (murder during a specified felony, here, while defendant engaged in arson) and (e)(10) (use of hazardous weapon to endanger multiple others) were both properly submitted to the jury because they addressed different aspects of the murder, although they both relied on the same evidence. Aggravating circumstance (e)(5) addresses the fact that the defendant committed murder while engaging in another felony, arson. Aggravating circumstance (e)(10) addresses a distinct aspect of the defendant's character—he not only intended to kill a particular person when setting fire to the apartment building, but he also disregarded the value of every human life in the building by using an accelerant to set the fire in the middle of the night.

State v. Green, 321 N.C. 594 (1988). In a first-degree murder prosecution for the murders of victims A, B, and C at a bar, the trial judge properly submitted the (e)(4) aggravating circumstance (prevent murder to arrest or effect escape) in the sentencing for the murder of C, since the evidence showed that C (who was in a defenseless position) was killed to eliminate him as a witness in the killings of A and B. The court also ruled, based on *State v. Hutchins*, 303 N.C. 321 (1981), discussed below, that it was proper to submit both this aggravating circumstance and (e)(11) (course of violent conduct). The (e)(11) aggravating circumstance involved the factual circumstances of the defendant's crimes, while the (e)(4) aggravating circumstance involved the defendant's motive in shooting a person in a defenseless position.

State v. Hutchins, 303 N.C. 321 (1981). The court ruled that it was not error to submit two aggravating circumstances in this case—(e)(4) (murder to prevent arrest or effect escape) and (e)(8) (murder of law enforcement officer or specified others performing duties)—even though they may have been based on the same evidence. The court stated that it is not error to submit multiple aggravating circumstances if the inquiry prompted by their submission is directed at distinct aspects of the defendant's character or the murder for which the defendant is to be punished. The (e)(4) aggravating circumstance focuses on the defendant's motivation in pursuing his or her course of conduct. The (e)(8) aggravating circumstance focuses on the factual circumstances of the crime. The court distinguished its ruling in *State v. Goodman*, 298 N.C. 1 (1979), discussed below.

Case Summaries: Multiple Aggravating Circumstances Improperly Submitted

State v. Howell, 335 N.C. 457 (1994). Relying on *State v. Quesinberry*, 319 N.C. 228 (1987), discussed immediately below, the court ruled that the trial judge erred in submitting both (e)(5) (murder during a specified felony, here, while defendant was committing burglary) and (e)(6) (murder for pecuniary gain) when these aggravating circumstances were supported by the same evidence. In this case, pecuniary gain was the motive for committing the burglary.

State v. Quesinberry, 319 N.C. 228 (1987). The defendant was convicted of first-degree murder based on premeditation and deliberation and felony murder, the underlying felony being armed robbery. Aggravating circumstances (e)(5) (murder during a specified felony, in this case, robbery) and (e)(6) (murder for pecuniary gain) were both submitted and found by the jury. The court ruled that the circumstances were redundant, since the motive of pecuniary gain provided the impetus for the robbery itself, and therefore it was error to submit both circumstances to the jury. *See also* State v. Davis, 325 N.C. 607 (1989) (similar ruling).

State v. Vereen, 312 N.C. 499 (1985). The trial judge erred in submitting two aggravating circumstances because they were based on the same evidence—the attempted rape of the murder victim's daughter—considering the jury instructions in this case. The jury instruction for (e)(5) (murder during a specified felony) set out that the murder was committed while the defendant committed the crime of first-degree burglary *or attempted rape.* The jury instruction for (e)(11) (course of violent conduct) set out that the murder was part of a course of conduct that included the defendant's commission of violent crimes against others, including felonious assault *and attempted rape.*

State v. Goodman, 298 N.C. 1 (1979). There was sufficient evidence to support the (e)(4) aggravating circumstance (murder to prevent arrest or effect escape) when, after the victim was shot and cut but before he was killed, the defendant stated that he "was afraid if the police found [the victim] that he would tell what he had done to him." The defendant and an accomplice then planned to bury the victim. Later they decided to shoot him and place him on a railroad track where his body would be mangled by a passing train. However, it was error to submit both (e)(4) and the (e)(7) aggravating circumstance (murder to hinder governmental function or law enforcement) since they were based on the same evidence. The submission of both was an unnecessary duplication of circumstances that resulted in an automatic accumulation of aggravating circumstances against the defendant. The court noted that sometimes the same evidence may support the finding of more than one aggravating circumstance; for example, an aggravating circumstance showing the defendant's motive and a different aggravating circumstance showing a factual event (see the later case of *State v. Hutchins*, 303 N.C. 321 (1981), discussed above).

B. Aggravating Circumstance (e)(1): Murder Committed by Incarcerated Defendant

G.S. 15A-2000(e)(1) states: "The capital felony was committed by a person lawfully incarcerated." This aggravating circumstance applies in cases like *State v. Braxton*,[27] where the defendant, in prison because of prior murder convictions, stabbed another inmate to death. In *State v. Rich*,[28] the North Carolina Supreme Court considered the relationship between (e)(1) and (e)(3) (previous conviction of violent felony). The defendant in *Rich* was serving a prison sentence for murder when he killed another inmate. On appeal, he argued that the jury could have relied on the same evidence—his prior murder conviction—to find both (e)(1) and (e)(3). Thus, the defendant contended, the trial court committed plain error in failing to instruct the jury that it could not rely on the same evidence to find multiple aggravating circumstances. The supreme court disagreed, stating that there was no risk that the jury relied on the same evidence to find the two factors. In essence, it reasoned that the fact of the defendant's imprisonment, not the nature of the prior conviction, established (e)(1), while the nature of the prior conviction, not the fact of the defendant's imprisonment, established (e)(3).

It is unclear whether this aggravating circumstance applies only to a murder committed within a prison or other detention facility or whether it also would apply to an escapee who commits a murder.[29]

C. Aggravating Circumstance (e)(2): Defendant Previously Convicted of Capital Felony

G.S. 15A-2000(e)(2) states: "The defendant had been previously convicted of another capital felony or had been previously adjudicated delinquent in a juvenile proceeding for committing an offense that would be a capital felony if committed by an adult."

What Constitutes a Capital Felony

To qualify as a capital felony under (e)(2), the felony must have been punishable by death when the defendant was convicted or perhaps when the defendant committed the felony. The state need not have sought the death penalty for that felony, nor must the defendant have been sentenced to death.[30] However, if the death penalty was not an authorized punishment for the felony at the time of the defendant's conviction because the death penalty had been declared unconstitutional, the conviction

---

27. 352 N.C. 158 (2000).

28. 346 N.C. 50 (1997).

29. *See, e.g.*, Duckett v. State, 919 P.2d 7 (Okla. Crim. App. 1995) (court interpreted the aggravating circumstance that the murder was committed while the defendant was "serving a term of imprisonment" to include a murder committed by an escapee from prison) (citation to Oklahoma statute omitted).

30. State v. Cummings, 352 N.C. 600 (2000) (summarized in the text below).

cannot be used as an aggravating circumstance under (e)(2).[31] Of course, it may still support aggravating circumstance (e)(3) (prior violent felony).

Consider the following case concerning what constitutes a capital felony.

> **State v. Cummings, 352 N.C. 600 (2000).** The court ruled, distinguishing *State v. Bunning*, 338 N.C. 483 (1994) (first-degree murder conviction in Virginia was not a capital felony conviction because the death penalty was not in effect at the time of conviction), that the trial judge did not err in submitting aggravating circumstance (e)(2) based on a 1966 North Carolina first-degree murder conviction because the death sentence could have been imposed for first-degree murder in 1966. Although the defendant had pleaded guilty in 1966 under a statute which precluded the death penalty as a punishment if the prosecutor agreed to the plea and it was approved by the presiding judge, the court noted that the test for determining the existence of this aggravating circumstance is not the punishment actually imposed but, rather, the maximum punishment that could have been imposed. A crime that is considered a "capital felony" under this aggravating circumstance maintains that status even if a defendant's case is not tried as a "capital case." The court stated that the defendant's plea to first-degree murder did not alter the classification of the offense as a capital felony. The court also rejected the defendant's argument that there was not a constitutional death penalty statute when the defendant entered his guilty plea because the statute was later ruled to be unconstitutional. The court stated that the ruling did not affect the validity of the defendant's conviction of a capital crime but merely affected the imposition of the death sentence.

What Constitutes a Conviction

The North Carolina Supreme Court has not decided whether a capital felony conviction that is being appealed qualifies as a prior capital felony conviction under aggravating circumstance (e)(2).[32]

A plea of no contest and the entry of judgment imposing a sentence as a result of that plea will constitute a conviction as long as the no contest plea (in a North Carolina state court) was entered on or after July 1, 1975.[33]

Each prior conviction may be a separate aggravating circumstance.[34]

---

31. State v. Bunning, 338 N.C. 483 (1994) (defendant's Virginia conviction for first-degree murder was not an aggravating circumstance under (e)(2) because, at the time of the conviction, the Virginia Supreme Court had ruled that the death penalty was unconstitutional).

32. The court noted but did not decide the issue (under aggravating circumstance (e)(3) (previous conviction of violent felony)) in *State v. Silhan*, 302 N.C. 223 (1981). The Structured Sentencing Act specifically includes a conviction being appealed as a prior conviction for the purpose of sentencing. G.S. 15A-1340.11(7). If the state uses a conviction that is being appealed and the appeal is ultimately successful, any death sentence based in part on the conviction may be subject to attack. *See* Johnson v. Mississippi, 486 U.S. 578 (1988).

33. State v. Holden, 321 N.C. 125 (1987). Although Holden was decided under aggravating circumstance (e)(3) (previous conviction of violent felony), its ruling would apply as well to this aggravating circumstance. Although the court did not say so in *Holden*, a plea of no contest (at least in a North Carolina state court) must have been entered on or after July 1, 1975, to constitute a prior conviction, based on the reasoning in the later case of *State v. Outlaw*, 326 N.C. 467 (1990) (in deciding whether a no contest plea constituted a conviction under North Carolina Rule of Evidence 609, the court noted that July 1, 1975, was the effective date of G.S. 15A-1022(c), which requires that a judge must determine that there was a factual basis for a no contest plea; thus, this determination and the entry of judgment constitute an adjudication of guilt and a conviction). If a no contest plea was entered in a court other than a North Carolina state court, an examination of the court's procedures in taking such a plea may be necessary.

34. State v. Moseley, 338 N.C. 1 (1994). Although *Moseley* was decided under aggravating circumstance (e)(3) (previous conviction of violent felony), its ruling would apply as well to this aggravating circumstance.

In 1994, the General Assembly added the language in (e)(2) concerning juvenile adjudications. It applies only to sentencing for a first-degree murder committed on or after May 1, 1994, but both the conduct forming the basis of the juvenile adjudication and the adjudication itself may have occurred before May 1, 1994.[35]

Timing of the Prior Capital Felony

To qualify as a conviction for this aggravating circumstance, the capital felony must have been *committed* before the commission of the first-degree murder for which the defendant is being sentenced. However, the *conviction* of that capital felony may occur at any time before the trial of the first-degree murder for which the defendant is being sentenced.[36]

Method of Proof

A prior conviction under this aggravating circumstance may be proved by the original court judgment, a certified copy of the court judgment, a stipulation by the state and the defendant, an admission by the defendant during the trial or sentencing hearing, testimony by a state's witness, or any other reliable method. In addition, the state may offer evidence of the circumstances underlying the prior conviction. The North Carolina Supreme Court has stated that the defendant may not—by offering to stipulate to the prior conviction—foreclose the state's offer of other evidence.[37] Thus, the state may offer the testimony of witnesses and law enforcement officers about the crime that resulted in the prior conviction, although the trial judge may exercise his or her discretion to prevent the sentencing hearing from becoming a mini-trial about the prior capital felony.[38]

Case Summaries: Submission of (e)(3) Rather Than (e)(2)

State v. Prevatte, 356 N.C. 178 (2002). The defendant was convicted of capital murder in Georgia in 1974. He was subsequently convicted of first-degree murder in North Carolina. The state asked the trial judge to submit aggravating circumstance (e)(3) (previous conviction of violent felony) rather than (e)(2) "as a way of simplifying [issues regarding the constitutionality of the Georgia statute under which the defendant was sentenced]." The court agreed. This was permissible; the state's request did not diminish the "integrity of the capital sentencing scheme."

Case Summaries: Propriety of Submitting Multiple Aggravating Circumstances

State v. Flowers, 347 N.C. 1 (1997). A capital sentencing jury found aggravating circumstance (e)(2), based on a prior first-degree murder conviction in which the death penalty could have been imposed, and aggravating circumstance (e)(3) (previous conviction of violent felony), based on five other violent felony convictions arising from the same trial in which the first-degree

---

Two aggravating circumstances were found under (e)(2) for two prior murders in *State v. Braxton*, 352 N.C. 158 (2000), though the propriety of that finding was not at issue on appeal.

35. State v. Leeper, 356 N.C. 55 (2002). Although *Leeper* was decided under aggravating circumstance (e)(3) (previous conviction of violent felony), its ruling would apply as well to this aggravating circumstance. *See also* State v. Wiley, 355 N.C. 592 (2002) (no ex post facto violation in applying legislative amendment to adjudication occurring before May 1, 1994).

36. State v. Warren, 348 N.C. 80 (1998) (relying on similar rulings involving aggravating circumstance (e)(3) (previous conviction of violent felony), the court ruled that it was proper to submit aggravating circumstance (e)(2) even though the conviction for the prior capital felony occurred after the date of the murder for which the defendant was being sentenced).

37. State v. Cummings, 323 N.C. 181 (1988).

38. *Id.*

murder conviction had occurred. The court ruled that separate evidence properly supported these two aggravating circumstances. The court rejected the defendant's argument that the same evidence was used to support both aggravating circumstances because the first-degree murder and the other five felonies arose from the same transaction.

D. Aggravating Circumstance (e)(3): Defendant Previously Convicted of Violent Felony

G.S. 15A-2000(e)(3) states: "The defendant had been previously convicted of a felony involving the use or threat of violence to the person or had been previously adjudicated delinquent in a juvenile proceeding for committing an offense that would be a Class A, B1, B2, C, D, or E felony involving the use or threat of violence to the person if the offense had been committed by an adult." The constitutionality of this aggravating circumstance has been upheld.[39] This aggravating circumstance is similar to the noncapital aggravating circumstance set forth in G.S. 15A-1340.16(d)(18a), though the latter is limited to prior juvenile adjudications, presumably because prior adult convictions are reflected in the defendant's prior record level under Structured Sentencing.

What Constitutes a Violent Felony

To qualify under this circumstance, the felony offense may be either (1) one in which the use or threat of violence is an element of the felony, in which case proof that the defendant used violence in committing the offense is unnecessary,[40] or (2) one in which the use or threat of violence, although not an element, was involved in the commission of the offense.[41] An example of the latter would be a defendant convicted of committing a felonious breaking or entering while pointing a gun at the homeowner.[42] The use or threat of violence is not an element of felonious breaking or entering, but in the example, it was part of the commission of that offense. If a defendant's prior felony conviction occurred in a court other than a North Carolina state court, then the offense of conviction must also constitute a felony in North Carolina.[43] A conviction by a general court martial is included within (e)(3).[44]

Consider the following cases relevant to this issue.

State v. Garcell, 363 N.C. 10 (2009). At the defendant's capital sentencing hearing, the state introduced evidence that the defendant had previously been convicted of common law robbery and two counts of second-degree kidnapping. It did not introduce evidence about the facts surrounding the convictions, but a defense witness and defense counsel briefly stated that the three convictions arose from a single incident. The trial judge submitted a single (e)(3) aggravating circumstance and instructed the jury that it could consider any or all of the prior convictions when deciding whether to find the circumstance. The jury found the circumstance, and the defendant was sentenced to death. On appeal, he argued that the trial judge erred in submitting

39. State v. Brown, 320 N.C. 179 (1987) (holding that the definition of aggravating circumstance (e)(3) is not unconstitutionally vague or overbroad).

40. State v. Green, 336 N.C. 142 (1994).

41. State v. McDougall, 308 N.C. 1 (1983).

42. *Id.* The court in *McDougall* gave other examples in footnote 1 of its opinion.

43. State v. Taylor, 304 N.C. 249 (1983); *Green*, 336 N.C. 142.

44. *Green*, 336 N.C. 142.

the kidnapping convictions because "second-degree kidnapping does not by definition involve the use or threat of violence to the person." The state supreme court (1) stated that it had never squarely ruled on that issue and (2) noted the "well-reasoned conclusions of federal courts" as well as suggestions in its own precedents that kidnapping is inherently violent, but (3) declined to rule on the issue in the abstract because in this case, the defense testimony and statements of counsel showed that the kidnappings were "committed in the same course of action as the inherently violent crime of common law robbery," making the kidnappings violent as well. In any event, (4) any error would have been harmless because the common law robbery alone provided sufficient support for the finding of the circumstance.

State v. Morgan, 359 N.C. 131 (2004). The trial court submitted the (e)(3) aggravator based on the defendant's Georgia conviction of "robbery by sudden snatch." A former officer testified that the defendant grabbed a woman's purse; that she attempted to hold onto it; that they "fought"; and that he "slung her down" and made off with the purse. The North Carolina Supreme Court ruled that the aggravator was properly submitted: "While the act of purse snatching may not invariably involve the use or threat of violence, [the officer's] testimony as to the circumstances surrounding this prior felony was sufficient to prove that violence was actually used during the commission of the crime."

State v. Jones, 339 N.C. 114 (1994). Relying on *State v. McDougall,* 308 N.C. 1 (1983), the court ruled that the trial judge, in instructing the jury on aggravating circumstance (e)(3), did not err in stating that robbery is a felony that by definition involves the use or threatened use of violence. In this case, the defendant had been previously convicted of common law robbery.

State v. Keel, 337 N.C. 469 (1994). Involuntary manslaughter is a violent felony under (e)(3); a killing need not be intentional to constitute a violent felony.

State v. Holden, 338 N.C. 394 (1994). The defendant's conviction of attempted second-degree rape under North Carolina law was automatically a prior violent felony conviction under aggravating circumstance (e)(3); it was not necessary to present evidence that violence was used in committing the offense.

State v. Green, 336 N.C. 142 (1994). For submission of (e)(3) to be proper, the state's evidence must show that (1) the defendant had been convicted of a felony, (2) the felony for which the defendant was convicted involved the "use or threat of violence to the person," and (3) the conduct underlying the conviction occurred before the date of the first-degree murder being tried. The state need not show that the defendant in fact acted violently in the prior felony; it need only show that the prior felony involved the use *or threat of* violence. It is sufficient if the prior felony (a) has an element of the use or threat of violence to the person, such as rape or armed robbery, or (b) was actually committed by the use or threat of violence to the person. The defendant here was convicted of attempted rape by a general court martial. The court ruled that attempted rape was defined as a violent crime by military case law and therefore qualified as a prior violent felony conviction under (e)(3) without the necessity of a showing that the defendant used violence in committing the offense.

State v. Rose, 335 N.C. 301 (1994). (1) A Mississippi conviction of attempted rape, proved by certified court records, was sufficient evidence of a felony involving the "use or threat of violence to the person." Rape under Mississippi law involves the use or threat of violence to the person, since an element of the offense is forcible ravishment. And since attempted rape requires a direct act toward forcible ravishment, it involves the use or threat of violence. (2) The trial judge in this case did not err in peremptorily instructing the jury that if it found that the defendant had committed attempted rape, this would constitute a felony within aggravating circumstance (e)(3).

State v. Artis, 325 N.C. 278 (1989). An assault with intent to commit rape is, as a matter of law, an offense involving the use or threat of violence to the person.

State v. Brown, 320 N.C. 179 (1987). The defendant's conviction of discharging a firearm into occupied property was sufficient evidence of (e)(3).

State v. Hamlette, 302 N.C. 490 (1981). The defendant's conviction of armed robbery was sufficient to prove (e)(3), since this offense involves the threat or use of violence. The court rejected the defendant's argument that the state must prove that the defendant acted violently in committing this offense.

What Constitutes a Conviction

The North Carolina Supreme Court has not decided whether a felony conviction that is being appealed qualifies as a prior felony conviction under aggravating circumstance (e)(3).[45]

A plea of no contest and the entry of judgment imposing a sentence as a result of that plea constitute a conviction as long as the no contest plea (in a North Carolina state court) was entered on or after July 1, 1975.[46]

Each prior conviction may be a separate aggravating circumstance.[47] However, it is not error to submit multiple prior violent felony convictions in support of a single aggravating circumstance; the jury need not be unanimous with respect to the predicate conviction.[48]

In 1994, the North Carolina General Assembly added the language in G.S. 15A-2000(e)(3) concerning juvenile adjudications.[49] It applies only to sentencing for a first-degree murder committed on

---

45. The court noted but did not decide the issue in *State v. Silhan,* 302 N.C. 223 (1981). The Structured Sentencing Act specifically includes a conviction being appealed as a prior conviction for the purpose of sentencing; *see* G.S. 15A-1340.11(7). If the state uses a conviction that is being appealed, and the appeal is ultimately successful, any death sentence based on the conviction may be subject to attack. *See* Johnson v. Mississippi, 486 U.S. 578 (1988).

46. State v. Holden, 321 N.C. 125 (1987). Although the court did not say so in *Holden,* a plea of no contest (at least in a North Carolina state court) must have been entered on or after July 1, 1975, to constitute a prior conviction, based on the reasoning in the later case of *State v. Outlaw,* 326 N.C. 467 (1990) (in deciding whether a no contest plea constituted a conviction under North Carolina Rule of Evidence 609, the court noted that July 1, 1975, was the effective date of G.S. 15A-1022(c) (2001), which requires that a judge must determine that there was a factual basis for a no contest plea; thus, this determination and the entry of judgment constitute an adjudication of guilt and a conviction). If a no contest plea was entered in a court other than a North Carolina state court, an examination of the court's procedures in taking such a plea may be necessary.

47. State v. Larry, 345 N.C. 497 (1997); State v. Moseley, 338 N.C. 1 (1994).

48. State v. DeCastro, 342 N.C. 667 (1996) (disjunctive jury instruction concerning two violent felony convictions submitted as one aggravating circumstance was not error); *see also* State v. Garcell, 363 N.C. 10 (2009).

49. The statute is silent on (1) whether to classify offenses resulting in juvenile adjudications as they were classified under the Fair Sentencing Act (if the offenses occurred when that act was effective, on or after July 1, 1981, until September 30, 1994) and (2) how to classify offenses that were not classified at all (those offenses that occurred before the Fair Sentencing Act became effective on or after July 1, 1981). A likely interpretation is to classify all these offenses in the same way they are classified under the Structured Sentencing Act, as provided for sentencing under that act. *See* G.S. 15A-1340.14(c). Presumably, out-of-state adjudications would be classified as the same class to which they are substantially similar, with the state having the burden of proving that a particular out-of-state adjudication was substantially similar to a Class A through E felony under North Carolina law. *Cf.* G.S. 15A-1340.14(e).

or after May 1, 1994, but both the conduct forming the basis for the adjudication and the adjudication itself may have occurred before May 1, 1994.[50] A prosecutor who wants to use the record of a defendant's juvenile adjudications must follow the provisions of G.S. 7B-3000(f).[51] Adult convictions incurred while the defendant was under 18 years old may be used to support aggravating circumstance (e)(3).[52]

Consider the following cases concerning what constitutes a conviction for purposes of (e)(3).

State v. White, 355 N.C. 696 (2002). The court ruled that the defendant's felonious assault conviction, obtained when, as a juvenile, he was tried as an adult, was properly submitted under aggravating circumstance (e)(3).

Johnson v. Mississippi, 486 U.S. 578 (1988). The defendant was convicted of murder and sentenced to death in a Mississippi state court. One of the aggravating circumstances supporting the death sentence was the defendant's prior violent felony conviction in a New York state court. After the defendant's conviction and death sentence was affirmed by the Mississippi Supreme Court, the New York Court of Appeals reversed the defendant's New York conviction. The defendant then filed a motion in the Mississippi Supreme Court seeking to set aside the death sentence based on the reversal of his New York conviction. The court denied the motion, ruling that the New York conviction provided adequate support for the death sentence, even if it was invalid. The United States Supreme Court ruled that allowing the defendant's death sentence to remain in effect, based in part on the invalid New York conviction, violated the Eighth Amendment to the United States Constitution.

State v. Beal, 311 N.C. 555 (1984). The defendant's prior adjudication of rape as a (non-juvenile) youthful offender under the Alabama Youthful Offender Act was not a prior felony conviction under aggravating circumstance (e)(3). The court relied on the Alabama statutory provision (and case law interpreting that provision) that the youthful offender adjudication "shall not be deemed a conviction of crime."

Timing of the Prior Violent Felony

To qualify as a conviction for this aggravating circumstance, the prior violent felony must have occurred before the commission of the first-degree murder for which the defendant is being sentenced. However, the *conviction* of that violent felony may occur at any time before the trial of the first-degree murder for which the defendant is being sentenced.[53]

---

50. State v. Leeper, 356 N.C. 55 (2002); *see also* State v. Wiley, 355 N.C. 592 (2002) (no ex post facto violation in applying legislative amendment to adjudication occurring before May 1, 1994).

51. The statute provides in part that such a record may be used "only by order of the court in the subsequent criminal proceeding, upon motion of the prosecutor, after an in camera hearing to determine whether the record in question is admissible."

52. *Garcell*, 363 N.C. 10 (finding no constitutional bar to the use of convictions based on offenses committed by the defendant when he was 16 years and 2 days old); State v. White, 355 N.C. 696 (2002).

53. State v. Squires, 357 N.C. 529 (2003) (relying on *State v. Burke*, 343 N.C. 129 (1996), the court ruled that the conviction for the prior violent felony may take place after the defendant commits the first-degree murder); State v. Warren, 347 N.C. 309 (1997); State v. Lyons, 343 N.C. 1 (1996).

Method of Proof

A prior conviction under this aggravating circumstance may be proved by the original court judgment, a certified copy of the court judgment, a stipulation by the state and the defendant, an admission by the defendant during the trial or sentencing hearing,[54] testimony by a state's witness, or any other reliable method.

The following cases address the method of proof of prior convictions.

State v. Thompson, 359 N.C. 77 (2004). The trial judge submitted seven (e)(3) aggravating circumstances based on the defendant's seven prior convictions. Two of the circumstances were based on armed robberies of Bojangles restaurants, but the trial judge instructed the jury to consider whether the defendant had been convicted of armed robberies against "Billy Adams" and "April Dobbins," the Bojangles employees who were present during the crimes. On appeal, the defendant argued that the evidence showed armed robberies against Bojangles, not Adams and Dobbins, and that the court's instructions created a fatal variance, rendering the state's evidence insufficient. The North Carolina Supreme Court disagreed, noting that the essence of armed robbery is the danger to human life and that variances concerning the specific owner of the property taken are immaterial. The court stated that all the evidence showed that the defendant had been convicted of armed robberies that involved threatening the lives of Adams and Dobbins, supporting the jury's finding of the aggravating circumstances.

State v. Carroll, 356 N.C. 526 (2002). The defendant was convicted of first-degree murder and sentenced to death. The court ruled that the state properly proved a Florida robbery conviction to support aggravating circumstance (e)(3). The court noted that the North Carolina Rules of Evidence do not apply in a capital sentencing hearing. The state called a North Carolina deputy clerk who identified several documents as certified copies of Florida court records involving a person with a name different than the defendant. The documents included a set of fingerprints from the person who had been convicted of robbery in Florida. The state called a fingerprint expert who had compared those fingerprints with a set of the defendant's North Carolina fingerprints and testified that they were made by the same person. The court noted that even if the rules of evidence were applicable, the Florida documents would be admissible under Rule 902 (self-authenticating documents) and the fingerprint card would have been admissible as a business record under the hearsay exception set forth in Rule 803(6).

State v. McLaughlin, 341 N.C. 426 (1995). The defendant was convicted of first-degree murder and sentenced to death. During the sentencing hearing, the defendant stipulated that he had previously been convicted of involuntary manslaughter and that the crime involved the use of violence, thereby establishing aggravating circumstance (e)(3). The North Carolina Supreme Court ordered a new sentencing hearing based on an error in jury instructions. At the begin-

54. As to admissions by defense counsel, consider *State v. Al-Bayyinah,* 359 N.C. 741 (2005). In *Al-Bayyinah,* the state sought to submit three separate (e)(3) aggravating circumstances based on the defendant's three separate prior convictions. The defendant authorized his attorneys to admit the existence of the three convictions but not to admit that he had, in fact, committed the crimes. However, his attorneys essentially admitted the latter during closing arguments. On appeal, the defendant argued that this amounted to ineffective assistance of counsel. The state supreme court disagreed, noting (1) that it had previously ruled that *State v. Harbison,* 315 N.C. 175 (1985), does not apply to sentencing hearings, (2) that the defendant "did consent to the overall strategy of admitting the convictions themselves," *Al-Bayyinah,* 359 N.C. at 757, and (3) that given the convictions, the jury was certainly going to find the aggravating circumstances regardless of the exact wording of the defense arguments.

ning of the new sentencing hearing, the defendant moved to withdraw the stipulation. Without an objection from the state, the judge allowed the withdrawal. However, during the sentencing hearing, the state sought to reintroduce the stipulation after it presented eyewitness testimony about the circumstances of the shooting that led to the prior conviction. The court ruled that the stipulation was properly admitted into evidence. The court rejected the defendant's argument that it was an impermissible stipulation about a matter of law. The court concluded that although the stipulation used the language "involved the use of violence," this language addressed the factual circumstances supporting the prior conviction, rather than a legal standard.

State v. Thomas, 331 N.C. 671 (1992). An Administrative Office of the Courts Criminal Record Check form was insufficient evidence of a prior violent felony conviction based on facts in this case. The partially completed form contained a disclaimer that the office of the clerk "cannot guarantee that the records listed herein belong to the individual for whom such record is sought." Neither the file number nor the date of birth of the named person was provided.

State v. Cummings, 323 N.C. 181 (1988). The court stated that although a prior conviction may be proved by the original certified copy of the court record or by stipulation, the state is not precluded from other methods of proof.

State v. Holden, 321 N.C. 125 (1987). Proof of a no contest plea and a final judgment in which a sentence was imposed as a result of that plea constitute a conviction under aggravating circumstance (e)(3). Although the court did not say so in this case, a plea of no contest (at least in a North Carolina state court) must have been entered on or after July 1, 1975, to constitute a prior conviction, based on the reasoning in the later case of *State v. Outlaw*, 326 N.C. 467 (1990) (in deciding whether a no contest plea constituted a conviction under North Carolina Rule of Evidence 609, the court noted that July 1, 1975, was the effective date of G.S. 15A-1022(c), which requires that a judge must determine that there was a factual basis for a no contest plea; thus, this determination and the entry of judgment constitute an adjudication of guilt and a conviction). If a no contest plea was entered in a court other than a North Carolina state court, an examination of the court's procedures in taking such a plea may be necessary.

State v. Hamlette, 302 N.C. 490 (1981). The defendant's testimony during the guilt-innocence phase that he had been convicted of armed robbery five years before the commission of the murder being tried was sufficient proof of a prior conviction under aggravating circumstance (e)(3). *See also* State v. McLaughlin, 323 N.C. 68 (1988) (similar ruling).

Proof of Circumstances Underlying the Conviction

The state may offer evidence of the circumstances underlying the defendant's previous conviction. The North Carolina Supreme Court has stated that the defendant may not—by offering to stipulate to the prior conviction—foreclose the state's offer of other evidence.[55] Thus, the state may offer the testimony of civilian witnesses and law enforcement officers about the conduct that resulted in the prior conviction. The defendant may attempt to mitigate the previous felony conviction through cross-examination or the introduction of other evidence.[56] However, the trial judge may exercise his

---

55. State v. Moseley, 336 N.C. 710 (1994); State v. McDougall, 308 N.C. 1 (1983).

56. *See, e.g.,* State v. Valentine, 357 N.C. 512 (2003) (the sole aggravating circumstance submitted at the penalty phase was (e)(3), based on the defendant's prior conviction for a felony assault; the defendant sought to cross-examine the victim of the assault about an affidavit the victim had signed that stated that the defendant

or her discretion to prevent the sentencing hearing from becoming a mini-trial about the prior violent felony.[57] Confrontation Clause issues may arise when attempting to prove the facts supporting a prior violent felony conviction.[58]

The following cases pertain to the introduction of evidence of the facts underlying the defendant's prior violent felony convictions.

State v. Campbell, 359 N.C. 644 (2005). The state introduced evidence that the defendant had a prior conviction of second-degree kidnapping and also introduced evidence about "domestic violence that occurred before the kidnapping and . . . evidence from the victim that defendant kidnapped her at gunpoint, made her drive to South Carolina, and raped her." The defendant argued that second-degree kidnapping is an inherently violent offense and that it was therefore unnecessary and improper to admit evidence about the facts surrounding the conviction. The North Carolina Supreme Court ruled, based on prior cases, that the state was entitled to present evidence of the surrounding circumstances and was not limited to the fact of conviction.

State v. Bell, 359 N.C. 1 (2004). The state introduced, in support of the (e)(3) aggravating circumstance, (1) evidence that the defendant had previously been convicted of common law robbery and (2) evidence about the facts of the crime. Among other evidence, the state elicited testimony from a police officer about the statement provided by the victim of the robbery. The state supreme court ruled that the victim's statement was testimonial and that its admission violated the Confrontation Clause but that the error was harmless because the other evidence offered by the state sufficiently supported the aggravating circumstance.

State v. Valentine, 357 N.C. 512 (2003). The sole aggravating circumstance submitted at the penalty phase was (e)(3), based on the defendant's prior conviction for a felony assault. The defendant sought to cross-examine the victim of the assault about an affidavit the victim had signed that stated that the defendant had not committed the assault, but the trial court prohibited the cross-examination. This was error, and a new sentencing hearing was required. The defendant has a right to rebut and to mitigate evidence submitted by the state concerning (e)(3).

State v. Nobles, 357 N.C. 433 (2003). The trial judge submitted aggravating circumstance (e)(3) to the jury based on the defendant's prior rape conviction. In support of the aggravating circumstance, the state introduced the victim's testimony from the rape trial. This violated the Confrontation Clause, as the state did not establish the victim's unavailability for the capital

---

had not committed the assault, but the trial court prohibited the cross-examination; this was error, and a new sentencing hearing was required because the defendant has a right to rebut and to mitigate evidence submitted by the state concerning (e)(3)); State v. Carter, 357 N.C. 345, 352 (2003) (stating that "both the state and the defendant may introduce evidence concerning the circumstances surrounding the defendant's prior crimes when those prior crimes support aggravating circumstances").

57. *Carter*, 357 N.C. 345 (trial judge properly limited defendant's cross-examination concerning his prior violent felony conviction when it became repetitive); State v. Strickland, 346 N.C. 443 (1997); *McDougall*, 308 N.C. 1.

58. *See, e.g.*, State v. Bell, 359 N.C. 1 (2004) (the admission of testimony from a police officer about a statement provided by the victim of the defendant's prior violent felony violated the Confrontation Clause because the victim's statement was testimonial, but the error was harmless given the other evidence in the case); State v. Nobles, 357 N.C. 433 (2003) (the defendant had a prior rape conviction; the state introduced the victim's testimony from the rape trial; this violated the Confrontation Clause, as the state did not establish the victim's unavailability for the capital sentencing hearing by showing that it had made a good faith attempt to procure her presence). The applicability of the Confrontation Clause in capital sentencing hearings is discussed further in Chapter 4, page 119.

sentencing hearing by showing that it had made a good faith but unsuccessful attempt to procure her presence.

State v. Carter, 357 N.C. 345 (2003). The state called a witness to testify about the facts surrounding the defendant's prior violent felony conviction. The defendant cross-examined the witness about prior statements the witness had made to the police that varied somewhat from her testimony at the defendant's sentencing hearing. Eventually, the trial judge forbade "further inquiry" and prohibited the defense from introducing a police report that the witness had signed that was inconsistent with her trial testimony. On appeal, the defendant argued that these rulings were error. The state supreme court affirmed. Although "both the state and the defendant may introduce evidence concerning the circumstances surrounding the defendant's prior crimes when those prior crimes support aggravating circumstances," and the defendant is generally allowed to attempt to "temper" the evidence of his or her prior crimes, these rights are not unlimited. Here, the trial court properly cut off repetitive cross-examination and precluded the defendant from introducing extrinsic evidence about minor inconsistencies in the witness's story.

State v. Strickland, 346 N.C. 443 (1997). Under aggravating circumstance (e)(3), the state offered a wife's testimony about a defendant's prior felony conviction for assaulting her husband. Most of her testimony described the circumstances of the defendant's assault on her husband based on her observations of the assault. She also testified that she was afraid that the defendant would have cut her with a knife if given the chance and that she is reminded daily of the assault. The court ruled, relying on *State v. Moseley*, 336 N.C. 710 (1994), that the wife's testimony was proper to establish for the jury the severity of the defendant's attack on the husband and the fear that the defendant caused.

State v. Rose, 339 N.C. 172 (1994). The state was properly permitted to introduce evidence surrounding the defendant's prior violent felony convictions, even though it had offered certified court judgments of those convictions.

State v. Jones, 339 N.C. 114 (1994). The court rejected the defendant's argument that the trial judge erred in allowing so much evidence of aggravating circumstance (e)(3) that its probative value was outweighed by its prejudicial effect. Three victims of three prior violent felonies committed by the defendant testified at the present sentencing hearing.

State v. Moseley, 336 N.C. 710 (1994). The court ruled that the trial judge properly allowed testimony about the details of the defendant's prior violent felony convictions from the victim of those crimes, even though the evidence was graphic and the defendant had stipulated to the convictions. For a similar ruling, see *State v. McDougall*, 308 N.C. 1 (1983) (court disavowed dictum in *State v. Silhan*, 302 N.C. 223 (1981), that victim's testimony should ordinarily not be allowed unless necessary to show crime involved violence; court also stated trial judge had discretion to prevent determination of aggravating circumstance (e)(3) from becoming "minitrial" of the previous charge).

Jury Instructions

The pattern jury instruction for this aggravating circumstance asks the judge to determine whether the defendant's prior conviction is for a felony that, "by definition[] involve[s] the threat or use of violence to the person."[59] If the judge resolves that issue in the affirmative, i.e., determines that the offense has as an element the use or threat of violence, then the jury must only determine whether the defendant was, in fact, previously convicted of the felony in question. It need not separately determine whether the felony in question involves the use or threat of violence, for that issue has been resolved by the trial judge as a matter of law. The cases support this procedure.[60]

Case Summaries: Propriety of Submitting Multiple Aggravating Circumstances

State v. Flowers, 347 N.C. 1 (1997). A capital sentencing jury found aggravating circumstance (e)(2) (previous conviction of capital felony), based on a prior first-degree murder conviction in which the death penalty could have been imposed, and aggravating circumstance (e)(3), based on five other violent felony convictions arising from the same trial in which the first-degree murder conviction had occurred. The court ruled that separate evidence properly supported these two aggravating circumstances. The court rejected the defendant's argument that the same evidence was used to support both aggravating circumstances because the first-degree murder and the other five felonies arose from the same transaction.

State v. Rose, 339 N.C. 172 (1994). The court ruled that separate evidence supported submission of both (e)(3) and (e)(11) (course of violent conduct). A prior Alabama murder conviction supported (e)(3), and a murder committed in North Carolina during the murder for which the defendant was being sentenced supported (e)(11).

State v. Rich, 346 N.C. 50 (1997). Separate evidence supported (e)(1) (murder by incarcerated defendant) and (e)(3) and both were properly submitted. The defendant was lawfully incarcerated when he committed the murder, which supported (e)(1), and he had previously been convicted of second-degree murder and discharging a firearm into occupied property, which supported (e)(3).

E. Aggravating Circumstance (e)(4): Murder Committed to Prevent Arrest or to Effect Escape

G.S. 15A-2000(e)(4) states: "The capital felony was committed for the purpose of avoiding or preventing a lawful arrest or effecting an escape from custody." This circumstance is almost identical to the noncapital aggravating circumstance set forth at G.S. 15A-1340.16(d)(3). Appellate case law on this circumstance has focused primarily on whether there was sufficient evidence that the first-degree murder was committed to avoid or to prevent a lawful arrest. Generally, evidence is sufficient if the

59. N.C.P.I. Crim.—105.10.

60. *See, e.g.*, State v. Rose, 335 N.C. 301 (1994) (holding that the trial judge did not err in peremptorily instructing the jury that if it found that the defendant had committed attempted rape, this would constitute a felony within aggravating circumstance (e)(3)); State v. Artis, 325 N.C. 278 (1989) (holding that an assault with intent to commit rape is, as a matter of law, an offense involving the use or threat of violence to the person). *Cf.* State v. Holden, 346 N.C. 404 (1997) (the state introduced a judgment showing the defendant's prior conviction of attempted second-degree rape but did not introduce evidence of the underlying facts; the judge's jury instruction on aggravating circumstance (e)(3) was erroneous when it described the felony as involving the use of violence, leaving out the words "or threat," because under some circumstances, attempted rape may involve only the threat of violence; but the error did not rise to the level of plain error).

murder was committed to eliminate a witness to a crime or to prevent a law enforcement officer from arresting the defendant. This need not be the defendant's sole purpose in committing the murder, however.[61]

Evidence that a killing merely occurred is insufficient.[62] On the other hand, sufficient evidence may include a defendant's statements before, during, or after the murder that showed the need to kill the victim to prevent, for example, the revelation of another crime to law enforcement or others.[63] In multiple murders, this circumstance may exist when the defendant kills a second or third person to eliminate them as witnesses to the first killing.[64] This circumstance also may exist when the defendant kills the victim to prevent the arrest of the defendant's accomplice.[65] In some cases, the facts surrounding the murder and the manner of the killing may provide sufficient evidence of this circumstance even absent any express statement by the defendant regarding the purpose of the murder.[66]

Case Summaries: Sufficient Evidence of Aggravating Circumstance (e)(4)

State v. Goss, 361 N.C. 610 (2007). The defendant admitted that he killed the victim only after she stated that she was going to call the police, that he was "going to pay" for assaulting her, and that he was "going to jail." This was sufficient evidence to support the jury's finding of aggravating circumstance (e)(4).

State v. Fowler, 353 N.C. 599 (2001). The defendant was convicted of first-degree murder and sentenced to death. The court ruled, relying on *State v. Green*, 321 N.C. 594 (1988), that there was sufficient evidence of aggravating circumstance (e)(4). The murder was committed during an armed robbery. The court noted that there was no evidence that the victim either posed a threat to the defendant or tried to resist during the robbery. The defendant shot the victim from behind from close range with a .44 caliber handgun. The victim was on the ground when he was shot. The court stated that the jury could reasonably infer from these facts that the defendant shot the victim to avoid being apprehended.

State v. Hardy, 353 N.C. 122 (2000). The court ruled that there was sufficient evidence of aggravating circumstance (e)(4) involving a murder committed during an armed robbery. The court stated that the defendant's comment to a co-worker that "[the victim] won't be able to tell it" because "I'm going to kill him" could lead a reasonable jury to find that one purpose in killing the victim was to avoid apprehension.

State v. Lemons, 348 N.C. 335 (1998). The court reiterated its ruling in *State v. Hunt*, 323 N.C. 407 (1988), that aggravating circumstance (e)(4) may be proved by showing that the murder was committed to avoid or prevent a lawful arrest of the defendant's accomplice; it need not be the defendant's arrest. The court ruled that the evidence was sufficient in this case. Although the

61. State v. Hardy, 353 N.C. 122, 135 (2000) (stating that a trial judge may properly submit aggravating circumstance (e)(4) where there is substantial evidence "from which the jury can infer that at least one of defendant's purposes for the killing" was to prevent arrest or to effect escape).

62. State v. Reese, 319 N.C. 110 (1987).

63. *See, e.g.*, State v. McCollum, 334 N.C. 208 (1993). *But see* State v. Williams, 304 N.C. 394 (1981) (defendant's statements were insufficient).

64. *See, e.g.*, State v. McLaughlin, 323 N.C. 68 (1988); State v. Green, 321 N.C. 594 (1988).

65. State v. Lemons, 348 N.C. 335 (1998); State v. Hunt, 323 N.C. 407 (1988).

66. State v. Fowler, 353 N.C. 599 (2001) (where the defendant killed a prone and non-threatening victim after a robbery, the jury could properly infer that the purpose of the killing was to eliminate a witness).

defendant testified that one of his accomplices shot one of the murder victims, he conceded that she was killed to eliminate her as a witness to the earlier murder of the other victim.

State v. McCarver, 341 N.C. 364 (1995). The defendant told two people that he planned to rob an old man who worked at a cafeteria and who had testified against him on a prior occasion. The defendant also told one of these people that if the old man saw him, the defendant would have to kill him because he had testified against the defendant before and was certain to do so again. The defendant robbed and murdered the old man. The court ruled that this was sufficient evidence of aggravating circumstance (e)(4), since one of the defendant's purposes for the murder was the desire to eliminate a witness who the defendant believed would testify against him.

State v. Gregory, 340 N.C. 365 (1995). The defendant was convicted of the murders of A and B. The court ruled that there was sufficient evidence of (e)(4) for both murders. Shortly after the defendant choked and snapped the neck of victim A until she was dead, he told an accomplice that he killed her "so we would never have to go to prison." After victim B screamed, the defendant told an accomplice to "take care of business" and instructed him to use a shotgun instead of a pistol "because if you use the pistol you are going to have to shoot her three or four times."

State v. McCollum, 334 N.C. 208 (1993). The defendant and his accomplices each raped an 11-year-old child. One of the accomplices then said, "we got to kill her to keep her from telling the cops on us." The defendant then participated in killing her. The court ruled that the defendant's actions after his accomplice's statement were evidence of his adoption of the accomplice's stated motive for killing her. Therefore, this was sufficient evidence of aggravating circumstance (e)(4).

State v. Hunt, 323 N.C. 407 (1988). (1) The evidence was sufficient to support aggravating circumstance (e)(4) in the defendant's murder trial for killing victim B when the defendant aided and abetted the co-defendant in killing victim B to avoid being arrested for the murder of victim A. The defendant was aware that victim B was talking to people about the murder of victim A. He also said after the killing of victim B, "That man was about to cause me to pull a life sentence." (2) The court rejected the defendant's argument that the submission of (e)(4) was improper because the motive for killing victim B was the factual basis for (e)(4). The court noted that the defendant's motive was not an element of the murder, and the ruling in *State v. Cherry*, 298 N.C. 86 (1979) (merger rule involving felony murder and use of underlying felony as an aggravating circumstance), did not preclude its use as an aggravating circumstance. (3) Aggravating circumstance (e)(4) may be found if the defendant acted with the purpose of avoiding his arrest or the arrest of his co-defendant, who was his accomplice in committing the murder.

State v. McLaughlin, 323 N.C. 68 (1988). The defendant was convicted of the murders of A (on March 26, 1984), B (on April 29, 1984), and C (on April 29, 1984). Aggravating circumstance (e)(4) was properly found in the sentencing hearing for the murders of B and C. The evidence showed that the defendant and his accomplice killed B to prevent her from exposing their involvement in killing A. They then killed C to prevent her from identifying them as the men who murdered B, her mother.

State v. Green, 321 N.C. 594 (1988). In a first-degree murder prosecution for the murders of A, B, and C at a bar, the trial judge properly submitted aggravating circumstance (e)(4) in the murder of C, since the evidence showed that C (who was shot while in a defenseless position) was killed to eliminate him as a witness in the killings of A and B. The court rejected the defendant's argument that (e)(4) may be found only when the defendant stated before the killing that a fear of arrest was a motivating factor for the killing. The court reviewed prior cases and stated that (e)(4) has been upheld in two situations: when the murder was committed to prevent the murder victim from capturing the defendant and when the murder was committed to eliminate a witness.

State v. Holden, 321 N.C. 125 (1987). The defendant's statements that he would have to kill a woman he raped so she would not tell anyone were sufficient evidence of (e)(4).

State v. Oliver, 309 N.C. 326 (1983). This case involved two murder defendants, Moore and Oliver, who were sentenced to death. The court noted that it had approved the submission of (e)(4) when there was evidence that one of the purposes of the murder was defendant Oliver's desire to avoid detection and apprehension for some underlying crime (in this case, armed robbery). The evidence was sufficient in defendant Moore's case in the murder of the armed robbery victim because Moore said (in recounting the incident to a fellow inmate) "you would have to be crazy to leave any witnesses." The evidence was also sufficient in defendant Oliver's case for his murder of a bystander to the robbery who was outside the store where the robbery occurred. The evidence was insufficient, however, in defendant Oliver's case for the murder of the armed robbery victim because Moore's statement was inadmissible against Oliver: it was made after the conspiracy had ended and other evidence was insufficient to show that Oliver intended to eliminate the victim as a witness.

State v. Goodman, 298 N.C. 1 (1979). There was sufficient evidence to support (e)(4) when, after the victim was shot and cut but before he was killed, the defendant stated that he "was afraid if the police found [the victim] that he would tell what had been done to him."

Case Summaries: Insufficient Evidence of Aggravating Circumstance (e)(4)

State v. Reese, 319 N.C. 110 (1987). There was insufficient evidence of aggravating circumstance (e)(4) when the only evidence to support it was the killing itself.

State v. Oliver, 309 N.C. 326 (1983). See the above discussion of this case, in which the court found that the evidence was insufficient for aggravating circumstance (e)(4) in defendant Oliver's case for the murder of the armed robbery victim.

State v. Williams, 304 N.C. 394 (1981). The defendant was convicted of the murder and armed robbery of a convenience store employee. The court ruled that the evidence was insufficient to submit (e)(4). The defendant's statement, as related by a state's witness, that he wanted to leave the convenience store parking lot at a slow rate of speed to avoid attracting attention did not support an inference that one purpose motivating the killing was the defendant's desire to avoid later detection and apprehension for his robbery. This statement was made after the killing and likely reflected the defendant's wish to avoid detection. However, the statement did not show his motivation before or at the time of the killing.

Case Summaries: Propriety of Submitting Multiple Aggravating Circumstances

State v. Maness, 363 N.C. 261 (2009). The court ruled that it was not plain error for the trial judge to submit both (e)(4) and (e)(8) (murder of law enforcement officer or specified others performing duties) where the defendant killed a law enforcement officer to avoid arrest. *See also* State v. Polke, 361 N.C. 65 (2006) (similar).

State v. Berry, 356 N.C. 490 (2002). The court ruled that the trial judge did not err in submitting both (e)(4) and (e)(11) (course of violent conduct). The (e)(4) aggravating circumstance focused on the defendant's motive for killing victim A—to prevent her from talking about the defendant's murder of victim B that he had committed seven weeks earlier. The (e)(11) aggravating circumstance required the jury to review the objective facts of the two murders to determine whether the offenses constituted a course of conduct.

State v. Golphin, 352 N.C. 364 (2000). The court ruled, relying on *State v. Hutchins,* 303 N.C. 321 (1981), that the trial judge did not err in submitting both (e)(4) and (e)(8) (murder of law enforcement officer or specified others performing duties). The two circumstances were directed at distinct aspects of the charged crimes. The (e)(4) circumstance was supported by the defendants' motivation to avoid arrest for the theft of a vehicle. The (e)(8) circumstance involved the two murdered officers' official duties: one officer had stopped one of the defendants for not wearing a seat belt and the other officer had assisted the first officer. *See also* State v. Nicholson, 355 N.C. 1 (2002) (similar ruling).

State v. Sanderson, 336 N.C. 1 (1994). Distinguishing *State v. Quesinberry,* 319 N.C. 228 (1987), the court ruled that the trial judge properly submitted, and the jury could properly find, both the (e)(4) and (e)(5) (murder during a specified felony, here, a kidnapping) aggravating circumstances because these circumstances were supported by different evidence.

State v. Green, 321 N.C. 594 (1988). The court ruled that the submission of both (e)(4) and (e)(11) (course of violent conduct) was proper; they were not based on the same evidence. The (e)(11) circumstance concerned the factual circumstances of the defendant's crimes, while the (e)(4) circumstance concerned the defendant's motive in shooting a person in a defenseless position to eliminate him as a witness in the killings of two other people.

State v. Hutchins, 303 N.C. 321 (1981). It was not error to submit both (e)(4) and (e)(8) (murder of law enforcement officer or specified others performing duties). The court stated that it is not error to submit multiple aggravating circumstances if the inquiry prompted by their submission is directed at distinct aspects of the defendant's character or the crime for which the defendant is to be punished. The (e)(4) circumstance focuses on the defendant's motivation in pursuing a course of conduct. The (e)(8) circumstance focuses on the factual circumstances of the crime. The court distinguished its ruling in *State v. Goodman,* 298 N.C. 1 (1979), discussed immediately below.

State v. Goodman, 298 N.C. 1 (1979). There was sufficient evidence to support aggravating circumstance (e)(4) when, after the victim was shot and cut but before he was killed, the defendant stated that he "was afraid if the police found [the victim] that he would tell what had been done to him." The defendant and an accomplice then planned to bury the victim. Later they decided to shoot him and to place him on a railroad track where his body would be mangled by a passing train. However, it was error to submit both (e)(4) and (e)(7) (murder to hinder governmental function or law enforcement), since they were based on the same evidence. This resulted in an automatic accumulation of aggravating circumstances against the defendant.

F. Aggravating Circumstance (e)(5): Murder Committed During Specified Felony

G.S. 15A-2000(e)(5) states: "The capital felony was committed while the defendant was engaged, or was an aider or abettor, in the commission of, or an attempt to commit, or flight after committing or attempting to commit, any homicide, robbery, rape or a sex offense, arson, burglary, kidnapping, or aircraft piracy or the unlawful throwing, placing, or discharging of a destructive device or bomb." This aggravating circumstance applies to a defendant who commits first-degree murder while also committing, attempting to commit, or fleeing after committing or attempting to commit specified felonies.[67]

Felony Murder and (e)(5)

If the jury convicts the defendant of first-degree murder based solely on the felony murder theory, aggravating circumstance (e)(5) may not be submitted at the sentencing hearing based on the underlying felony or felonies submitted as a basis for felony murder.[68] If the jury convicts the defendant of first-degree murder based on premeditation and deliberation as well as felony murder, then (e)(5) based on the felony involved in the felony murder may be submitted at the sentencing hearing.[69] If both theories—premeditation and deliberation and felony murder—are submitted and the jury convicts the defendant of first-degree murder without specifying which theory or theories support its verdict, then (e)(5) may not be submitted at the sentencing hearing based on the underlying felony or felonies submitted under the felony murder theory.[70]

When a defendant pleads guilty without limitation to first-degree murder, he or she is guilty of all theories of first-degree murder that are supported by sufficient evidence.[71] Thus, if evidence supports both a theory of felony murder and a theory of premeditation and deliberation, then the submission of aggravating circumstance (e)(5) for the underlying felony of felony murder would be proper.

Consider the following cases regarding the relationship between the theory or theories supporting the first-degree murder conviction and the propriety of submitting (e)(5).

> **Schiro v. Farley, 510 U.S. 222 (1994).** The jury returned on a verdict sheet a verdict of guilty of felony murder (based on rape) but left blank its verdict on the charge of intentional murder. The trial judge imposed a death sentence, finding as a statutory aggravating factor that the defendant intentionally killed the victim while committing rape. (1) The United States Supreme Court rejected the defendant's argument that the Double Jeopardy Clause was violated because his

---

67. The meaning of some of the terms used in G.S. 15A-2000(e)(5) is not completely clear. For example, it is uncertain whether indecent liberties is a "sex offense" or whether that term refers only to the "sexual offenses" set out in G.S. 14-27.2 *et seq.*

68. State v. Taylor, 304 N.C. 249 (1981); State v. Oliver, 302 N.C. 28 (1981); State v. Cherry, 298 N.C. 86 (1979). However, these rulings do not appear to bar the use under (e)(5) of another felony or other felonies that were not submitted to the jury under the felony murder theory at the guilt phase if there is sufficient evidence to support its/their submission. *See* State v. Richardson, 342 N.C. 772 (1996) (proper to submit armed robbery under aggravating circumstance (e)(5) when defendant was convicted of first-degree murder based solely on felony murder theory and the only underlying felony supporting the conviction was first-degree rape). In addition, if the jury specifically indicated in its verdict that it found two felonies to support the felony murder theory, it would appear that one of them could be submitted to support aggravating circumstance (e)(5).

69. State v. Rook, 304 N.C. 201 (1981). Of course, any other felony or felonies not submitted to the jury under the felony murder theory at the guilt phase also could be submitted under aggravating circumstance (e)(5) if there is sufficient evidence to support its/their submission.

70. State v. Silhan, 302 N.C. 223 (1981).

71. State v. Meyer, 353 N.C. 92 (2000); State v. Johnson, 298 N.C. 47 (1979); *Silhan*, 302 N.C. 223.

sentencing proceeding constituted a successive prosecution for intentional murder. The clause does not apply to a single prosecution in which a sentencing hearing follows a trial. (2) The Court did not address the defendant's argument that principles of collateral estoppel would bar the use of the "intentional murder" aggravating factor because the defendant failed to meet his burden of establishing the factual predicate for applying those principles. That is, the defendant failed to establish that the jury's act in leaving the verdict blank for intentional murder was an acquittal of that theory of murder.

State v. Stroud, 345 N.C. 106 (1996). The defendant was convicted of murder based on the theories of torture and felony murder, with kidnapping as the underlying felony. The court ruled that it was proper to submit kidnapping to support aggravating circumstance (e)(5).

State v. Richardson, 342 N.C. 772 (1996). The defendant was convicted of first-degree murder based solely on the felony murder theory, and the only underlying felony supporting the conviction was first-degree rape. The court ruled that it was proper to submit armed robbery to support aggravating circumstance (e)(5).

State v. Upchurch, 332 N.C. 439 (1992). The jury convicted the defendant of first-degree murder based on premeditation and deliberation but rejected first-degree murder based on felony murder (first-degree burglary). However, the jury convicted the defendant of first-degree burglary. The court ruled, based on *State v. Cherry*, 298 N.C. 86 (1979), that the trial judge properly submitted aggravating circumstance (e)(5) based on burglary.

State v. Reese, 319 N.C. 110 (1987). The defendant was convicted of first-degree murder based on the theories of premeditation and deliberation and felony murder, and the underlying felony was armed robbery. On appeal, the court ruled that there was insufficient evidence of premeditation and deliberation to support the first-degree murder conviction based on that theory. Therefore, the submission of aggravating circumstance (e)(5) based on armed robbery was error.

State v. Rook, 304 N.C. 201 (1981). When the defendant was convicted of first-degree murder on both premeditation and deliberation and felony murder theories, the trial judge did not err in submitting aggravating circumstance (e)(5) based on rape, which was the underlying felony of the felony murder theory. For similar rulings, see *State v. Gregory*, 340 N.C. 365 (1995); *State v. Davis*, 340 N.C. 1 (1995); *State v. Sexton*, 336 N.C. 321 (1994); *State v. McNeil*, 324 N.C. 33 (1989); *State v. Williams*, 308 N.C. 47 (1983); and *State v. Goodman*, 298 N.C. 1 (1979).

State v. Silhan, 302 N.C. 223 (1981). If both a premeditation and deliberation theory and a felony murder theory are submitted and the jury convicts the defendant of first-degree murder without specifying which theory or theories support its verdict, then aggravating circumstance (e)(5) may not be submitted based on the underlying felony or felonies submitted under the felony murder theory.

State v. Oliver, 302 N.C. 28 (1981). When a defendant is convicted of first-degree murder based solely on the felony murder theory, the trial judge may not submit the underlying felony used in the felony murder theory as an aggravating circumstance under (e)(5). In this case, the trial judge erred in submitting (e)(5) based on armed robbery when the defendants were convicted of first-degree murder based on the felony murder theory only, and armed robbery was the underlying felony. *See also* State v. Taylor, 304 N.C. 249 (1981) (similar ruling but error was harmless beyond a reasonable doubt); State v. Cherry, 298 N.C. 86 (1979).

Connection between Murder and the Specified Felony

Evidence is sufficient to support aggravating circumstance (e)(5) even if the felony is committed after the murder victim is killed, as long as the felony occurs during a continuous series of events surrounding the victim's death.[72] For example, (e)(5) based on the felony of armed robbery may be submitted to the jury if the evidence shows that the defendant took a person's wallet after shooting and killing the person, and this is so even if the taking is an afterthought to the murder rather than its motive.[73]

Consider the following cases on this issue.

> **State v. Campbell, 359 N.C. 644 (2005).** The defendant and the victim were seen together at a liquor store one evening. The next evening, the defendant "was in possession of the victim's car, wallet, boom box, and other personal property," the victim was dead in his home, the defendant had the victim's blood on his pants, and the defendant's DNA was in the victim's home. The defendant was convicted of felony murder based on robbery. The North Carolina Supreme Court ruled that the evidence, although circumstantial, was sufficient to support the conviction. The jury could reasonably infer that the murder and the robbery were part of the same continuous transaction. For the same reason, the evidence was sufficient to support the (e)(5) aggravating circumstance, which was submitted based on the robbery. (The defendant was also convicted of first-degree murder on the theory of premeditation and deliberation.)
>
> **State v. Haselden, 357 N.C. 1 (2003).** The defendant shot and killed a neighbor, stealing her purse, clothes, and car. He was convicted of first-degree murder based on premeditation and deliberation and on felony murder, as well as armed robbery. Aggravating circumstance (e)(5) was submitted and found based on the robbery. On appeal, the defendant claimed that there was insufficient evidence of the aggravating circumstance because there was no evidence that the taking of the victim's property was part of a continuous transaction with the murder. The North Carolina Supreme Court disagreed, finding that the defendant's own statements before the crime, to the effect that he wanted to take someone's car at gunpoint, provided the necessary connection.
>
> **State v. Holden, 346 N.C. 404 (1997).** The defendant was sentenced to death at a capital resentencing hearing. The court ruled that four prior unadjudicated sexual assaults, virtually identical to the circumstances surrounding the attempted rape of the murder victim, were properly admitted to show intent in proving aggravating circumstance (e)(5) (here, murder committed during attempted rape). The court also ruled that the defendant's offer to stipulate to intent to commit rape did not bar the state from offering this evidence.
>
> **State v. Richardson, 342 N.C. 772 (1996).** The court ruled that the state is not required to prove that the commission of the felony constituting aggravating circumstance (e)(5) was the motivation for the murder, rejecting the defendant's argument that "the (e)(5) circumstance excludes robberies committed as afterthoughts." It is sufficient evidence of (e)(5) that the felony and the murder were part of the same criminal transaction.
>
> **State v. Carter, 338 N.C. 569 (1994).** The court ruled that the evidence was sufficient to submit (e)(5) based on the felony of attempted rape. When the murder victim's body was discovered, her left pant leg was completely off, her panties were down, and her bra was above her breasts.

72. State v. Robbins, 319 N.C. 465 (1987).
73. State v. Richardson, 342 N.C. 772 (1996).

She had multiple abrasions and lacerations. Blood of the same type as the victim's was on the defendant's clothes. In addition, there was evidence that the defendant raped another woman shortly after he committed the murder. This evidence was sufficient to support the inferences that the defendant knocked the murder victim to the ground and forcibly removed her pants and panties in an attempt to rape her.

State v. Jennings, 333 N.C. 579 (1993). There was sufficient evidence in this case to submit (e)(5) when the felony was sexual offense (penetrating the murder victim's anus with an object by force and against the victim's will).

State v. McDowell, 329 N.C. 363 (1991). The (e)(5) aggravating circumstance was erroneously submitted because there was insufficient evidence of the underlying felony of attempted armed robbery. *See also* State v. Irwin, 304 N.C. 93 (1981) (similar ruling; insufficient evidence of underlying felony of kidnapping).

State v. Robbins, 319 N.C. 465 (1987). There was sufficient evidence to support the finding of aggravating circumstance (e)(5) based on armed robbery. Relying on *State v. Fields*, 315 N.C. 191 (1985), the court ruled that the intent to steal and the taking of property may occur after the victim is killed, as long as the taking occurred during a continuous transaction with the killing of the victim. However, the jury found existence of (e)(5) based on *both* armed robbery *and* first-degree kidnapping, but the reviewing court ruled that evidence of first-degree kidnapping was insufficient. Thus, the submission of kidnapping as a basis for (e)(5) was error. The court ruled that the defendant was entitled to a new sentencing hearing.

Finding of Multiple (e)(5) Circumstances

The jury may properly find multiple circumstances under (e)(5) if they are supported by separate evidence. For example, the jury may properly find two aggravating circumstances under (e)(5) based on a murder committed while the defendant was committing first-degree rape and first-degree sexual offense, even though these felonies were committed against the same victim.[74]

The following cases address the propriety of submitting multiple (e)(5) aggravating circumstances.

State v. Murrell, 362 N.C. 375 (2008). The defendant told several acquaintances that he was planning to commit a robbery. He approached the victim, who was seated in his parked car, and shot him. The defendant took control of the vehicle, placed the victim in the passenger seat, and began driving. The victim was still alive, so the defendant shot him again. The defendant stole the victim's watch and money. This was sufficient to support two (e)(5) aggravating circumstances, one for armed robbery and one for kidnapping.

State v. Smith, 359 N.C. 199 (2005). The defendant entered the victim's home, choked him into unconsciousness, bound his wrists and ankles, covered his face with tape, pushed him under a bed, and left him to die of asphyxiation while the defendant ransacked his house. At the defendant's capital sentencing proceeding, the trial judge submitted aggravating circumstance (e)(5) twice, once for kidnapping and once for robbery. The defendant argued on appeal that the aggravating circumstances were based on the same evidence and were duplicative. The North Carolina Supreme Court ruled that separate evidence supported each circumstance because the

74. State v. Moseley, 338 N.C. 1 (1994); *see also* State v. Cheek, 351 N.C. 48 (1999) (robbery and kidnapping); State v. Bond, 345 N.C. 1 (1996) (kidnapping of victim A, kidnapping of victim B, and robbery).

"binding and taping [of the victim] was not an inherent, inevitable part of the robbery. Rather, these forms of restraint exposed the victim to a greater danger than that inherent in the robbery and constituted a kidnapping."

State v. Cheek, 351 N.C. 48 (1999). The defendant and his accomplice abducted a taxicab driver in Jacksonville, put her in the taxicab's trunk, and drove the taxicab to Wilmington. The accomplice then shot the victim and set fire to the taxicab, and the victim died. The court ruled, relying on *State v. Trull*, 349 N.C. 428 (1998), that the trial judge properly submitted both kidnapping and armed robbery as separate aggravating circumstances under (e)(5).

State v. Moseley, 338 N.C. 1 (1994). The court ruled that the jury properly found two statutory aggravating circumstances under (e)(5) because the murder here was committed while the defendant was engaged in the commission of (1) first-degree sexual offense and (2) first-degree rape. Both aggravating circumstances were supported by distinct and separate evidence, even though they involved the same victim. *See also* State v. Bond, 345 N.C. 1 (1996) (separate evidence supported three aggravating circumstances for three felonies committed during murder).

Relationship between Aggravating Circumstances (e)(5) and (e)(6)

The North Carolina Supreme Court has ruled that both (e)(5) and (e)(6) (murder for pecuniary gain) may not be submitted if the motive for the felony supporting (e)(5) is pecuniary gain. For example, if the defendant killed the victim during the course of a robbery in which the defendant sought the victim's money and the defendant was convicted of first-degree murder based on both a theory of premeditation and deliberation and a theory of felony murder, then the trial judge may submit to the jury either (e)(5) (based on the robbery) or (e)(6), but not both.[75] If, however, the defendant was convicted of first-degree murder based only on the felony murder theory and the underlying felony was robbery, the trial judge does not have a choice of which of the two circumstances to submit to the jury—the judge may only submit (e)(6).[76]

The North Carolina Supreme Court has upheld the submission of both (e)(5) and (e)(6) when separate evidence supports each. For example, in *State v. East*,[77] the defendant committed two murders in the course of stealing money from the victims and also in stealing the keys to the victims' car. While pecuniary gain was the motive in stealing the money, which supported (e)(6), there was no evidence that the motive for the theft of the car keys was pecuniary gain. The defendant stole the keys so he could use the car as transportation either to visit his girlfriend or to evade law enforcement, not to sell the car and convert it to cash. Thus, the theft of the keys supported robbery under (e)(5), and this evidence was separate from the evidence supporting (e)(6).

The following cases address the relationship between aggravating circumstances (e)(5) and (e)(6).

State v. Raines, 362 N.C. 1 (2007). The defendant lived with a friend and the friend's wife. One night, he killed the couple and stole their guns, credit cards, checks, and truck. At the penalty phase of his capital trial, the trial judge submitted aggravating circumstances (e)(5) and (e)(6). This was proper because "the trial court instructed the jury to consider only the theft of the firearms, credit cards, and checks in determining whether the (e)(6) . . . circumstance was

75. State v. Quesinberry, 319 N.C. 228 (1987).
76. *Id.*; State v. Oliver, 302 N.C. 28 (1981).
77. 345 N.C. 535 (1997).

present and to not consider the vehicle theft in making that determination. As to . . . (e)(5) . . . the trial court instructed the jury to consider only the evidence related to the theft of the truck."

State v. Miller, 357 N.C. 583 (2003). The defendant and an accomplice asked the victim for a ride. When the victim agreed, the defendant drew a knife and forced the victim to drive to a remote area. The defendant and his accomplice killed the victim and stole money he had been planning to deposit in a bank. The trial judge submitted aggravating circumstances (e)(5) and (e)(6). The basis for (e)(5) was kidnapping, for the purpose of facilitating robbery. Citing the factually similar case of *State v. Call*, 349 N.C. 382 (1998), the North Carolina Supreme Court held that this was proper because (e)(5) concerns the factual circumstances of the crime, while (e)(6) concerns the defendant's motive. [*Author's note*: To the extent that the court's reasoning suggests that it is generally permissible to submit (e)(5) and (e)(6) on the same evidence, *Miller* is inconsistent with *State v. Quesinberry*, 319 N.C. 228 (1987), discussed below, and its progeny.]

State v. White, 355 N.C. 696 (2002). The court ruled that separate evidence supported the submission of both (e)(5) and (e)(6). The theft of the victim's keys and car supported (e)(5). The defendant stole the car for transportation, not to sell it. The defendant's theft of the victim's money supported (e)(6). Thus, separate, independent evidence supported submission of these aggravating circumstances. The court noted that the jury instructions properly limited the jury's consideration of the evidence supporting each circumstance.

State v. Davis, 353 N.C. 1 (2000). The court ruled, citing *State v. Gay*, 334 N.C. 467 (1993), and other cases, that the trial judge did not err in submitting both (e)(5) and (e)(6) because they were not supported by the same evidence. The jury instructions carefully distinguished between the property that was the subject of the armed robbery aggravating circumstance and the different property that was the subject of the pecuniary gain aggravating circumstance.

State v. East, 345 N.C. 535 (1997). The court ruled that it was proper to submit aggravating circumstances (e)(5) and (e)(6) because these circumstances were supported by separate evidence. The court noted that the defendant murdered the victims while engaged in two robberies. The defendant committed the murders not only in the course of stealing money from the victims, but also in the course of stealing the keys to the victims' car. While there was evidence of a pecuniary gain motive in stealing the money, there was no evidence that the motive for the theft of the car keys was pecuniary gain. The evidence showed that the defendant stole the keys to use the car as transportation either to visit his girlfriend or to evade law enforcement, not to sell the car and convert it into cash. Thus, the theft of money supported (e)(6) and the theft of the keys supported (e)(5).

State v. Howell, 335 N.C. 457 (1994). Relying on *State v. Quesinberry*, 319 N.C. 228 (1987), the court ruled that the trial judge erred in submitting both (e)(5) and (e)(6) when these aggravating circumstances were supported by the same evidence. In this case, pecuniary gain was the motive for committing the burglary that supported (e)(5).

State v. Quesinberry, 319 N.C. 228 (1987). The defendant was convicted of first-degree murder based on premeditation and deliberation and felony murder, the underlying felony being armed robbery. The jury found both aggravating circumstances (e)(5) and (e)(6). The court ruled that the circumstances were redundant since the motive of pecuniary gain provided the impetus for the robbery itself, and therefore it was error to submit both circumstances to the jury. *See also* State v. Davis, 325 N.C. 607 (1989) (similar ruling).

Case Summaries: Propriety of Submitting Multiple Aggravating Circumstances

State v. Waring, 364 N.C. 443 (2010). The defendant and an accomplice stole the victim's wallet, raped her, and murdered her by stabbing her repeatedly. The trial judge submitted aggravating circumstances (e)(5) (here, murder during a rape), (e)(6) (murder for pecuniary gain), and (e)(9) (especially heinous, atrocious, or cruel). Separate evidence supported each submission, and the prosecutor's argument did not ask the jury to find more than one aggravating circumstance based on the same evidence.

State v. Elliott, 360 N.C. 400 (2006). The defendant raped and murdered an elderly woman and stole her possessions. He was convicted of, inter alia, first-degree felony murder based on the rape and first-degree burglary. At his capital sentencing proceeding, the trial judge submitted the (e)(5) aggravating circumstance based on the burglary, and the jury found it. The trial judge also submitted, and the jury also found, aggravating circumstance (e)(9) (especially heinous, atrocious, or cruel). Although some of the evidence supporting (e)(5) and (e)(9) overlapped, the evidence was not completely overlapping; it was therefore proper to submit both circumstances.

State v. Tirado, 358 N.C. 551 (2004). The defendant and others stole a car from victim A, shooting her nonfatally. Then they stole a car from victims B and C, forcing the victims into the trunk and later stealing their jewelry and killing them. The trial judge did not plainly err in submitting aggravating circumstances (e)(5) (based on the kidnapping of victims B and C), (e)(6) (murder for pecuniary gain, based on the theft of jewelry from victims B and C), and (e) (11) (course of violent conduct, based, as to each murder, on the others). Separate evidence supported each aggravating circumstance.

State v. Miller, 357 N.C. 583 (2003). The defendant and an accomplice asked the victim for a ride. When the victim agreed, the defendant drew a knife and forced the victim to drive to a remote area. The defendant and his accomplice killed the victim and stole money he had been planning to deposit in a bank. The trial judge submitted aggravating circumstances (e)(5) and (e)(6) (murder for pecuniary gain). The basis for (e)(5) was kidnapping, for the purpose of facilitating robbery. Citing the factually similar case of *State v. Call*, 349 N.C. 382 (1998), the North Carolina Supreme Court held that this was proper because (e)(5) concerns the factual circumstances of the crime, while (e)(6) concerns the defendant's motive. [See the author's note regarding this section of the court's opinion in the section above concerning the relationship between aggravating circumstances (e)(5) and (e)(6).] The trial judge also submitted aggravating circumstance (e)(9) (especially heinous, atrocious, or cruel). The supreme court ruled that separate evidence supported (e)(5) and (e)(9): beyond the kidnapping, the "defendant made the victim take off his clothes, put a ball into the victim's mouth, and put electrical tape around the victim's head to secure the ball . . . completely cut[ting] off the victim's oxygen supply. . . . Defendant then stabbed the victim ten to 30 times while the victim was alive."

State v. Holmes, 355 N.C. 719 (2002). "In this case, separate evidence supported both the (e)(5) and (e)(11) [course of violent conduct] aggravating circumstances. The jury found defendant guilty of the first-degree murder of [victim A], the attempted first-degree murder of [victim B], and robbery with a firearm. Based upon these verdicts, separate, independent evidence supported each aggravating circumstance: the robbery supported the (e)(5) aggravating circumstance, while the attempted murder of [victim B] supported the (e)(11) aggravating circumstance."

State v. Smith, 347 N.C. 453 (1998). The defendant was convicted of first-degree murder for setting fire to an apartment building by lighting kerosene, killing one person and seriously injuring others. Distinguishing *State v. Quesinberry*, 319 N.C. 228 (1987), the court ruled that aggravating circumstances (e)(5) (here, murder committed while defendant engaged in arson) and (e)(10) (use of hazardous to endanger multiple others) were both properly submitted to the jury because they addressed different aspects of the defendant's murder, although they both relied on the same evidence. Aggravating circumstance (e)(5) addresses the fact that the defendant committed murder while engaging in another felony, arson. Aggravating circumstance (e)(10) addresses a distinct aspect of the defendant's character—he not only intended to kill a particular person when setting fire to the apartment building, but he also disregarded the value of every human life in the building by using an accelerant to set the fire in the middle of the night.

State v. Daughtry, 340 N.C. 488 (1995). The court ruled that separate evidence supported the submission of aggravating circumstances (e)(5) (here, murder committed during commission of a sex offense) and (e)(9) (especially heinous, atrocious, or cruel). Evidence supporting (e)(5) showed that some object had been inserted into the victim's rectum or vagina. Evidence supporting (e)(9) showed severe blunt trauma wounds to the head and many abrasions about her body.

State v. Conaway, 339 N.C. 487 (1995). The court reviewed the evidence at the sentencing hearing and ruled that separate substantial evidence supported each of the following three aggravating circumstances in a double murder case: (e)(5) (here, murder committed during the commission of kidnapping), (e)(6) (murder for pecuniary gain, by taking money from a cash register during an armed robbery), and (e)(11) (course of violent conduct, by killing multiple victims).

State v. Rouse, 339 N.C. 59 (1994). Separate evidence supported the submission of both (e)(5) (here, murder committed during attempted rape and attempted armed robbery) and (e)(9) (especially heinous, atrocious, or cruel). The victim was stabbed seventeen times and suffered for fifteen minutes as she lost half of her blood. The court noted that evidence supporting each aggravating circumstance may overlap as long as the same evidence doesn't support more than one aggravating circumstance.

State v. Sanderson, 336 N.C. 1 (1994). Distinguishing *State v. Quesinberry*, 319 N.C. 228 (1987), the court ruled that the trial judge properly submitted, and the jury could properly find, both (e)(4) (murder to prevent arrest or effect escape) and (e)(5) (here, murder committed while the defendant was engaged in a kidnapping) because these circumstances were supported by different evidence.

State v. Gibbs, 335 N.C. 1 (1993). The trial judge did not err in submitting both aggravating circumstance (e)(5) (here, murder during the course of a burglary) and aggravating circumstance (e)(11) (course of violent conduct). These circumstances were not supported by the same evidence. Proof that the defendant committed a murder during the burglary did not also require proof of the commission of violence toward the other victims (two other people were murdered). And the defendant need not have engaged in a violent course of conduct to have committed a murder in the course of the burglary.

State v. Jennings, 333 N.C. 579 (1993). The trial judge properly submitted two aggravating circumstances—(e)(5) (here, murder during a sex offense) and (e)(9) (especially heinous, atrocious, or cruel)—because they were not based on the same evidence. There was substantial evidence of the especially heinous, atrocious, or cruel nature of the murder (the savage beating of the victim) apart from the evidence that the murder was committed while attempting to penetrate the victim's anus with an object.

State v. Vereen, 312 N.C. 499 (1985). Considering the jury instructions in this case, the trial judge erred in submitting two aggravating circumstances because they were based on the same evidence, namely, the attempted rape of the murder victim's daughter. The jury instruction for the first aggravating circumstance, (e)(5), set out that the murder was committed while the defendant committed the crime of first-degree burglary *or attempted rape.* The jury instruction for the second, (e)(11) (course of violent conduct), set out that the murder was part of a course of conduct that included the defendant's commission of violent crimes against others, including felonious assault *and attempted rape.*

Case Summaries: Miscellaneous Matters

State v. Polke, 361 N.C. 65 (2006). The defendant shot and killed an officer who was attempting to arrest him. He also shot a second officer, who survived. After the defendant was sentenced to death, he argued on appeal that the evidence at trial supported aggravating circumstance (e)(5), apparently on the theory that the murder took place during the defendant's attempted murder of the second officer. The defendant further argued that the trial judge's failure to submit an aggravating circumstance that was supported by the evidence was arbitrary and constituted structural error requiring the defendant's death sentence to be vacated. The state supreme court disagreed, holding that even if the evidence supported the submission of (e)(5), failure to do so was not structural error.

State v. Davis, 353 N.C. 1 (2000). The court ruled that the trial judge's jury instruction (which was not the pattern jury instruction) on (e)(5) was erroneous. The instruction did not require that the murder must have been committed while the defendant was engaged in the commission of an armed robbery.

G. Aggravating Circumstance (e)(6): Murder Committed for Pecuniary Gain

G.S. 15A-2000(e)(6) states: "The capital felony was committed for pecuniary gain." This aggravating circumstance has been upheld over several constitutional challenges.[78]

Connection between the Murder and the Pecuniary Gain

Aggravating circumstance (e)(6) applies when a motive for the first-degree murder is pecuniary gain—for example, when a defendant kills a person to facilitate a theft, a defendant is paid to kill a person, or a defendant kills a person to obtain life insurance proceeds. Financial gain need not be the defendant's

78. State v. Jennings, 333 N.C. 579 (1993) (jury instruction not unconstitutionally vague); State v. Williams, 317 N.C. 474 (1986) (finding aggravating circumstance (e)(6) in a case where the defendant was convicted of first-degree murder based solely on the felony murder theory—the underlying felony was armed robbery—did not violate the Eighth Amendment; a killing committed for pecuniary gain is a circumstance that effectively differentiates between all people convicted of first-degree murder and those few who are deserving of the death penalty); State v. Oliver, 309 N.C. 326 (1983) (aggravating circumstance (e)(6) not unconstitutionally vague).

sole, or even primary, motivation.[79] Nor must the defendant actually succeed in obtaining anything of value as a result of the murder.[80] Finally, if the defendant commits a murder for another reason, then takes or attempts to take the victim's property opportunistically after the fact, this aggravating circumstance does not apply.[81]

Consider the following cases, which address the connection between the murder and the pecuniary gain sought.

State v. Taylor, 362 N.C. 514 (2008). The defendant and an accomplice robbed a small grocery store. A gunfight broke out between the proprietors and the robbers. One of the proprietors died. The defendant was convicted of first-degree murder both by premeditation and by felony murder, as well as two counts of armed robbery. At sentencing, the jury found aggravating circumstance (e)(6). (1) The trial judge did not commit plain error in instructing the jury that it could find the circumstance if, "when the defendant killed the victim . . . he intended or expected to obtain money or other things of value" as a result. (2) The prosecutor's argument to the jury—"you have already found that aggravating circumstance [(e)(6)] because you have found the defendant guilty of conspiracy to commit robbery of the store and also robbery of the store"—was not so grossly improper as to require the trial judge to intervene ex mero motu. (Note, however, that the argument misstated applicable law.) (3) Given the "abundant" evidence supporting aggravating circumstance (e)(6), defense counsel did not render ineffective assistance of counsel by briefly conceding the issue in closing argument. (4) Because aggravating circumstance (e)(6) concerns the defendant's motive, there is no "requirement that the defendant actually take money from the victim," i.e., that the defendant succeed in obtaining pecuniary gain.

State v. Murrell, 362 N.C. 375 (2008). The defendant told several acquaintances that he was planning to commit a robbery and that he knew of a "chop shop" where he could take a stolen vehicle. He approached the victim, who was seated in his parked car, and shot him, eventually making off with the vehicle. At the penalty phase of the defendant's capital trial, the judge instructed the jury that if it found "that when the defendant killed the victim, the defendant took or intended to take the victim's automobile," then it should find aggravating circumstance (e)(6). The defendant argued that the instruction allowed the jury to find the circumstance even if it concluded that the taking of the vehicle was a mere act of opportunism after a murder committed for another reason. The state supreme court disagreed, noting that the trial judge had also instructed "that the pecuniary gain must have been '[obtained] as compensation for committing [the murder]' or '[intended or expected] as a result of the death of the victim.'"

State v. Allen, 360 N.C. 297 (2006). The defendant shot and killed a friend while walking through a forest, perhaps after some sort of disagreement. The defendant then took the victim's truck, which he soon sold, and had his girlfriend steal the victim's wallet and ATM card from his residence. At the penalty phase of the defendant's trial, the jury found aggravating circumstance (e)(6). On appeal, the defendant argued that the evidence was insufficient to support the circumstance because he did not take almost $2,000 in cash that the victim was carrying. The state supreme court rejected this argument and affirmed, noting that the victim was armed and

79. State v. Davis, 353 N.C. 1 (2000).

80. *See, e.g.,* State v. Taylor, 362 N.C. 514 (2008).

81. Aggravating circumstance (e)(5) (murder during a specified felony) often will apply on these facts, as the taking will often constitute an armed robbery. *See supra* notes 72–73 and accompanying text.

apparently survived the shooting for some period of time, and thus "the jury could have reasonably believed defendant did not take the money because of fear of his victim."

State v. Bell, 359 N.C. 1 (2004). The defendant and two accomplices assaulted the victim, stole her car, eventually forced her into the trunk, took her purse, and killed her. At the penalty phase of the defendant's capital trial, the judge submitted aggravating circumstance (e)(5) (murder during a specified felony), on the basis of the kidnapping and the related larceny of the car, and aggravating circumstance (e)(6), on the basis of the theft of the purse and the money it contained. The defendant argued on appeal that the evidence was insufficient to support (e)(6), but the North Carolina Supreme Court disagreed: "The . . . defendant wished to leave Newton Grove but had no car and no job. . . . [I]n order to leave town, defendant needed a means of transportation and money to finance his trip. It is reasonable to infer . . . that defendant acted for his own pecuniary gain when he kidnapped the victim . . . and took her money. While obtaining a car may have been defendant's primary motivation, it may be reasonably inferred from the evidence that he was also motivated by the need for money." Further, "[t]he fact that defendant killed the victim after he had obtained the money from her purse is irrelevant. . . . The hope of pecuniary gain motivated the murder which was ultimately committed in an effort to enjoy the fruits of the crime" by preventing the victim from contacting law enforcement.

State v. Maske, 358 N.C. 40 (2004). The defendant was convicted of first-degree murder based on premeditation and deliberation and felony murder, the felony being robbery. After killing the victim, the defendant took personal property from the apartment where the victim lived. The court ruled that the trial judge erred in instructing on aggravating circumstance (e)(6). After quoting from the pattern jury instruction's general description of the aggravating circumstance, the trial judge stated, "If you find from the evidence beyond a reasonable doubt that when the defendant killed the victim, the defendant took $200 from the victim's purse, you would find this aggravating circumstance . . . ." The court stated that while the general description of the aggravating circumstance was a correct statement of the law, the quoted sentence removed from the jury the requirement that it make a finding as to whether there was a connection between the killing and the taking of something of value. Because the instruction allowed the jury to find the aggravating circumstance even if the taking had no causal relationship to the killing—in other words, if the taking was a "mere act of opportunism committed after a murder was perpetrated for another reason"—it was erroneous.

State v. Jones, 357 N.C. 409 (2003). The defendant was convicted of two counts of first-degree felony murder, based on the underlying felony of armed robbery. The state supreme court ruled that the trial judge committed plain error in instructing the jury on aggravating circumstance (e)(6), by stating in part that "[i]f you find from the evidence beyond a reasonable doubt . . . that when the defendant killed the victim, the defendant was in the commission of robbery with a deadly weapon, you would find this aggravating circumstance . . ." The court noted that the judge's instruction failed to explain what would constitute pecuniary gain and erroneously stated that the jury's finding of robbery with a dangerous weapon would automatically mandate the finding of this aggravating circumstance.

State v. Chandler, 342 N.C. 742 (1996). The defendant was convicted of first-degree murder based solely on the felony murder theory, and the underlying felony was first-degree burglary. The court ruled that the trial judge properly submitted aggravating circumstance (e)(6) because the evidence showed that the defendant broke into and entered the victim's home with the intent to steal. The court stated that it was irrelevant whether the defendant wanted to steal the victim's purse or marijuana to satisfy his drug dependency because the burglary was motivated by pecuniary gain in either event. The court also ruled that (e)(6) was properly submitted even though the underlying felony was first-degree burglary and one of its elements was larceny. Pecuniary gain under (e)(6) reflects the motive for committing the murder, and pecuniary gain is not an element of first-degree burglary.

State v. Daniels, 337 N.C. 243 (1994). The evidence was sufficient to support aggravating circumstance (e)(6). The defendant confessed that he intended to and did ask the victim for money. When the victim did not give it to him, he killed her and then took money from her purse. For additional cases finding sufficient evidence of (e)(6), see *State v. Carter*, 342 N.C. 312 (1995); *State v. Alston*, 341 N.C. 198 (1995); *State v. Hunt*, 323 N.C. 407 (1988); and *State v. Jerrett*, 309 N.C. 239 (1983).

State v. Bacon, 337 N.C. 66 (1994). The evidence was sufficient to support aggravating circumstance (e)(6) when the defendant was to share in the proceeds of insurance money to be paid to his accomplice, the wife of the murder victim.

State v. Moore, 335 N.C. 567 (1994). The evidence was sufficient to support (e)(6) when the defendant sought to be named executor of the murder victim's will and obtained a one-third share of the insurance proceeds plus her distribution from the estate, all as a direct result of the victim's death. It is not required for the submission of this aggravating circumstance that the defendant's primary motivation for the murder is financial gain.

State v. McLaughlin, 323 N.C. 68 (1988). The evidence was sufficient to support (e)(6) when the defendant was paid to murder the victim.

State v. Oliver, 309 N.C. 326 (1983). The (e)(6) aggravating circumstance was properly submitted. Although the first-degree murder verdict was supported by the felony murder theory of armed robbery, "double jeopardy does not preclude the submission of pecuniary gain when the underlying felony is armed robbery." *See also* State v. Taylor, 304 N.C. 249 (1981); State v. Irwin, 304 N.C. 93 (1981). Nor is aggravating circumstance (e)(6) unconstitutionally vague.

State v. Oliver, 302 N.C. 28 (1981). The defendant murdered a convenience store employee during an armed robbery. After leaving the store, the defendant murdered a bystander who was there to purchase gas. The court rejected the defendant's argument that aggravating circumstance (e)(6) should not be submitted for the murder of the bystander because the money had already been obtained from the convenience store employee. The court concluded that the hope of pecuniary gain provided the impetus for the murder of both victims. This hope and the two murders were inextricably intertwined.

Relationship between Aggravating Circumstances (e)(5) and (e)(6)

The North Carolina Supreme Court has ruled that both (e)(5) (murder during a specified felony) and (e)(6) may not both be submitted if the motive for the felony supporting (e)(5) is pecuniary gain. For example, if the defendant killed the victim during the course of a robbery in which the defendant sought the victim's money and the defendant was convicted of first-degree murder based on both a theory of premeditation and deliberation and a theory of felony murder, then the trial judge may submit to the jury either (e)(5) (based on the robbery) or (e)(6), but not both.[82] If, however, the defendant was convicted of first-degree murder based only on the felony murder theory and the underlying felony was robbery, the trial judge does not have a choice of which of the two circumstances to submit to the jury—the judge may only submit (e)(6).[83]

The North Carolina Supreme Court has upheld the submission of both (e)(5) and (e)(6) when separate evidence supports each. For example, in *State v. East*,[84] the defendant committed two murders in the course of stealing money from the victims and also in stealing the keys to the victims' car. While pecuniary gain was the motive in stealing the money, which supported (e)(6), there was no evidence that the motive for the theft of the car keys was pecuniary gain. The defendant stole the keys so he could use the car as transportation either to visit his girlfriend or to evade law enforcement, not to sell the car and convert it to cash. Thus, the theft of the keys supported robbery under (e)(5), and this evidence was separate from the evidence supporting (e)(6).

The following cases address the relationship between aggravating circumstances (e)(5) and (e)(6).

State v. Raines, 362 N.C. 1 (2007). The defendant lived with a friend and the friend's wife. One night, he killed the couple and stole their guns, credit cards, checks, and truck. At the penalty phase of his capital trial, the trial judge submitted aggravating circumstances (e)(5) and (e)(6). This was proper because "the trial court instructed the jury to consider only the theft of the firearms, credit cards, and checks in determining whether the (e)(6) . . . circumstance was present and to not consider the vehicle theft in making that determination. As to . . . (e)(5) . . . the trial court instructed the jury to consider only the evidence related to the theft of the truck."

State v. Miller, 357 N.C. 583 (2003). The defendant and an accomplice asked the victim for a ride. When the victim agreed, the defendant drew a knife and forced the victim to drive to a remote area. The defendant and his accomplice killed the victim and stole money he had been planning to deposit in a bank. The trial judge submitted aggravating circumstances (e)(5) and (e)(6). The basis for (e)(5) was kidnapping for the purpose of facilitating robbery. Citing the factually similar case of *State v. Call*, 349 N.C. 382 (1998), the North Carolina Supreme Court held that this was proper because (e)(5) concerns the factual circumstances of the crime, while (e)(6) concerns the defendant's motive. [*Author's note*: To the extent that the court's reasoning suggests that it is generally permissible to submit (e)(5) and (e)(6) on the same evidence, *Miller* is inconsistent with *State v. Quesinberry*, 319 N.C. 228 (1987), discussed below, and its progeny.]

State v. White, 355 N.C. 696 (2002). The court ruled that separate evidence supported the submission of both (e)(5) and (e)(6). The theft of the victim's keys and car supported (e)(5). The defendant stole the car for transportation, not to sell it. The defendant's theft of the victim's money supported (e)(6). Thus, separate, independent evidence supported submission of these aggravating circumstances. The court noted that the jury instructions properly limited the jury's consideration of the evidence supporting each circumstance.

State v. Davis, 353 N.C. 1 (2000). The court ruled, citing *State v. Gay*, 334 N.C. 467 (1993), and other cases, that the trial judge did not err in submitting both (e)(5) and (e)(6). The jury instructions carefully distinguished between the property that was the subject of the armed robbery

82. State v. Quesinberry, 319 N.C. 228 (1987).
83. *Id.*; State v. Oliver, 302 N.C. 28 (1981).
84. 345 N.C. 535 (1997).

aggravating circumstance and the different property that was the subject of the pecuniary gain aggravating circumstance.

State v. East, 345 N.C. 535 (1997). The defendant was convicted of two murders. The court ruled that it was proper to submit aggravating circumstances (e)(5) and (e)(6) because these circumstances were supported by separate evidence. The court noted that the defendant murdered the victims while engaged in two robberies. The defendant committed the murders not only in the course of stealing money from the victims, but also in the course of stealing the keys to the victims' car. While there was evidence of a pecuniary gain motive in stealing the money, there was no evidence that the motive for the theft of the car keys was pecuniary gain. The evidence showed that the defendant stole the keys to use the car as transportation either to visit his girlfriend or to evade law enforcement, not to sell the car and convert it into cash. Thus, the theft of money supported (e)(6) and the theft of the keys supported (e)(5).

State v. Howell, 335 N.C. 457 (1994). Relying on *State v. Quesinberry*, 319 N.C. 228 (1987), discussed immediately below, the court ruled that the trial judge erred in submitting both (e)(5) and (e)(6) when these aggravating circumstances were supported by the same evidence. In this case, pecuniary gain was the motive for committing the burglary.

State v. Quesinberry, 319 N.C. 228 (1987). The defendant was convicted of first-degree murder based on premeditation and deliberation and felony murder, the underlying felony being armed robbery. Both aggravating circumstances (e)(5) and (e)(6) were submitted and found by the jury. The court ruled that the circumstances were redundant, since the motive of pecuniary gain provided the impetus for the robbery itself, and therefore it was error to submit both circumstances to the jury. Only one of the circumstances should have been submitted. *See also* State v. Davis, 325 N.C. 607 (1989) (similar ruling).

Case Summaries: Propriety of Submitting Multiple Aggravating Circumstances

State v. Waring, 364 N.C. 443 (2010). The defendant and an accomplice stole the victim's wallet, raped her, and murdered her by stabbing her repeatedly. The trial judge submitted aggravating circumstances (e)(5) (murder during a specified felony, in this case, rape), (e)(6), and (e)(9) (especially heinous, atrocious, or cruel). Separate evidence supported each, and the prosecutor's argument did not ask the jury to find more than one aggravating circumstance based on the same evidence.

State v. Tirado, 358 N.C. 551 (2004). The defendant and others stole a car from victim A, shooting her nonfatally. Then they stole a car from victims B and C, forcing the victims into the trunk and later stealing their jewelry and killing them. The trial judge did not plainly err in submitting aggravating circumstances (e)(5) (murder during a specified felony, based on the kidnapping of victims B and C), (e)(6) (based on the theft of jewelry from victims B and C), and (e)(11) (course of violent conduct, based, as to each murder, on the others). Separate evidence supported each aggravating circumstance.

State v. Jones, 327 N.C. 439 (1990). Distinguishing *State v. Quesinberry*, 319 N.C. 228 (1987), discussed above, the court ruled that the submission of aggravating circumstances (e)(6) and (e)(11) (course of violent conduct) was proper. The aggravating circumstances were not improperly supported by the same evidence. Evidence of the robbery of a convenience store employee supported (e)(6). Evidence that the defendant killed the victim, wounded another, and fired shots endangering others supported (e)(11).

State v. Conaway, 339 N.C. 487 (1995). The court reviewed the evidence at the sentencing hearing and ruled that separate substantial evidence supported each of the following three aggravating circumstances in this double murder case: (e)(5) (murder during a specified felony, in this case kidnapping), (e)(6) (pecuniary gain by taking money from a cash register during an armed robbery), and (e)(11) (course of violent conduct, by killing multiple victims).

H. Aggravating Circumstance (e)(7): Murder Committed to Hinder Governmental Function or Law Enforcement

G.S. 15A-2000(e)(7) states: "The capital felony was committed to disrupt or hinder the lawful exercise of any governmental function or the enforcement of laws." This aggravating circumstance is substantially identical to the noncapital aggravating circumstance set forth at G.S. 15A-1340.16(d)(5). This aggravating circumstance may apply when a defendant commits a murder to prevent (1) a law enforcement officer from arresting the defendant, (2) a person from giving information to law enforcement about the defendant's criminal offenses, or (3) a potential witness from testifying against the defendant.[85] Of course, similar evidence often will also support aggravating circumstance (e)(4) (murder to prevent arrest or effect escape). However, if the same evidence supports both (e)(7) and (e)(4), only one of the aggravating circumstances may be submitted to the jury.[86] Aggravating circumstance (e)(7) has been discussed only infrequently in appellate cases, suggesting that prosecutors or judges may typically prefer to submit (e)(4) when the same evidence could support either circumstance.[87]

Case Summaries: Aggravating Circumstance (e)(7)

State v. Anthony, 354 N.C. 372 (2001). The defendant was convicted of first-degree murder and sentenced to death for the murder of his wife. A domestic violence protective order had been issued after the murder victim had filed a domestic violence complaint against the defendant. The victim was murdered on the day before she was scheduled to return to court. The defendant was aware of this hearing and was extremely upset about it. Although the court ruled that there was evidence to support the submission of both aggravating circumstances (e)(7) and (e)(8) (murder of law enforcement officer or specified others performing duties, in this case, murder of witness because of exercise of official duty as witness), the court also ruled that the trial judge erred in submitting both aggravating circumstances because they were based on the same evidence. Both circumstances referred to the domestic violence matter previously initiated by the murder victim and scheduled for hearing the day after the murder. The relationship between the defendant, the murder victim, and their children was one reason that the victim had instituted the action and why she was to be a witness at the upcoming hearing. The court distinguished *State v. Gray*, 347 N.C. 143 (1997), discussed immediately below, in which the court upheld the submission of both (e)(7) and (e)(8). [*Author's note*: The statements in *Gray* about the kind of evidence that may support aggravating circumstance (e)(8) were disavowed in *State v. Long*, 354 N.C. 534 (2001). See the discussion of *Long* under aggravating circumstance (e)(8), below.]

---

85. *See generally, e.g.*, State v. Goodman, 298 N.C. 1 (1979); State v. Maynard, 311 N.C. 1 (1984) (Frye, J., concurring and dissenting).

86. *Goodman*, 298 N.C. 1.

87. One possible reason for this is that (e)(4) may be submitted together with (e)(8) (murder of law enforcement officer or specified others performing duties) based on the same evidence, while (e)(7) may not be submitted together with (e)(8) based on the same evidence.

State v. Gray, 347 N.C. 143 (1997). The court ruled that sufficient evidence supported aggravating circumstance (e)(7) where the defendant killed his wife to "disrupt[] . . . divorce proceedings." The defendant had refused to answer interrogatories in the divorce case concerning the parties' finances and had been served with an order to answer the interrogatories or show cause why he should not be held in contempt. Discovery was to have been completed one week after the defendant killed his wife. The evidence showed that the defendant was determined that his wife get nothing from the marriage; he had liquidated marital property and put the proceeds in his name. The court ruled that the jury could reasonably find that one reason he killed his wife was to stop the divorce action against him. [*Author's note*: The court's statements about the kind of evidence that may support aggravating circumstance (e)(8) (murder of law enforcement officer or specified others performing duties) were disavowed in *State v. Long*, 354 N.C. 534 (2001). See the discussion of *Long* under aggravating circumstance (e)(8), below.]

State v. Gregory, 340 N.C. 365 (1995). The court ruled that the judge's instruction on aggravating circumstance (e)(7), based on the pattern jury instruction, was not error.

State v. Goodman, 298 N.C. 1 (1979). There was sufficient evidence to support aggravating circumstance (e)(4) (murder to prevent arrest or effect escape) when, after the victim was shot and cut but before he was killed, the defendant stated that he "was afraid if the police found [the victim] that he would tell what had been done to him." The defendant and an accomplice then planned to bury the victim. Later they decided to shoot him and place him on a railroad track where his body would be mangled by a passing train. However, it was error to submit both (e)(4) and (e)(7) because they were based on the same evidence. The submission of both was an unnecessary duplication of circumstances that resulted in an automatic accumulation of aggravating circumstances against the defendant.

I. Aggravating Circumstance (e)(8): Murder Committed Against Law Enforcement Officer or Specified Others

G.S. 15A-2000(e)(8) states: "The capital felony was committed against a law enforcement officer, employee of the Division of Adult Correction of the Department of Public Safety, jailer, fireman, judge or justice, former judge or justice, prosecutor or former prosecutor, juror or former juror, or witness or former witness against the defendant, while engaged in the performance of his official duties or because of the exercise of his official duty." This aggravating circumstance is similar to the noncapital aggravating circumstance set forth in G.S. 15A-1340.16(d)(6), although the latter encompasses several additional categories of persons.

In *State v. Long*,[88] the North Carolina Supreme Court ruled that this aggravating circumstance has two prongs. It applies when a member of one of the groups listed in the statute is killed (1) while engaged in the performance of his or her official duties (the "engaged in" prong) or (2) because of the exercise of his or her official duty (the "because of" prong).

To submit the "engaged in" prong, the state must show that the victim was actively engaged at the time of the murder in performing a duty expected of a member of the protected group. For example, if the victim was a witness against the defendant in a pending case, the state would need to show that

88. 354 N.C. 534 (2001).

at the time of the murder, the victim was engaged in an activity such as swearing out a warrant, discussing the case with a prosecutor, going to court to testify, or actively testifying. The court explicitly disavowed language in *State v. Gray*[89] that implied that a witness is engaged in his or her official duties from the time the witness swears out a warrant until the witness completes his or her testimony.

To submit the "because of" prong, the state must show that the defendant's motivation for killing the victim was that he or she was performing a duty expected of a member of the protected group.

The North Carolina Supreme Court has ruled that this aggravating circumstance applies to the murder of a law enforcement officer who was working off-duty, in uniform, pursuant to department regulations, and was killed while performing law enforcement–related duties.[90] Although the state supreme court has not decided whether this circumstance requires proof that the defendant knew or had reasonable grounds to know that the victim was a member of the protected group, the state court of appeals has interpreted the similar noncapital aggravating circumstance not to require such knowledge with respect to the "engaged in" prong.[91]

The court has also ruled that it is permissible for a jury to find both (e)(8) and (e)(4) (murder to prevent arrest or effect escape) because these circumstances focus on different aspects of sentencing. Aggravating circumstance (e)(4) focuses on the defendant's motivation, while (e)(8) focuses on the factual circumstances of the murder.[92]

Case Summaries: Aggravating Circumstance (e)(8)

State v. Carter, __ N.C. App. __, 711 S.E.2d 515 (2011). The defendant, injured in a melee at a nightclub, sprayed the assembled crowd indiscriminately with bullets, killing a law enforcement officer who had responded to the fracas. The defendant was convicted of second-degree murder, and the jury found the noncapital aggravating circumstance set forth in G.S. 15A-1340.16(d)(6), which is similar to capital aggravating circumstance (e)(8). Deciding an issue of first impression, the state court of appeals ruled that the "engaged in" prong was properly submitted, regardless of whether the defendant knew that the victim was a law enforcement officer. In an extensive analysis, the court reasoned that the "engaged in" prong focuses on objective facts, and so "does not require the State to prove that the defendant knew or reasonably should have known that the victim was a member of the protected class."

State v. Augustine, 359 N.C. 709 (2005). The defendant told acquaintances that he wanted to shoot a police officer because the defendant's brother had recently been sentenced to prison. The defendant proceeded to shoot an officer fatally with no warning and no provocation. This evidence "fully support[ed]" aggravating circumstance (e)(8).

State v. Long, 354 N.C. 534 (2001). The defendant lived with his mother and had a history of violently abusing her. As a result of one incident, the defendant was charged with assault on a female. Five days before the trial on that charge was scheduled to begin, the defendant fatally assaulted his mother. At his capital sentencing hearing, the trial judge submitted aggravating circumstance (e)(8) on the theory that the defendant had killed his mother while she was "engaged in" her official duties as a witness against him. On appeal, the defendant argued that

89. 347 N.C. 143 (1997).

90. State v. Gaines, 332 N.C. 461 (1992).

91. State v. Carter, __ N.C. App. __, 711 S.E.2d 515 (2011). *But cf.* State v. Avery, 315 N.C. 1 (1985) (requiring such knowledge in a prosecution for the criminal offense of assault on a law enforcement officer).

92. *See, e.g.,* State v. Maness, 363 N.C. 261 (2009); State v. Polke, 361 N.C. 65 (2006); State v. Nicholson, 355 N.C. 1 (2002); State v. Golphin, 352 N.C. 364 (2000); State v. Hutchins, 303 N.C. 321 (1981).

the circumstance should not have been submitted because his mother was not actively engaged in being a witness at the time of the murder. The state, citing *State v. Gray*, 347 N.C. 143 (1997), contended that "a witness is engaged in the official performance of her duties from the time she swears out a warrant until the time she testifies." The North Carolina Supreme Court ruled for the defendant. Although his mother may have been a witness against him, she was not "actively engaged at the time of the murder in the performance of a duty expected of a witness, such as swearing out a warrant, discussing the case with a prosecutor, going to court to testify, or actively testifying," so the "engaged in" prong of (e)(8) was not met. The court stated that it was not "intend[ing] to suggest that the fact a victim witness has not yet testified precludes submission of the 'because of' prong of the (e)(8) aggravator."

State v. Anthony, 354 N.C. 372 (2001). The defendant was convicted of first-degree murder and sentenced to death for the murder of his wife. A domestic violence protective order had been issued after the murder victim had filed a domestic violence complaint against the defendant. The victim was scheduled to return to court the morning after her murder. The defendant was aware of this hearing and was extremely upset about it. Although the court ruled that there was evidence to support the submission of both (e)(7) (murder to hinder governmental function or law enforcement) and (e)(8), the court also ruled that the trial judge erred in submitting both aggravating circumstances because they were based on the same evidence. Both circumstances referred to the domestic violence matter previously initiated by the murder victim and scheduled for hearing the day after the murder. The relationship between the defendant, the murder victim, and their children was one reason the victim had instituted the action and why she was to be a witness at the upcoming hearing. The court distinguished *State v. Gray*, 347 N.C. 143 (1997), in which the court upheld the submission of both (e)(7) and (e)(8). [*Author's note*: The statements in *Gray* about the kind of evidence that may support aggravating circumstance (e)(8) were disavowed in *State v. Long*, 354 N.C. 534 (2001). See the discussion of *Long*, above.]

State v. Guevara, 349 N.C. 243 (1998). The defendant was convicted of the first-degree murder of Officer A and felonious assault of Officer B. The court ruled that the trial judge did not err in submitting aggravating circumstance (e)(8), even assuming that Officer A illegally entered the defendant's home to arrest him, because the defendant had no right to use deadly force under the circumstances. The court noted that even if the officer in some way improperly performed his official duties, the defendant was still not justified under G.S. 15A-401(f) in using deadly force against the officer.

State v. Alston, 341 N.C. 198 (1995). The murder victim, who had an ongoing relationship with the defendant, was found dead two days after testifying against the defendant in a trial for an assault against her. The court ruled that this was sufficient evidence of aggravating circumstance (e)(8).

State v. Gaines, 332 N.C. 461 (1992). A Charlotte police officer was working for a motel while off-duty, in uniform, and pursuant to department regulations. The defendants left the motel after a dispute with the officer about their visiting a particular motel room. They later returned and killed the officer by shooting him while he sat in the motel lobby. The court ruled that aggravating circumstance (e)(8) includes as victims duly sworn law enforcement officers when they are performing off-duty, secondary law enforcement–related duties when it is clear that these duties and compensation are incidental and supplemental to their primary duties of law enforcement on behalf of the general public. The evidence in this case was sufficient to submit (e)(8) under both prongs: the murder was committed against the law enforcement officer (1) while the officer was engaged in the performance of his official duties and (2) because the officer was exercising his official duties.

State v. Hutchins, 303 N.C. 321 (1981). The court ruled that it was not error to submit two aggravating circumstances in this case—(e)(4) (murder to prevent arrest or effect escape) and (e)(8)—even though they may have been based on the same evidence. The court stated that it is not error to submit multiple aggravating circumstances if the inquiry prompted by their submission is directed at distinct aspects of the defendant's character or the murder for which the defendant is to be punished. The (e)(4) aggravating circumstance focuses on the defendant's motivation in pursuing his or her course of conduct. The (e)(8) aggravating circumstance focuses on the factual circumstances of the crime. The court distinguished its ruling in *State v. Goodman*, 298 N.C. 1 (1979). *See also* State v. Maness, 363 N.C. 261 (2009) (similar ruling); State v. Polke, 361 N.C. 65 (2006) (similar ruling); State v. Nicholson, 355 N.C. 1 (2002) (similar ruling); State v. Golphin, 352 N.C. 364 (2000) (similar ruling).

J. Aggravating Circumstance (e)(9): Murder Especially Heinous, Atrocious, or Cruel

G.S. 15A-2000(e)(9) states: "The capital felony was especially heinous, atrocious, or cruel."

The North Carolina Supreme Court has repeatedly ruled that aggravating circumstance (e)(9) and the pattern jury instruction defining it are constitutional.[93] The court has noted that under this circumstance a murder must not be merely heinous, atrocious, or cruel—descriptions that might apply to all first-degree murders—but must be *especially* heinous, atrocious, or cruel. The supreme court has described several types of murders that may warrant submission of this aggravating circumstance to the jury:

1. a murder physically agonizing or otherwise dehumanizing to the victim;
2. a murder less violent than described in item 1, immediately above, but conscienceless, pitiless, or unnecessarily torturous to the victim, including a murder that leaves the victim in his or her last moments aware of, but helpless to prevent, impending death;
3. a murder that demonstrates a defendant's unusual depravity of mind exceeding what is normally present in first-degree murder cases; and
4. a murder committed in a fashion beyond what was necessary to effectuate the victim's death.[94]

Among the factors that the state supreme court has discussed in connection with aggravating circumstance (e)(9) are the victim's age, i.e., whether the victim was very young or very old;[95] whether

93. *See, e.g.*, State v. Duke, 360 N.C. 110 (2005) (reaffirming constitutionality after *Ring v. Arizona*, 536 U.S. 584 (2002)); State v. Smith, 359 N.C. 199 (2005) (based on prior precedent, aggravating circumstance (e)(9) not unconstitutionally vague); State v. Syriani, 333 N.C. 350 (1993).

94. State v. Golphin, 352 N.C. 364 (2000); State v. Gibbs, 335 N.C. 1 (1993).

95. State v. Lane, 365 N.C. 7 (2011) (5-year-old victim); State v. Garcell, 363 N.C. 10 (2009) (71-year-old victim); State v. Jones, 358 N.C. 330 (2004) (14-year-old victim); State v. Bell, 359 N.C. 1 (2004) (89-year-old victim); State v. Huff, 325 N.C. 1 (1989) (9-month-old victim); State v. Williams, 339 N.C. 1 (1994) (68-year-old victim).

the defendant had a racial[96] or satanic[97] motivation; whether the victim was helpless;[98] the number of wounds inflicted by the defendant;[99] the extent to which the defendant planned the murder in advance;[100] whether the victim died a slow death;[101] whether the victim anticipated his or her death;[102] whether the defendant invaded the sanctuary of the victim's home;[103] whether children saw, or were likely to see, the murder or its aftermath;[104] and whether the defendant desecrated the victim's body.[105]

There have been many appellate cases on aggravating circumstance (e)(9). Quite a few are summarized below. The North Carolina Supreme Court reversed several cases for insufficient evidence of (e)(9) in the early 1980s. Since 1984, however, the court has found insufficient evidence of (e)(9) in just one case.[106]

Case Summaries: Constitutional Issues

Maynard v. Cartwright, 486 U.S. 356 (1988). The United States Supreme Court ruled that the Oklahoma aggravating circumstance of "especially heinous, atrocious, or cruel" was unconstitutionally vague when those words on their face did not offer sufficient guidance to the jury and Oklahoma courts had not adopted a limiting construction that cured the infirmity.

Godfrey v. Georgia, 446 U.S. 420 (1980). The defendant shot his wife in the forehead with a shotgun, killing her instantly. He then shot his mother-in-law in the head with the shotgun, killing her instantly. The jury, based on this evidence, found as an aggravating factor that the murder was "outrageously or wantonly vile, horrible and inhuman." The United States Supreme Court ruled that the Georgia Supreme Court in this case had not applied a constitutional construction of this aggravating factor. The defendant's crimes did not reflect a consciousness materially more "depraved" than that of any person guilty of murder. His victims were killed instantaneously.

---

96. *Golphin*, 352 N.C. 364.

97. State v. White, 355 N.C. 696 (2002) (satanic motive may show a depravity of mind and thus is relevant in proving this aggravating circumstance).

98. State v. Murrell, 362 N.C. 375 (2008); State v. Hurst, 360 N.C. 181 (2006).

99. State v. Goss, 361 N.C. 610 (2007) (defendant stabbed victim more than fifty times); State v. Morgan, 359 N.C. 131 (2004) (forty-eight separate wounds).

100. *Hurst*, 360 N.C. 181.

101. *Goss*, 361 N.C. 610 (defendant paused while stabbing victim, prolonging her suffering); State v. Elliott, 360 N.C. 400, 425 (2006) (defendant killed victim "by strangulation, a method of murder which takes several minutes").

102. *Elliott*, 360 N.C. at 425 (victim was "aware of her impending death but helpless to prevent it"); State v. Allen, 360 N.C. 297 (2006) (incapacitated victim was aware of his impending death); State v. Bell, 359 N.C. 1 (2004) (victim trapped in the trunk of her own car for hours, awaiting her death); State v. Tirado, 358 N.C. 551 (2004) (similar).

103. State v. Garcell, 363 N.C. 10, 66 (2009) (defendant killed victim "within the perceived sanctuary of her own residence"); State v. Cummings, 361 N.C. 438, 477 (2007) (defendant murdered victim "while she was in the supposed safety of her own home"); *Bell*, 359 N.C. at 44 (noting that the victim "was kidnapped from her own home").

104. *Goss*, 361 N.C. at 628 ("[D]efendant left the victim's three-year-old grandson alone in the residence after the murder, making it highly probable that the child would awaken to discover his grandmother['s body]."); State v. McNeill, 360 N.C. 231 (2006) (defendant shot victim in front of many witnesses, including children).

105. *Garcell*, 363 N.C. at 66 (defendant "desecrated [the victim's] remains by riding her limp body like a horse"); *McNeill*, 360 N.C. 231 (the defendant shot the victim, then, as a final insult, kicked her before leaving her to die).

106. State v. Lloyd, 354 N.C. 76 (2001) (victim was shot four times on her front porch by her ex-boyfriend after a brief argument; her death was relatively rapid; and while her son and 5-year-old grandson were in the house, they did not witness the shooting).

There was no principled way to distinguish this case, in which the death penalty was imposed, from the many cases in which it was not.

State v. Duke, 360 N.C. 110 (2005). The court reaffirmed, after *Ring v. Arizona*, 536 U.S. 584 (2002), that the pattern instruction for aggravating circumstance (e)(9) sufficiently narrows and refines the circumstance to render it constitutional.

State v. Smith, 359 N.C. 199 (2005). Based on prior precedent, the court held that aggravating circumstance (e)(9) is not unconstitutionally vague.

State v. Syriani, 333 N.C. 350 (1993). The court ruled that the (e)(9) aggravating circumstance and the pattern jury instruction on (e)(9) were constitutional. *See also* State v. Huff, 325 N.C. 1 (1989).

State v. Fullwood, 323 N.C. 371 (1988). The court, upholding the constitutionality of aggravating circumstance (e)(9) when the pattern jury instruction was given, distinguished the ruling in *Maynard v. Cartwright*, 486 U.S. 356 (1988), discussed above, by noting that the unconstitutional jury instruction in *Maynard*, unlike the North Carolina pattern jury instruction, did not limit this aggravating circumstance to the "conscienceless or pitiless crime which is unnecessarily torturous to the victim." *See also* Fullwood v. Lee, 290 F.3d 663 (4th Cir. 2002) (holding that the pattern instruction provides sufficient guidance to the jury to render aggravating circumstance (e)(9) constitutional). *But cf.* Smith v. Dixon, 14 F.3d 956 (4th Cir. 1994) (en banc) (stating that the trial judge's very brief jury instruction on aggravating circumstance (e)(9) was unconstitutionally vague but that the issue was not properly preserved, and in any event, the error was harmless; the unconstitutional instruction was not the North Carolina pattern jury instruction).

Case Summaries: Jury Instruction Issues

State v. Oliver, 309 N.C. 326 (1983). The trial judge erred in the instruction on aggravating circumstance (e)(9) when the instruction indicated that the jury could find this circumstance based *solely* on evidence that the murder victim begged for his life, since this factor alone does not always necessitate a finding that a murder was especially heinous, atrocious, or cruel.

State v. Jennings, 333 N.C. 579 (1993). When the defendant was convicted of first-degree murder based on both torture and premeditation and deliberation, the trial judge properly submitted (e)(9). [*Author's note*: It is possible that if a defendant were convicted of first-degree murder based only on torture, the court would rule that (e)(9) may not be submitted, based on the principles set out in *State v. Cherry*, 298 N.C. 86 (1979) (improper to submit underlying felony as (e)(5) aggravating circumstance (murder during a specified felony) when defendant is convicted of first-degree murder based solely on felony murder theory since there is an automatic aggravating circumstance of the underlying felony), because this circumstance is directed at the conscienceless or pitiless crime that is *unnecessarily torturous* to the victim. *Cf.* State v. Moore, 335 N.C. 567 (1994) (aggravating circumstance (e)(9) properly submitted where defendant was convicted of first-degree murder by poisoning; poisoning not inherently torturous).]

Case Summaries: Sufficient Evidence of Aggravating Circumstance (e)(9)

State v. Murrell, 362 N.C. 375 (2008). The defendant told several acquaintances that he was planning to commit a robbery. He approached the victim, who was seated in his parked car, and shot him. The defendant took control of the vehicle, placed the victim in the passenger seat, and began driving. The defendant "fired a second, fatal shot at the helpless victim as he lay upside down on the front passenger side of the vehicle and after he begged defendant to put him out of his misery." This supported the jury's finding of aggravating circumstance (e)(9).

State v. Raines, 362 N.C. 1 (2007). The defendant lived with a friend and the friend's wife. One night, he killed the couple and stole their guns, credit cards, checks, and truck. There was sufficient evidence of aggravating circumstance (e)(9) where the defendant brutally beat his friend with a wrench and then shot him three times because it was "just better to kill him."

State v. Goss, 361 N.C. 610 (2007). The defendant's neighbor, the victim here, confronted the defendant about whether he had raped her daughter. The defendant then assaulted the victim, beating her unconscious several times. Then he "needlessly stabbed her over fifty times . . . pausing several times between series of stabs, thereby prolonging the victim's suffering. Only [then] did defendant finally inflict a wound calculated to end her life, slitting her throat as she was gasping her final breaths. Lastly, defendant left the victim's three-year-old grandson alone in the residence after the murder, making it highly probable that the child would awaken to discover his grandmother['s body]." This supported the jury's finding of aggravating circumstance (e)(9).

State v. Cummings, 361 N.C. 438 (2007). The defendant murdered the victim "while she was in the supposed safety of her own home, stabbing her numerous times in the face and leaving her bleeding after rendering her helpless to prevent her impending death." This supported the jury's finding of aggravating circumstance (e)(9).

State v. Forte, 360 N.C. 427 (2006). The prosecutor's argument in support of aggravating circumstance (e)(9) presented a "plausible scenario" and so was not improper. The state contended that the evidence showed that the defendant entered the home of an elderly couple, attacked and killed the husband as he lay in bed, then killed and sexually assaulted the blind wife as she attempted to come to her husband's aid. The state supreme court also stated that the evidence was sufficient to support (e)(9).

State v. Allen, 360 N.C. 297 (2006). The defendant shot a friend twice while walking through a forest, perhaps after some sort of disagreement. One of the shots was to the victim's knee, incapacitating him. The defendant's girlfriend testified that the victim survived for a period of time and that the defendant periodically threw rocks at him to determine whether he was still alive. The throwing of the rocks, together with the incapacitated victim's awareness of his impending death, supported aggravating circumstance (e)(9).

State v. McNeill, 360 N.C. 231 (2006). The defendant's wife left him and began dating another man. The defendant attacked her at a friend's home in front of many witnesses, including children. He shot her and chased her around the yard as she begged for her life. When she fell to the ground, he shot her many more times and, as a final insult, kicked her before leaving her to die. The evidence was sufficient to support aggravating circumstance (e)(9).

State v. Hurst, 360 N.C. 181 (2006). The prosecutor's closing argument at the penalty phase of the defendant's trial emphasized that the defendant had planned in advance to kill the victim and that the defendant fired a final shot to the victim's face as he lay helpless on his back. These statements were relevant to aggravating circumstance (e)(9) and were not improper.

State v. Bell, 359 N.C. 1 (2004). There was sufficient evidence of aggravating circumstance (e)(9) where "the victim, an eighty-nine year old woman, was kidnapped from her own home, repeatedly beaten, and placed in the trunk of her own car to await most certain death. The victim fought to free herself from the trunk of her car, only to have the trunk lid repeatedly slammed down upon her. The victim was trapped in her car for hours, helpless and obviously in fear for her life[,] . . . ultimately . . . dying alone in the trunk of her own car, which defendant had set on fire."

State v. Barden, 356 N.C. 316 (2002). The defendant was convicted of first-degree murder and sentenced to death. The court ruled that the evidence was sufficient to support aggravating circumstance (e)(9). The defendant bludgeoned the victim in the head many times, apparently changing weapons during the course of the attack, and the defendant acknowledged that the victim may have been alive after the attack and that he took no steps to assist him. In addition, the defendant instituted the attack only after the victim, who had already loaned the defendant money once that night, refused to make a second loan of $20. The defendant's attack began after the victim had turned his back to the defendant to resume his work duties.

State v. Hooks, 353 N.C. 629 (2001). The defendant was convicted of first-degree murder and sentenced to death. The court ruled that there was sufficient evidence of aggravating circumstance (e)(9). The defendant and the victim were arguing. The defendant stated that he was going to "f-k [the victim] up." When the victim began to back away, the defendant pulled a .38 caliber handgun out of his pocket and pointed it at the victim's face. The victim then said, "Oh, you're going to shoot me now," and after a moment of silence, the defendant shot the victim four times. The victim then fell to the ground, and the defendant began to kick him in the face and chest, pistol-whip him, and taunt him by repeating, "you thought I was playing." The defendant then fled the scene. The victim remained conscious and was clearly in extreme pain for at least fifteen minutes.

State v. Brewington, 352 N.C. 489 (2000). The defendant was convicted of two counts of first-degree murder involving the murders of his grandmother and nephew. The murders were committed by his fiancée and a person he had hired. Although the defendant was not present during the commission of the murders, he planned the manner in which they were to be carried out: the victims were to be stabbed and their home set on fire. Based on the plan, it was reasonable to infer that the deaths of one or both victims would not be instantaneous. The court ruled that there was sufficient evidence to prove aggravating circumstance (e)(9).

State v. Golphin, 352 N.C. 364 (2000). Two defendants were convicted of the first-degree murders of two law enforcement officers and sentenced to death for both murders. The court ruled that the evidence was sufficient to support aggravating circumstance (e)(9) against Defendant A. Defendant B shot an officer, causing him to become incapacitated. This enabled Defendant A to shake himself free of the officer's grasp and retrieve the officer's pistol. He then shot the officer multiple times as he lay on the ground moaning. Because the officer had the presence of mind to attempt to grab Defendant A after he had been shot, this evidence showed that the officer was aware of his fate and unable to prevent his impending death.

State v. Cheek, 351 N.C. 48 (1999). The state's pathologist testified that he believed the victim in this case was alive when her taxicab was set on fire because of the presence of soot in her air passages and nose. He also testified that the cause of death was carbon monoxide poisoning. The evidence was unclear as to whether the victim was conscious when the fire began. The court ruled that the evidence, although not conclusive, was sufficient for the jury to find that not only was the victim alive when the taxicab was set on fire, but also that she was aware of her impending death. Thus, there was sufficient evidence to submit (e)(9).

State v. Flippen, 349 N.C. 264 (1998). The defendant was sentenced to death for the first-degree murder of his 2-year-old stepdaughter. The court ruled that the trial judge did not err in submitting (e)(9). The defendant was the victim's primary caregiver on the day he killed her. The court stated that the child was particularly vulnerable and at the defendant's mercy. The defendant inflicted many blows on her head, neck, and abdomen; the resulting injuries went beyond what would have been necessary to kill her.

State v. Atkins, 349 N.C. 62 (1998). The defendant was convicted of the first-degree murder of his 8-month-old son and sentenced to death. Four medical experts testified about the severity of the murder victim's injuries in comparison to other injuries occurring to other children that the experts had treated in their respective medical practices. The court ruled that such evidence was admissible in proving aggravating circumstance (e)(9).

State v. Moseley, 336 N.C. 710 (1994). When determining the sufficiency of the evidence to support aggravating circumstance (e)(9), the court stated that the state is entitled to all reasonable inferences that can be drawn from the evidence. Thus, the court stated that it must assume that the victim received many of her injuries while she was alive. The following evidence was sufficient: the victim was manually strangled, stabbed twelve times, tortured by incisions on her chest and neck, sexually assaulted with a blunt object, and beaten about her body. The murder was characterized by excessive brutality, physical pain, psychological suffering, and dehumanizing aspects not normally found in a first-degree murder.

State v. Ingle, 336 N.C. 617 (1994). The defendant was convicted of first-degree murder after he, wholly unprovoked, beat an elderly man to death with an ax handle. (He also was convicted at the same trial of first-degree murder of the man's wife; that murder was committed in a similar manner.) The defendant argued that because the evidence showed that the murder victim was unaware of his presence and was rendered unconscious by the first blow, he did not suffer any of the physical or psychological torture that would cause his murder to be considered sufficient evidence of aggravating circumstance (e)(9). The court rejected this argument, noting that (e)(9) does not entirely depend on the experience endured by the victim during the killing. The court stated that when a murderer attacks an elderly victim by surprise and repeatedly hits the victim in the head with an ax handle without the slightest provocation, it may be inferred that the murder was conscienceless and pitiless. Evidence that the defendant committed a similar set of murders six weeks later, after a boastful discussion of his murderous capabilities, was further evidence of a lack of pity for his victims. The facts of this murder suggest a depravity of mind not easily matched by even the most egregious of slayings, found the court, as well as a level of brutality that exceeded that ordinarily present in first-degree murder.

State v. Sexton, 336 N.C. 321 (1994). The following evidence was sufficient to support aggravating circumstance (e)(9): the murder victim was sexually assaulted and then strangled with her stockings; she would have known what was happening for at least ten seconds before losing consciousness. The murder was physically agonizing and involved psychological terror not normally present in murder cases. For similar sexual assault and strangulation cases in which the (e)(9) circumstance was properly submitted, see *State v. Artis*, 325 N.C. 278 (1989) (manual strangulation during forcible sexual assault) and *State v. Johnson*, 298 N.C. 47 (1979) (defendant tried to strangle victim with "fish stringer," then sexually assaulted her while she was unconscious; when defendant discovered victim was still alive, he stabbed her to death).

State v. Moore, 335 N.C. 567 (1994). The evidence was sufficient to support aggravating circumstance (e)(9) in a poisoning murder in which the victim suffered prolonged physical agony. The court rejected the defendant's argument that the rationale of the ruling in *State v. Cherry*, 298 N.C. 86 (1979) (underlying felony may not be used as an aggravating circumstance when defendant is convicted of first-degree murder based on felony murder only), should apply to bar this aggravating circumstance from being used in a first-degree murder by poisoning, since this aggravating circumstance will always be present. The court noted that neither the fact that poison is administered in small doses over extended periods of time nor the type of poison used—slow or fast acting—are elements of the offense.

State v. Lee, 335 N.C. 244 (1994). The evidence was sufficient to support (e)(9). The victim was kidnapped at gunpoint, stripped naked, and driven to another location where she was forced to walk or run to the place where she was beaten on the head, kicked in the throat, and strangled by the defendant. The defendant said that the victim died a slow and painful death.

State v. Gibbs, 335 N.C. 1 (1993). The court ruled that the evidence was sufficient to support (e)(9). The murder victim, tied and gagged at the defendant's direction, suffered under knowledge that her death was imminent. She was helpless and terrorized. The defendant, standing within a few feet of her, placed the muzzle of his rifle on her forehead. Evidence that the defendant shot the victim because her crying made him nervous showed that he acted in a conscienceless, pitiless manner in killing her.

State v. Syriani, 333 N.C. 350 (1993). The evidence was sufficient to support (e)(9) when the victim had been subjected to domestic violence by the defendant (her husband), who stabbed her twenty-eight times with a screwdriver, leading to her death twenty-eight days later.

State v. Oliver, 309 N.C. 326 (1983). Evidence was sufficient to support aggravating circumstance (e)(9) when the defendant killed the robbery victim in cold blood as the victim was pleading "please don't shoot me." The defendant showed no remorse and later boasted to fellow inmates that he had pointed the gun at the robbery victim, who begged not to be shot and offered the defendant more money, and that he "kind of liked the idea of it" (apparently referring to killing the victim). The court reaffirmed its earlier ruling, made in the defendant's first appeal, on the sufficiency of evidence of (e)(9), *State v. Oliver*, 302 N.C. 28 (1981).

The following are brief summaries of some other cases in which the court ruled that evidence of aggravating circumstance (e)(9) was sufficient:

State v. Lane, 365 N.C. 7 (2011) (aggravating circumstance (e)(9) was supported by the evidence where the defendant raped a 5-year-old child "before putting her, while still alive, in a garbage bag sealed with duct tape, wrapping her in a tarp, and discarding her body in a creek").

State v. Garcell, 363 N.C. 10 (2009) (aggravating circumstance (e)(9) was supported by the evidence where the defendant "manhandled, brutally choked, and strangled his victim, a 71-year-old woman, to death within the perceived sanctuary of her own residence" then "desecrated her remains by riding her limp body like a horse").

State v. Morgan, 359 N.C. 131 (2004) (sufficient evidence of aggravating circumstance (e)(9) where the defendant, angry because the victim used his drugs but then refused to give him oral sex, murdered the victim by inflicting forty-eight separate wounds, apparently with a broken beer bottle).

State v. Tirado, 358 N.C. 551 (2004) (defendant and others stole a car from the victims, forcing them into the trunk and later stealing their jewelry and killing them as they pleaded for their lives; there was sufficient evidence to support aggravating circumstance (e)(9), given the extreme depravity of the killings and the victims' awareness of their impending deaths).

State v. Holman, 353 N.C. 174 (2000) (defendant's method in carrying out the killing of his wife—chasing her in his car, ramming her car, and then approaching her and killing her with his shotgun—was conscienceless and pitiless, inflicting excessive fear and psychological terror).

State v. Anderson, 350 N.C. 152 (1999) (victim was 2-1/2 years old, defendant was her primary caregiver, and victim was brutally beaten and severely abused by defendant and another person).

State v. Fleming, 350 N.C. 109 (1999) (victim was repeatedly assaulted with a blunt object in his home; as victim struggled to defend himself, defendant continued to hit victim on the head as victim moved about the house; defendant also manually strangled victim so that his hyoid bone was fractured; evidence supported a reasonable inference that victim remained conscious during his ordeal and suffered great physical pain and torture).

State v. Hipps, 348 N.C. 377 (1998) (victim was stabbed thirty-four times and existence of defensive wound on victim's hand suggested that victim was conscious and aware of what was happening).

State v. Kandies, 342 N.C. 419 (1996) (victim was savagely beaten, strangled, and sexually assaulted by defendant, whom she knew and trusted).

State v. Robinson, 342 N.C. 74 (1995) (defendant forced murder victim, by putting sawed-off shotgun to victim's neck, to drive to certain location; victim kept begging and pleading with defendant and accomplice not to hurt him because he had no money; defendant and accomplice directed victim to side street where he was told to lie down; accomplice shot victim in the face and defendant took his wallet; murder was physically agonizing or otherwise dehumanizing to the victim).

State v. Frye, 341 N.C. 470 (1995) (defendant murdered victim, who knew and trusted defendant; defendant stabbed victim repeatedly, causing pain but not unconsciousness; this amounted to "psychological torture" and supported (e)(9)).

State v. Burr, 341 N.C. 263 (1995) (defendant's murder of defenseless 4-month-old baby was not only pitiless, but it also betrayed the special role that the defendant had been given in the child's family; the injuries inflicted on the child were numerous, in excess of what was necessary to kill the victim, and brutal).

State v. Alston, 341 N.C. 198 (1995) (defendant repeatedly beat the victim about her face with a hammer or similar blunt object and, while she was conscious, suffocated her with a pillow placed against her face; based on these and other facts, the court ruled that evidence supported a finding that the killing was physically agonizing and involved psychological torture not normally present in murder).

State v. Lynch, 340 N.C. 435 (1995) (defendant shot 12-year-old victim nine times, continually shooting her while she tried to crawl across a street to a safe place; victim was aware that she was going to die but was unable to prevent her impending death).

State v. Williams, 339 N.C. 1 (1994) (defendant inflicted seven different wounds to the 68-year-old victim; four of these head injuries would have been sufficient to disorient or confuse the victim but not render him unconscious; the three remaining head injuries exceeded the normal brutality found in first-degree murder cases; the victim could have remained conscious throughout all seven blows and have been aware of, while incapable of preventing, his impending death; court noted that the victim's age is a factor in determining whether to submit aggravating circumstance (e)(9)).

State v. Carter, 338 N.C. 569 (1994) (the defendant administered abrasions and lacerations all over the victim's body as she struggled with him; the victim asked the defendant several times not to kill her; he then silenced her by strangling her; she fought him for at least two minutes before losing consciousness and dying; the defendant then pounded her head several times with a brick).

State v. Rose, 335 N.C. 301 (1994) (defendant inflicted multiple stab wounds to victim's body and manually strangled her to death; victim was conscious while defendant inflicted lesser knife wounds on her body and could have remained so after she was struck on the head; defendant's strangulation of victim took between four and five minutes).

State v. Quick, 329 N.C. 1 (1991) (defendant stabbed a practically helpless 78-year-old man seventeen times in the chest area; seven or eight wounds extended through the heart and right lung; victim could have lived up to ten minutes after sustaining stab wounds).

State v. Bonney, 329 N.C. 61 (1991) (defendant murdered his daughter; victim had twenty-seven gunshot entrance wounds all over her body; wounds to her face and chest occurred before she died; victim was alive and aware of her fate while many of the shots were fired).

State v. Huff, 325 N.C. 1 (1989) (defendant buried 9-month-old infant son alive; jury may properly consider victim's age in determining weight to give (e)(9)).

State v. Laws, 325 N.C. 81 (1989) (both murder victims were unable to defend themselves because of extreme intoxication, and the defendant beat them mercilessly with a hammer).

State v. McNeil, 324 N.C. 33 (1989) (defendant not only choked and shot the victim, he also beat and stabbed her and hit her in the face with a wooden frame which had nails sticking out of it).

State v. McLaughlin, 323 N.C. 68 (1988) (defendant beat victim with a pipe, stuffed her mouth with a rag, dragged her into a bathroom, forced her head under water, and held it there while she struggled for her life).

State v. Lloyd, 321 N.C. 301 (1988) (defendant stabbed victim seventeen times and kicked him with such force as to cause his brain to swell and hemorrhage, ultimately causing his death; victim did not die immediately, lingering for at least five to ten minutes).

State v. Spruill, 320 N.C. 688 (1987) (defendant stalked victim and cut her two separate times, the second time causing her to drown in her own blood).

State v. Reese, 319 N.C. 110 (1987) (defendant repeatedly stabbed robbery victim as if in a "frenzy"; victim remained conscious for many minutes before dying).

State v. Stokes, 319 N.C. 1 (1987) (defendant and accomplices beat robbery victim severely on and about his head; blows fractured his skull and caused hemorrhaging into his brain; victim remained in a semiconscious state for over twelve hours before dying).

State v. Johnson, 317 N.C. 343 (1986) (defendant stabbed victim, took her from car and sexually assaulted her, stabbed her fifty-five times more, and fifteen to twenty minutes elapsed from the first stabbing until the victim died).

State v. Gladden, 315 N.C. 398 (1986) (defendant slashed victim's throat, shot him twice, dragged him into a ditch, and then shot him twice more in the head; victim choked to death slowly and suffered extreme pain and anxiety before his death).

State v. Brown, 315 N.C. 40 (1985) (defendant took robbery victim from convenience store to secluded area five miles from the store, bound her hands, and shot her six times; victim may have lived as long as fifteen minutes after being shot).

State v. Huffstetler, 312 N.C. 92 (1984) (murder victim died as a result of blows with a cast-iron skillet so severe that they fractured her skull, neck, jaw, and collarbone and caused her skull to be pushed into her brain).

State v. Craig, 308 N.C. 446 (1983) (court rejected defendant's argument that murder was not especially heinous, atrocious, or cruel because the victim, with a blood alcohol level of 0.29, was so intoxicated that she must have been practically anesthetized against the torture of the thirty-seven stab wounds he inflicted upon her with a pocket knife).

State v. Brown, 306 N.C. 151 (1982) (the defendant stabbed two victims to death; the number, severity, and character of the wounds supported (e)(9); also, the victims' bodies were grossly mutilated).

State v. Pinch, 306 N.C. 1 (1982) (defendant, through the execution of a deliberate plan and with a grin on his face, shot two victims, one of whom pleaded for his life).

State v. Smith, 305 N.C. 691 (1982) (defendant kidnapped, robbed, and raped the victim during several-hour ordeal and then killed her by striking her on the head with a cinder block).

State v. Rook, 304 N.C. 201 (1981) (defendant beat victim, hit her with a tire tool, cut her with a knife, raped her, ran over her with a car, and then left her alone to die).

State v. Martin, 303 N.C. 246 (1981) (during twenty-five-minute ordeal, defendant fired shots at victim, one of which severed her spine; hit her on the head and face repeatedly with his fist and pistol; fired shots at her in her son's presence; and then shot her to death).

State v. Silhan, 302 N.C. 223 (1981) (victim was stripped from the waist down, had her hands tied behind her back and her brassiere tied around her neck, was marched at knife-point into the woods, and was forced to lie down while she was beaten and murdered).

State v. McDowell, 301 N.C. 279 (1980) (with a two-foot machete, defendant entered victim's house, threatened to rape victim's 14-year-old sister, and struck at 4-year-old victim while she was in her sister's arms, wounding her nine times and killing her).

State v. Johnson, 298 N.C. 355 (1979) (the defendant offered a 10-year-old boy $10 to have sex with him, and when the boy refused, the defendant strangled him with a nylon fish stringer; during or after the killing, the defendant sexually assaulted the victim).

State v. Barfield, 298 N.C. 306 (1979) (defendant placed arsenic in victim's tea and beer because she feared victim would report her forgery of checks drawn on the victim's bank account).

State v. Johnson, 298 N.C. 47 (1979) (defendant tried to strangle the victim, rendered her unconscious, sexually molested her, and, realizing she was not dead, stabbed her to death).

State v. Goodman, 298 N.C. 1 (1979) (victim was shot several times and cut repeatedly with a knife, placed alive in a car trunk, and begged for his life; he was then driven to another county, taken out of the trunk, and shot twice in the head).

Case Summaries: Insufficient Evidence of Aggravating Circumstance (e)(9)

State v. Lloyd, 354 N.C. 76 (2001). The defendant shot the victim four times, and the victim's death was relatively rapid. The court conducted a detailed review of its cases involving aggravating circumstance (e)(9) and ruled that the evidence was insufficient to support this aggravator.

State v. Hamlet, 312 N.C. 162 (1984). The evidence was insufficient to support the submission of aggravating circumstance (e)(9). The defendant shot the victim in the head immediately after the victim entered a vestibule. The victim was unaware of the defendant's presence until he had entered the vestibule. The victim was unconscious and unable to feel any pain after the shot to his head. He was shot six more times after the shot to the head. He died about five hours later without regaining consciousness.

State v. Moose, 310 N.C. 482 (1984). The evidence was insufficient to support (e)(9). The defendant, who was in his pickup truck, followed the victim's car down a road and repeatedly honked his horn and bumped the back of the victim's car at an intersection. The victim and another person in the car wondered who was behind them and pulled into a drugstore parking lot. The pickup truck pulled beside the car, the defendant pointed a shotgun at both occupants in the car, and the victim said "Oh God, what are they going to do?" The defendant then fired the shotgun, shooting the victim in the head and killing him. The court stated that there was no evidence that either the victim or the other person in the car believed that the ultimate result of the pickup truck following their vehicle would be death. There was insufficient evidence that the victim was stalked and feared that death was likely to result.

State v. Stanley, 310 N.C. 332 (1984). The evidence was insufficient to support aggravating circumstance (e)(9). The court stated that there was no evidence that the defendant stalked his victim, his estranged wife; the evidence simply showed that the defendant drove past her house several times. The victim and her family, knowing of the defendant's presence in the area, nevertheless went outside the house for a walk. The court stated that obviously they were not being tortured psychologically by the defendant's actions. At no time before the shooting did the defendant threaten the victim or any of her family. Rather, he shot the victim suddenly, nine times in rapid succession, and she was rendered unconscious within minutes and died shortly thereafter. There was no evidence that the defendant intended that the victim suffer a prolonged, torturous death or that she in fact suffered such a death. Although there was evidence that the victim said "Please Stan" before she was shot, there was no evidence that the defendant heard it or what the words may have referred to.

State v. Oliver, 309 N.C. 326 (1983). A statement by the defendant's accomplice, made after the conspiracy had ended, that the murder victim had said "Please don't shoot me" was inadmissible against the defendant. Considering all the evidence in this case, there was insufficient proof to support aggravating circumstance (e)(9) in the sentencing hearing of the defendant (although it was sufficient as to the defendant's accomplice).

State v. Hamlette, 302 N.C. 490 (1981). The evidence was insufficient to support aggravating circumstance (e)(9) when the defendant, after riding around drinking beer most of the evening, saw the victim and shot him three times from behind without any established motive. Although the victim lingered for twelve days and died from the gunshot wounds, the court concluded that this murder was not *especially* heinous.

State v. Oliver, 302 N.C. 28 (1981). The evidence was insufficient to support (e)(9). The defendant, running from a convenience store after committing an armed robbery, shot and killed an innocent bystander who was there to purchase gas. The killing was a sudden act, and the victim died instantaneously. The victim did not suffer unusual pain or suffering. The court concluded that the brutality of this killing did not exceed that normally present in first-degree murder cases.

Case Summaries: Propriety of Submitting Multiple Aggravating Circumstances

State v. Waring, 364 N.C. 443 (2010). The defendant and an accomplice stole the victim's wallet, raped her, and murdered her by stabbing her repeatedly. The trial judge submitted aggravating circumstances (e)(5) (murder during a specified felony, in this case, rape), (e)(6) (murder for pecuniary gain), and (e)(9). Separate evidence supported each, and the prosecutor's argument did not ask the jury to find more than one aggravating circumstance based on the same evidence.

State v. Elliott, 360 N.C. 400 (2006). The defendant beat, raped, and murdered an elderly woman in her own home. The beating was brutal and left extensive blood spatter in the victim's home. The defendant killed the victim "by strangulation, a method of murder which takes several minutes, leaving [the victim] aware of her impending death but helpless to prevent it." This was sufficient evidence to support aggravating circumstance (e)(9), and while some of this evidence may have overlapped with the evidence used to support aggravating circumstance (e)(5) (murder during a specified felony, here, burglary), the overlap was not complete.

State v. Jones, 358 N.C. 330 (2004). The defendant shot and killed his wife, then killed his 14-year-old stepson. There was sufficient evidence to support aggravating circumstance (e)(9) as to the murder of the stepson, given the child's age and the parental relationship between the victim and the defendant. There was separate evidence, namely, the murder of the defendant's wife, to support aggravating circumstance (e)(11) (course of violent conduct).

State v. DeCastro, 342 N.C. 667 (1996). The court ruled that separate evidence supported the submission of aggravating circumstances (e)(9) and (e)(11) (course of violent conduct). Evidence supporting (e)(9) included the defendant's infliction of twenty-three stab wounds on the victim. The victim did not die a quick, painless death but remained conscious during the five to ten minutes that elapsed before she died. In addition, her jeans and panties had been pulled to her ankles, her shirt torn open, and her bra pulled above her breasts, exposing her breasts, torso, and lower body. The evidence supporting (e)(11) was entirely different from the evidence supporting (e)(9): before killing the victim, the defendant robbed, beat, and murdered the victim's husband.

State v. Daughtry, 340 N.C. 488 (1995). The court ruled that separate evidence supported the submission of aggravating circumstances (e)(5) (murder during a specified felony, here, a sex offense) and (e)(9). Evidence supporting (e)(5) showed that some object had been inserted into the victim's rectum or vagina. Evidence supporting (e)(9) showed severe blunt trauma wounds to the victim's head and many abrasions about her body.

State v. Rouse, 339 N.C. 59 (1994). Separate evidence supported the submission of both (e)(5) (murder during a specified felony, in this case, attempted rape and attempted armed robbery) and (e)(9). The victim was stabbed seventeen times and suffered for fifteen minutes as she lost half of her blood. The court noted that evidence supporting each aggravating circumstance may overlap as long as the same evidence doesn't support more than one aggravating circumstance.

State v. Jennings, 333 N.C. 579 (1993). The trial judge properly submitted aggravating circumstances (e)(5) (murder during a specified felony, here, a sex offense) and (e)(9) because they were not based on the same evidence. There was substantial evidence of the especially heinous, atrocious, or cruel nature of the murder (the savage beating of the victim) apart from the evidence that the murder was committed while attempting to penetrate the victim's anus with an object.

K. Aggravating Circumstance (e)(10): Defendant's Use of Hazardous Weapon to Endanger Multiple Others

G.S. 15A-2000(e)(10) states: "The defendant knowingly created a great risk of death to more than one person by means of a weapon or device which would normally be hazardous to the lives of more than one person." This aggravating circumstance is identical to the noncapital aggravating circumstance set forth in G.S. 15A-1340.16(d)(8).

In *State v. Moose*,[107] the North Carolina Supreme Court ruled that there was sufficient evidence of aggravating circumstance (e)(10) when a defendant fired a shotgun at close range toward two people who were in a motor vehicle. Although the court in that case emphasized that a shotgun is "capable of firing more than one, and in fact, many projectiles in a pattern over a wide impact area rather than a specifically aimed single projectile such as from a rifle or pistol,"[108] it appears that firearms other than shotguns may also support the submission of aggravating circumstance (e)(10),[109] at least if they are not single-shot devices. Fire bombs and other weapons of mass destruction may also be included within (e)(10).[110] Under some circumstances, a motor vehicle may be a qualifying weapon or device.[111]

107. 310 N.C. 482 (1984); *see also* State v. Jones, 339 N.C. 114 (1994).

108. *Moose*, 310 N.C. at 497.

109. State v. Brown, 357 N.C. 382 (2003) (evidence supported aggravating circumstance (e)(10) where the defendant shot and killed his girlfriend and an infant with a pistol while both victims slept in the same bed); State v. Sellars, 363 N.C. 112 (2009) (discussing the noncapital aggravating circumstance set forth in G.S. 15A-1340.16(d)(8) and finding ample evidence supporting the circumstance where the defendant fired a semiautomatic weapon at three police officers); State v. Davis, 349 N.C. 1 (1998) (aggravating circumstance (e)(10) properly found in case involving a .30 caliber rifle); *see also* State v. Bruton, 344 N.C. 381 (1996) (holding that the trial judge did not err, in a noncapital case, in applying a Fair Sentencing Act aggravating circumstance similar to (e)(10) based on the defendant's use of a nine-millimeter semiautomatic pistol). It may also be worth noting that in footnote 2 in *Moose*, the court cited two Georgia cases upholding the findings of that state's similarly worded aggravating circumstance. The defendant in one case used two pistols and in another case used a .32 caliber automatic pistol. *But cf.* State v. Nobles, 350 N.C. 483 (1999) (error for trial judge to instruct jury that a semiautomatic pistol is a weapon that would normally be hazardous to the lives of more than one person because this relieved the state of its burden of proof).

110. State v. Norwood, 344 N.C. 511 (1996) (can of gasoline plus burning paper bag, when thrown into a store).

111. State v. Lopez, 363 N.C. 535 (2009) (discussing the noncapital aggravating circumstance set forth in G.S. 15A-1340.16(d)(8), the court stated that a vehicle may be a device that is hazardous to the lives of multiple people, as when it is driven recklessly by an intoxicated driver).

Case Summaries: Sufficient Evidence of Aggravating Circumstance (e)(10)

State v. Brown, 357 N.C. 382 (2003). Without discussion, the court stated that the evidence supported aggravating circumstance (e)(10) where the defendant shot and killed his girlfriend and an infant while both victims slept in the same bed.

State v. Lopez, 363 N.C. 535 (2009). Discussing the noncapital aggravating circumstance set forth in G.S. 15A-1340.16(d)(8), the court stated that a motor vehicle may be a device that is hazardous to the lives of multiple people, as when it is driven recklessly by an intoxicated driver.

State v. Sellars, 363 N.C. 112 (2009). Discussing the noncapital aggravating circumstance set forth in G.S. 15A-1340.16(d)(8), the court found ample evidence supporting the circumstance where the defendant fired a semiautomatic weapon at three police officers.

State v. Norwood, 344 N.C. 511 (1996). The defendant threw a burning paper bag and gasoline into a convenience store during business hours while there were at least two people inside. The store exploded into flames after the defendant escaped. The court ruled that this evidence was sufficient to prove aggravating circumstance (e)(10). The court held that a can of gasoline, when used with a burning paper bag, "has the potential to kill more than one person."

State v. Moose, 310 N.C. 482 (1984). The (e)(10) aggravating circumstance addresses two considerations: a great risk of death that the defendant knowingly created and the weapon by which it was created. The following evidence in this case was sufficient to support this circumstance. The defendant knew that there were two people in the front seat of the victim's car. The defendant's firing of a shotgun into the front seat created a risk of death to both of them, even though only one of the occupants was killed. The crucial consideration in determining whether a weapon or device fits with this aggravating circumstance is its potential to kill more than one person if the weapon is used in its normal fashion—that is, in the manner in which it was designed. A shotgun is such a weapon.

State v. Jones, 339 N.C. 114 (1994). The evidence was sufficient to support aggravating circumstance (e)(10) when the defendant, from a distance of ten feet, fired a 12-gauge shotgun into the rear seat of a vehicle occupied by the murder victim and three other people. The blast immediately killed one passenger and injured another.

Case Summaries: Propriety of Submitting Multiple Aggravating Circumstances

State v. Smith, 347 N.C. 453 (1998). The defendant was convicted of first-degree murder after setting fire to an apartment building by lighting kerosene, killing one person and seriously injuring others. Distinguishing *State v. Quesinberry*, 319 N.C. 228 (1987), the court ruled that aggravating circumstances (e)(5) (murder during a specified felony, in this case, while defendant engaged in arson) and (e)(10) were both properly submitted to the jury because they addressed different aspects of the defendant's murder, although they both relied on the same evidence. Aggravating circumstance (e)(5) addresses the fact that the defendant committed murder while engaging in another felony—arson. Aggravating circumstance (e)(10) addresses a distinct aspect of the defendant's character—he not only intended to kill a particular person when setting fire to the apartment building, but he also disregarded the value of every human life in the building by using an accelerant to set the fire in the middle of the night.

State v. Davis, 349 N.C. 1 (1998). The defendant, using a .30 caliber M1 carbine rifle, killed three people and injured two others. He was convicted of three counts of first-degree murder and sentenced to death for each. The court ruled that the trial judge did not err in submitting both (e)(10) and (e)(11) (course of violent conduct). There was independent evidence to support both aggravating circumstances, even though some of the evidence may have overlapped.

Case Summaries: Jury Instruction on Aggravating Circumstance (e)(10)

State v. Nobles, 350 N.C. 483 (1999). The trial judge instructed the jury that, concerning aggravating circumstance (e)(10), "a Lorcin 380 caliber semi-automatic pistol is a weapon which would normally be hazardous to the lives of more than one person." The court ruled that the judge erred in giving this instruction because it improperly relieved the state of its burden to prove this element of the aggravating circumstance.

L. Aggravating Circumstance (e)(11): Murder Part of Course of Violent Conduct

G.S. 15A-2000(e)(11) states: "The murder for which the defendant stands convicted was part of a course of conduct in which the defendant engaged and which included the commission by the defendant of other crimes of violence against another person or persons." The constitutionality of this aggravating circumstance has been upheld.[112] It is not necessary that the defendant be charged with, or have been convicted of, the other crime(s) of violence for this aggravating circumstance to apply.[113]

The North Carolina Supreme Court has stated that the following are some of the factors to consider in determining whether the first-degree murder and other violent crime(s) were part of a course of conduct under (e)(11): the temporal proximity of the crimes to one another; a recurrent modus operandi; a similar motivation to commit the crimes; and a connection, common scheme, or some pattern or psychological thread that ties them together.[114] The closer the temporal proximity of the first-degree murder and the other violent crime(s), the more likely that the acts are a part of a plan or course of action. The further apart the violent acts, the more one must carefully consider other factors, such as modus operandi and motivation. However, the court also has stated that temporal proximity affects the weight of the evidence, not its admissibility.[115]

Case Summaries: Sufficient Evidence of Aggravating Circumstance (e)(11)

State v. Phillips, 365 N.C. 103 (2011). Aggravating circumstance (e)(11) was "fully supported" where the defendant and his accomplices killed four people and seriously injured another during an attempt to rob a drug dealer and his friends.

State v. Wilkerson, 363 N.C. 382 (2009). The court briefly reaffirmed that when a defendant is convicted of multiple murders, each may be used to support aggravating circumstance (e)(11) as to the other(s).

State v. Raines, 362 N.C. 1 (2007). The state's "evidence showed that defendant's actions in murdering each victim [a husband and a wife] were part of the course of conduct which resulted

---

112. State v. Roper, 328 N.C. 337 (1991) (aggravating circumstance (e)(11) not unconstitutionally vague or overbroad on its face or as applied); State v. Williams, 305 N.C. 656 (1982); State v. Pinch, 306 N.C. 1 (1982) (no double jeopardy violation in submitting each of two murders as an (e)(11) aggravating circumstance for the other).

113. State v. Boyd, 343 N.C. 699 (1996).

114. State v. Price, 326 N.C. 56 (1990); State v. Cummings, 332 N.C. 487 (1992).

115. *Cummings*, 332 N.C. 487.

in other crimes of violence to another person—the other victim. This is sufficient to satisfy the (e)(11) aggravating circumstance."

State v. Jones, 358 N.C. 330 (2004). The defendant killed his wife and stepson. The killing of each victim supported the finding of aggravating circumstance (e)(11) as to the other victim. The North Carolina Supreme Court stated that "the fact that the victims were related to each other and to the accused supports submission of the course of conduct aggravator."

State v. Moses, 350 N.C. 741 (1999). The defendant was convicted of two first-degree murders that had been committed two months apart. The court ruled that the trial judge did not err in submitting aggravating circumstance (e)(11) for each first-degree murder conviction. The evidence showed that the drug-related murders had a common *modus operandi* and motivation.

State v. Hoffman, 349 N.C. 167 (1998). The defendant was convicted of first-degree murder and armed robbery of a jewelry store that occurred on November 27, 1995. In support of aggravating circumstance (e)(11), the state offered evidence of two bank robberies that occurred on October 20, 1995, and September 18, 1995. The court ruled that the trial judge did not err in submitting this aggravating circumstance. The court noted that the time span between the robberies was sufficiently close to be considered part of the same course of conduct. Also, there was a similar *modus operandi*—all the robberies occurred in small towns near Charlotte and in daylight hours while the businesses were open, shared the same motive (pecuniary gain), and the same sawed-off shotgun, green bag, ski mask, and white Nissan were used.

State v. Cummings, 346 N.C. 291 (1997). The defendant was convicted of first-degree murder for a killing (victim A) that occurred during an armed robbery on April 22, 1994. At the capital sentencing hearing, the state offered evidence of aggravating circumstance (e)(11) that was based on a pending charge of murder (victim B) that occurred on April 19, 1994. The court ruled that there was sufficient evidence of the murder of victim B and a sufficient link between the murders to support (e)(11). Both murders occurred within several days of each other. The evidence showed that both murders were committed to obtain money for cocaine and involved elderly victims. The defendant had a plan involving the murders of both victims.

State v. Boyd, 343 N.C. 699 (1996). The court ruled that a defendant need not be convicted of or charged with the "other crimes of violence" to prove (e)(11). The court also ruled that evidence that the defendant assaulted a person with a deadly weapon with intent to kill during the murder of another person supported the finding of (e)(11).

State v. Chapman, 342 N.C. 330 (1995). There was sufficient evidence to submit aggravating circumstance (e)(11) for two murders committed about two months apart. The murders shared a common *modus operandi*. Both murder victims were young women with drug habits; the defendant knew both and had smoked crack with each. One victim was nude when found, and the other was nude from the waist down. Both victims suffered blunt-force trauma injuries to the head; one victim died of strangulation, and the pathologist could not exclude the possibility that the other victim had also been strangled. Each body was found in the lowest part of a vacant house; the houses were within two blocks of each other.

State v. Walls, 342 N.C. 1 (1995). There was sufficient evidence to submit aggravating circumstance (e)(11) when, over a period of two days, the defendant physically battered the mother of the 3-year-old murder victim, threatened to kill her, and ultimately tried to drown her on the day he succeeded in drowning her 3-year-old son.

State v. Garner, 340 N.C. 573 (1995). The defendant's fatal shooting of a convenience store clerk four days before the double murders for which he was being tried, and the shooting of a taxicab driver eighteen days after the commission of the double murders, together were proper evidence to support the submission of aggravating circumstance (e)(11). The events were close in time and the *modus operandi* was similar because the defendant used the same pistol to kill or attempt to kill each victim and had one or two accomplices with him during each crime. Also, the same motive (committing robbery to obtain money for drugs) existed for all these crimes.

State v. Skipper, 337 N.C. 1 (1994). The defendant's fatal shooting of two people within seconds of each other was sufficient evidence of (e)(11). *See also* State v. Gregory, 340 N.C. 365 (1995) (sufficient evidence of (e)(11) when defendant killed two people and seriously wounded a third person).

State v. Lee, 335 N.C. 244 (1994). The defendant was convicted of first-degree murder for kidnapping, sexually assaulting, and murdering a female jogger (victim A) on September 24, 1989. The state offered evidence under (e)(11) that on September 29, 1989, the defendant kidnapped, raped, sodomized, and robbed another female jogger (victim B), who managed to escape. Relying on *State v. Cummings*, 332 N.C. 487 (1992), summarized immediately below, the court ruled that this evidence was sufficient to support (e)(11) when the defendant's motivation and *modus operandi* were the same for both crimes, they were committed within five days of each other, and the defendant believed that both victims were members of an associated group (female joggers from a local university).

State v. Cummings, 332 N.C. 487 (1992). The court ruled that evidence of the defendant's murder of two sisters (one of whom was the murder victim in this case), where the killings were committed twenty-six months apart, was sufficient to support aggravating circumstance (e)(11). The court noted (1) that the defendant had a similar motivation to commit both murders, namely, an overpowering desire to assert his relationship with his children (both victims were mothers of his children), and (2) that the victims were sisters. The evidence also showed that the defendant had another motive to kill the victims: he believed they had taken advantage of him in a cocaine deal. Also, the *modus operandi* was the same for both murders. Both victims were shot in the back of the head, were naked when killed, were wrapped in similar plastic and sheets, and were buried in shallow graves.

State v. Price, 326 N.C. 56 (1990). The defendant's commission of arson of a former girlfriend's home when she was in the home and a violent hostage-taking incident, both occurring within days after the commission of the murder being tried, were sufficient evidence to support (e)(11).

State v. McLaughlin, 323 N.C. 68 (1988). Aggravating circumstance (e)(11) was properly submitted for each of two murders (mother and daughter were killed during the same night) committed by the defendant.

State v. Rogers, 316 N.C. 203 (1986). There was sufficient evidence to submit (e)(11) when the defendant shot and killed victim A and then fired his weapon at victim B, intending to kill him.

State v. Williams, 305 N.C. 656 (1982). There was sufficient evidence to submit (e)(11) when the defendant—after robbing and murdering the victim in Gastonia—drove to Concord, where he robbed and murdered a convenience store employee.

Case Summaries: Propriety of Submitting Multiple Aggravating Circumstances

State v. Tirado, 358 N.C. 551 (2004). Aggravating circumstances (e)(11), (e)(5) (murder during the commission of a specified felony), and (e)(6) (murder for pecuniary gain) were all properly submitted. Separate evidence supported each.

State v. Berry, 356 N.C. 490 (2002). The court ruled that the trial judge did not err in submitting both (e)(4) (murder to prevent arrest or effect escape) and (e)(11). The (e)(4) aggravating circumstance focused on the defendant's motive for killing victim A—to prevent her from talking about the defendant's murder of victim B that he had committed seven weeks earlier. The (e)(11) aggravating circumstance required the jury to review the objective facts of the two murders to determine whether the offenses constituted a course of conduct.

State v. Davis, 349 N.C. 1 (1998). The defendant, using a .30 caliber M1 carbine rifle, killed three people and injured two others. He was convicted of three counts of first-degree murder and sentenced to death for each. The court ruled that the trial judge did not err in submitting both (e)(10) (use of hazardous weapon to endanger multiple others) and (e)(11). There was independent evidence to support both aggravating circumstances, even though some of the evidence may have overlapped.

State v. DeCastro, 342 N.C. 667 (1996). The court ruled that separate evidence supported the submission of aggravating circumstances (e)(9) (especially heinous, atrocious, or cruel) and (e)(11). Evidence supporting (e)(9) included the defendant's infliction of twenty-three stab wounds on the victim. The victim did not die a quick, painless death but remained conscious during the five to ten minutes that elapsed before she died. In addition, her jeans and panties had been pulled to her ankles, her shirt torn open, and her bra pulled above her breasts, exposing her breasts, torso, and lower body. The evidence supporting (e)(11) was entirely different from the evidence supporting (e)(9): before killing the victim, the defendant robbed, beat, and murdered the victim's husband.

State v. Gibbs, 335 N.C. 1 (1993). The trial judge did not err in submitting both (e)(5) (murder during a specified felony, here, a burglary) and (e)(11). These circumstances were not supported by the same evidence. Proof that the defendant committed a murder during the burglary did not also require proof of the commission of violence toward the other victims (two other people were murdered). And the defendant need not have engaged in a violent course of conduct to have committed a murder in the course of the burglary.

State v. Gay, 334 N.C. 467 (1993). The court stated that a trial judge should instruct the jury to ensure that it does not use the same evidence to find more than one aggravating circumstance. *See also* State v. Rouse, 339 N.C. 59 (1994) (failure to request such an instruction limited appellate review to plain error analysis, and court did not find plain error in this case).

State v. Jones, 327 N.C. 439 (1990). Distinguishing *State v. Quesinberry*, 319 N.C. 228 (1987), the court ruled that the submission of both (e)(6) (murder for pecuniary gain) and (e)(11) was proper. The aggravating circumstances were not supported by the same evidence. Evidence of the robbery of a convenience store supported (e)(6). Evidence that the defendant killed the victim, wounded another, and fired shots endangering others supported (e)(11).

State v. Green, 321 N.C. 594 (1988). In a first-degree murder prosecution for the murders of victims A, B, and C at a bar, the trial judge properly submitted the (e)(4) aggravating circumstance (prevent murder to arrest or effect escape) in the sentencing for the murder of C, since the evidence showed that C (who was in a defenseless position) was killed to eliminate him as a witness in the killings of A and B. The court also ruled, based on *State v. Hutchins*, 303 N.C. 321 (1981), that it was proper to submit both aggravating circumstance (e)(4) and aggravating circumstance (e)(11). The (e)(11) aggravating circumstance involved the factual circumstances of the defendant's crimes, while the (e)(4) aggravating circumstance involved the defendant's motive in shooting a person in a defenseless position.

State v. Vereen, 312 N.C. 499 (1985). Considering the jury instructions in this case, the trial judge erred in submitting two aggravating circumstances because they were based on the same evidence, namely, the attempted rape of the murder victim's daughter. The jury instruction for aggravating circumstance (e)(5) (murder during a specified felony) set out that the murder was committed while the defendant committed the crime of first-degree burglary *or attempted rape*. The jury instruction for (e)(11) set out that the murder was part of a course of conduct that included the defendant's commission of violent crimes against others, including felonious assault *and attempted rape*.

State v. Conaway, 339 N.C. 487 (1995). The court reviewed the evidence at the sentencing hearing and ruled that separate substantial evidence supported each of the following three aggravating circumstances in double murder case: (e)(5) (murder during a specified felony, here, kidnapping), (e)(6) (murder for pecuniary gain, in this case, by taking money from a cash register during an armed robbery), and (e)(11) (in this case, the defendant killed a second person). The court stated that when there is separate substantial evidence to support each aggravating circumstance, it is proper for each circumstance to be submitted even though evidence supporting each may overlap. *See also* State v. Rose, 339 N.C. 172 (1994) (separate evidence supported submission of both (e)(3) (previous conviction of violent felony) and (e)(11)).

Case Summaries: What Constitutes a Crime of Violence

State v. Price, 326 N.C. 56 (1990). Arson of a house when the defendant knew people were inside was an act of violence under aggravating circumstance (e)(11).

State v. Jerrett, 309 N.C. 239 (1983). The kidnapping of another was a crime of violence when the evidence showed that the defendant, after shooting and killing the murder victim, pointed a gun at another person and forced her to come with him in a car.

Case Summaries: Jury Instruction on Aggravating Circumstance (e)(11)

State v. Berry, 356 N.C. 490 (2002). The court ruled that the trial judge erred in the jury instruction on aggravating circumstance (e)(11). The instruction allowed the jury to find the aggravating circumstance without also finding that the murder of victim A was part of the course of conduct that included the earlier murder of victim B.

Chapter 6

Mitigating Circumstances

Chapter 6

Mitigating Circumstances

This chapter discusses mitigating circumstances, both statutory and nonstatutory, and the case law interpreting them. Very generally, a mitigating circumstance is anything in the defendant's character or background, or any aspect of the charged offense, that might support a sentence other than death.[1] In the words of the pertinent North Carolina Pattern Jury Instruction (hereinafter N.C.P.I.), a mitigating circumstance is defined as "a fact or group of facts, which do not constitute a justification or excuse for a killing, or reduce it to a lesser degree of crime than first degree murder, but which may be considered as extenuating or reducing the moral culpability of the killing or making it less deserving of extreme punishment than other first degree murders."[2] A mitigating circumstance need not have a nexus to the offense, that is, it may concern the defendant but not the crime.[3]

Mitigating circumstances are addressed in subsection (f) of Section 15A-2000 of the North Carolina General Statutes (hereinafter G.S.). The mitigating circumstances listed in subdivisions (1) through (8) of G.S. 15A-2000(f) are commonly known as *statutory* mitigating circumstances. These mitigating circumstances are as follows:

- (f)(1) The defendant has no significant history of prior criminal activity.
- (f)(2) The defendant committed the murder while under the influence of a mental or emotional disturbance.
- (f)(3) The victim was a voluntary participant in the murder or consented to the murder.
- (f)(4) The defendant was an accomplice in or accessory to a murder committed by another person and the defendant's participation was relatively minor.
- (f)(5) The defendant acted under duress or under the domination of another person.
- (f)(6) The defendant's capacity to appreciate the criminality of the conduct or to conform his or her conduct to the requirements of law was impaired.
- (f)(7) The defendant's age at the time of the murder.
- (f)(8) The defendant aided in the apprehension of another capital felon or testified truthfully for the state in another prosecution of a felony.

1. Eddings v. Oklahoma, 455 U.S. 104 (1982) (citing Lockett v. Ohio, 438 U.S. 586 (1978)).
2. N.C.P.I. Crim.—150.10.
3. Tennard v. Dretke, 542 U.S. 274, 287 (2004) ("[W]e cannot countenance the suggestion that low IQ evidence is not relevant mitigating evidence . . . unless the defendant also establishes a nexus to the crime.").

G.S. 15A-2000(f)(9) also defines as a mitigating circumstance "[a]ny other circumstance arising from the evidence which the jury deems to have mitigating value." This is commonly called the *catchall* mitigating circumstance.

Defendants often ask the trial judge to submit, either under the umbrella of (f)(9) or pursuant to a defendant's constitutional right to have the jury consider all relevant mitigating circumstances, specific mitigating circumstances not enumerated in the statute, such as the fact that the defendant was abused by his or her parents. Such circumstances are commonly known as *nonstatutory* mitigating circumstances. Even when specific nonstatutory mitigating circumstances are submitted to the jury, the judge also should submit the catchall language of subdivision (9) as a separate, additional mitigating circumstance.[4]

A. General Rules Concerning Mitigating Circumstances

The pattern jury instruction provides that the defendant has the burden of proving a mitigating circumstance by a preponderance of evidence.[5] The North Carolina Supreme Court has ruled that it is constitutional to place the burden of proof on the defendant.[6]

The United States Supreme Court has ruled that the Eighth and Fourteenth Amendments to the United States Constitution require that the sentencer—the jury, in North Carolina—may not be precluded from considering as a mitigating circumstance any relevant aspect of the defendant's character or record and any of the circumstances of the offense that the defendant offers as a basis for a sentence less than death.[7] Accordingly, a trial judge must instruct on a mitigating circumstance when substantial evidence supports the circumstance such that a juror could reasonably find the circumstance.[8] The North Carolina Supreme Court has stated that a trial judge should resolve in the defendant's favor any reasonable doubt as to whether or not to submit a mitigating circumstance to the jury.[9]

The North Carolina Supreme Court has ruled that, when evidence offered by the defendant is sufficient to support a finding of a statutory mitigating circumstance, a trial judge must submit that circumstance to the jury, regardless of whether or not there has been a request to do so and even if

---

4. N.C.P.I. Crim.—150.10.

5. *Id.* The instruction also states that the evidence of a mitigating circumstance must "satisfy you" that the mitigating circumstance exists. The North Carolina Supreme Court has held that this does not create a higher standard than a preponderance of the evidence, nor is the instruction too vague to be understood. *See, e.g.*, State v. Elliott, 360 N.C. 400 (2006); State v. Payne, 337 N.C. 505 (1994).

6. State v. Moore, 335 N.C. 567 (1994); State v. Lloyd, 321 N.C. 301 (1988). *See also* Walton v. Arizona, 497 U.S. 639 (1990) (a state may constitutionally place on the defendant the burden of proving mitigating evidence).

7. Lockett v. Ohio, 438 U.S. 586 (1978); Eddings v. Oklahoma, 455 U.S. 104 (1982). *See also* State v. Cherry, 298 N.C. 86 (1979).

8. The court has described the test somewhat differently in various cases. In *State v. Laws*, 325 N.C. 81, 98 (1989), and *State v. Skipper*, 337 N.C. 1, 53 (1994), the court used the term "substantial evidence." In *State v. Price*, 331 N.C. 620, 632 (1992), the court used the term "jury could reasonably find," although "jury" should be replaced by "juror" in light of the ruling in *McKoy v. North Carolina*, 494 U.S. 433 (1990) (jury need not be unanimous regarding mitigating circumstances). *See also* State v. Fullwood, 329 N.C. 233 (1991). Of course, a defense counsel's mere assertion of facts at a charge conference is not probative of the existence of a mitigating circumstance to support its submission to the jury. State v. Mickey, 347 N.C. 508 (1998). Although a trial judge has a duty under North Carolina law to instruct on mitigating circumstances, the Eighth Amendment does not require a specific instruction. Buchanan v. Angelone, 522 U.S. 269 (1998).

9. State v. Pinch, 306 N.C. 1 (1982). *See also* State v. Payne, 328 N.C. 377 (1991).

the defendant does not want the judge to submit that circumstance.[10] The same is true if the evidence offered by the state is sufficient to support a finding of a statutory mitigating circumstance.[11] (See the discussion later in this chapter under "Mitigating Circumstance (f)(1): No Significant Prior Criminal History" on special jury instructions when a defendant objects to the submission of a statutory mitigating circumstance.) The erroneous failure to submit a statutory mitigating circumstance will require a new sentencing hearing unless the state can prove that the error was harmless beyond a reasonable doubt.[12] Generally, the submission of a nonstatutory mitigating circumstance that is similar to a statutory mitigating circumstance does not cure the error because the jury is not required to give mitigating value to a nonstatutory mitigating circumstance it finds.[13] When a trial judge allows a defendant's request for the submission of a statutory mitigating circumstance, any error in submitting the circumstance is invited error not reviewable on appeal.[14] Erroneous submission of a statutory mitigating circumstance other than at the defendant's request is usually harmless error.[15]

A trial judge's duty to submit nonstatutory mitigating circumstances to the jury is more limited. A judge's failure to submit such a circumstance is not error absent a defendant's timely written request to the judge to submit the circumstance.[16] A *timely* written request likely means that the request must be made by the time of the jury charge conference at the sentencing hearing.[17] A trial judge must include appropriate nonstatutory mitigating circumstances in writing on the issues and recommendation form when the defendant makes a timely written request to do so.[18] Absent such a request, the

---

10. State v. Hurst, 360 N.C. 181, 197 (2006) (trial judge did not err in following defendant's request not to submit mitigating circumstance (f)(1) (no significant criminal history); although the invited error doctrine is inapplicable to failure to submit statutory mitigating circumstances and the trial judge must submit any circumstances that are supported by the record regardless of a defendant's request, it is also true that "a whole record review will necessarily include consideration of the parties' positions as to whether the instruction should be given"); State v. Walker, 343 N.C. 216 (1996); State v. Holden, 338 N.C. 394 (1994) (error not to instruct on (f)(7) (defendant's age) where the defendant was 30 years old but a psychologist testified to a mental age of 10 years, even though defendant withdrew request for submission); *Price*, 331 N.C. 620 (error, but harmless, to grant defendant's request not to submit the first prong of (f)(6) (impaired capacity to appreciate the criminality of conduct) and to submit only the second prong (impaired capacity to conform conduct to the law), where evidence supported both prongs).

11. State v. Stokes, 308 N.C. 634 (1983).

12. *See, e.g.*, State v. Quick, 337 N.C. 359 (1994).

13. *Id. See also generally Hurst*, 360 N.C. 181.

14. State v. Polke, 361 N.C. 65 (2006) (judge submitted (f)(1) (no significant criminal history) at the defendant's request; defendant could not challenge submission on appeal).

15. State v. Phillips, 365 N.C. 103 (2011) (concerning erroneous submission of (f)(4) (minor participation)).

16. State v. Rouse, 339 N.C. 59 (1994) (after the defendant submitted a list of proposed nonstatutory mitigating circumstances, the trial judge stated that he would submit thirteen nonstatutory mitigating circumstances and provided the state and the defendant with a copy of all circumstances to be submitted; defense counsel endorsed the judge's proposed submissions; although the judge did not include all of the defendant's requested circumstances, the state supreme court ruled that defense counsel's express approval of the judge's submissions and counsel's failure to object to the circumstances not submitted rendered any error in failing to submit the other circumstances invited error under G.S. 15A-1443(c)); State v. Hill, 331 N.C. 387 (1992); State v. Johnson, 298 N.C. 47 (1979).

17. *Cf.* State v. McNeil, 350 N.C. 657 (1999) (trial judge informed defense counsel at the jury charge conference that instructions on (f)(2) (mental or emotional disturbance) and (f)(6) (impaired capacity) would include references to the defendant's alcoholism and personality disorder; after the jury had begun its deliberations, defense counsel contended that organic brain damage should have been included; trial judge properly refused to reinstruct the jury because Rule 21 of the General Rules of Practice for the Superior and District Courts does not permit the defendant to propose a new evidentiary matter if the defendant had the opportunity to raise that issue at the charge conference).

18. State v. Cummings, 326 N.C. 298 (1990). Of course, a judge would have the duty to do so with *statutory* mitigating circumstances even absent a request from the defendant.

trial judge's failure to list the circumstances on the form is not error.[19] Furthermore, a trial judge may decline to submit a nonstatutory mitigating circumstance that is subsumed in other statutory or nonstatutory mitigating circumstances that are submitted or may combine two nonstatutory mitigating circumstances into one circumstance.[20] The recent trend among trial judges appears to be away from attempting to combine or reduce the number of nonstatutory mitigating circumstances, however.

As with aggravating circumstances, evidence admitted during the guilt-innocence phase is competent and admissible to support the submission of mitigating circumstances; there is no need to readmit the evidence at the capital sentencing hearing.[21]

In *McKoy v. North Carolina*,[22] the United States Supreme Court held that it was unconstitutional to require a jury to find a mitigating circumstance unanimously before a juror could consider that circumstance during the process of determining whether the jury's recommendation should be death or life imprisonment. The Court ruled that individual jurors must be allowed to consider the mitigating circumstances each juror finds regardless of whether other jurors agree.[23] As a result of the *McKoy* ruling, N.C.P.I.—Crim. 150.10 was rewritten. It now provides that in connection with Issue Two (determination of whether mitigating circumstances exist) on the Issues and Recommendation as to Punishment Form, if one or more jurors finds by a preponderance of evidence that a particular mitigating circumstance exists, the jury must indicate "yes" in the appropriate place on the form. In deciding Issue Three (the weighing of aggravating circumstances with mitigating circumstances), it provides that each juror may[24] consider any mitigating circumstance or circumstances the juror has determined to exist. It provides a similar instruction for deciding Issue Four (whether aggravating

---

19. *Id.*

20. State v. Robinson, 355 N.C. 320, 340 (2002) ("For each of the omitted proposed mitigating circumstances, a corresponding mitigating circumstance that subsumed the proposed one was submitted to the jury. Also, the jury could have availed itself of the opportunity to consider any evidence of mitigating value under the (f)(9) catchall mitigating circumstance."); State v. Taylor, 354 N.C. 28 (2001) (similar); State v. Walls, 342 N.C. 1 (1995) (proposed nonstatutory mitigating circumstances were properly subsumed in both statutory and other nonstatutory mitigating circumstances); State v. McLaughlin, 341 N.C. 426, 445 (1995) (nonstatutory mitigating circumstances that the defendant "was of low intelligence with poor judgment and limited insight," "was under a pattern of substance abuse at the time of the commission of the crime," and had "limited mental capacity at the time of the trial [that] significantly reduced his culpability for the offense" were subsumed in the submitted statutory mitigating circumstances (f)(2) (mental or emotional disturbance) and (f)(6) (impaired capacity) and the catchall mitigating circumstance (f)(9)); State v. Spruill, 338 N.C. 612 (1994) (trial judge did not err in combining two aspects of the defendant's educational background into one nonstatutory mitigating circumstance); State v. Lee, 335 N.C. 244 (1994) (trial judge did not err in not submitting the nonstatutory mitigating circumstance that the defendant's inability to conform his conduct to the requirements of the law was by reason of his mental defect and not of his own making; it was subsumed by mitigating circumstances (f)(2) (mental or emotional disturbance) and (f)(6) (impaired capacity) and by a nonstatutory mitigating circumstance concerning whether the defendant appreciated his mental condition and dangerousness); State v. Benson, 323 N.C. 318 (1988) (similar); State v. Fullwood, 323 N.C. 371 (1988) (similar); State v. Greene, 324 N.C. 1 (1989) (similar).

21. G.S. 15A-2000(a)(3).

22. 494 U.S. 433 (1990). *McKoy* was based on the earlier case of *Mills v. Maryland*, 486 U.S. 367 (1988). For a more recent Supreme Court case discussing *Mills* and *McKoy*, see *Smith v. Spisak*, 558 U.S. 139 (2010).

23. However, the North Carolina Supreme Court has ruled that a jury must be unanimous in answering "yes" or "no" to Issues One, Three, and Four on the issues and recommendation form. State v. McCarver, 341 N.C. 364 (1995) (Issue One asks jurors to indicate whether they have found one or more listed aggravating circumstances; Issues Three and Four are briefly described in the text following this note).

24. N.C.P.I.–Crim. 150.10, in describing the weighing process required by Issue Three, states that "each juror may consider" any mitigating circumstance that he or she found to exist. In *Lee*, 335 N.C. 244, the court ruled that the use of the term "may" in the instruction did not impermissibly allow jurors to ignore mitigating circumstances that they had found to exist. The court noted that the instruction also states that the jury "must" weigh aggravating circumstances against mitigating ones.

circumstances are sufficiently substantial to impose the death penalty when considered with mitigating circumstances). The North Carolina Supreme Court has ruled that there is no constitutional requirement that a juror must consider a mitigating circumstance found by another juror to exist. Therefore, the court found these instructions constitutionally valid because they give each juror the opportunity to consider and to weigh—in deciding Issue Three and Issue Four—whatever mitigating circumstances he or she individually finds in deciding Issue Two.[25]

The state high court has also rejected the argument that capital sentencing jury instructions, because they allow different jurors to reach different conclusions regarding the existence of mitigating circumstances, violate a defendant's right to a unanimous jury verdict under Article I, Section 24, of the North Carolina Constitution. The court ruled that while the state constitution does require a unanimous verdict to convict a defendant of a crime, it does not apply to sentencing recommendations.[26]

Any juror who finds the existence of a *statutory* mitigating circumstance must give it some weight in the process of making the sentence recommendation, though the amount of weight to give the circumstance is left to each juror's discretion.[27]

Any juror who finds the existence of a *nonstatutory* mitigating circumstance must decide whether or not to give any weight to that circumstance in the process of making the sentence recommendation.[28] Thus a nonstatutory mitigating circumstance is mitigating only if a juror considers it to have mitigating value.

The court has ruled that this procedure in giving weight to mitigating circumstances is constitutional.[29] Many cases reiterate these basic holdings.[30]

B. Peremptory Jury Instructions for Mitigating Circumstances

If credible, uncontroverted evidence is presented to support the existence of a mitigating circumstance, whether statutory or nonstatutory, a trial judge must give a peremptory jury instruction on that circumstance upon the defendant's timely written[31] request. In order to be timely, the request must be made by the time of the jury charge conference at the sentencing hearing.

Even if the trial judge gives a peremptory instruction on a statutory or nonstatutory mitigating circumstance, a juror may decline to find the existence of that circumstance because the supporting

25. State v. Skipper, 337 N.C. 1 (1994); *Lee*, 335 N.C. 244.

26. State v. Baldwin, 330 N.C. 446 (1992).

27. State v. Howell, 343 N.C. 229 (1996) (judge erred in informing jury that they could give no weight to statutory mitigating circumstance); State v. Keel, 337 N.C. 469 (1994).

28. *Keel*, 337 N.C. 469.

29. *Id.*

30. *See, e.g.,* State v. Walters, 357 N.C. 68 (2003); State v. Flippen, 349 N.C. 264 (1998); *Howell*, 343 N.C. 229; State v. Jaynes, 342 N.C. 249 (1995); State v. Baker, 338 N.C. 526 (1994); State v. Reeves, 337 N.C. 700 (1994); State v. Robinson, 336 N.C. 78 (1994); *Keel*, 337 N.C. 469; State v. Hill, 331 N.C. 387 (1992); State v. Fullwood, 323 N.C. 371 (1988).

31. G.S. 15A-1231 allows a party to "tender written instructions" for the court's consideration. Cases noting the requirement of a written submission include *State v. Raines*, 362 N.C. 1, 23 (2007) ("Neither party has pointed us to, nor can we find in the record, defendant's written request for [a peremptory] instruction."), and *State v. Duke*, 360 N.C. 110, 131 (2005) (ruling that the trial judge properly declined to give a peremptory instruction in part because "there is nothing in the record or the transcript to indicate such a request was made in writing by defendant").

evidence is not credible or convincing.[32] In addition, a juror may decline to find the existence of a nonstatutory mitigating circumstance because the juror does not consider the circumstance to have mitigating value.[33]

N.C.P.I.—Crim. 150.11 provides language for a peremptory instruction on a *statutory* mitigating circumstance. It is not an appropriate instruction for a *nonstatutory* mitigating circumstance because a juror may decide that the nonstatutory mitigating circumstance does not have mitigating value even though the juror finds it to exist.[34] In *State v. Lynch*,[35] the North Carolina Supreme Court approved the following peremptory instruction for a nonstatutory mitigating circumstance: "All of the evidence tends to show [named mitigating circumstance]. Accordingly, as to this mitigating circumstance, I charge that if you find the facts to be as all the evidence tends to show, you will answer, 'Yes,' as to the mitigating circumstance Number [#] on the issue and recommendation form if one or more of you deems it to have mitigating value." N.C.P.I.—Crim. 150.12 contains a variant of this instruction with slightly different language.

When the state stipulates to the existence of a mitigating circumstance, the judge must give the jury a *mandatory* peremptory instruction that requires the jury to find the mitigating circumstance. In such a case, the judge must instruct the jury to answer "yes" on the issues and recommendation form to the finding of that mitigating circumstance.[36] The North Carolina Supreme Court has ruled that a defendant is not entitled to a directed verdict on a statutory mitigating circumstance even if the evidence in support of the circumstance is substantial, manifestly credible, and uncontradicted.[37]

Case Summaries: Evidence Did Not Support Peremptory Instruction

State v. Waring, 364 N.C. 443 (2010). The trial judge did not err in declining to give peremptory instructions on mitigating circumstances (f)(2) (mental or emotional disturbance), (f)(6) (impaired capacity), and (f)(8) (assistance to the state). The first two mitigating circumstances, though supported by the defendant's experts, were contested by "evidence presented during the guilt portion of the trial, the cross-examination of defendant's experts, and the rebuttal testimony presented on behalf of the State by [the state's expert]." As to the (f)(8) mitigating circumstance, "[a]lthough some evidence supported defendant's claim that he aided in the apprehension of [a co-defendant], other evidence indicated that defendant provided several different names and identities for the other man involved in the murder, led police officers on a wild goose chase[,] . . . and stated that he was not going to snitch."

State v. Maness, 363 N.C. 261 (2009). The trial judge did not err in declining to give peremptory instructions as to two nonstatutory mitigating circumstances, namely, (1) that the defendant

32. State v. Thompson, 359 N.C. 77 (2004); State v. Alston, 341 N.C. 198 (1995); State v. Rouse, 339 N.C. 59 (1994); State v. Holden, 338 N.C. 394 (1994); State v. Gay, 334 N.C. 467 (1993); State v. McCollum, 334 N.C. 208 (1993); State v. Johnson, 298 N.C. 47 (1979).

33. *Thompson*, 359 N.C. 77; *Gay*, 334 N.C. 467.

34. State v. Green, 336 N.C. 142 (1994); State v. Gregory, 340 N.C. 365 (1995).

35. 340 N.C. 435, 476 (1995).

36. State v. Flippen, 344 N.C. 689 (1996); State v. Hill, 347 N.C. 275 (1997). *Cf.* State v. Garcell, 363 N.C. 10 (2009) (defendant was not entitled to a mandatory peremptory instruction on mitigating circumstance (f)(7) (defendant's age), as the state did not stipulate to that circumstance).

37. *Garcell*, 363 N.C. at 55 n.8 ("A mandatory peremptory instruction on a particular circumstance is akin to a directed verdict, but a directed verdict is not the appropriate device in this context."); State v. Holden, 346 N.C. 404 (1997); State v. Carter, 342 N.C. 312 (1995). In *Holden*, the court effectively disavowed the suggestion in *Rouse*, 339 N.C. 59, that a directed verdict might be appropriate. It is now clear that a peremptory instruction is the appropriate instruction when there is uncontradicted evidence supporting a mitigating circumstance.

was cooperative with officers after being taken into custody and was polite during interviews and (2) that the defendant has accepted responsibility for his criminal conduct. The evidence on the defendant's cooperation and politeness was conflicting. The defendant's admission that he had killed the victim and that he was guilty of second-degree murder was more an attempt to avoid the death penalty than an acceptance of responsibility.

State v. Raines, 362 N.C. 1 (2007). The trial judge properly declined to give a peremptory instruction on mitigating circumstance (f)(2) (mental or emotional disturbance), as the evidence was conflicting. Concerning the preservation of the issue, the court stated, "[n]either party has pointed us to, nor can we find in the record, defendant's written request for such an instruction."

State v. Forte, 360 N.C. 427 (2006). The trial judge properly declined to give a peremptory instruction on mitigating circumstances (f)(2) (mental or emotional disturbance) and (f)(6) (impaired capacity). The defendant's evidence consisted mainly of the testimony of his expert witnesses. The state supreme court, quoting *State v. Barden*, 356 N.C. 316 (2002), stated that "the testimony of an expert witness who has prepared an analysis of a defendant in preparation for trial 'lacks the indicia of reliability based on the self-interest inherent in obtaining appropriate medical treatment' and, because not 'manifestly credible,' does not support a peremptory instruction." Furthermore, the evidence was not uncontroverted because, inter alia, "[s]everal of defendant's friends and family testified that they never saw any signs that defendant had a mental or emotional disturbance."

State v. Duke, 360 N.C. 110 (2005). The trial judge properly declined to give a peremptory instruction on mitigating circumstances (f)(2) (mental or emotional disturbance) and (f)(6) (impaired capacity). First, "[t]here [wa]s nothing in the record or the transcript to indicate such a request was made in writing by defendant." Second, the evidence on both circumstances was conflicting.

State v. Bonnett, 348 N.C. 417 (1998). The court ruled that the trial judge did not err in not giving a peremptory instruction on mitigating circumstance (f)(4) (minor participation). The evidence was not uncontroverted. The court noted that the evidence tended to show that the defendant supplied the murder weapon and took the money box during the robbery and murder for which he was being sentenced.

State v. Stephens, 347 N.C. 352 (1997). The court ruled that, based on the following evidence, the trial judge did not err in failing to give a peremptory instruction for mitigating circumstance (f)(1) (no significant criminal history). The defendant was being sentenced for convictions of murders committed on January 20, 1995. The defendant was convicted (1) in 1982 of hit-and-run involving property damage and driving under the influence; (2) in 1983 of driving while license suspended; and (3) in 1986 of driving under the influence. Also, the defendant had a long history of purchasing and using illegal drugs.

State v. Buckner, 342 N.C. 198 (1995). The court ruled that the defendant was not entitled to a peremptory instruction on the nonstatutory mitigating circumstance that the defendant was a hard worker because there was evidence that the defendant stole from two of his employers and stopped working for another employer after being involved in a fight at work.

State v. Simpson, 341 N.C. 316 (1995). The court examined the evidence supporting mitigating circumstances (f)(1) (no significant criminal history), (f)(2) (mental or emotional disturbance), (f)(6) (impaired capacity), and (f)(7) (defendant's age) and ruled that the trial judge properly refused to give peremptory instructions because the evidence concerning these mitigating circumstances was not uncontroverted.

State v. McLaughlin, 341 N.C. 426 (1995). The court examined the evidence supporting several nonstatutory mitigating circumstances and ruled that the trial judge did not err (except in regard to one circumstance, discussed in a separate summary in the next section, below) in refusing to give peremptory instructions because the evidence supporting the circumstances was not uncontroverted and manifestly credible.

State v. Lynch, 340 N.C. 435 (1995). The trial judge did not err in failing to give a peremptory instruction on the (f)(2) (mental or emotional disturbance) and (f)(6) (impaired capacity) mitigating circumstances. The evidence offered to support these circumstances was not uncontroverted.

State v. Rouse, 339 N.C. 59 (1994). The court ruled that even when a defendant is entitled to a peremptory instruction on a mitigating circumstance because the evidence is uncontroverted, the jury is still free to reject the circumstance if it does not find the evidence credible or convincing. (The court disapproved of language in *State v. Kirkley*, 308 N.C. 196 (1983), that was inconsistent with this ruling.) The court concluded that the jury could have found that the evidence from mental health experts was not credible or convincing on (f)(6) (impaired capacity). The court stated that a defendant may be entitled to a directed verdict on a statutory mitigating circumstance if the evidence in support of the circumstance is substantial, manifestly credible, and uncontradicted but that the evidence in this case did not support such a procedure; this suggestion has subsequently been disavowed, as discussed in the text above.

State v. Lee, 335 N.C. 244 (1994). The trial judge did not err in failing to issue a peremptory instruction concerning mitigating circumstance (f)(6) (impaired capacity). The evidence was not uncontroverted. *See also* State v. Johnson, 298 N.C. 47 (1979) (similar ruling).

State v. Holden, 321 N.C. 125 (1987). The trial judge did not err in failing to give peremptory instructions for four statutory mitigating circumstances: (f)(1) (no significant criminal history); (f)(2) (mental or emotional disturbance); (f)(6) (impaired capacity); and (f)(7) (defendant's age). As to the first three circumstances, the evidence was conflicting. As to the last, the court ruled that "the jury could find that the defendant's age, 30, was not a mitigating factor. The judge also did not err in declining to give peremptory instructions concerning eleven nonstatutory mitigating circumstances, six of which the jury did not find.

State v. Spruill, 320 N.C. 688 (1987). The defendant was not entitled to a peremptory instruction on mitigating circumstance (f)(2) (mental or emotional disturbance) when the expert testimony about the defendant's mental and emotional condition was equivocal.

State v. Gladden, 315 N.C. 398 (1986). The defendant was not entitled to a peremptory instruction on mitigating circumstance (f)(1) (no significant criminal history) based on evidence of his prior criminal convictions and prior criminal history in this case. In addition, the defendant failed to make a timely request for the instruction (in fact, the defendant failed to make a request for the instruction at all). The court also ruled that the defendant was not entitled to a peremptory instruction on (f)(3) (victim voluntary participant). The state produced ample evidence to contradict the defendant's assertion that the victim initially attacked him with a knife. In addition, the defendant failed to make a timely request to give this instruction (in fact, the defendant failed to make a request for the instruction).

State v. Noland, 312 N.C. 1 (1984). The trial judge did not err in failing to give a peremptory instruction on mitigating circumstance (f)(1) (no significant criminal history) since there was evidence of a conviction for communicating threats and prior acts of communicating threats and assaulting a female. The trial judge also did not err in failing to give a peremptory instruction on (f)(2) (mental or emotional disturbance) since conflicting evidence was offered by the defendant and the state.

State v. Gardner, 311 N.C. 489 (1984). The trial judge did not err in failing to give a peremptory instruction on mitigating circumstance (f)(7) (defendant's age). The defendant was 24 years old at the time of the murders. *See also* State v. Oliver, 309 N.C. 326 (1983) (similar ruling; defendant was 19 years, 11 months old).

State v. Smith, 305 N.C. 691 (1982). The trial judge did not err in failing to give a peremptory instruction on mitigating circumstance (f)(6) (impaired capacity) when the testimony of two eyewitnesses suggested that the defendant was in complete control of his faculties when he committed the murder, in contrast to the defendant's expert testimony that his faculties were impaired.

Case Summaries: Evidence Supported Peremptory Instruction

State v. Lloyd, 354 N.C. 76 (2001). The court ruled that the trial judge erred in not submitting a peremptory instruction for mitigating circumstance (f)(8) (assistance to the state). The defendant's evidence in the capital sentencing hearing showed that his truthful testimony at another trial was both uncontroverted and credible.

State v. McLaughlin, 341 N.C. 426 (1995). The court ruled that the trial judge erred in not giving a peremptory instruction concerning the nonstatutory mitigating circumstance that the defendant had achieved a position as a cook in the prison kitchen since the evidence about this circumstance was both uncontroverted and manifestly credible. (The court, however, found the error to be harmless beyond a reasonable doubt.)

State v. Jones, 339 N.C. 114 (1994). The court ruled that the trial judge erred in not giving a peremptory instruction on sixteen nonstatutory mitigating circumstances. (The court, however, found the error to be harmless beyond a reasonable doubt; the jury found six of the circumstances, and unanimously rejected the remainder, leading the reviewing court to conclude that "the jury rejected the mitigating circumstances not found because they determined these circumstances had no mitigating value, not because they rejected the factual basis for the[m].")

State v. Holden, 338 N.C. 394 (1994). The court ruled that the defendant offered uncontroverted evidence of mitigating circumstance (f)(2) (mental or emotional disturbance) and that the trial judge erred in denying the defendant's request for a peremptory instruction. The court also ruled that the error was not harmless beyond a reasonable doubt. Although one or more jurors found that the mitigating circumstance existed, it was not known whether all jurors found that it existed. It is possible that had the peremptory instruction been given, more jurors or all jurors would have done so. And that could have affected the balancing of mitigating circumstances against aggravating circumstances, thereby affecting the sentencing recommendation.

State v. Gay, 334 N.C. 467 (1993). At the sentencing hearing, the defendant submitted a written request for peremptory instructions for all mitigating circumstances. The court ruled that the trial judge must, if requested, give a peremptory instruction for any mitigating circumstances—

statutory or nonstatutory—if supported by uncontroverted evidence. The court granted a new sentencing hearing because the trial judge erred in failing to give a peremptory instruction for several nonstatutory mitigating circumstances supported by uncontroverted evidence. (The court noted that individual jurors may still reject a mitigating circumstance if the supporting evidence was not convincing or—with a nonstatutory mitigating circumstance—they do not consider it to have mitigating value.)

Case Summaries: Content of Peremptory Instruction

State v. Taylor, 362 N.C. 514 (2008). Relying on *State v. Trull*, 349 N.C. 428 (1998), the court rejected the defendant's argument that "the trial court committed plain error by failing to give individualized instructions and explanations for each of the thirty-two nonstatutory mitigating circumstances submitted to the jury and by giving a single peremptory instruction for those mitigating circumstances." This procedure did not devalue the nonstatutory mitigating circumstances, and indeed, one or more jurors found thirty of the circumstances to exist.

State v. Lynch, 340 N.C. 435 (1995). The court ruled that the following peremptory instruction for a nonstatutory mitigating circumstance was proper: "All of the evidence tends to show [named mitigating circumstance]. Accordingly, as to this mitigating circumstance, I charge that if you find the facts to be as all the evidence tends to show, you will answer, 'Yes,' as to the mitigating circumstance Number [#] on the issue and recommendation form if one or more of you deems it to have mitigating value."

State v. Green, 336 N.C. 142 (1994). The trial judge did not err in refusing the defendant's request to give—for *nonstatutory* mitigating circumstances—the peremptory instruction in N.C.P.I.—CRIM. 150.11 because that instruction is only appropriate for *statutory* mitigating factors. Although a peremptory instruction on a nonstatutory mitigating circumstance may direct the jurors that the evidence supports the factual existence of the circumstance, each juror—before finding the circumstance—must also decide that the circumstance has mitigating value.

Case Summaries: Timely Written Request for Peremptory Instruction

State v. Garcell, 363 N.C. 10 (2009). Trial counsel did not request a peremptory instruction on certain nonstatutory mitigating circumstances, and the state supreme court held that the defendant thereby waived any claim of error concerning the lack of a peremptory instruction.

State v. Raines, 362 N.C. 1 (2007). The trial judge properly declined to give a peremptory instruction on mitigating circumstance (f)(2) (mental or emotional disturbance) as the evidence was conflicting. Concerning the preservation of the issue, the court stated, "[n]either party has pointed us to, nor can we find in the record, defendant's written request for such an instruction."

State v. Duke, 360 N.C. 110 (2005). The trial judge properly declined to give a peremptory instruction on mitigating circumstances (f)(2) (mental or emotional disturbance) and (f)(6) (impaired capacity), in part because "[t]here is nothing in the record or the transcript to indicate such a request was made in writing by defendant."

State v. Johnson, 298 N.C. 47 (1979). The court ruled that a defendant must make a timely request for a peremptory instruction for a mitigating circumstance. *See also* State v. Gladden, 315 N.C. 398 (1986) (defendant failed to request peremptory instruction); State v. Gay, 334 N.C. 467 (1993) (trial judge erred in not giving peremptory instructions on mitigating circumstances supported by uncontroverted evidence when defendant had made written request for such instructions).

State v. Skipper, 337 N.C. 1 (1994). The defendant made a written request for a peremptory instruction for all mitigating circumstances. However, on the trial judge's oral inquiry, the defendant asked for peremptory instructions on just two mitigating circumstances. The court ruled that, based on the defendant's response to the trial judge's oral inquiry, the judge did not err in giving peremptory instructions only for these two mitigating circumstances.

Case Summaries: Content of Request for Peremptory Instruction

State v. Womble, 343 N.C. 667 (1996). At a capital sentencing hearing, the defendant made a general request that peremptory instructions be given for any uncontroverted mitigating circumstances. On appeal, the defendant argued that the trial judge erred in failing to give a peremptory instruction for the nonstatutory mitigating circumstance that nothing was taken from the murder victim's residence. The court noted that the defendant failed to make a specific request that a peremptory instruction be given for this particular mitigating circumstance and ruled, relying on *State v. Skipper*, 337 N.C. 1 (1994), discussed in the section immediately above, that the trial judge did not err in failing to give a peremptory instruction for this circumstance.

State v. Gregory, 340 N.C. 365 (1995). The defendant made a general written request for peremptory instructions for all his requested mitigating circumstances but did not clearly specify that he was seeking a different peremptory instruction for statutory and nonstatutory mitigating circumstances (nor did the defendant propose a different instruction for the nonstatutory mitigating circumstances). Also, the defendant did not specify which nonstatutory mitigating circumstances were supported by uncontroverted evidence and, therefore, entitled him to a peremptory instruction. On appeal, the defendant argued that the trial judge erred in not giving peremptory instructions on twenty-three nonstatutory mitigating circumstances. The court ruled that the defendant's request for peremptory instructions was inadequate under *State v. Green*, 336 N.C. 142 (1994) (different peremptory instructions required for statutory and nonstatutory mitigating circumstances), and that, therefore, the trial judge did not err in not giving peremptory instructions.

C. Mitigating Circumstances and Resentencing Hearings

The North Carolina Supreme Court has issued rulings that involve the submission of mitigating circumstances at capital resentencing hearings. A defendant is not entitled, under the collateral estoppel doctrine, to a jury instruction at a capital resentencing hearing that mitigating circumstances unanimously found by the jury at the first capital sentencing hearing are established as a matter of law.[38] A defendant is also not entitled to a peremptory jury instruction for a mitigating circumstance based on the state's stipulation of its existence at a prior capital sentencing hearing.[39]

D. Mitigating Circumstance (f)(1): No Significant Prior Criminal History

G.S. 15A-2000(f)(1) states: "The defendant has no significant history of prior criminal activity."

In deciding whether to submit this mitigating circumstance to the jury, a trial judge must determine whether any rational juror could conclude based on the evidence that the defendant had no significant history of prior criminal activity. A defendant's criminal history is considered "significant" if it is likely to affect or influence the jury's determination of its recommended sentence; it is not merely the number of prior criminal activities but the nature and recency of these activities that is considered in determining whether to submit this circumstance.[40] In 2006, the North Carolina Supreme Court suggested that trial judges had been leaning too far in the direction of submitting this circumstance, especially in cases in which the defendant had a criminal record and objected to the submission of this circumstance.[41]

Evidence relevant to the submission of this mitigating circumstance may come from evidence offered at the guilt phase or at the sentencing hearing, including, for example, evidence offered by the state or elicited on its cross-examination of the defendant.[42] Relevant evidence includes the commission of uncharged or unadjudicated crimes as well as criminal convictions;[43] criminal activity prior to age 18 also may be considered.[44] However, such relevant evidence is limited to criminal activity that was committed before the date of the murder for which the defendant is being sentenced.[45]

If neither the state nor the defendant presents any evidence regarding whether or not the defendant has any criminal history, then the trial judge should not submit this circumstance.[46] When a defendant presents general evidence concerning his or her background and upbringing, and that evidence does not include an express discussion of the defendant's criminal history or lack thereof, the mere fact that evidence of prior criminal activity is absent from the defendant's case is not enough to warrant submission of mitigating circumstance (f)(1).[47]

---

38. State v. Adams, 347 N.C. 48 (1997). *Cf.* Bobby v. Bies, 556 U.S. 825 (2009) (even if the defendant's mental retardation was established at his capital sentencing hearing, which took place prior to *Atkins v. Virginia*, 536 U.S. 304 (2002), the state was not collaterally estopped from contesting the defendant's retardation in post-*Atkins* proceedings, in part because the finding of retardation was not "necessary to the judgment," i.e., to the defendant's death sentence, and in fact cut against that judgment; this reasoning implies that any mitigating circumstance found in a case in which the defendant was sentenced to death is likewise not "necessary to the judgment" and not eligible for collateral estoppel).

39. State v. Flippen, 349 N.C. 264 (1998).

40. State v. Jones, 339 N.C. 114 (1994); State v. Sexton, 336 N.C. 321 (1994).

41. State v. Hurst, 360 N.C. 181 (2006).

42. State v. Quick, 337 N.C. 359 (1994); State v. Walls, 342 N.C. 1 (1995).

43. State v. Ingle, 336 N.C. 617 (1994).

44. State v. Garcell, 363 N.C. 10 (2009) (the trial judge did not commit plain error in instructing the jury to consider the defendant's prior convictions for robbery and second-degree kidnapping, offenses he committed when he was 16 years old; nothing in *Roper v. Simmons*, 543 U.S. 551 (2005), which prohibits the imposition of the death penalty on a defendant who was under 18 years old when he or she committed murder, limits the jury's ability to consider prior offenses committed by the defendant when he or she was under 18).

45. State v. Forte, 360 N.C. 427 (2006); State v. Sidden, 347 N.C. 218 (1997); State v. Coffey, 336 N.C. 412 (1994).

46. State v. Gibbs, 335 N.C. 1 (1993); Delo v. Lashley, 507 U.S. 272 (1993); State v. Laws, 325 N.C. 81 (1989); State v. Fullwood, 323 N.C. 371 (1988).

47. State v. Taylor, 362 N.C. 514 (2008).

Sometimes a defendant, as a matter of strategy, will not request—or will even object to—the submission of this circumstance in an attempt to preserve credibility with the jury or to avoid giving the state the right to present evidence of the defendant's prior criminal history. As noted earlier in this chapter, a trial judge must submit a statutory mitigating circumstance when it is supported by sufficient evidence, even if the defendant does not request its submission or even objects to its submission.[48] However, the North Carolina Supreme Court has set out guidelines for judges and prosecutors for when this circumstance is submitted despite the defendant's objection:

- A prosecutor must not argue to the jury that a defendant has requested that a particular mitigating circumstance be submitted or has sought to have the jury find that circumstance.
- The trial judge should instruct the jury that the defendant did not request that the mitigating circumstance be submitted.
- The trial judge also should instruct the jury that the submission of the mitigating circumstance is required as a matter of law because there is some evidence from which the jury could, but is not required to, find the mitigating circumstance to exist.[49]

The state may offer evidence of the defendant's prior criminal activity to rebut the defendant's evidence in support of mitigating circumstance (f)(1). The evidence may consist of testimony by witnesses to this criminal activity and court records of convictions.[50] However, the North Carolina Supreme Court has ruled that the state's evidence may be offered only in the rebuttal stage of the sentencing hearing, not in the state's case-in-chief.[51] If the defendant does not present any evidence in support of (f)(1), the state has no right to present rebuttal evidence.

Case Summaries: Sufficient Evidence of Mitigating Circumstance (f)(1)

State v. Phillips, 365 N.C. 103 (2011). The defendant committed murder in 2003. The trial judge properly submitted (f)(1) where the defendant had prior convictions for "felony breaking and entering in 1999, felony larceny in 1998, driving under the influence in 1996, larceny in 1993, sale of marijuana in 1991, and sale of a narcotic or controlled substance in 1990." The state supreme court noted that the defendant's "prior convictions were somewhat remote in time and do not appear to involve violence against a person."

State v. Waring, 364 N.C. 443 (2010). The trial judge submitted (f)(1) over the defendant's objection. His criminal history consisted of "breaking and entering a motor vehicle (a Class I felony) and several misdemeanors, including misdemeanor larceny, public disturbance, defrauding an innkeeper, trespassing, carrying a concealed weapon, and possession of marijuana. There was also evidence of unspecified theft activity, mostly at school. Because the evidence . . . was limited to minor offenses, the trial court" properly submitted the circumstance.

---

48. *See supra* nn. 10–13 and accompanying text. *See also* State v. Quick, 337 N.C. 359 (1994) (listing cases). In *State v. Walls*, 342 N.C. 1 (1995), the court ruled that the defendant was not denied his Sixth Amendment right to the effective assistance of counsel when his attorney argued to the jury that he was not asking them to find in favor of the (f)(1) mitigating circumstance based on the facts in that case. The court rejected the defendant's argument that because no juror found (f)(1), the jurors used that finding as a *de facto* aggravating circumstance.

49. State v. Walker, 343 N.C. 216 (1996). The court also stated that absent extraordinary facts, the erroneous submission of a mitigating circumstance is harmless. *See also* State v. Bone, 354 N.C. 1 (2001) (no extraordinary facts existed that rendered any possible error by trial judge in submitting mitigating circumstance prejudicial to defendant).

50. State v. Maynard, 311 N.C. 1 (1984); State v. Roper, 328 N.C. 337 (1991); State v. Holden, 321 N.C. 125 (1987).

51. State v. Brown, 315 N.C. 40 (1985); State v. Taylor, 304 N.C. 249 (1981).

State v. Cummings, 361 N.C. 438 (2007). The defendant neither requested nor objected to the submission of (f)(1). The trial judge did not err in submitting the circumstance. The defendant's criminal history apparently consisted of (1) "underage alcohol and illegal drug use," which the jury might have viewed as minor, and (2) a robbery that took place about a month before the robbery and murder that resulted in the capital trial, which the jury might have viewed as an aberration from the defendant's generally law-abiding behavior.

State v. Parker, 354 N.C. 268 (2001). The court ruled, relying on *State v. Rowsey*, 343 N.C. 603 (1996), and other cases, that the trial judge did not err in submitting (f)(1). The defendant was convicted in 1995 of sixteen counts of obtaining property by false pretenses, nonviolent crimes that arose during one brief period of the defendant's life. The court stated that a rational jury could have concluded that the defendant had no significant prior criminal history.

State v. Blakeney, 352 N.C. 287 (2000). The defendant's prior criminal history included evidence of drug abuse and a conviction of an armed robbery committed in 1989 in which he struck the robbery victim in the head with his gun. Based on this evidence, the court ruled that the trial judge did not err in submitting (f)(1). The court also rejected, citing *State v. Ball*, 344 N.C. 290 (1996), the defendant's argument that this mitigating circumstance should not have been submitted because the court also submitted the statutory aggravating circumstance set forth in G.S. 15A-2000(e)(3) (previous conviction of violent felony).

State v. Williams, 350 N.C. 1 (1999). The court ruled that the judge did not err in submitting (f)(1) over the defendant's objection. The defendant had been convicted of many misdemeanor assaults on females (one in 1995, four in 1992, and one in 1989) and other offenses such as communicating threats, trespass, and burglary. The court concluded that a rational juror could have found that the defendant's prior criminal activity was insignificant.

State v. Fletcher, 348 N.C. 292 (1998). The court ruled that the trial judge erred in not submitting (f)(1). The court stated that its analysis in *State v. Jones*, 346 N.C. 704 (1997) (sufficient evidence to submit (f)(1)), discussed immediately below, had emphasized that the defendant's prior convictions in that case consisted of property crimes rather than violent crimes. A common theme in cases in which (f)(1) should have been submitted is the defendants' predominantly nonviolent criminal histories. The court noted that while the defendant's prior criminal history showed that he stole from others for most of his life and had appeared in recent years to have largely supported himself by stealing and occasionally selling drugs, his breaking and enterings and larcenies were not connected to any violent behavior.

State v. Jones, 346 N.C. 704 (1997). The defendant at his capital sentencing hearing argued against the submission of mitigating circumstance (f)(1) and the trial judge did not submit it. The court here ruled that the judge below erred as to (f)(1) because the following evidence supported its submission. In 1988 the defendant was convicted of four misdemeanor larcenies involving stealing from his employer over a period of four or five years. In 1993 the defendant was convicted of two or three felony larcenies for stealing jewelry from a motel in which he worked. The defendant did not receive a prison sentence for any of these convictions. He had smoked marijuana since middle school and had used cocaine since 1988. There was no evidence that he had committed any violent crimes before the murder of the victim in 1993.

State v. Geddie, 345 N.C. 73 (1996). The court ruled that the trial judge did not err in submitting (f)(1), even though the defendant had two prior felonious assault convictions and an attempted robbery conviction. The assault convictions occurred ten and fifteen years, respectively, before the trial of the present case, while the robbery conviction was five years old. The court stated that a rational juror could have found the existence of (f)(1) under these facts.

State v. Walls, 342 N.C. 1 (1995). The defendant had convictions for driving while impaired, assault, communicating threats, escape, nonfelonious breaking and entering, receiving stolen goods, possessing a stolen vehicle, and possessing stolen credit cards. The court ruled that the trial judge did not err in submitting (f)(1) and noted that it had previously upheld the submission of this circumstance based on criminal activities equal to or greater than the defendant's in this case, citing *State v. Turner*, 330 N.C. 249 (1991), and *State v. Wilson*, 322 N.C. 117 (1988). The court stated that an important factor in the trial judge's determination of whether a rational juror could reasonably find this mitigating circumstance is the nature and age of the prior criminal activities, rather than the mere number of them.

State v. Quick, 337 N.C. 359 (1994). Evidence presented at a resentencing hearing showed that the defendant had illegally used drugs and had been convicted of larceny, receiving stolen goods, and forgery. The court ruled, relying on *State v. Mahaley*, 332 N.C. 583 (1992), and *State v. Wilson*, 322 N.C. 117 (1988), both summarized below, that the trial judge erred in not submitting (f)(1) and that the error was not harmless "beyond reasonable doubt." The court also ruled that the submission of a nonstatutory mitigating circumstance that was similar to (f)(1) did not cure the error since a jury is not required to give mitigating value to a nonstatutory mitigating circumstance.

State v. Ingle, 336 N.C. 617 (1994). The defendant objected to the trial judge's submission of (f)(1) and assigned the judge's submission as error on appeal. The court here ruled that the trial judge properly submitted (f)(1), relying on its rulings in *State v. Mahaley*, 332 N.C. 583 (1992), *State v. Wilson*, 322 N.C. 117 (1988), and *State v. Lloyd*, 321 N.C. 301 (1988), all summarized below. Evidence of the defendant's prior criminal history consisted principally of his use of illegal drugs and the fact that his aunt "took out warrants on him" for communicating threats and trespassing. The court noted that it was proper to consider unadjudicated crimes in determining the sufficiency of evidence under (f)(1). *See also* State v. Frye, 341 N.C. 470 (1995) (trial judge properly submitted (f)(1) when evidence showed defendant's extensive use of illegal drugs and his many prior periods of incarceration).

State v. Mahaley, 332 N.C. 583 (1992). The evidence showed that the defendant had no record of criminal convictions and her prior criminal history consisted of using illegal drugs and stealing money and credit cards to support her drug habit. The court ruled that this evidence required the trial judge to submit (f)(1) without regard to the wishes of the state or the defendant. The court ordered a new sentencing hearing because the state did not prove that the failure to submit (f)(1) was harmless beyond a reasonable doubt.

State v. Turner, 330 N.C. 249 (1991). There was sufficient evidence from which a reasonable juror could find (f)(1). Adjudicated criminal activity consisted solely of the misdemeanor offenses of receiving stolen goods, larceny, assault with a deadly weapon, and worthless check. Unadjudicated criminal activity included possession of marijuana, theft when the defendant was a juvenile, sale of marijuana to the victim that led to the murder, and possession of a sawed-off shotgun.

State v. McNeil, 327 N.C. 388 (1990). The court ruled that a reasonable juror could find (f)(1) based on evidence that the defendant's only prior conviction was for voluntary manslaughter, a conviction incurred seven years before the defendant's murder trial.

State v. Wilson, 322 N.C. 117 (1988). The court ruled that the trial judge erred in not submitting (f)(1) when the defendant had a prior felony conviction for the second-degree kidnapping of his former wife (who was not the murder victim in this case), incurred four years before the murder being tried, had stored illegal drugs in his shed, and had participated in a theft with the murder victim.

State v. Lloyd, 321 N.C. 301 (1988). The court ruled that the trial judge did not err in submitting (f)(1) over the defendant's objection when the defendant had two felony convictions about twenty years before the murder for which he was being sentenced and had seven alcohol-related misdemeanor convictions over an eleven-year period up to the time of the murder. *See also* State v. Buckner, 342 N.C. 198 (1995) (no error in submitting (f)(1) when defendant had been convicted of seven felonious breaking and entering offenses, one common law robbery offense, and one drug trafficking offense over a six-month period that occurred two years before the commission of the first-degree murder for which he was being sentenced; court stated that all of this criminal activity occurred within a brief period of time, most of it was nonviolent, and the defendant received probation for the convictions). However, *Lloyd* was criticized in the later case of *State v. Hurst*, 360 N.C. 181 (2006), summarized in the next section, below.

State v. Brown, 315 N.C. 40 (1985). The court ruled that the trial judge did not err in submitting (f)(1) over the defendant's objection when the defendant had eighteen prior felony convictions, and these convictions had occurred in 1963 and 1965, when the defendant was under 21 years old. However, *Brown* was criticized in the later case of *State v. Hurst*, 360 N.C. 181 (2006), summarized in the next section, below.

Case Summaries: Insufficient Evidence of Mitigating Circumstance (f)(1)

State v. Lane, 365 N.C. 7 (2011). The trial court did not err in refusing to submit (f)(1). The defendant had prior convictions for DWI and for felonious restraint. If the judge had submitted (f)(1), the state would have called the defendant's ex-wife, the victim of the felonious restraint, to testify about the incident, during which the defendant abducted his ex-wife and forced her into sexual activity. The North Carolina Supreme Court noted that the defendant did not request the submission of (f)(1) and stated that "the forecast evidence . . . supports the trial court's . . . determination that no rational jury would have found that defendant's prior criminal activity was insignificant."

State v. Taylor, 362 N.C. 514 (2008). At his capital sentencing hearing, the defendant called two mental health experts and three former teachers who testified generally regarding his background and his impoverished upbringing. "Defendant offered no evidence of his criminal record, and defense counsel twice indicated to the trial court that defendant was not seeking submission of the (f)(1) mitigating circumstance. Nevertheless, defendant [argued on appeal that] he was entitled to an (f)(1) instruction because the testimony of his sentencing witnesses allegedly depicted a comprehensive life history from which significant criminal activity was absent." The state supreme court rejected this argument, stating that "testimony that defendant used marijuana but not other drugs, drank while underage but was never charged, and did not get in many fights at school is not substantial evidence that defendant lacked a significant history of prior criminal activity." To support (f)(1), the defendant would have needed to develop his evidence further; the absence of evidence about a defendant's criminal history is not evidence that the defendant has no significant criminal history.

State v. Forte, 360 N.C. 427 (2006). Although the trial judge erroneously considered the defendant's conduct after the murder for which he was being sentenced in refusing to submit (f)(1), the decision not to submit the circumstance was correct based only on the defendant's conduct prior to the murder, which included "felonious larceny and possession of stolen property . . . , driving while impaired . . . , resisting and assaulting a police officer during a fight in a club . . . , and driving while license revoked," as well as drug use, probation and parole violations, and aggressive behavior.

State v. Hurst, 360 N.C. 181 (2006). The defendant asked the trial judge not to submit (f)(1) and to submit as a nonstatutory mitigating circumstance the fact that "[p]rior to this offense, the defendant had no significant history of violent criminal activity." The trial judge did so. On appeal, the defendant argued that the trial judge erred in failing to submit (f)(1). The state supreme court first rejected the idea that any error was invited by the defendant. Because G.S. 15A-2000(b) states that a trial judge "shall" instruct on any mitigating circumstance that is supported by the evidence, "the doctrine of invited error cannot apply" when a judge erroneously grants a defendant's request not to instruct on a mitigating circumstance. (However, the court stated that when reviewing a trial judge's decision not to instruct on a mitigating circumstance, it would consider the whole record, including whether the defendant requested an instruction.) Next, the court strongly suggested that (f)(1) was being submitted too often, i.e., that it was being submitted in too many cases in which the defendant's criminal history was substantial and in which the submission of (f)(1) could work to the defendant's disadvantage. In keeping with that reasoning, the court ruled that the trial judge correctly declined to submit (f)(1) in this case, where the defendant had "broken into a residence . . . a few months before the instant murder and stolen a firearm"; had several prior breaking or entering convictions; had abused marijuana, crack cocaine, and Oxycontin; and had a pending charge of driving under the influence. Finally, the court overruled *State v. Rouse*, 339 N.C. 59 (1994), to the extent that *Rouse* suggested "that if the evidence pertaining to a defendant's criminal history is offered in a context other than for the purpose of determining whether an (f)(1) instruction should be given, the defendant might not be entitled to the instruction." In fact, an instruction on (f)(1) may be based on any relevant evidence in the record.

State v. Thompson, 359 N.C. 77 (2004). The trial judge properly declined to submit (f)(1) where the defendant "had twice previously committed armed robbery of a . . . restaurant and, in the process, kidnapped five victims."

State v. King, 353 N.C. 457 (2001). The state presented evidence at the capital sentencing hearing that the defendant had previously been convicted of first-degree murder of a former wife (the killing occurred in 1967). The court ruled, relying on *State v. McNeil*, 350 N.C. 657 (1999), summarized below, that the trial judge did not err in not submitting mitigating circumstance (f)(1).

State v. Greene, 351 N.C. 562 (2000). The defendant beat his father to death in order to steal money from him. The court ruled that the trial judge did not err in failing to submit (f)(1). The court noted that much of the defendant's prior criminal activity was recurrent, recent, and similar to his conduct the day of the robbery and murder of his father, and thus it was significant.

Most of the criminal activity that resulted in the defendant's prior convictions occurred after the defendant was 30 years old and within seven years of the murder of his father. Before robbing his father and beating him to death with a shotgun, the defendant habitually sneaked into his father's house and stole money while his father was outside working. During the same time period, the defendant would assault his girlfriend. Thus, the defendant had a significant history of recurrent and escalating criminal conduct, much of which was close in time to the murder.

State v. Hamilton, 351 N.C. 14 (1999). The defendant was convicted of a first-degree murder committed in 1994. The court ruled that the trial judge did not err in failing to submit (f)(1). The defendant had been convicted in 1988 of two counts of rape of a 15-year old in which he pulled a knife on the victim; the evidence showed that the defendant raped the victim twice in North Carolina (for which he was convicted) and then raped her twice in South Carolina. The defendant had also been convicted of an unprovoked second-degree murder in 1974 and, in 1987, of misdemeanor assault on a female and misdemeanor escape. The court noted the defendant's second-degree murder conviction and its ruling in *State v. McNeil*, 350 N.C. 657 (1999), summarized immediately below.

State v. McNeil, 350 N.C. 657 (1999). The court ruled that the trial judge did not err in failing to submit (f)(1). Although the court in a prior appeal of this case, 327 N.C. 388 (1990), had stated that there was evidence to support the submission of this mitigating circumstance, the court here noted that the state in the resentencing hearing offered new evidence of prior serious criminal activity (burglary, larceny, and hit-and-run) in addition to a voluntary manslaughter conviction. This evidence was more extensive and significant than the proof presented at the first trial and supported the trial judge's ruling not to submit the mitigating circumstance.

State v. Bonnett, 348 N.C. 417 (1998). The court ruled that the trial judge did not err in failing to submit (f)(1). The defendant's prior criminal convictions included accessory after the fact to murder, two counts of accessory after the fact to felonious assault, several drug convictions, and larceny of an automobile. The court distinguished *State v. Jones*, 346 N.C. 704 (1997), summarized in the previous section, above, on the basis that the defendant in *Jones* had not been convicted of any violent crimes.

State v. Atkins, 349 N.C. 62 (1998). The court ruled that the trial judge did not err in failing to submit (f)(1). The court noted that the defendant had a significant history of violent attacks, including fights in the military and repeated assaults on the victim's mother, even while she was pregnant. He also repeatedly and viciously beat his own son, a completely defenseless infant and the victim of the murder in this case.

State v. Sidden, 347 N.C. 218 (1997). The defendant murdered a father and his two sons. The father was murdered several hours before the sons. The defendant was tried only for the murders of the two sons and was convicted. At the death sentencing hearing, the trial judge considered the murder of the father in determining whether to submit (f)(1) in sentencing the defendant for the murder of the two sons. The court here, relying on *State v. Coffey*, 336 N.C. 412 (1994) (only crimes committed before the murder being sentenced may be considered in deciding whether to submit (f)(1)), ruled that the judge properly considered the murder of the father in considering this mitigating circumstance. The court rejected the defendant's argument that the father's murder could not be considered because it was part of the course of conduct during which the two sons were murdered. The court ruled that the judge acted properly in not submitting (f)(1) because, in addition to the defendant's murder of the father, the defendant had been involved in the illegal sale of alcohol and drugs during his entire adult life.

State v. Powell, 340 N.C. 674 (1995). The trial judge properly did not instruct on (f)(1) when there was insubstantial evidence about the defendant's prior criminal history. The only evidence consisted of testimony about the defendant's cocaine use and a witness's passing reference that the defendant was temporarily released from jail to attend his father's funeral (nothing was mentioned about the offense for which the defendant was in jail). Neither the state nor the defendant mentioned the defendant's criminal record or introduced it into evidence.

State v. Daughtry, 340 N.C. 488 (1995). The trial judge properly did not instruct on (f)(1) when the evidence showed that the defendant often beat the murder victim, shot an acquaintance in the leg, and was convicted of driving under the influence and assault inflicting serious injury (in which the defendant struck a man on the head with a large stick, causing a concussion and breaking his jaw and ribs). No rational juror could have found that the defendant had no significant history of prior criminal activity. The court cited its ruling in *State v. Sexton*, 336 N.C. 321 (1994), summarized below.

State v. Jones, 339 N.C. 114 (1994). The trial judge properly did not instruct on (f)(1) when the evidence showed that the defendant had three prior violent felony convictions: two counts of felonious assault and one count of robbery. No rational juror could have found that the defendant had no significant history of prior criminal activity.

State v. Rouse, 339 N.C. 59 (1994). The court ruled that the evidence did not entitle the defendant to the submission of (f)(1). The defendant's mother testified that the defendant sustained a head injury in an automobile accident; he had been drinking at the time of the accident and had a 0.19 blood alcohol concentration. The defendant's mother drove him to work because he "lost his driver's license," and the defendant did not attempt to regain his license because he did not want to. The defendant's mother also testified about his attempted suicide. After his arrest for murder, the defendant became "very combative" with the arresting officer. The defendant used illegal drugs for many years. The court found that the references in this case to the defendant's criminal activity were "cursory and unsubstantiated," and the court stated that testimony about it was "elicited in contexts in which the jury would not have considered it as bearing" on this mitigating circumstance or on the defendant's character. For example, evidence of the defendant's drug abuse was offered to show that the defendant was mentally impaired at the time of the murder. However, this aspect of the court's analysis was subsequently overruled in *State v. Hurst*, 360 N.C. 181 (2006), as detailed above.

State v. Skipper, 337 N.C. 1 (1994). The court ruled that the trial judge did not err in refusing to submit (f)(1). The defendant had been convicted in 1978, 1982, and 1984 of assault with a deadly weapon inflicting serious injury. The court concluded that these convictions, which occurred within twelve years of the murder being tried and which were similar to the murder, were evidence that the defendant had a significant record. Therefore, a juror could not have rationally found this mitigating circumstance, particularly since the jury unanimously found these prior felony assault convictions as an aggravating circumstance under G.S. 15A-2000(e)(3) (previous conviction of violent felony).

State v. Sexton, 336 N.C. 321 (1994). The evidence of the defendant's prior criminal activity was a conviction of forgery and uttering on May 1, 1989, and a conviction for two counts of assault on a female on October 22, 1989. The court noted that one of these counts was an assault by choking of a female that occurred less than one year before the strangulation of the murder victim. The defendant testified he did not remember choking the assault victim, a circumstance strikingly similar to his professed lack of memory about the details of the strangulation of the murder victim. The court stated that "[g]iven the nature and recency of his record of assault, we cannot say that the trial court erred in determining that no reasonable juror could have concluded defendant's criminal history was insignificant." Therefore, the trial judge did not err in failing to submit (f)(1). [*Author's note*: Compare the rulings in the following cases in which the court found the evidence sufficient to support the submission of (f)(1): *State v. Williams*, 350 N.C. 1 (1999); *State v. Walls*, 342 N.C. 1 (1995); *State v. Mahaley*, 332 N.C. 583 (1992); *State v. Wilson*, 322 N.C. 117 (1988); *State v. Lloyd*, 321 N.C. 301 (1988).]

State v. Jones, 336 N.C. 229 (1994). The trial judge properly refused to submit (f)(1), based on the following evidence, because a jury could not have rationally found the existence of this circumstance. The defendant was using illegal drugs for several weeks before the murder. He had broken into a particular convenience store "six or seven times" and had stolen various articles. He had broken into a pawn shop and stolen several guns. He sold some of the guns and used one of them to kill the victim in this case. Members of the defendant's family testified that he had shoplifted and "hustled" as a child.

State v. Robinson, 336 N.C. 78 (1994). The trial judge properly refused to submit (f)(1), based on the following evidence, because a jury could not have rationally found the existence of this circumstance. The defendant had been involved in criminal activity since adolescence. (The defendant was 31 years old at the time of the sentencing hearing.) He had been a drug user since age 13. He made his living selling drugs, and he sometimes earned $4,000 to $5,000 a week doing so. He had been seen selling illegal drugs—including cocaine, marijuana, and PCP—in Maryland and two North Carolina cities. Three years before the murder for which he was being sentenced, he was convicted of robbery of a business and of two of its employees. Evidence also showed that the defendant, in connection with the present murder, had come from Maryland to sell drugs and to commit a robbery.

State v. Gibbs, 335 N.C. 1 (1993). The trial judge properly refused to submit (f)(1) when neither the state nor the defendant presented any evidence about the defendant's criminal history. The court followed *State v. Laws*, 325 N.C. 81 (1989), and *Delo v. Lashley*, 507 U.S. 272 (1993). *See also* State v. Fullwood, 323 N.C. 371 (1988) (similar ruling).

State v. McHone, 334 N.C. 627 (1993). The court ruled that the trial judge did not err in refusing to instruct on (f)(1). The defendant, who was 20 years old, had prior convictions for a provisional license violation; failure to stop at the scene of an accident; possession of alcoholic beverage by a person under 21; drunk and disruptive in public; fourteen counts of felonious breaking and entering; thirteen counts of felonious larceny; and conspiracy to break and enter. The defendant's psychiatrist testified that the defendant told him that he had been convicted at age 17 for stealing a woman's pocketbook to get drugs and had also broken into about sixty houses to support his drug problem. The court concluded that no rational juror could have found that the defendant had no significant history of prior criminal activity.

State v. Artis, 325 N.C. 278 (1989). The trial judge did not err in failing to submit this mitigating circumstance when the defendant had many prior convictions for assault and other offenses.

The judge made the determination not to submit this circumstance after conducting a hearing outside the jury's presence to learn of the defendant's prior criminal history.

State v. Laws, 325 N.C. 81 (1989). A witness's cursory and unsubstantiated reference to the defendant's use of marijuana was not substantial evidence to support the submission of (f)(1).

State v. Stokes, 308 N.C. 634 (1983). The court ruled that no reasonable jury could find (f)(1) based on the following criminal activity of the defendant prior to committing murder in 1981: two break-ins in 1974, a break-in in 1975, assault on a female and two larcenies in 1979, and a break-in in 1981. In addition, the defendant admitted that he sold and possessed marijuana on many occasions and he also had stolen marijuana from other drug dealers.

State v. Hutchins, 303 N.C. 321 (1981). The defendant's evidence that he had a good reputation in the community in which he lived was not sufficient evidence by itself to require the trial judge to submit (f)(1).

Case Summaries: Evidence Did Not Support Peremptory Instruction

State v. Stephens, 347 N.C. 352 (1997). The court ruled that the trial judge did not err in failing to give a peremptory instruction for (f)(1). The defendant was sentenced to death for convictions of murders committed on January 20, 1995. The defendant had been convicted of (1) hit-and-run involving property damage and driving under the influence in 1982; (2) driving while license suspended in 1983; and (3) driving under the influence in 1986. Also, the defendant had a long history of purchasing and using illegal drugs.

State v. Gladden, 315 N.C. 398 (1986). Based on evidence of his prior criminal convictions and prior criminal history, the defendant was not entitled to a peremptory instruction on (f)(1). In addition, the defendant failed to make a timely request for the instruction.

State v. Noland, 312 N.C. 1 (1984). The trial judge did not err in refusing to give a peremptory instruction for (f)(1) since there was evidence that the defendant had been convicted of communicating threats and had committed prior acts of communicating threats and assaulting a female. *See also* State v. Simpson, 341 N.C. 316 (1995) (similar ruling).

Case Summaries: Requirement That Criminal Activity Occur before Commission of Murder

State v. Forte, 360 N.C. 427 (2006). Although the trial judge erroneously considered the defendant's conduct after the murder for which he was being sentenced in refusing to submit (f)(1), the decision not to submit the circumstance was correct based only on the defendant's conduct prior to the murder, which included "felonious larceny and possession of stolen property . . . , driving while impaired . . . , resisting and assaulting a police officer during a fight in a club . . . , and driving while license revoked," as well as drug use, probation and parole violations, and aggressive behavior.

State v. Gell, 351 N.C. 192 (2000). Relying on *State v. Coffey*, 336 N.C. 412 (1994), summarized below, the court ruled that it was error to permit the jury to consider a defendant's larceny conviction in connection with mitigating circumstance (f)(1) because the larceny occurred after the murder for which the defendant was being sentenced. The court rejected the state's argument that the larceny was properly considered because it was part of a continuous transaction with the murder.

State v. Sidden, 347 N.C. 218 (1997). The defendant murdered a father and his two sons. The father was murdered several hours before the sons. The defendant was tried only for the murders of the two sons and was convicted. At the death sentencing hearing, the trial judge considered the murder of the father in determining whether to submit (f)(1) in sentencing the defendant for the murder of the two sons. The court here, relying on *State v. Coffey*, 336 N.C. 412 (1994), summarized below, ruled that the judge properly considered the murder of the father in considering this mitigating circumstance. The court rejected the defendant's argument that the father's murder could not be considered because it was part of the course of conduct during which the two sons were murdered. The court ruled that the judge acted properly in not submitting (f)(1) because, in addition to the defendant's murder of the father, the defendant had been involved in the illegal sale of alcohol and drugs during his entire adult life.

State v. Coffey, 336 N.C. 412 (1994). The court ruled that the only evidence of criminal activity that may be considered under (f)(1) is criminal activity committed before the date of the murder for which the defendant is being sentenced.

Case Summaries: State's Evidence Offered in Rebuttal to (f)(1)

State v. Williams, 350 N.C. 1 (1999). The court ruled that the trial judge was not required to determine, before the state presented rebuttal evidence on (f)(1), that a rational juror could find from the evidence that the defendant had no significant history of criminal activity. This determination need only be made before deciding whether to submit this mitigating circumstance. The court also ruled that the trial judge is not required to make findings of fact to explain his or her decision to submit this mitigating circumstance.

State v. Roper, 328 N.C. 337 (1991). The court ruled that the trial judge properly permitted the state to offer testimony of a person who alleged the defendant raped her before the murder being tried because the testimony was offered in rebuttal to the defendant's request that (f)(1) be submitted to the jury. The testimony of the alleged rape was admissible even though the defendant had never been convicted of the crime. (The court noted that the defendant withdrew his request for (f)(1) after this evidence was presented.)

State v. Holden, 321 N.C. 125 (1987). The state properly was permitted during the sentencing hearing to offer rebuttal evidence to (f)(1) by offering the testimony of five witnesses who described the defendant's prior criminal activity; more specifically, they testified as to two rapes and three assaults.

State v. Brown, 315 N.C. 40 (1985). The trial judge erred in allowing the state to introduce evidence in its case-in-chief at the sentencing hearing in rebuttal to the submission of this mitigating circumstance. (The court ruled, however, that the error was harmless beyond a reasonable doubt.) *See also* State v. Taylor, 304 N.C. 249 (1981) (similar ruling).

State v. Maynard, 311 N.C. 1 (1984). The trial judge properly allowed the state to offer, as its rebuttal evidence on (f)(1) and to counter the defendant's good character evidence, a court clerk's testimony, which consisted of the clerk reading the entire judgment (including the original charges) of conviction for the defendant's prior offenses. The state also was properly permitted to offer testimony setting forth the details of these crimes.

Case Summaries: Procedural Issues

State v. Williams, 350 N.C. 1 (1999). The court ruled that the trial judge was not required to determine, before the state presented rebuttal evidence on (f)(1), that a rational juror could find from the evidence that the defendant had no significant history of criminal activity. This determination need only be made before deciding whether to submit this mitigating circumstance. The court also ruled that the judge is not required to make findings of fact to explain his or her decision to submit this mitigating circumstance.

E. Mitigating Circumstance (f)(2): Under the Influence of a Mental or Emotional Disturbance

G.S. 15A-2000(f)(2) states: "The capital felony was committed while the defendant was under the influence of mental or emotional disturbance."

As stated in the jury instruction on this circumstance, N.C.P.I.—CRIM. 150.10, a defendant is under the influence of a mental or emotional disturbance if he or she is in any way affected or influenced by such a disturbance at the time of the murder being tried.[52] The defendant must show some nexus or connection between the disturbance and the murder.[53]

The North Carolina Supreme Court has stated that although evidence of some sort of provocation or triggering event will usually be present when the defendant suffers from a mental or emotional disturbance, evidence of such provocation is not a prerequisite to the submission of this mitigating circumstance to the jury.[54]

The court has also ruled that voluntary intoxication by alcohol or drugs at the time of the murder does not qualify by itself as a mental or emotional disturbance under mitigating circumstance (f)(2), nor does drug or alcohol withdrawal stemming from voluntary intoxication.[55] In addition, an inability to control one's drug or alcohol habits is neither a mental nor an emotional disturbance.[56] However, a defendant may present evidence that an underlying mental or emotional condition was exacerbated by alcohol or drug consumption.[57] Voluntary intoxication, to the extent it affects a defendant's ability to understand and to control his or her actions, is evidence that may support statutory mitigating circumstance (f)(6), commonly known as the impaired capacity circumstance.[58]

Evidence sometimes will support both the (f)(2) and (f)(6) mitigating circumstances and will require that both circumstances be submitted to the jury.[59]

The North Carolina Supreme Court has been somewhat inconsistent concerning whether evidence of explosive anger or uncontrolled temper is sufficient to support (f)(2). The court has said that evidence of a defendant's "plain inability . . . to control his temper" is not sufficient.[60] Yet the court

52. For an extensive discussion of this circumstance, see *State v. Greene*, 329 N.C. 771 (1991).
53. State v. Bonnett, 348 N.C. 417 (1998); State v. Hill, 347 N.C. 275 (1997).
54. *Greene*, 329 N.C. 771.
55. State v. Irwin, 304 N.C. 93 (1981); State v. Moose, 310 N.C. 482 (1984); State v. Miller, 339 N.C. 663 (1995).
56. State v. Ward, 338 N.C. 64 (1994); *Moose*, 310 N.C. 482.
57. *Greene*, 329 N.C. 771; State v. Brogden, 329 N.C. 534 (1991).
58. *Irwin*, 304 N.C. 93.
59. *Greene*, 329 N.C. 771; State v. Stokes, 308 N.C. 634 (1983).
60. State v. Badgett, 361 N.C. 234, 257 (2007). *See also* State v. Strickland, 346 N.C. 443 (1997); *Ward*, 338 N.C. 64, 112 (trial court properly declined to submit mitigating circumstance (f)(2) where the defendant's forensic psychiatrist testified that the defendant had a "short fuse"; the supreme court stated that "[i]nability to control

also found that there was sufficient evidence to support (f)(2) in at least one older case in which the most relevant evidence was that the defendant was explosive and sometimes became enraged and threatening.[61]

Case Summaries: Sufficient Evidence of Mitigating Circumstance (f)(2)

State v. Fletcher, 348 N.C. 292 (1998). The court ruled that the trial judge erred in not submitting (f)(2). The defendant's psychologist testified that under times of stress, the defendant might not perceive reality correctly and that it was likely that the defendant had been in a stress overload situation for a very long time based on his environment and psychological problems. He also testified that, given the defendant's lack of any violent history, the defendant must have been "in a very psychotic state or really out of it on drugs" to attack and kill in the manner in which the victim was killed.

State v. Greene, 329 N.C. 771 (1991). (1) The evidence was sufficient to support (f)(2) when it showed that the defendant suffered from organic brain damage that resulted in his having poor judgment and a lack of impulse control. The defendant's condition was exacerbated by alcohol consumption, and he had been drinking on the day he killed his father, with whom there was ill will. (2) The court stated that although some provocation of the defendant will almost always be present when the defendant suffers from a mental or emotional disturbance as set out in (f)(2), evidence of provocation is not a prerequisite to the submission of (f)(2) to the jury. The court disavowed a contrary statement in *State v. Irwin*, 304 N.C. 93 (1981).

State v. Brogden, 329 N.C. 534 (1991). The court ruled that the following evidence was sufficient to support the submission of (f)(2): the defendant drank heavily in the time leading up to the murder and testified that the alcohol was having an effect on him. More importantly, according to the court, the defendant's wife testified that the defendant was explosive and subject to mood changes in which he would become enraged and threaten her.

State v. Stokes, 308 N.C. 634 (1983). The court ruled that there was sufficient evidence to require the submission of (f)(2). This proof included the following: there was expert testimony that the defendant was mildly mentally retarded (he had an IQ of 63 and read at grade level 2.9) and had an antisocial personality disorder which had been unsuccessfully treated with medication. The court apparently concluded that the defendant suffered from the emotional disturbance of antisocial personality disorder at the time of the murder for which he was being sentenced. *See also* State v. Robinson, 327 N.C. 346 (1990) (similar ruling).

Case Summaries: Insufficient Evidence of Mitigating Circumstance (f)(2)

State v. Badgett, 361 N.C. 234 (2007). The defendant argued that the trial judge erred in refusing to submit (f)(2) based on evidence that the defendant suffered from intermittent explosive disorder. However, only one of the defendant's three experts suggested that diagnosis, and that expert did so only as a "preliminary" diagnosis from which she later "retreated." Further, this expert failed to explain the symptoms of the disorder or how they affected the defendant at the time of the crime for which he was being sentenced. The defendant's evidence mainly showed a "plain inability . . . to control his temper," which is insufficient to support (f)(2). The evidence

---

one's drug habits or temper is neither mental nor emotional disturbance as contemplated by this mitigating circumstance").

61. *Brogden*, 329 N.C. 534.

overall "signal[led] deliberation, not the influence of an emotional or mental disturbance at the time of the crime."

State v. Polke, 361 N.C. 65 (2006). The defendant resisted arrest, was sprayed with pepper spray, and shot and killed an officer. On appeal he argued that "the pain and disabling effects caused by the pepper spray resulted in a mental or emotional disturbance" and that (f)(2) should have been submitted. Noting the absence of expert testimony supporting this theory, and concluding that the defendant shot the officer for the purpose of evading arrest, the state supreme court disagreed.

State v. Hooks, 353 N.C. 629 (2001). The court ruled, relying on *State v. Geddie*, 345 N.C. 73 (1996), and distinguishing *State v. Greene*, 329 N.C. 771 (1991), that the trial judge did not err in failing to submit (f)(2). The court stated that the evidence tended to show that the defendant's impoverished skills, which resulted from chronic substance abuse, led to poor impulse control and a failure to understand the consequences of his actions. This evidence showed diminished capacity rather than any mental disturbance at the time of the killing for which the defendant was being sentenced. The court noted that despite the American Psychiatric Association's listing alcohol and drug abuse as mental disorders, the court has consistently ruled that voluntary intoxication is not a mental disturbance under (f)(2).

State v. Bonnett, 348 N.C. 417 (1998). The court ruled that the trial judge did not err in failing to submit (f)(2). The court noted that one of the defendant's experts testified that testing showed the defendant to be disturbed psychologically and to be socially alienated with a poor self-image, insecurity, and feelings of inadequacy. However, neither of the defendant's experts' testimony suggested any nexus between the defendant's personality characteristics and the crimes he committed or any mental or emotional disturbance at the time of the killing being tried.

State v. Hill, 347 N.C. 275 (1997). The court ruled that the evidence was insufficient to submit (f)(2). The defendant's expert witnesses did not provide a nexus between the defendant's personality characteristics and the crimes he committed. The manner of the killing for which he was being sentenced and the defendant's later actions indicated that he was not under the influence of a mental or emotional disturbance at the time of the killing. The evidence showed that the defendant raped the victim and deliberately set fire to her body to destroy the evidence. The defendant then returned to the house where he had attacked the victim and set it on fire. Later, the defendant drove to a pond, where he threw the gun used in the murder into the water.

State v. Strickland, 346 N.C. 443 (1997). The court ruled that the evidence was insufficient to submit (f)(2). After examining the evidence (the defendant shot the victim because he was angry), the court noted that it had previously ruled, citing *State v. Ward*, 338 N.C. 64 (1994), that an inability to control one's temper is neither a mental nor an emotional disturbance under this mitigating circumstance.

State v. Miller, 339 N.C. 663 (1995). (1) The defendant contended that the evidence showed that at the time of the murder being tried, he suffered from cocaine and opiate withdrawal, which is a defined psychiatric disorder. He also argued that this disorder made him more vulnerable to the provocation that led him to shoot the victim. The court ruled that drug withdrawal from voluntary intoxication does not qualify as a mental or emotional disturbance under mitigating circumstance (f)(2). The court cited *State v. Irwin*, 304 N.C. 93 (1981), and *State v. Greene*,

329 N.C. 771 (1991). (2) The defendant also contended that a racial slur spoken by the victim provoked him to shoot, indicating that he suffered from a mental disturbance that made him particularly susceptible to provocation. The court noted that although abnormal susceptibility to provocation can show a mental or emotional disturbance (citing *Greene*), the defendant admitted that he committed the murder for money, not as a result of the racial slur.

State v. Ward, 338 N.C. 64 (1994). The court ruled that the trial judge did not err in refusing to submit (f)(2). The defendant's psychiatric expert directly refused to opine that the defendant was under the influence of a mental or emotional disturbance on the night he committed the murder for which he was being sentenced; instead he stated that the defendant was under the influence of drugs or alcohol. There was no evidence suggesting a link between the defendant's mental condition and substance abuse, which is required under *State v. Irwin*, 304 N.C. 93 (1981). Voluntary intoxication properly may be considered instead under mitigating circumstance (f)(6) (impaired capacity). The court stated that the inability to control one's drug habits or temper is neither a mental nor an emotional disturbance under (f)(2). The court cited *State v. Moose*, 310 N.C. 482 (1984), and *State v. Pinch*, 306 N.C. 1 (1982).

State v. Brown, 306 N.C. 151 (1982). The defendant's use of alcohol and drugs on the night of the murder being tried was not sufficient evidence of (f)(2). The trial judge properly instructed on mitigating circumstance (f)(6) (impaired capacity).

State v. Irwin, 304 N.C. 93 (1981). The court ruled that evidence of the defendant's use of a central nervous system depressant and consumption of beer within hours of the murder for which he was being sentenced was insufficient evidence to support the submission of (f)(2). Voluntary intoxication by alcohol or drugs at the time of the murder is not by itself sufficient evidence of (f)(2). It may properly be considered under mitigating circumstance (f)(6) (impaired capacity). *See also* State v. Chandler, 342 N.C. 742 (1996) (defendant's voluntary use of alcohol on the night of the murder was insufficient evidence to require submission of (f)(2)).

Case Summaries: Evidence Supported Peremptory Instruction

State v. Holden, 338 N.C. 394 (1994). The court ruled that the trial judge erred in denying the defendant's request for a peremptory instruction when the defendant offered uncontroverted evidence of (f)(2) by mental health experts. The court also ruled that the error was not harmless beyond a reasonable doubt. Although one or more jurors found that (f)(2) existed, it was not known whether all jurors found that it existed. It is possible that had the peremptory instruction been given, more jurors or all jurors would have done so. And that could have affected the balancing of mitigating circumstances against aggravating circumstances, thereby affecting the sentencing recommendation. The court ordered a new sentencing hearing.

Case Summaries: Evidence Did Not Support Peremptory Instruction

State v. Waring, 364 N.C. 443 (2010). The trial judge did not err in refusing to give a peremptory instruction on (f)(2). The defendant called two mental health experts who testified in support of (f)(2), but their testimony was contradicted by the state's expert and by some of the circumstances of the murder.

State v. Taylor, 362 N.C. 514 (2008). The trial judge did not plainly err in failing to give a peremptory instruction on (f)(2). The defendant did not request such an instruction, and absent a request, a peremptory instruction is not required.

State v. Raines, 362 N.C. 1 (2007). It appeared that the defendant did not properly request a peremptory instruction on (f)(2), but even if he did, he was not entitled to it. The defendant's evidence, including expert testimony that he suffered from depression, attachment disorder, and explosive anger, was not uncontroverted. The state did not present expert testimony, but the facts of the crime being tried showed that the defendant "created a ruse to enter the [victims'] residence and had the mental capacity at the time of the murders to steal various items of personal property from the residence," facts consistent with premeditation rather than emotional disturbance.

State v. Forte, 360 N.C. 427 (2006). The trial judge did not err in refusing to give a peremptory instruction on (f)(2). The defendant's evidence came from three mental health experts, all hired by the defense in anticipation of trial. Citing *State v. Barden*, 356 N.C. 316 (2002), the state supreme court ruled that such evidence is not manifestly credible and does not support a peremptory instruction. Furthermore, several friends and family members of the defendant testified that they never saw any evidence that the defendant was disturbed.

State v. Duke, 360 N.C. 110 (2005). The trial judge did not err in refusing to give a peremptory instruction on (f)(2). The defendant's mental health expert testified that the defendant suffered from a mental or emotional disturbance but also "admitted on cross-examination [that] two clinicians could come to different conclusions" and acknowledged that different experts had given the defendant inconsistent diagnoses in the past. This did not amount to uncontroverted evidence.

State v. Roache, 358 N.C. 243 (2004). The trial judge did not commit plain error in failing to give a peremptory instruction on (f)(2) and defense counsel did not render ineffective assistance of counsel in failing to request such an instruction. The defendant's evidence supporting (f)(2) came exclusively from a mental health expert "hired by defendant in preparation for . . . trial." The North Carolina Supreme Court, citing *State v. Richmond*, 347 N.C. 412 (1998), stated that evidence from such a witness is not manifestly credible and does not require a peremptory instruction.

State v. Spruill, 320 N.C. 688 (1987). The defendant was not entitled to a peremptory instruction on (f)(2) when the testimony of two defense experts about the defendant's mental and emotional condition was equivocal.

State v. Noland, 312 N.C. 1 (1984). The trial judge did not err in refusing to give a peremptory instruction on (f)(2) since conflicting evidence was offered by the defendant and the state. *See also* State v. Simpson, 341 N.C. 316 (1995) (similar ruling; conflicting evidence elicited by state's cross-examination of defense expert).

Case Summaries: Miscellaneous Issues Concerning Mitigating Circumstance (f)(2)

State v. Murrell, 362 N.C. 375 (2008). The defendant argued that the portion of the pattern jury instruction that analogizes mitigating circumstance (f)(2) to acting in the heat of passion upon adequate provocation was erroneous. The North Carolina Supreme Court rejected the defendant's argument, relying on *State v. Wilkinson*, 344 N.C. 198 (1996).

State v. McKoy, 323 N.C. 1 (1988). The jury's failure to find (f)(2) was not error because evidence of this circumstance was neither uncontradicted nor inherently credible.

State v. Taylor, 354 N.C. 28 (2001). The defendant was convicted of first-degree murder and sentenced to death. The court ruled that the trial judge in the capital sentencing hearing did not err in prohibiting a defense sociologist from testifying about the defendant's mental capacity to appreciate the criminality of his conduct or whether the defendant was under the influence of a mental or emotional disturbance. The court noted that although the sociologist was clearly qualified to give his opinion about the possible cultural effects of living in a drug-infested environment, he was not qualified—based on his training and experience—to give, in essence, a medical opinion about any possible mental defect of the defendant.

F. Mitigating Circumstance (f)(3): Victim Voluntary Participant in Murder

G.S. 15A-2000(f)(3) states: "The victim was a voluntary participant in the defendant's homicidal conduct or consented to the homicidal act." Perhaps not surprisingly, there are few cases on point. This circumstance would appear to apply, for example, in a case in which a wife kills her husband, who is suffering from a painful and terminal illness, with her husband's consent. This mitigating circumstance is similar to the noncapital mitigating circumstance set forth in G.S. 15A-1340.16(e)(6).

Case Summaries: Mitigating Circumstance (f)(3)

State v. Locklear, 349 N.C. 118 (1998). The defendant and the victim got into an altercation inside the home where both lived. The victim "invited defendant outside," and the two began to fight. The defendant was winning. The victim stopped fighting and moved towards a storage shed, stating that he would be "right back." The defendant then entered the residence, retrieved a shotgun, shot the victim in the back, and shot him again as he lay on the ground. The court ruled that the trial judge did not err in refusing to submit (f)(3), noting that the defendant "presented no evidence that he knew the victim kept a weapon in the shed or that the victim reinitiated the fight."

State v. Larry, 345 N.C. 497 (1997). The defendant robbed a grocery store while an off-duty police officer was there as a customer. The officer chased the defendant as he ran from the store. A struggle ensued, and the defendant killed the officer. The defendant was convicted of first-degree murder. The court ruled that this evidence did not support the submission of (f)(3).

State v. Gladden, 315 N.C. 398 (1986). The defendant was not entitled to a peremptory instruction on (f)(3). The state produced ample evidence to contradict the defendant's assertion that the victim initially attacked him with a knife. In addition, the defendant failed to make a timely request to give this instruction.

G. Mitigating Circumstance (f)(4): Defendant's Participation Was Relatively Minor

G.S. 15A-2000(f)(4) states: "The defendant was an accomplice in or accessory to the capital felony committed by another person and his participation was relatively minor." This mitigating circumstance is somewhat similar to the noncapital mitigating circumstance set forth in G.S. 15A-1340.16(e)(2).

Case Summaries: Sufficient Evidence of Mitigating Circumstance (f)(4)

State v. Robinson, 327 N.C. 346 (1990). The court ruled that the defendant's testimony at his sentencing hearing (and other evidence in the case) that he was following his accomplice's instructions and plan to murder the victims was sufficient evidence of (f)(4) to require its submission.

State v. Stokes, 308 N.C. 634 (1983). The state offered the defendant's purported confession that tended to show that the defendant was a lookout but did not deliver the fatal blows in the murder being tried. There was other evidence that the defendant actually delivered the blows that caused the victim's death. The defendant testified at trial that he did not participate in the murder. The court ruled that this conflicting testimony required submission of (f)(4).

Case Summaries: Insufficient Evidence of Mitigating Circumstance (f)(4)

State v. Phillips, 365 N.C. 103 (2011). The defendant and several accomplices killed multiple victims during a robbery. The defendant shot one of the victims in the neck and instructed an accomplice to stab the victim. The stab wounds to the victim's chest were the fatal wounds. The defendant requested, and the trial court gave, a jury instruction on (f)(4) as to that murder. No juror found the circumstance. On appeal, the court agreed with the defendant that the trial judge erred in submitting the circumstance but concluded that the error, "whether invited or not, was harmless."

State v. Watts, 357 N.C. 366 (2003). The defendant and another man forced their way into the victim's home and then robbed and killed her. A defense witness testified that the co-defendant had admitted to the witness that he had killed the victim and that the defendant had participated only in the break-in and robbery. However, "[s]everal disinterested witnesses discredited [the witness's] testimony," including the defendant's sister, who described the defendant's clothes after the incident as being covered in blood, and witnesses who testified that the defendant had taken the lead in selling the proceeds of the robbery. The defendant's evidence was insufficiently substantial to require the submission of (f)(4).

State v. Roseboro, 351 N.C. 536 (2000). The court ruled that the trial judge did not err in failing to submit (f)(4). It noted that "[t]he record discloses no evidence from which the jury could have found defendant guilty of premeditated murder of [the victim] without finding that he actually killed her" and that the trial judge had not instructed the jury on an aiding and abetting theory. The defendant was not entitled to relitigate under (f)(4) the question of whether he or his accomplice had actually committed the murder.

State v. Anderson, 350 N.C. 152 (1999). The court ruled that the evidence was insufficient to support the submission of (f)(4). Although the defendant may not have inflicted the closed-head injury on the night the child victim died, she significantly abused her over a long period of time.

Case Summaries: Miscellaneous Issues Concerning Mitigating Circumstance (f)(4)

State v. Al-Bayyinah, 359 N.C. 741 (2005). The defendant was convicted of felony murder after fatally stabbing a store owner during an attempted robbery. The evidence at trial indicated that a single individual committed the robbery. The defendant contended at the guilt phase that the perpetrator was an acquaintance of his, but the jury apparently rejected this contention. At the penalty phase, the trial judge submitted (f)(4) even though the defendant did not request it and had asked that the jury be told he did not request it. The state supreme court held that defense counsel did not perform deficiently in telling the jury that the defendant had not requested (f)(4) and that the jury should disregard the circumstance; this was part of counsel's strategy to preserve credibility with the jury.

State v. Bonnett, 348 N.C. 417 (1998). The court ruled that the trial judge did not err in failing to give a peremptory instruction on (f)(4). The evidence was not uncontroverted. The court noted that the evidence tended to show that the defendant supplied the murder weapon and took the money box during the robbery and murder being tried.

H. Mitigating Circumstance (f)(5): Under Duress or Domination of Another Person

G.S. 15A-2000(f)(5) states: "The defendant acted under duress or under the domination of another person." This mitigating circumstance is somewhat similar to the noncapital mitigating circumstance set forth in G.S. 15A-1340.16(e)(1).

Case Summaries: Mitigating Circumstance (f)(5)

State v. Nicholson, 355 N.C. 1 (2002). The defendant assaulted his wife, and a magistrate issued a warrant for his arrest. The defendant's wife called the defendant and asked him to come to their trailer to retrieve his clothing. As he arrived, she called the police, and an officer came to the trailer to serve the arrest warrant. The defendant shot and killed both his wife and the officer. The North Carolina Supreme Court ruled that the trial judge did not err in failing to submit (f)(5). Although the defendant presented evidence that he suffered from borderline intellectual functioning, that he was generally under the domination of his wife, and that his wife induced him to come to the trailer to be arrested, "there is no evidence showing that [his wife's] actions pressured defendant into using deadly force against her or [the officer] through duress or dominance."

State v. Fletcher, 354 N.C. 455 (2001). The defendant contended that he committed a robbery and murder under the domination of his older girlfriend and presented expert testimony to the effect that he had a passive personality and tended to follow others. The trial judge did not err in failing to submit (f)(5). "At most defendant's testimony shows that [his girlfriend] suggested commission of the crime and that defendant readily agre ed and participated. This is not the equivalent of duress or domination."

State v. Cheek, 351 N.C. 48 (1999). The defendant and another man went on a crime spree that included murdering a cab driver. The defendant contended that he participated only out of fear of his accomplice. The trial judge submitted (f)(5) but did not give a peremptory instruction on it, and this was not error. "Defendant's evidence supporting his contention that he acted only out of fear . . . is undermined by the evidence showing defendant's efforts to reunite with [his accomplice] once they were separated after [eluding police after] the murder."

State v. Anderson, 350 N.C. 152 (1999). The court ruled that the evidence was insufficient to support the submission of (f)(5). The defendant and her boyfriend repeatedly abused a young child in their care, killing her. Although the boyfriend had been prosecuted for assaulting the defendant and there was evidence that he was in "complete control" in their relationship, this evidence concerned "general aspects of [the] defendant's relationship with" the boyfriend and did not show that the fatal acts of abuse were committed under duress or under his domination.

State v. Barnes, 330 N.C. 104 (1991). The court ruled that there was sufficient evidence of (f)(5) to require its submission. There was evidence that in many circumstances surrounding the commission of the murders the accomplice ordered the defendant around—e.g., telling him what to do, where to sit, what to wear—and that the defendant complied. In addition, a psychiatric expert testified that the defendant was passive and was more a follower than a leader.

State v. Robinson, 327 N.C. 346 (1990). The court ruled that the defendant's testimony at his sentencing hearing (and other evidence in the case) that he was following his accomplice's instructions and plan to murder the victims was sufficient evidence of (f)(5) to require its submission.

State v. McLaughlin, 323 N.C. 68 (1988). The trial judge did not err in failing to submit (f)(5) when the evidence failed to show that the defendant was an excessive user of drugs or alcohol to an extent that might have brought him under his accomplice's influence in committing the three murders involved in this case.

I. Mitigating Circumstance (f)(6): Defendant's Impaired Capacity

G.S. 15A-2000(f)(6) states: "The capacity of the defendant to appreciate the criminality of his conduct or to conform his conduct to the requirements of law was impaired." There is no noncapital mitigating circumstance that closely tracks this circumstance.[62]

This mitigating circumstance has two separate prongs: (1) impairment of the defendant's capacity to appreciate the criminality of his or her conduct; and (2) impairment of the defendant's capacity to conform his or her conduct to the requirements of law.[63] Evidence may be sufficient to require the submission of only one prong or it may be sufficient for both prongs. It is error if the trial judge submits only one prong when the evidence was sufficient for both.[64] Also, evidence sometimes will support both (f)(2) (mental or emotional disturbance) and (f)(6). In such a case, both circumstances must be submitted to the jury.[65]

The North Carolina Supreme Court has stated that the (f)(6) mitigating circumstance

> may exist even if a defendant has capacity to know right from wrong, to know that the act he committed was wrong, and to know the nature and quality of that act. It would exist even under these circumstances if the defendant's capacity to appreciate (to fully comprehend or be fully sensible of) the criminality (wrongfulness) of his conduct was impaired (lessened or diminished), or if defendant's capacity to follow the law and refrain from engaging in the illegal conduct was likewise impaired (lessened or diminished).[66]

---

62. The circumstance set forth in G.S. 15A-1340.16(e)(4) is probably the most similar of the noncapital mitigating circumstances. That provision reads as follows: "The defendant's age, immaturity, or limited mental capacity at the time of commission of the offense significantly reduced the defendant's culpability for the offense."

63. State v. Price, 331 N.C. 620 (1992).

64. *Id.*

65. State v. Greene, 329 N.C. 771 (1991); State v. Stokes, 308 N.C. 634 (1983).

66. State v. Johnson, 298 N.C. 47, 68 (1979).

The court has noted that evidence supporting this circumstance must link the defendant's impaired capacity to the time of the murder.[67]

One recurrent issue concerns the role of low intelligence in supporting (f)(6). In *State v. Artis*,[68] the North Carolina Supreme Court stated that evidence of low intelligence, while perhaps sufficient to support submission of a *nonstatutory* mitigating circumstance, "is simply insufficient, without more," to require the submission of (f)(6).[69] At least one subsequent case has reaffirmed that holding.[70] However, it does not seem that very much "more" must be shown in order for the submission of (f)(6) to be appropriate. The court has endorsed submission of the circumstance based on a combination of low intelligence and the following: antisocial personality disorder,[71] a history of substance abuse,[72] low self-esteem and anguish,[73] and alcohol consumption.[74]

A second issue that arises frequently concerns the relationship between drug and alcohol use and mitigating circumstance (f)(6). Defendants often claim impaired capacity based on voluntary intoxication. However, it is not sufficient for the defendant to show a history of drug and alcohol consumption without showing consumption near the time of the murder.[75] Even a showing that the defendant consumed drugs or alcohol near the time of the murder is insufficient if the defendant does not establish that he or she consumed a large quantity of intoxicants or that the quantity limited his or her ability to understand or control his or her actions.[76] However, if the defendant is able to show that he or she consumed a large quantity of intoxicants or that the intoxicants substantially affected his or her faculties, many cases hold that the defendant is entitled to an instruction on (f)(6).[77]

---

67. *See, e.g.,* State v. Lyons, 343 N.C. 1 (1996); State v. Ward, 338 N.C. 64 (1994).

68. 325 N.C. 278 (1989). The evidence in *Artis* suggested that the defendant was mentally retarded, with an IQ of 67. Under *Atkins v. Virginia*, 536 U.S. 304 (2002), he would be ineligible for the death penalty. However, the *Artis* court's remarks remain relevant for defendants who are of low intelligence but who are not mentally retarded.

69. *Artis*, 325 N.C. at 313.

70. State v. Williams, 339 N.C. 1, 48 (1994) (submission of (f)(6) not required where evidence suggested that the defendant had an IQ in the borderline intellectual functioning range but had no "treatable mental disorder").

71. State v. Stokes, 308 N.C. 634 (1983).

72. State v. Quick, 329 N.C. 1 (1991).

73. State v. Fullwood, 329 N.C. 233 (1991).

74. State v. Artis, 329 N.C. 679 (1991). This is a later opinion in the same *Artis* case that is discussed in the text above. This opinion does not discuss the holding in the original opinion, however, and treats (f)(6) only briefly.

75. *See, e.g.,* State v. Garner, 340 N.C. 573, 599 (1995) (evidence that the defendant "showed up at Army formations with alcohol on his breath, . . . drank beer with an Army buddy regularly, and . . . had failed a random drug test" was insufficient to support submission of (f)(6)); State v. Miller, 339 N.C. 663, 687 (1995) (evidence that "defendant ingested drugs on 30 September and immediately after the murder on 5 October" failed to show "that he was impaired by drugs or withdrawal therefrom at the time of the murder" and so did not warrant the submission of (f)(6)).

76. *See, e.g.,* State v. Strickland, 346 N.C. 443, 464 (1997) ("Mere evidence that a defendant has consumed alcohol or drugs prior to the murder does not constitute substantial evidence supporting the (f)(6) mitigating circumstance" absent a showing of the effect on the defendant and, where the evidence showed only that "defendant had consumed about six beers and a few drinks of liquor," submission of (f)(6) was not warranted); State v. Hunt, 330 N.C. 501, 514, 514–15 (1992) (although there was evidence that the defendant drank "some whiskey" prior to the murder being tried, the court noted that there was "a dearth of evidence as to how much of this whiskey defendant actually consumed, and thus [it found that] nothing in the record would permit [it] or a jury to speculate as to the effect that defendant's alcohol consumption had on his abilities").

77. *See, e.g.,* State v. Cummings, 329 N.C. 249 (1991) (sufficient evidence of (f)(6) based on consumption of alcohol); State v. Payne, 328 N.C. 377 (1991) (similar, based on alcohol and gasoline); State v. Quesinberry, 328 N.C. 288 (1991) (similar, based on alcohol and marijuana).

Finally, the North Carolina Supreme Court has stated that although it never has ruled that expert testimony is required to establish the existence of this circumstance,[78] it has been found to be supported by the court only where there was evidence from some source of some mental disorder, disease, or defect or proof of voluntary intoxication by alcohol or drugs, to the degree that it affected the defendant's ability to understand and control his or her actions.[79]

Case Summaries: Sufficient Evidence of Mitigating Circumstance (f)(6)

State v. Price, 331 N.C. 620 (1992). The trial judge submitted only the second prong of (f)(6), the defendant's impaired capacity to conform his conduct to the requirements of law. The defendant specifically requested that the judge not submit the first prong, the defendant's impaired capacity to appreciate the criminality of his conduct. The court ruled that the trial judge erred in not submitting the first prong because there was sufficient evidence to support its submission and a trial judge has a duty to submit a statutory mitigating circumstance regardless of the defendant's wishes. A psychologist's testimony that the defendant suffered from a mental illness that impaired his ability to make judgments, have appropriate mood responses, and be in touch with reality, considered with evidence of the defendant's past psychiatric problems resulting in hospitalization, was sufficient evidence of the first prong. (However, the court ruled that the error in not submitting the first prong was harmless beyond a reasonable doubt.)

State v. McLaughlin, 330 N.C. 66 (1991). The court ruled that there was sufficient evidence to submit (f)(6) when the defendant had an IQ of 72 and on the day of the murder had used marijuana and LSD and ingested wine and beer.

State v. Artis, 329 N.C. 679 (1991). The court ruled that the evidence was sufficient to support (f)(6). On the day of the murder the defendant was "high . . . from beer" and "drunk." The defendant's IQ was 67, which placed him in the upper range of mentally retarded people.

State v. Wynne, 329 N.C. 507 (1991). The court ruled that evidence was sufficient to support both prongs of (f)(6). The defendant suffered from an alcohol problem for some time before the murder, and shortly before the commission of the murder the defendant had consumed alcohol and smoked marijuana. Also, the defendant recently had been examined for psychological problems by a mental health professional. The evidence could support a reasonable inference that the defendant had psychological problems and was intoxicated at the time of the murder. As a result, his ability to appreciate the criminality of his conduct or to conform his conduct to the requirements of the law was impaired.

State v. Thomas, 329 N.C. 423 (1991). Evidence that the defendant was under the influence of heroin at the time of the murder, had blacked out, and had awakened to find the victim dead was sufficient, along with his prior drug use, to submit (f)(6) to the jury.

State v. Cummings, 329 N.C. 249 (1991). The court ruled that there was sufficient evidence, even though no mental health expert testified, to submit (f)(6) when the evidence showed that the defendant had consumed a large quantity of alcohol on the day of the murder and suffered from alcoholism for a number of years.

---

78. *Cummings*, 329 N.C. 249, 253 (sufficient evidence of (f)(6) although no mental health expert testified; evidence from the defendant and his family showed his excessive consumption of alcohol, and the defendant could not say exactly what happened the day of the murder because he was "pretty well loaded").

79. State v. Syriani, 333 N.C. 350 (1993).

State v. Fullwood, 329 N.C. 233 (1991). The court ruled that the evidence was sufficient to support the submission of (f)(6). A defense psychologist testified that the defendant had an IQ of 80, which is a borderline level between low normal intelligence and mentally retarded. The defendant suffered from very low feelings of self-esteem and "inadequate personality." Another defense psychologist testified that the defendant lacked verbal abilities and that his ability to understand and be understood through words was severely limited. Also, the defendant's emotional anguish at the time of the murder aggravated his already limited reasoning ability, low feelings of self-esteem, and inadequate personality. The defendant's judgment was very poor at the time of the murder.

State v. Quick, 329 N.C. 1 (1991). The court ruled that the evidence was sufficient to support the submission of (f)(6). A psychologist testified that the defendant's IQ placed him in the borderline range of intellectual functioning and his low intelligence limited his understanding of social rules and customs. In addition, the psychologist stated that the defendant's history of substance abuse could "compromise the abilities he has."

State v. Huff, 328 N.C. 532 (1991). The court ruled that the evidence was sufficient to support the submission of (f)(6). Expert testimony showed that the defendant suffered from paranoid schizophrenia and at the time of the murder was unable to understand the difference between right and wrong and the nature and quality of his acts.

State v. Payne, 328 N.C. 377 (1991). The court ruled that there was sufficient evidence to submit (f)(6). The evidence showed that the defendant had inhaled gasoline from a can on more than one occasion, and he had been drinking alcohol the night before the murder victim's body was found. After the murder, sheriff's deputies found the defendant smelling like beer and lying in a barn loft strewn with a gasoline can and several beer cans, which could support a reasonable inference that he was intoxicated at the time of the murder.

State v. Quesinberry, 328 N.C. 288 (1991). The court ruled that there was sufficient evidence to submit (f)(6) when the evidence showed that the defendant habitually abused alcohol and drugs for eight years and, over a six-hour period immediately before the murder, he consumed two beers and smoked five marijuana cigarettes.

State v. Sanderson, 327 N.C. 397 (1990). The court ruled that there was sufficient evidence to submit (f)(6) when the evidence showed that the defendant consumed large amounts of drugs on the day the murder was committed and said that he had injected two syringes of "dope" just before stabbing the victim. He also told law enforcement officers that he committed the murder because he was under the influence of drugs.

State v. McNeil, 327 N.C. 388 (1990). The court ruled that there was sufficient evidence to submit (f)(6) when the evidence showed that the defendant had consumed substantial amounts of alcohol on the weekend of the murders being tried and expert testimony indicated that the defendant was an alcoholic whose consumption of alcohol impaired his judgment and contributed to his behavior.

State v. Sanders, 327 N.C. 319 (1990). The court ruled that there was sufficient evidence to submit (f)(6) when the evidence showed that the defendant had significant mental illness, possibly schizophrenia-paranoid type, and had manic depressive–like symptoms. He also suffered rapid mood changes, resisted medical treatment, and exhibited antisocial traits. His IQ was 72, which indicates borderline mental retardation.

State v. Stokes, 308 N.C. 634 (1983). The court ruled that there was sufficient evidence to require the submission of (f)(6). Expert testimony showed that the defendant was mildly mentally retarded and had an antisocial disorder. The defendant had a long history of treatment for mental problems that began when he was 10 years old.

Case Summaries: Insuffcient Evidence of Mitigating Circumstance (f)(6)

State v. Badgett, 361 N.C. 234 (2007). The defendant argued that the trial judge erred in refusing to submit (f)(6) based on evidence that the defendant suffered from intermittent explosive disorder. However, only one of the defendant's three experts suggested that diagnosis, and that expert did so only as a "preliminary" diagnosis from which she later "retreated." Further, this expert failed to explain the symptoms of the disorder or how they affected the defendant at the time of the crime. The defendant's evidence showed only that he could not control his temper, not that he suffered from impaired capacity. The court also stated that the "defendant's . . . lies to police about his involvement in the murder and his washing and disposal of the murder weapon . . . tend to show that defendant fully appreciated the criminality of his conduct."

State v. Polke, 361 N.C. 65 (2006). The defendant resisted arrest, was sprayed with pepper spray, and shot and killed an officer. On appeal he argued that the pain and disabling effects caused by the pepper spray "impaired his mental capacity during the shooting" and merited the submission of (f)(6). Noting the absence of expert testimony supporting this theory, and concluding that the defendant shot the officer for the purpose of evading arrest, the state supreme court disagreed.

State v. Kemmerlin, 356 N.C. 446 (2002). The court ruled that the trial judge did not err in declining to submit (f)(6). The court noted that the judge submitted mitigating circumstance (f)(2) (mental or emotional disturbance). The court stated that the evidence showed that the defendant was depressed and suffering from borderline personality disorder and thus was under the influence of a mental or emotional disturbance. However, the defendant's expert testified that this disturbance did not prevent the defendant from appreciating the criminality of her conduct or controlling her conduct as required by law.

State v. Strickland, 346 N.C. 443 (1997). The court ruled that the evidence was insufficient to submit (f)(6). The court noted that mere evidence that a defendant has consumed alcohol or drugs before a murder does not constitute substantial evidence supporting this mitigating circumstance. The court stated that there was no evidence that the defendant's consumption of alcohol so impaired him as to prevent his understanding of the criminality of his conduct or that the consumption of alcohol affected his ability to control his actions.

State v. Hill, 347 N.C. 275 (1997). The court ruled that the evidence was insufficient to submit (f)(6). The testimony of both of the defendant's experts did not establish that his personality characteristics affected his ability to understand and control his actions. The court noted that, in fact, the experts testified to the contrary.

State v. Lyons, 343 N.C. 1 (1996). The defendant's psychologist testified that the defendant suffered from bipolar disorder, antisocial personality disorder, and substance abuse. However, the psychologist never testified that the defendant was unable to conform his conduct to the requirements of the law or that the defendant was suffering from antisocial personality disorder *at the time of the murder being tried.* The court stated that it is not enough for a defense expert to proffer a general definition of a disorder without any testimony about the specific symptoms from which a particular defendant suffers. The court ruled that, based on the testimony here, the trial judge did not err in not submitting (f)(6).

State v. Garner, 340 N.C. 573 (1995). The defendant presented evidence of his voluntary intoxication through witnesses who testified that he appeared at army formations with alcohol on his breath, drank beer regularly with an army buddy, and had failed a random drug test. His family and friends testified that he underwent a radical and abrupt character change in the month before the murders being tried that was indicative of a mental breakdown. The court ruled that this evidence by itself was insufficient to support the submission of (f)(6).

State v. Miller, 339 N.C. 663 (1995). The defendant presented evidence that he ingested drugs on September 30, 1985, as well as immediately after the murder for which he was being sentenced, which occurred on October 5, 1985. The defendant asked for medicine for withdrawal symptoms while in the hospital on October 6, 1985. A defense psychologist testified that the defendant was prone to addiction, lacked appropriate judgment, and had low-average intelligence. The court ruled that this evidence was insufficient to support the submission of (f)(6) because there was no evidence that the defendant was impaired by drugs or drug withdrawal at the time of the murder or that any of the withdrawal symptoms he may have experienced impaired his capacity. None of the defendant's witnesses, including the psychologist, testified that his capacity to appreciate the wrongfulness of his conduct or to conform his conduct to the law was impaired. The court cited *State v. Williams*, 305 N.C. 656 (1982), summarized below.

State v. Williams, 339 N.C. 1 (1994). The court ruled that the trial judge did not err in failing to submit (f)(6). The defendant was a fair student with average grades until age 15, after which he barely passed his classes. His ninth-grade school year was interrupted so he could attend a "sheltered workshop . . . for the handicapped and retarded." His IQ tests placed him in the borderline range of intelligence. However, there was no evidence of any treatable mental disorder. The court relied on its ruling in *State v. Artis*, 325 N.C. 278 (1989), summarized below.

State v. Ward, 338 N.C. 64 (1994). The court ruled that the trial judge did not err in failing to submit (f)(6). There was no evidence that would support an inference that the defendant's mental capacity was impaired at the time of the murder being tried. The defendant's smoking crack cocaine more than eight hours before he committed the murder, considered in light of his sister's testimony that he was acting "normal" within one and one-half hours of the murder, was not sufficient evidence of this circumstance. The defendant's own expert witness "could not conclude unconditionally" that the defendant met this circumstance. The court noted that although the evidence tended to show that the defendant historically abused drugs, there was no evidence to support an inference that his mental capacity was impaired at the time of the murder.

State v. Syriani, 333 N.C. 350 (1993). The defendant's testimony that his judgment was affected by his emotional disturbance was insufficient in this case to support submission of (f)(6) to the jury.

State v. Hunt, 330 N.C. 501 (1992). The court ruled that there was insufficient evidence that the defendant's alcohol consumption required submission of either prong of (f)(6). The court noted that there was a dearth of evidence about how much alcohol the defendant had consumed and regarding the effect that the defendant's alcohol consumption had on his abilities. *See also* State v. DeCastro, 342 N.C. 667 (1996); State v. Jones, 342 N.C. 457 (1996).

State v. Artis, 325 N.C. 278 (1989). The court ruled that the evidence was insufficient to support the submission of (f)(6) when evidence of the defendant's mild retardation failed to suggest any link between the retardation and the defendant's inability to appreciate the criminality of his conduct or to conform his conduct to the requirements of the law. The court distinguished its ruling in *State v. Stokes,* 308 N.C. 634 (1983), discussed in the previous section, above. The court noted that a low IQ by itself may justify the submission of a nonstatutory mitigating circumstance.

State v. Allen, 323 N.C. 208 (1988). The court ruled that the evidence was insufficient to support the submission of (f)(6) when the evidence only showed that the defendant may have taken a drug several hours before the murder being tried or may have drunk some beer. The court noted that there was no expert testimony about the defendant's condition.

State v. Williams, 305 N.C. 656 (1982). The court ruled that the evidence was insufficient to support the submission of (f)(6) when there was no expert psychiatric or other evidence to show that the defendant's capacity to appreciate the criminality of his conduct was impaired by his consumption of alcohol on the night of the murder for which he was being sentenced. The mere ingestion of alcohol, by itself, was not sufficient evidence of (f)(6).

Case Summaries: Evidence Did Not Support Peremptory Instruction

State v. Forte, 360 N.C. 427 (2006). The trial judge did not err in refusing to give a peremptory instruction on (f)(6). The defendant's evidence came from three mental health experts, all hired by the defense in anticipation of trial. Citing *State v. Barden,* 356 N.C. 316 (2002), the state supreme court ruled that such evidence is not manifestly credible and does not support a peremptory instruction. Furthermore, several friends and family members of the defendant testified that they never saw any evidence that the defendant was disturbed.

State v. Duke, 360 N.C. 110 (2005). The trial judge did not err in failing to give a peremptory instruction on (f)(6), even if such an instruction had been requested. The defendant's evidence supporting (f)(6) was not uncontroverted. The defendant attempted to cover up his crime, attempted to destroy evidence, and attempted to establish a bogus alibi, all of which could have led a jury to find that the defendant appreciated the criminality of his actions.

State v. Roache, 358 N.C. 243 (2004). The trial judge did not commit plain error in failing to give a peremptory instruction on (f)(6) and defense counsel did not render ineffective assistance of counsel in failing to request one. The defendant's evidence supporting (f)(6) came exclusively from a mental health expert "hired by defendant in preparation for . . . trial." The North Carolina Supreme Court, citing *State v. Richmond,* 347 N.C. 412 (1998), stated that evidence from such a witness is not manifestly credible and does not require a peremptory instruction.

State v. Smith, 305 N.C. 691 (1982). The trial judge did not err in failing to give a peremptory instruction on (f)(6) because the evidence was conflicting on this circumstance. The evidence of the murder being tried, presented through the testimony of two eyewitnesses, suggested that the defendant was in complete control of his faculties when he committed the murder. In contrast, the defendant's experts testified that his faculties were impaired. *See also* State v. Johnson, 298 N.C. 47 (1979) (similar ruling); State v. Lynch, 340 N.C. 435 (1995) (similar ruling); State v. Simpson, 341 N.C. 316 (1995) (evidence insufficient to support peremptory instruction).

Case Summaries: Jury Instruction Issues

State v. Rouse, 339 N.C. 59 (1994). To the extent that the trial judge's statement in the jury instruction indicated that the defendant had to show *both* a personality disorder *and* intoxication to establish (f)(6), it was error. While the consumption of alcohol or drugs may show impaired capacity, it is unnecessary to establish (f)(6).

State v. Johnson, 317 N.C. 343 (1986). The jury instruction on (f)(6) was not erroneous when it required that the defendant must be "substantially" impaired by alcohol.

State v. Johnson, 298 N.C. 47 (1979). The jury instruction on (f)(6) was erroneous because it failed to explain the difference between the defendant's capacity to know right from wrong and the impairment of the defendant's capacity to appreciate the criminality of his or her conduct or to conform that conduct to the requirements of law. *See also* State v. Johnson, 298 N.C. 355 (1979) (similar ruling).

State v. Goodman, 298 N.C. 1 (1979). The jury instruction on (f)(6) was not erroneous. The instruction properly explained that in order to establish this circumstance a defendant must establish intoxication "to a degree that it affects defendant's ability to understand and control his actions." The General Assembly did not intend that intoxication, "however slight," should be a mitigating circumstance. *See also* State v. Taylor, 304 N.C. 249 (1981).

Case Summaries: Qualifications of Expert to Testify about Mitigating Circumstance (f)(6)

State v. Taylor, 354 N.C. 28 (2001). The defendant was convicted of first-degree murder and sentenced to death. The court ruled that the trial judge in the capital sentencing hearing did not err in prohibiting a defense sociologist from testifying about the defendant's mental capacity to appreciate the criminality of his conduct or whether the defendant was under the influence of a mental or emotional disturbance. The court noted that although the sociologist was clearly qualified to give his opinion about the possible cultural effects of living in a drug-infested environment, he was not qualified—based on his training and experience—to give, in essence, a medical opinion about any possible mental defect of the defendant.

J. Mitigating Circumstance (f)(7): Defendant's Age at Time of Murder

G.S. 15A-2000(f)(7) states: "The age of the defendant at the time of the crime." The noncapital mitigating circumstance set forth in G.S. 15A-1340.16(e)(4) encompasses the age of the defendant, though it also encompasses other matters such as limited mental capacity.

While not every defendant suffers from a mental or emotional disturbance or has committed a prior capital felony, every defendant is of *some* age. Because it does not establish a specific age cutoff, mitigating circumstance (f)(7) appears to have been written to allow each juror some latitude to decide for him or herself what age qualifies as a mitigating circumstance. Accordingly, the pattern jury instruction for (f)(7) states that "[t]he mitigating effect of the age of the defendant is for you to determine."[80] Defendants have sometimes argued that this instruction allows a juror to give no weight

80. N.C.P.I.—Crim. 150.10.

to a defendant's age, in violation of the rule that jurors must give some weight to statutory mitigating circumstances,[81] but the North Carolina Supreme Court has rejected this argument.[82]

The court has also ruled that chronological age is not alone determinative when deciding whether evidence is sufficient to submit this circumstance to the jury. A defendant's immaturity, youthfulness, or lack of emotional or intellectual development at the time of the murder must also be considered.[83] Accordingly, the court has found sufficient evidence of (f)(7) for a 30-year-old defendant[84] and insufficient evidence of (f)(7) for a 20-year-old defendant.[85]

Although (f)(7) most often arises in connection with youthful defendants, a defendant's advanced age may also require submission of this circumstance.[86]

Case Summaries: Sufficient Evidence of Mitigating Circumstance (f)(7)

State v. Zuniga, 348 N.C. 214 (1998). The court ruled, relying on *State v. Holden*, 338 N.C. 394 (1994), summarized immediately below, that the trial judge erred in failing to submit (f)(7). The defendant was 27 years old at the time of the murder being tried. However, a mental health expert testified that the defendant had an IQ of 56, signifying an intellectual age of 7.4 years, a history of mild to moderate mental retardation, and moderate organic brain syndrome. Another mental health expert testified that the defendant had an IQ of 64, suffered from mild mental retardation, and had chronic brain damage. Both experts said that the defendant was mentally impaired at the time of the murder.

State v. Holden, 338 N.C. 394 (1994). The court ruled that the trial judge erred in failing to instruct on (f)(7), despite the defendant's withdrawal of his requested instruction on this circumstance, because the evidence supported its submission. Although the defendant was 30 years old at the time of the murder for which he was being sentenced, a psychologist testified that the defendant's mental age was 10 years and that his problem-solving skills were closer to those of a 10-year-old.

State v. Turner, 330 N.C. 249 (1991). The court ruled that the defendant's age of 22 and proof that he was neglected and abused as a youth were sufficient in this case to submit (f)(7).

Case Summaries: Insufficient Evidence of Mitigating Circumstance (f)(7)

State v. Hurst, 360 N.C. 181 (2006). The trial judge did not err in failing to submit (f)(7). The defendant was 23 years old at the time he committed the murder being tried. He presented some evidence of emotional immaturity, including an expert's testimony about his emotional instability. However, there was also evidence of maturity, including the defendant's work history and the fact that he had shown responsibility in caring for family members and others. On balance, the court concluded, "the record demonstrates that his maturity was consistent with his chronological age," and submission of (f)(7) was therefore not required.

State v. Thompson, 359 N.C. 77 (2004). The trial judge did not err in failing to submit (f)(7). The defendant was 32 years old when he committed the murder being tried, but he presented expert testimony that he came from a chaotic background, behaved in a childlike manner,

---

81. *See supra* note 27 and accompanying text.
82. State v. Maske, 358 N.C. 40 (2004); State v. Rouse, 339 N.C. 59 (1994).
83. State v. Bowie, 340 N.C. 199 (1995).
84. State v. Holden, 338 N.C. 394 (1994).
85. *Bowie*, 340 N.C. 199.
86. State v. Hill, 331 N.C. 387 (1992).

"lacked internal skills to respond maturely to stressful situations, and functioned emotionally as an adolescent." However, he was a high school graduate of normal intelligence who held a job and who functioned as a father and a spouse. The state supreme court found that this evidence counterbalanced the evidence of emotional immaturity.

State v. Peterson, 350 N.C. 518 (1999). The court ruled that the trial judge did not err in not submitting (f)(7). The court noted that while the defendant presented evidence that he led a restrained childhood under a strict guardian and did not make many friends, there was no evidence from which a jury could conclude that the defendant was mentally immature. He had completed his GED, had normal reading skills, a stable marital relationship, handled his own finances, and had a good employment record.

State v. Atkins, 349 N.C. 62 (1998). The court ruled that the trial judge did not err in failing to submit (f)(7). The defendant was 23 years old, had an IQ of 107, was functioning in the average to high-average range of intelligence, and had a relatively good understanding of social nuances. The court stated that while the defendant presented evidence that he suffered from conditions or disorders commonly found in adolescents and participated in an activity or activities often enjoyed by some youngsters, its review of the record revealed no evidence that the defendant exhibited decisional skills and understanding equivalent to those of an adolescent.

State v. Bonnett, 348 N.C. 417 (1998). The court ruled that the trial judge did not err in failing to submit (f)(7). The defendant had introduced evidence that he was 26 years old at the time of the murder being tried, was abandoned at birth by his mother, grew up in a dysfunctional family, and had an IQ of 86 and a learning disability. The court noted that chronological age is not determinative of this mitigating circumstance, citing *State v. Daughtry*, 340 N.C. 488 (1995), discussed immediately below. The court stated that the defendant did not introduce substantial evidence of his immaturity, youthfulness, or lack of emotional or intellectual development at the time of the murder, and the evidence showed that the defendant had only slightly below-normal intelligence, with no major disturbance of mood or thinking.

State v. Daughtry, 340 N.C. 488 (1995). The court ruled that there was no error in failing to submit (f)(7). The defendant was 27 years old at the time of the murder being tried. He had completed high school, had average intelligence, with no major disturbance of mood or thinking, and was gainfully employed before his arrest. Testimony did not link his impulsive nature and immaturity to his age; rather, these traits apparently stemmed from a personality disorder and somewhat dysfunctional family life.

State v. Bowie, 340 N.C. 199 (1995). The court ruled that there was no error in failing to submit (f)(7). The defendant was 20 years old when the murder being tried was committed. He was placed in a foster home when he was 12 years old; he then developed at a normal rate. He graduated from high school and took classes at a community college. He related well to other students and had many friends. His teachers, coaches, and principal testified that he was polite, cooperative, and able to handle criticism and follow rules. His social worker considered him trustworthy enough that she lent him $2,000 to purchase a truck for which he regularly made payments. The court relied on *State v. Johnson*, 317 N.C. 343 (1986), summarized below, and distinguished its ruling in *State v. Turner*, 330 N.C. 249 (1991).

State v. Spruill, 338 N.C. 612 (1994). The court ruled that the trial judge did not err in failing to submit (f)(7). The defendant was 31 years old, had worked as an auto mechanic and in a shipyard, moved on to a better position, attended church, and functioned quite well in the community. The defendant contended that he was an immature and dependent person who had borderline intelligence. However, the court noted, relying on *State v. Johnson*, 317 N.C. 343 (1986), discussed below, that evidence showing emotional immaturity is not viewed in isolation, particularly when other evidence shows more mature qualities and characteristics.

State v. Hill, 331 N.C. 387 (1992). The court ruled that the trial judge did not err in failing to submit (f)(7). The defendant's chronological age of 54 did not, standing alone, entitle him to have this mitigating circumstance submitted. The court stated that advanced age may qualify under (f)(7). However, the defendant in this case had argued—but did not present supporting evidence—that his physiological age was 75 to 80 years old.

State v. Porter, 326 N.C. 489 (1990). The court ruled that the trial judge did not err in failing to submit (f)(7). Although the defendant was 61 years old and had a borderline IQ of 71, he had a youthful interest in his victim, he vigorously responded to the prosecutor's cross-examination, and he showed physical prowess in his attempts to escape.

State v. Laws, 325 N.C. 81 (1989). The court ruled that the trial judge did not err in failing to submit (f)(7). Although the defendant was 23 years old, there was no substantial evidence of his immaturity, youthfulness, or lack of emotional or intellectual development at the time of the murder for which he was being sentenced. The court stated that chronological age is not the determining factor with this mitigating circumstance. *See also* State v. DeCastro, 342 N.C. 667 (1996); State v. Richardson, 342 N.C. 772 (1996).

State v. Johnson, 317 N.C. 343 (1986). The court ruled that the trial judge did not err in failing to submit (f)(7) when the evidence showed that the defendant was 23 years old and had an apparently normal physical and intellectual development, although he was emotionally immature for his age.

Case Summaries: Evidence Did Not Support Peremptory Instruction

State v. Garcell, 363 N.C. 10 (2009). The defendant was 18 years and 5 months old at the time he committed the murder being tried. He was not entitled to a *mandatory* peremptory instruction on (f)(7). Such an instruction is appropriate only when the state stipulates to a mitigating circumstance, which it did not do in this case. Further, while the defendant's expert testified that the defendant was emotionally immature, there was also evidence of calculated behavior and leadership by the defendant.

State v. Taylor, 362 N.C. 514 (2008). The defendant did not request a peremptory instruction on (f)(7), so the trial judge did not err in failing to give one.

State v. Gardner, 311 N.C. 489 (1984). The court ruled that the trial judge did not err in failing to give a peremptory instruction on (f)(7). The defendant was 24 years old at the time of the murders for which he was being sentenced. *See also* State v. Oliver, 309 N.C. 326 (1983) (similar ruling; defendant was 19 years and 11 months old at the time of the murder being tried); State v. Simpson, 341 N.C. 316 (1995) (similar ruling; defendant was soon to become a father, had held several jobs, had a criminal background, and was 21 years old at the time of the murder being tried).

Case Summaries: Jury Instruction Issues

State v. Maske, 358 N.C. 40 (2004). The trial judge did not err in instructing the jury that it should "consider whether the age of the defendant at the time of this murder is a mitigating factor" and that "[t]he mitigating effect of the age of the defendant is for you to determine from all of the facts." Following *State v. Rouse*, 339 N.C. 59 (1994), the state supreme court ruled that this instruction did not have the effect of converting (f)(7) into a nonstatutory mitigating circumstance.

State v. Simpson, 341 N.C. 316 (1995). The court ruled that the trial judge properly did not give the defendant's requested instruction on mitigating circumstance (f)(7), which was as follows: "The statutory mitigating circumstance relating to the age of the defendant is not limited to the defendant's chronological age at the time of the murder. You must also consider the defendant's mental or emotional age at the time of the offense." This instruction improperly dictated a set formula for determining whether the defendant's age had mitigating value. The court ruled that the pattern jury instruction given by the judge properly allowed a broader consideration of factors.

State v. Skipper, 337 N.C. 1 (1994). The trial judge used the pattern jury instruction for (f)(7), which stated that "the mitigating effect of the age of the defendant is for you to determine." The court ruled that this instruction did not unconstitutionally permit a juror to refuse to consider evidence about age as a mitigating circumstance. The actual weight that a jury chooses to give the circumstance is a reflection of the weight given to it by each individual juror. The court examined the evidence (defendant's chronological age was 48, his mental age was 6, but he had been married, ran his own business, and supported himself and his children) and ruled that the jury was not required to find that this circumstance existed.

K. Mitigating Circumstance (f)(8): Defendant's Assistance to the State

G.S. 15A-2000(f)(8) states: "The defendant aided in the apprehension of another capital felon or testified truthfully on behalf of the prosecution in another prosecution of a felony." This mitigating circumstance is similar to the noncapital mitigating circumstance set out in G.S. 15A-1340.16(e)(7).[87]

Case Summaries: Mitigating Circumstance (f)(8)

State v. Lloyd, 354 N.C. 76 (2001). The court ruled that the trial judge erred in not giving a peremptory instruction on (f)(8). The defendant's evidence in the capital sentencing hearing showed that his truthful testimony at another trial was both uncontroverted and credible.

87. That circumstance reads, "[t]he defendant aided in the apprehension of another felon or testified truthfully on behalf of the prosecution in another prosecution of a felony." The appellate cases regarding that circumstance are demanding. *See, e.g.,* State v. Wiggins, 159 N.C. App. 252, 270 (2003) (trial judge did not err in refusing to find the circumstance where the defendant told the police where an accomplice was staying but "previously lied to police and cooperated only after being pressed by police"); State v. Brewington, 343 N.C. 448, 458 (1996) (trial judge did not err in refusing to find the mitigating circumstance even though, "[p]ursuant to a request by police officers, defendant called his accomplice by telephone and engaged him in a mutually inculpatory conversation" and allowed officers to listen to and to record the conversation; the defendant would not give officers the accomplice's name, and therefore he was not instrumental in the apprehension of the accomplice). In light of *State v. Bacon*, 326 N.C. 404 (1990), summarized below, it is doubtful that trial judges should read (f)(8) so restrictively.

[*Author's note*: Although not discussed by the court, the trial at which the defendant testified took place in 1994, while the defendant did not commit murder until 1998.]

State v. Bacon, 326 N.C. 404 (1990). The court ruled that there was sufficient evidence to support the submission of (f)(8). The defendant was romantically involved with the estranged wife of the victim. The defendant and the estranged wife killed the victim. The estranged wife told the police that she and the victim had been attacked by unknown assailants. The defendant, meanwhile, told police that he had killed the victim in front of the estranged wife, essentially in self-defense. Because the defendant's false exculpatory statement was inconsistent with the estranged wife's false exculpatory statement, the police began to view the estranged wife as a possible suspect rather than crediting her statement. Notwithstanding the fact that the defendant's statement "did not turn out to be totally accurate," the fact that his statement made officers suspicious of the estranged wife was sufficient to support submission of the circumstance. This ruling suggests that, at least in some circumstances, *unintentional* assistance in apprehending another capital felon is sufficient to support this circumstance. Although the trial judge instructed on this circumstance, the written issues to be answered by the jury listed the circumstance as aiding in the *prosecution* (instead of *apprehension*) of another capital felon, to which the jury answered "no." This was error, requiring a new capital sentencing hearing. [*Author's note*: At the defendant's second trial, a judge again refused to instruct on (f)(8) and, based on the less-developed record at the second trial, the North Carolina Supreme Court affirmed. State v. Bacon, 337 N.C. 66 (1994).]

L. Mitigating Circumstance (f)(9): Any Other Circumstance Having Mitigating Value

G.S. 15A-2000(f)(9) states: "Any other circumstance arising from the evidence which the jury deems to have mitigating value." There is a catchall mitigating circumstance for noncapital cases as well, though it is phrased somewhat differently.[88]

G.S. 15A-2000(f)(9) provides for the submission of mitigating circumstances that are not listed in (f)(1) through (f)(8). The trial judge has the duty to submit a specific nonstatutory mitigating circumstance when the defendant has made a timely written request, a juror could reasonably find that the circumstance had mitigating value, and sufficient evidence supports its submission.[89] In addition, the trial judge must submit the language of G.S. 15A-2000(f)(9) as a catchall mitigating circumstance.

There are many potential nonstatutory mitigating circumstances relating to the defendant's character or record or the circumstances of the murder being tried. Depending on the facts of the case and the defendant's trial strategy, a defendant may ask for the submission of only a few nonstatutory mitigating circumstances or dozens. Here is a partial list of nonstatutory mitigating circumstances that have been submitted:

- the defendant is a person of good character and reputation
- the defendant has been gainfully employed
- the defendant has been a good employee
- the defendant has engaged in work that provides direct assistance to others

88. G.S. 15A-1340.16(e)(21) ("Any other mitigating factor reasonably related to the purposes of sentences").
89. State v. Green, 336 N.C. 142 (1994).

- the defendant served in the military and was honorably discharged from military service
- the defendant has earned a high school diploma (college degree)
- the defendant is considerate and loving to his or her family (or specified individuals)
- the defendant has been a good parent
- the defendant has financially supported his or her spouse and children
- the defendant is involved in religious activities
- the defendant was abused by his or her parents
- the defendant was an illegitimate child and did not have much of a relationship with his or her natural parents
- the defendant is the product of a deprived and socially deviant environment
- the defendant has a low mental age
- the defendant's low IQ impairs his or her judgment
- the defendant has low emotional development
- the defendant has no history of violence or violent acts
- the defendant has exhibited good behavior in confinement (see Case Summaries section, below)
- the defendant has shown remorse for the murder
- the defendant cooperated with law enforcement officers
- the defendant voluntarily acknowledged his or her guilt (confessed) to a law enforcement officer
- the defendant acted under the domination of another during the commission of the murder
- the defendant's participation in the murder was relatively minor
- the defendant's character and prior conduct were inconsistent with the murder

Case Summaries: Defendant's Good Conduct in Jail or Prison or Adjustment to Prison Life

Skipper v. South Carolina, 476 U.S. 1 (1986). The United States Supreme Court ruled that evidence of the defendant's good conduct in jail awaiting trial must constitutionally be admitted as mitigating evidence of the defendant's disposition to make a well-behaved and peaceful adjustment to prison life. The Court cited *Eddings v. Oklahoma*, 455 U.S. 104 (1982) (constitutional error in not considering as mitigating evidence the defendant's turbulent family history, beatings by his father, and his severe emotional disturbance). [*Author's note*: In *State v. Robinson*, 336 N.C. 78 (1994), the court overruled *State v. Pinch*, 306 N.C. 1 (1982), to the extent that it conflicted with the ruling in *Skipper*.]

State v. Smith, 359 N.C. 199 (2005). The North Carolina Supreme Court ruled that the trial court did not err in excluding evidence concerning "how defendant's conduct and duties in jail related to other inmates' conduct and duties." This type of comparative evidence was not relevant to the defendant's character or record or to the circumstances of his crime The defendant was allowed to introduce evidence that he generally behaved well in jail.

State v. Bunning, 346 N.C. 253 (1997). The court ruled, citing *Skipper v. South Carolina*, 476 U.S. 1 (1986), discussed above, and *State v. Rouse*, 339 N.C. 59 (1994), discussed below, that the judge erred during the capital sentencing hearing in prohibiting a defense expert from testifying that the defendant would not be a danger in prison to himself or other inmates.

State v. Basden, 339 N.C. 288 (1994). The court held that the ruling in *Skipper v. South Carolina*, 476 U.S. 1 (1986), discussed above, does not prohibit the trial judge from instructing the jury that it could refuse to consider the nonstatutory mitigating circumstance of good conduct in jail if it considered the evidence to have no mitigating value. The court noted that the defendant here was allowed, in accordance with the *Skipper* ruling, to offer evidence of his good behavior in jail. *See also* State v. Burr, 341 N.C. 263 (1995) (similar ruling); State v. Garner, 340 N.C. 573 (1995) (similar ruling).

State v. McLaughlin, 341 N.C. 426 (1995). The court ruled that the trial judge erred in not giving a peremptory instruction concerning the nonstatutory mitigating circumstance that the defendant had achieved a position as a cook in the prison kitchen since the evidence about this circumstance was both uncontroverted and manifestly credible. (The court, however, found the error to be harmless beyond a reasonable doubt.) The court also ruled that the trial judge did not err in failing to give peremptory instructions concerning nonstatutory mitigating circumstances, such as the defendant's self-improvement during incarceration, his desirable prison record, and assisting other prison inmates to adjust to prison life, because the evidence was either controverted or not manifestly credible as to these circumstances.

State v. Rouse, 339 N.C. 59 (1994). The court ruled that the trial judge erred in not allowing a defense psychiatrist who had investigated the defendant's mental health to offer his opinion about the defendant's ability to adjust to prison life, which was proper evidence of a nonstatutory mitigating circumstance. The court disavowed dicta in *State v. Pinch*, 306 N.C. 1 (1982), that was inconsistent with its ruling in this case. The court cited *Skipper v. South Carolina*, 476 U.S. 1 (1986), summarized above.

State v. Robinson, 336 N.C. 78 (1994). The trial judge erred in not submitting as a nonstatutory mitigating circumstance the fact that the defendant, in a structured prison environment, was able to conform his behavior to prison rules and perform required tasks. The state supreme court overruled *State v. Pinch*, 306 N.C. 1 (1982), to the extent it conflicted with the United States Supreme Court's ruling in *Skipper v. South Carolina*, 476 U.S. 1 (1986), summarized above. However, the court found the error to be harmless beyond a reasonable doubt. *See also* State v. Green, 336 N.C. 142 (1994) (improper not to submit as nonstatutory mitigating circumstance that defendant "will continue to adjust well to prison life and will be a model prisoner").

Case Summaries: Mental Age of the Defendant

State v. Robinson, 330 N.C. 1 (1991). The court ruled that there was sufficient evidence to support the submission of the following nonstatutory mitigating circumstance: the mental age of the defendant at the time of the murder for which he was being sentenced. A psychologist testified that the defendant was mentally retarded with an IQ of 69, which placed him in the lowest 2 percent of the population.

Case Summaries: Defendant's Sentences for Other Criminal Convictions

State v. Squires, 357 N.C. 529 (2003). Trial judge did not err in refusing to submit, as a nonstatutory mitigating circumstance, the fact that the defendant was serving a 105-year Georgia sentence for other crimes: "a defendant's prison sentence for another crime is not relevant as a mitigating circumstance."

State v. Price, 337 N.C. 756 (1994). Distinguishing *Simmons v. South Carolina*, 512 U.S. 154 (1994), the court reaffirmed its ruling in *State v. Price*, 331 N.C. 620 (1992), that the trial judge properly refused to submit as a nonstatutory mitigating circumstance the fact that the defendant had been sentenced to life imprisonment for a Virginia murder conviction. The Virginia life sentence was not a circumstance that tends to justify a sentence of less than death for the first-degree murder for which the defendant was being sentenced. *See also* State v. Reeves, 337 N.C. 700 (1994) (similar ruling).

State v. Robinson, 336 N.C. 78 (1994). The court ruled that the trial judge properly refused to submit as nonstatutory mitigating circumstances the lengthy terms of imprisonment received by the defendant for convictions of offenses that were tried with the current first-degree murder case. Sentencing for other offenses was not a circumstance that tends to justify a sentence of less than death for the first-degree murder for which the defendant was being sentenced. Also, references to these additional sentences would necessarily and improperly inject parole eligibility into the determination of the sentencing recommendation of death or life imprisonment. *See also* State v. Jones, 336 N.C. 229 (1994) (similar ruling).

State v. Lee, 335 N.C. 244 (1994). The court ruled that the trial judge properly excluded the defendant's proffered evidence at his capital sentencing hearing that the trial judge would sentence the defendant (after the sentencing hearing) for the convictions of kidnapping of the murder victim and for noncapital crimes against another victim. Such evidence was irrelevant in deciding whether the defendant should be sentenced to death.

Case Summaries: Consideration of Accomplice's Sentence or Plea Bargain

State v. Roache, 358 N.C. 243 (2004). The defendant argued that the fact that a co-defendant received a life sentence should have been admitted to support mitigating circumstance (f)(9). The state supreme court disagreed, ruling that a co-defendant's sentence has no mitigating value in and of itself. It distinguished *State v. Roseboro*, 351 N.C. 536 (2000) (stating that "the jury may consider an accomplice's sentence as a mitigating circumstance under the 'catchall' instruction"), summarized below, by stating that *Roseboro* "applies in a case where evidence of the co-defendant's sentence is already before the court, such as where the co-defendant testified at trial and evidence of a plea bargain was presented by way of impeachment."

State v. Jaynes, 353 N.C. 534 (2001). The court reaffirmed prior rulings that a co-defendant's sentence is not a mitigating circumstance and rejected the argument that *State v. Roseboro*, 351 N.C. 536 (2000), summarized below, permitted evidence of a co-defendant's sentence as a mitigating circumstance.

State v. Meyer, 353 N.C. 92 (2000). The defendant was convicted of two counts of first-degree murder and was sentenced to death for both counts. The court ruled that the trial judge did not err in failing to admit evidence of an accomplice's life sentences for both murders and in declining to submit to the jury the nonstatutory mitigating circumstance that the defendant's accomplice received life sentences. The court, citing *State v. Smith*, 352 N.C. 531 (2000), discussed immediately below, and *State v. Sidden*, 347 N.C. 218 (1997), stated that it had repeatedly ruled that an accomplice's sentence for the same murder(s) is irrelevant in a capital sentencing hearing; it is neither an aspect of the defendant's character or record nor a mitigating circumstance. The court rejected the defendant's argument that *State v. Roseboro*, 351 N.C. 536 (2000), summarized below, acknowledged the relevance of such evidence.

State v. Smith, 352 N.C. 531 (2000). The court ruled, citing *State v. Williams*, 305 N.C. 656 (1982), and *State v. Ward*, 338 N.C. 64 (1994), that an accomplice's punishment is not an aspect of the defendant's character or record and therefore is not a mitigating circumstance. Thus, the trial judge properly did not instruct on the proposed mitigating circumstance that the co-defendant here did not receive a death sentence.

State v. Roseboro, 351 N.C. 536 (2000). The defendant's accomplice testified against the defendant. The accomplice acknowledged that he was serving three life sentences in connection with the charged offenses. During closing argument at the penalty phase, the prosecutor argued that the accomplice's sentence was not a mitigating circumstance as to the defendant. The state supreme court ruled that the argument was not improper, stating (1) that "[e]vidence of a co-defendant's sentence is not relevant to a defendant's character or record or to the circumstances of the killing; hence, such evidence is not relevant to show a mitigating circumstance"; and (2) that "the jury may consider an accomplice's sentence as a mitigating circumstance under the 'catchall' instruction." The court concluded that the prosecutor properly argued in opposition to the use of the accomplice's sentence under the catchall mitigating circumstance and that the prosecutor did not improperly argue that the accomplice's sentence was an aggravating circumstance.

State v. Bond, 345 N.C. 1 (1996). The defendant was convicted of first-degree murder based on the theory of accessory before the fact and sentenced to death. The principal, who was 16 years old when he killed the victim, was not eligible for the death penalty under G.S. 14-17. The court ruled that evidence that the principal was ineligible by age to receive the death penalty was inadmissible at the sentencing hearing because it was not a mitigating circumstance. The sentence imposed on an accomplice is not a mitigating circumstance for the defendant being sentenced.

State v. Ward, 338 N.C. 64 (1994). The court ruled that evidence that another participant in the murder received a lesser sentence is not a nonstatutory mitigating circumstance. The court rejected the defendant's argument that the ruling in *Parker v. Dugger*, 498 U.S. 308 (1991) (Florida Supreme Court acted arbitrarily by affirming death sentence without considering mitigating circumstances found by the trial judge, one of which was more lenient sentencing for accomplice), required the court to reconsider its prior rulings on this issue, such as *State v. Williams*, 305 N.C. 656 (1982) (it is not a mitigating circumstance that two accomplices of the defendant received a plea bargain in which their maximum punishment would be ten years' imprisonment); *State v. Irwin*, 304 N.C. 93 (1981) (similar ruling); and *State v. McLaughlin*, 341 N.C. 426 (1995) (similar ruling). *See also* State v. Garner, 340 N.C. 573 (1995) (it is not a nonstatutory mitigating circumstance that the defendant's accomplice had not been and may not be tried capitally); State v. Goode, 341 N.C. 513 (1995) (it is not a nonstatutory mitigating circumstance that the defendant's accomplice had an extensive prior criminal record for violent crimes).

Case Summaries: Absence of Aggravating Circumstance or Absence of Additional Theory of First-Degree Murder

State v. Miller, 339 N.C. 663 (1995). The court ruled that the trial judge did not err in failing to submit the nonstatutory mitigating circumstance that the defendant neither threatened nor harmed eyewitnesses during his commission of murder and robbery. Not only is the absence of an aggravating circumstance not a mitigating circumstance, but also the absence of bad conduct that could have occurred during the commission of crimes is not a mitigating circumstance. Mitigating circumstances, both statutory and nonstatutory, focus on positive aspects of a defendant's character or behavior, noted the court.

State v. Green, 336 N.C. 142 (1994). The defendant pled guilty to first-degree murder based on the felony murder theory only. The court ruled that the trial judge did not err in refusing to submit as a nonstatutory mitigating circumstance the fact that the defendant did not kill after premeditation and deliberation. The court pointed out that the absence of an alternative theory for establishing that a murder was first-degree murder is not a mitigating circumstance. *But cf.* State v. Blakeney, 352 N.C. 287 (2000) (error, but harmless, for trial judge to refuse to submit nonstatutory mitigating circumstance that the defendant "did not set out to kill" the victim).

State v. Hunt, 330 N.C. 501 (1992). The court ruled that it is not a nonstatutory mitigating circumstance that murder victims were not tortured. The mere absence of evidence to establish an aggravating circumstance (in this case, especially heinous, atrocious, or cruel) is not evidence of a mitigating circumstance, the court stated. *See also* State v. Brown, 306 N.C. 151 (1982) (even assuming murders were not committed for pecuniary gain, that fact is not a mitigating circumstance).

Case Summaries: Residual Doubt Concerning Defendant's Guilt

Oregon v. Guzek, 546 U.S. 517 (2006). A defendant does not have a federal constitutional right to present, during the penalty phase of a capital trial, evidence that he or she was innocent of the crime in question. A state may prohibit the introduction of such evidence as irrelevant to the sentencing issue.

State v. Hill, 331 N.C. 387 (1992). The court found that a juror's residual or lingering doubt about the defendant's guilt is not a nonstatutory mitigating circumstance since it does not involve the defendant's character or record or the circumstances of the murder being tried. The court cited *Franklin v. Lynaugh,* 487 U.S. 164 (1988) (submission of residual doubt as mitigating circumstance is not constitutionally required). *See also* State v. Goode, 341 N.C. 513 (1995) (similar ruling); State v. Walls, 342 N.C. 1 (1995) (similar ruling).

Case Summaries: Impact of Sentence on, or Opinion Regarding Sentence of, Third Parties

State v. Smith, 359 N.C. 199 (2005). The state supreme court ruled that the trial court did not err in excluding the following evidence as irrelevant to mitigation: evidence "about defendant's consideration of suicide and his feelings about his children and mother" and evidence that the defendant "had family members who would support him if he received a life sentence." Generally, the court viewed this evidence as irrelevant to the defendant's character or record or the circumstances of his crime.

State v. Nicholson, 355 N.C. 1 (2002). The court ruled that the trial judge properly excluded proffered defense evidence of how the defendant's death (if he were to be sentenced to death) would impact his family. Such evidence does not relate to an aspect of the defendant's character or record or the circumstances of the murder for which he was being sentenced.

State v. Hardy, 353 N.C. 122 (2000). The court ruled that the effect of the defendant's execution (if he were to be sentenced to death) on his friend is not a mitigating circumstance. Citing *State v. Locklear,* 349 N.C. 118 (1998), summarized below, the court noted that a third party's feelings are irrelevant as a mitigating circumstance.

State v. Bowman, 349 N.C. 459 (1998). The court ruled that the opinion of the murder victim's mother regarding whether the defendant should receive the death penalty is inadmissible as a mitigating circumstance. The court stated that such evidence has no bearing on the defendant's character, prior record, or the circumstances of his offense.

State v. Locklear, 349 N.C. 118 (1998). The court ruled that the trial judge did not err in failing to submit a proposed nonstatutory mitigating circumstance that the defendant continues to have family members who care for and support him. The court stated that the feelings, actions, and conduct of third parties do not have mitigating value as to the defendant and, therefore, are irrelevant in a capital sentencing hearing.

Case Summaries: Sympathy for the Defendant

State v. Keel, 337 N.C. 469 (1994). The court ruled that the trial judge properly rejected the following instruction proposed by the defendant: "you are entitled to base your verdict upon any sympathy or mercy you may have for the defendant that arises from the evidence presented in this case." Instead, the trial judge instructed the jury as to the definition of "mitigating circumstance" and told the panel that they should regard as such a circumstance "any aspect of the defendant's character or record . . . that the defendant contends [form] a basis for a sentence less than death and any other circumstance arising from the evidence which [they] deem[ed] to have mitigating value." Explaining the ruling in *California v. Brown*, 479 U.S. 538 (1987) (upholding constitutionality of jury instruction that jury "must not be swayed by mere sentiment, conjecture, sympathy, passion, prejudice, public opinion or public feeling"), the court ruled that the judge's instruction was proper in that it clearly informed the jury that they could consider any circumstance—including sympathy for the defendant—that arose from the evidence and that, in their estimation, had mitigating value. *See also* State v. Jones, 339 N.C. 114 (1994) (trial judge did not err by refusing to instruct the jury that it was entitled to base its recommendation on any sympathy or mercy it might have for the defendant that arises from the evidence presented in the case); State v. Hill, 331 N.C. 387 (1992) (court stated that trial judges should not refer to "sympathy" in instructions on mitigating circumstances to avoid giving jurors the suggestion that they have unbridled discretion in the sentencing decision).

State v. Jones, 336 N.C. 229 (1994). The court rejected the defendant's argument that the pattern jury instruction was improper when it informed the jury that it has a duty to return a recommendation of death if it answered "yes" to Issue Four (whether aggravating circumstances are sufficiently substantial to impose the death penalty when considered with mitigating circumstances) on the sentence recommendation form. The court cited *State v. McDougall*, 308 N.C. 1 (1983), and *State v. Maynard*, 311 N.C. 1 (1984). [*Author's Note*: The section in Chapter 4 entitled "Prosecutor's Reference to Mercy or Sympathy" may also be of interest in connection with the role that sympathy for the defendant may play in a capital sentencing hearing.]

Case Summaries: Miscellaneous Matters

State v. Garcell, 363 N.C. 10 (2009). The trial judge did not err in giving individualized instructions on each statutory mitigating circumstance but not doing so for each of twenty-seven nonstatutory mitigating circumstances. This was a "practical" way of instructing the jury that did not diminish the importance of the nonstatutory mitigating circumstances. *See also* State v. Taylor, 362 N.C. 514 (2008) (similar).

State v. Smith, 359 N.C. 199 (2005). The North Carolina Supreme Court ruled that the trial court did not err in excluding the following evidence as irrelevant to mitigation: testimony from the defendant's mother that "if it had not been for the crack," the defendant would have behaved differently; and evidence that a prison minister viewed the defendant as "dedicated" to religious services because he voluntarily helped other inmates. Generally, the court viewed this evidence as irrelevant to the defendant's character or record or the circumstances of his crime.

State v. Thompson, 359 N.C. 77 (2004). The trial judge did not err in refusing to submit, as a nonstatutory mitigating circumstance, the fact that the defendant was willing to plead guilty to first-degree murder and serve a life sentence. It was not clear that the defendant was actually willing to do so, and even if he was, it was not clear that his willingness reflected acceptance of responsibility rather than simply a desire to avoid the death penalty.

State v. Blakeney, 352 N.C. 287 (2000). The defendant broke into a house and stole some personal property. When the victim later arrived at the house, the defendant hid in the house as she entered it and then murdered her. A portion of the defendant's statement to law enforcement officers tended to show that he did not intend to kill the victim when he broke into the house. The court ruled, relying on *State v. Green*, 336 N.C. 142 (1994), that the trial judge erred in failing to submit the nonstatutory mitigating circumstance that the defendant did not set out to kill the victim when he entered the victim's home. However, the error was harmless beyond a reasonable doubt.

State v. Williams, 305 N.C. 656 (1982). The court found the following evidence to be irrelevant and therefore inadmissible as nonstatutory mitigating circumstances: the lack of any deterrent effect of the death penalty, the rehabilitative nature of people who have committed heinous crimes, and the manner of execution in North Carolina. *See also* State v. Taylor, 304 N.C. 249 (1981) (evidence that capital punishment is imposed in a racially discriminatory manner is not a nonstatutory mitigating circumstance); State v. Cherry, 298 N.C. 86 (1979) (evidence that innocent people have sometimes been executed and that capital punishment was objectionable on religious grounds are not nonstatutory mitigating circumstances).

Chapter 7

The Racial Justice Act

Chapter 7

The Racial Justice Act

This chapter addresses the Racial Justice Act, or RJA.[1] The RJA is relatively new. At this writing, in January 2013, there are no appellate decisions interpreting it. Therefore, of necessity, this chapter differs from the preceding chapters, which focus heavily on established law reflected in court opinions. This chapter is more speculative and forward-looking and should be viewed in that light.

Also, because this book is designed for use in connection with capital trials, this chapter discusses the impact of the RJA on pretrial proceedings in capital cases. RJA claims may also be made in post-conviction proceedings, but such proceedings generally are not discussed in this book.

A. Background

Claims of racial discrimination in capital cases have been made as long as the death penalty has existed in North Carolina. Prior to the enactment of the RJA, avenues for raising such claims included the following:

- ***Batson* claims.** Under *Batson v. Kentucky*,[2] a defendant may seek to prevent, or seek relief based on, racial discrimination by the state in exercising its peremptory challenges during jury selection.
- **Fair cross section claims.** Under *Duren v. Missouri*,[3] a defendant may seek relief on the grounds that the jury pool from which his or her jury was selected systematically excluded a distinctive racial group.
- **Claims of intentional racial discrimination under *McCleskey*.** In *McCleskey v. Kemp*,[4] the United States Supreme Court rejected equal protection and Eighth Amendment challenges brought by a death-sentenced defendant from Georgia who relied on a statistical study showing, in part, that African-American defendants who killed white victims were much more likely to receive the death penalty than other defendants. The Court stated that a defendant "must prove that the decisionmakers in *his* case acted with discriminatory

1. Sections 15A-2010 *et seq.* of the North Carolina General Statutes (hereinafter G.S.)
2. 476 U.S. 79 (1986). *Batson* claims are discussed in Chapter 3.
3. 439 U.S. 357 (1979). *Duren* claims are discussed in Chapter 2.
4. 481 U.S. 279 (1987).

purpose"[5] in order to establish an equal protection violation and that statistics alone can't show discrimination in any individual case. However, a defendant who can establish, for example, that a prosecutor elected to seek the death penalty in his or her case based on racial animus would be entitled to relief under *McCleskey*.

Some North Carolina legislators and others believed that these mechanisms for addressing discrimination were inadequate and that race continued to play a substantial role in the administration of the death penalty in the state. Apparently in response to these concerns, the General Assembly passed the Racial Justice Act on August 6, 2009. The vote in both chambers divided mostly along party lines, with Democrats supporting the bill and Republicans opposing it. It was signed into law by Governor Beverly Perdue on August 11, 2009.[6] In this chapter, the 2009 version of the RJA will sometimes be called the "original RJA."

Very generally, the original RJA allowed a defendant to attempt to establish, through statistical or other evidence, that race played a significant factor in decisions to seek or impose the death penalty in his or her county, prosecutorial district, or judicial division, or in the state as a whole. If he or she succeeded, the court was required to bar the state from seeking the death penalty against the defendant. (The original RJA also provided for post-conviction challenges to death sentences that had already been imposed. As noted at the outset, however, such claims are beyond the scope of this chapter.)

North Carolina was the second state to enact legislation specifically targeting racial discrimination in capital cases. Kentucky was the first; it adopted its racial justice act in 1998.[7] It is clear from looking at the text of both statutes that Kentucky's law served as a model for North Carolina's. However, North Carolina's original RJA was broader than Kentucky's statute in several important respects.[8]

Many North Carolina defendants charged with capital crimes filed claims under the original RJA. In general, as discussed in greater detail below, judges did not consider the merits of such claims, instead deferring consideration of the claims until after the defendants' trials.

Almost all death row inmates also filed claims under the original RJA. As of this writing, only a handful of such claims have been adjudicated, all by a single judge. The judge in each case has ruled for the defendant on the basis of discrimination by the state in jury selection.[9] The state has asked

---

5. *Id.* at 292 (emphasis in original).

6. S.L. 2009-464 (SB 461), *codified at* G.S. Chapter 15A, Article 101.

7. Ky. Rev. Stat. Ann. §§ 532.300 *et seq.*

8. For example, (1) Kentucky's law allows claims only at the pretrial stage, while the original RJA provided for both pretrial and post-conviction claims; (2) Kentucky's law requires that the defendant establish his or her claim by clear and convincing evidence, while North Carolina's statute did not incorporate that elevated burden of proof; (3) North Carolina's law allowed a defendant to show that "[r]ace was a significant factor in decisions to exercise peremptory challenges during jury selection," while Kentucky's does not provide for juror-based claims; and (4) while North Carolina allowed a defendant to show discrimination in the county, prosecutorial district, judicial division, or state as a whole, Kentucky's statute provides for state-level claims only. The Kentucky law has been criticized as ineffective by the American Bar Association (ABA). ABA, *Evaluating Fairness and Accuracy in State Death Penalty Systems: The Kentucky Death Penalty Assessment Report* vii (2011) (concluding that the Kentucky act "appears to have a number of restrictions limiting its effectiveness at identifying and remedying racial discrimination in the administration of the death penalty").

9. *See* Order Granting Motion for Appropriate Relief, *State v. Robinson*, Cumberland Cnty. Case No. 91 CRS 23143 (Apr. 20, 2012) (Weeks, J.) (hereinafter 4/20/12 Order, *Robinson*); Order Granting Motion for Appropriate Relief, *State v. Golphin*, Cumberland Cnty. Case No. 97 CRS 47314-15 (Dec. 13, 2012) (Weeks, J.) (hereinafter 12/13/12 Order, *Golphin*) (also adjudicating the claims of defendants Walters and Augustine and also addressing claims under the amended RJA).

the North Carolina Supreme Court to review the rulings.[10] Those involved in capital litigation will closely watch the outcome, alert to the possibility that either the trial court's ruling or the supreme court's decision might have some preclusive or precedential effect.

The original RJA was controversial, and the controversy grew when nearly all death-sentenced defendants filed claims under it. When control of the General Assembly shifted from Democrats to Republicans, efforts to amend or repeal the RJA began in earnest. After several failed attempts,[11] the General Assembly substantially amended the RJA on July 2, 2012.[12] In this chapter, the version of the RJA that resulted from the legislature's actions will sometimes be called the "amended RJA." The amended RJA curtails the original RJA in important respects. However, as discussed in greater detail below, the meaning and scope of the amended RJA are not completely clear.

The session law amending the RJA provides that it "is effective when it becomes law and applies to all capital trials held prior to, on, or after the effective date of this act and to all capital defendants sentenced to the death penalty prior to, on, or after the effective date of this act."[13] Therefore, this chapter focuses principally on the amended RJA. However, defendants charged with crimes that took place during the period when the original RJA was in effect may be entitled to have their claims heard under the original RJA. That possibility is discussed briefly at the end of this chapter.

B. Issues under the Amended RJA

Cognizable Claims

The original RJA encompassed claims of discrimination (1) based on the defendant's race, (2) based on the victim's race, and (3) in jury selection, and allowed proof of such discrimination at the level of (a) the county, (b) the prosecutorial district, (c) the judicial division, or (d) the state as a whole. The amended RJA appears to eliminate some of these claims from the scope of the law.

First, the amended RJA appears to rule out claims based on discrimination at the level of the judicial division or the state as a whole. Under new G.S. 15A-2011(c), "[t]he defendant has the burden of proving that race was a significant factor in decisions to seek or impose the sentence of death in the county or prosecutorial district at the time the [defendant's] death sentence was sought or imposed."[14]

Second, the amended RJA may rule out claims of discrimination based on the victim's race. New G.S. 15A-2011(d) states that "[e]vidence relevant to establish a finding that race was a significant factor in decisions to seek or impose the sentence of death . . . may include . . . evidence, that either (i) the race of the defendant was a significant factor or (ii) race was a significant factor in decisions to

---

10. *See, e.g.*, Petition for Writ of Certiorari, *State v. Robinson*, North Carolina Supreme Court Case No. 411A94-5 (July 10, 2012). As of this writing, the state has indicated that it will file a similar petition regarding the *Golphin* order.

11. During the 2010 legislative session, two bills were introduced that would have eliminated pretrial RJA claims and limited the scope of the RJA to post-conviction claims. Neither bill advanced very far in the legislative process. During the 2011 legislative session, both chambers of the General Assembly passed a bill (SB 9, HB 12) that would have "supersede[d] and nullifie[d] the provisions of [the RJA] that existed prior to the effective date of this act and which are repealed by this act." In effect, the bill would have rendered the RJA a statutory codification of the *McCleskey* rule. However, Governor Perdue vetoed the bill, and while the Senate overrode her veto, the House did not.

12. S.L. 2012-136 (SB 416).

13. *Id.* § 10.

14. *See also* G.S. 15A-2011(d) (again referring to "the county or prosecutorial district" as the relevant unit of consideration); G.S. 15A-2011(f) (same).

exercise peremptory challenges during jury selection." The victim's race is no longer mentioned as the basis of a possible claim in the statute, though the use of the phrase "may include" arguably does not exclude claims concerning types of discrimination other than those enumerated in the statute.[15] Further, the amended RJA retains several general statements concerning racial discrimination that could be interpreted to allow consideration of claims based on the race of the victim.[16]

Impact on the Defendant's Case

Under the original RJA, there was some uncertainty as to whether a defendant who could show a pattern of discrimination in, for example, a prosecutorial district, but who could not establish discrimination in his or her own case was entitled to relief.[17] When the RJA was amended, the phrase "in the defendant's case" was added to G.S. 15A-2011(a). The amendment may have been intended to resolve the uncertainty and to bring the amended RJA in line with the constitutional standard under *McCleskey*, in which the United States Supreme Court held that to establish an equal protection violation, "a criminal defendant must prove that . . . purposeful [racial] discrimination 'had a discriminatory effect' *on him*."[18] However, the exact meaning and intent of the statute remains somewhat opaque.

The reference to "the defendant's case" appears in this context:

> A finding that race was the basis of the decision to seek or impose a death sentence may be established if the court finds that race was a significant factor in decisions to seek or impose the death penalty in the defendant's case at the time the death sentence was sought or imposed. For the purposes of this section, "at the time the death

---

15. However, it may be significant that the same subsection goes on to say that admissible evidence "may include, but is not limited to," certain types of evidence listed in the statute. G.S. 15A-2011(d). The use of the phrase "but is not limited to" at that point in the subsection may suggest that the failure to use a similar phrase before the listing of possible claims (i.e., race-of-defendant claims and jury selection claims) is intentional and reflects a legislative desire to constrain RJA claims to the two enumerated types.

16. G.S. 15A-2010 ("No person shall be subject to or given a sentence of death . . . pursuant to any judgment that was sought or obtained on the basis of race."); G.S. 15A-2011(a) ("A finding that race was the basis of the decision to seek or impose a death sentence may be established if the court finds that race was a significant factor in decisions to seek or impose the death penalty in the defendant's case at the time the death sentence was sought or imposed.").

17. Then-G.S. 15A-2012(a)(3) stated that the court "shall" strike the death penalty if the defendant could establish discrimination at the county, prosecutorial district, judicial division, or state levels. Thus, relief appeared to be mandatory when the defendant established a pattern of discrimination, regardless of the court's conclusions about the existence or nonexistence of discrimination in the defendant's case. However, G.S. 15A-2011(a) stated that an RJA claim "may" be established when a defendant showed discrimination at the county, prosecutorial district, judicial division, or state levels. The use of the permissive term "may" seemed to leave open the possibility that a judge could find evidence of historical discrimination but still deny the defendant relief—for example, if the court determined that there was no discrimination in the defendant's case. Adding to this possibility was G.S. 15A-2011(c), which provided (and still provides) that "[t]he court may consider evidence of the impact upon the defendant's trial of any program the purpose of which is to eliminate race as a factor in seeking or imposing a sentence of death." If showing discrimination at the county, prosecutorial district, judicial division, or state levels were sufficient to require relief under the RJA, it is not clear why the existence or nonexistence of such a program would be relevant. Finally, the first sentence of the Act stated (and still states) that "[n]o person shall be subject to or given a sentence of death . . . pursuant to any judgment that was sought or obtained on the basis of race." G.S. 15A-2010. Arguably, that language suggested that the defendant's particular judgment must be tainted by racial bias. One superior court judge ruled that the original RJA did not require a showing of discrimination in the defendant's particular case (see 4/20/12 Order, *Robinson*, cited in full *supra* note 9). Another upheld the constitutionality of the RJA in part by concluding that the Act "does provide for consideration of the facts and circumstances of an individual case." Order Denying State's Motion to Dismiss on Constitutional Grounds, *State v. Moses*, Forsyth Cnty. Case No. 96 CRS 19456-57 (Feb. 24, 2011) (Wood, J.).

18. 481 U.S. 279, 292 (1987) (emphasis supplied).

> sentence was sought or imposed" shall be defined as the period from 10 years prior to the commission of the offense to the date that is two years after the imposition of the death sentence.[19]

First, the statute uses the permissive term "may" in the phrase "may be established if." That arguably leaves open the possibility of establishing discrimination by means other than showing an effect on the defendant's case.

Second, the statute confusingly juxtaposes the terms "in the defendant's case" and "at the time the death sentence was sought or imposed . . . defined as the period from 10 years prior to the commission of the offense to the date that is two years after the imposition of the death sentence." Defendants may argue that the multi-year time span encompassed by the "at the time" provision allows a court to consider patterns of discrimination even without a clear connection to the defendant's individual case. Or they may argue that the statute, in effect, defines discrimination taking place within the prescribed window of time as taking place "in the defendant's case."[20]

The state is likely to argue that, in the context of the political controversy over the RJA, the new phrase "in the defendant's case" is the key to the proper interpretation of the amended statute. It may contend that the "at the time" provision limits the scope of statistical evidence that a court may consider but does not undercut the requirement that the defendant ultimately must establish discrimination in his or her particular case.[21]

Timing of Claim

Under new G.S. 15A-2011(f)(1), a defendant may raise an RJA claim "at the pretrial conference," i.e., the Rule 24 hearing, which is discussed in detail in Chapter 2, "or in postconviction proceedings."

Pleading a Claim

Under the original RJA, a defendant was required to "state with particularity how the evidence supports" his or her RJA claim.[22] This language has been retained, albeit in a different statutory location, in the amended RJA.[23] The reference to "evidence" suggests that the particularity requirement demands more than simply identifying the type of discrimination (for example, discrimination in the exercise of peremptory challenges) that the defendant contends exists and the level (for example, the prosecutorial district) on which the defendant contends that discrimination took place. However, it

---

19. G.S. 15A-2011(a).

20. The only judge to have conducted a merits hearing under the amended RJA essentially adopted this interpretation. 12/13/12 Order, *Golphin,* cited in full *supra* note 9, at 17 ("Therefore, in order to appropriately give effect to all of the language in the amended RJA, the Court holds that 'in the defendant's case' does not require proof in the defendant's individual trial. Indeed, the amended RJA does not even use the word 'trial.' More importantly, a trial-specific requirement would read the temporal and geographic provisions out of the amended RJA by making evidence that satisfied those parameters entirely unnecessary to a claim for relief. This the Court cannot do. Instead, the Court concludes that 'in the defendant's case' requires defendants to prove that race was a significant factor within the temporal statutory window and the specified geographic areas."). Defendants may also point to G.S. 15A-2011(c), which states that "[t]he defendant has the burden of proving that race was a significant factor in decisions to seek or impose the sentence of death in the county or prosecutorial district at the time the death sentence was sought or imposed." It would seem that a defendant could carry that burden without presenting evidence focused on his or her individual case.

21. Appropriate statistical evidence is certainly relevant and admissible under the amended RJA, but G.S. 15A-2011(e) provides that such evidence "alone is insufficient" to establish an RJA claim.

22. Former G.S. 15A-2012(a).

23. G.S. 15A-2011(f).

is not clear exactly how detailed the defendant's discussion of the evidence must be or what quantum of supporting evidence must be forecast. It appears that an insufficiently specific claim is subject to dismissal under new G.S. 15A-2011(f)(2).[24]

Scheduling or Deferring a Hearing on a Claim

New G.S. 15A-2011(f) states that if the judge "finds that the defendant's motion fails to state a sufficient claim . . . then the court shall dismiss the claim without an evidentiary hearing," but that if the judge "finds that the defendant's motion states a sufficient claim . . . the court shall schedule a hearing on the claim." This raises the question: If a capital defendant sufficiently states an RJA claim, must the hearing be scheduled before trial or may the judge defer further proceedings on the claim until after trial?

Under the original RJA, the overwhelming practice among judges was to defer pretrial claims. Then-G.S. 15A-2012 provided that once an RJA claim was made, "[t]he court shall schedule a hearing." Most judges, reasoning that if the defendant were not sentenced to death the RJA claim would be moot, "schedule[d]" the hearing for after the trial. This also avoided any risk of delaying the trial unduly for protracted RJA proceedings. (Of course, deferral of the hearing was not mandatory, and a judge could have chosen to proceed on the RJA claim prior to trial, perhaps reasoning that if the RJA claim were successful the trial would be simpler by virtue of being noncapital.)

The same practice appears likely under the amended RJA. The language in new G.S. 15A-2011(f) requiring a court to "schedule a hearing on the claim" is similar to the "shall schedule a hearing" language of former G.S. 15A-2012 and presumably can accommodate the same mechanism of "schedul[ing]" a hearing for after the conclusion of the trial. If a judge elects to defer a pretrial RJA claim, the judge probably should find on the record that the defendant's claim has been timely filed and is preserved, so as to avoid any argument later that the defendant forfeited his or her rights under the RJA by failing to pursue his or her claim pretrial.

Discovery

Under the original RJA, defense counsel in some cases sought discovery regarding items such as the District Attorney's policy regarding when to pursue the death penalty; any efforts made to address the impact of race when deciding whether to pursue the death penalty; the race of the District Attorney's employees; the District Attorney's plea bargaining policies; any lawsuits against the District Attorney claiming racial discrimination in employment; information about all first-degree murder cases prosecuted by the office of the District Attorney within a specified time frame, including the race of the defendant, victim, and jurors; the history of plea negotiations; and other matters. Under the amended RJA, defense counsel might seek discovery of similar information.

The RJA does not address discovery for pretrial RJA claims. It is likely that a court has the inherent authority to order appropriate discovery.[25] However, it is also likely that a court has the inherent authority to limit discovery, i.e., to balance the defendant's need for information with the burden imposed on the state. The nature of the defendant's claims and the strength of the evidence forecast

---

24. G.S. 15A-2011(f)(2) states that "If the court finds that the defendant's motion fails to state a sufficient claim under [the RJA], then the court shall dismiss the claim without an evidentiary hearing."

25. *Cf., e.g.*, State v. Buckner, 351 N.C. 401 (2000) (authorizing the use of depositions in connection with motion for appropriate relief proceedings in appropriate cases); State v. Taylor, 327 N.C. 147 (1990) (discussing discovery and inherent authority).

by the defendant may be relevant considerations when deciding whether, and to what extent, to allow discovery.

If a court decides to defer a hearing on a defendant's RJA claims until after the trial, it probably should also defer discovery. If the defendant is not sentenced to death, the need for discovery will be obviated. Furthermore, the nature and extent of discovery may be influenced by any interpretation of the RJA that may be provided by the appellate courts between the time the pretrial claim is asserted and the time the post-conviction claim is considered.

Admissible Evidence

If a defendant makes an RJA claim prior to trial and the court elects to hear the claim prior to trial, the court must determine what type of evidence is admissible. The North Carolina Rules of Evidence[26] appear to apply to RJA hearings, as RJA hearings are "proceedings" under Rule 1101(a) and are not excluded from the scope of the rules by Rule 1101(b).

The RJA itself provides some additional guidance. Under G.S. 15A-2011(d):

> Evidence relevant to establish a finding that race was a significant factor in decisions to seek or impose the sentence of death in the county or prosecutorial district at the time the death sentence was sought or imposed may include statistical evidence derived from the county or prosecutorial district where the defendant was sentenced to death, or other evidence, that either (i) the race of the defendant was a significant factor or (ii) race was a significant factor in decisions to exercise peremptory challenges during jury selection. The evidence may include, but is not limited to, sworn testimony of attorneys, prosecutors, law enforcement officers, judicial officials, jurors, or others involved in the criminal justice system. A juror's testimony under this subsection shall be consistent with Rule 606(b) of the North Carolina Rules of Evidence, as contained in G.S. 8C-1.

Further, G.S. 15A-2011(e) provides that the state may offer rebuttal evidence, including statistical evidence.

Sufficient Evidence

A judge considering an RJA claim must determine whether the defendant's evidence is sufficient to warrant relief. The burden of proof rests with the defendant.[27] The statute does not directly specify the quantum of proof that is necessary, i.e., whether the defendant must show discrimination by a preponderance of the evidence, by clear and convincing evidence, or under some other standard. However, it is reasonably clear that the preponderance standard applies to post-conviction RJA claims,[28] and absent a specific provision to the contrary, it is likely that courts will apply the preponderance standard to pretrial RJA claims as well.[29]

---

26. G.S. 8C-1.

27. G.S. 15A-2011(c) ("The defendant has the burden of proving that race was a significant factor . . .").

28. New G.S. 15A-2011(f)(1) refers to the rules governing motions for appropriate relief in Article 89 of Chapter 15A of the General Statutes. Among those rules is G.S. 15A-1420(c)(5), which states that "[i]f an evidentiary hearing is held, the moving party has the burden of proving by a preponderance of the evidence every fact essential to support the motion." *See* 12/13/12 Order, *Golphin*, cited in full *supra* note 9, at 18 (applying the preponderance standard to post-conviction claims under the amended RJA because that is the standard that applies to motions for appropriate relief).

29. *Cf.* State v. Johnson, 304 N.C. 680, 684 (1982) (noting that "[t]he quantum of proof required to establish the voluntariness of a statement is not specified in G.S. 15A-977" and ruling that a preponderance of the evidence

As discussed above, it is not completely clear whether the defendant's evidence must show discrimination in his or her particular case. However, the amended RJA does state that "[s]tatistical evidence alone is insufficient to establish that race was a significant factor under [the RJA]."[30] This is somewhat similar to the conclusion of the United States Supreme Court in *McCleskey* that statistical evidence alone was "insufficient to support an inference that any of the decisionmakers in [the defendant's] case acted with discriminatory purpose."[31] The RJA does not state what type or quantum of additional evidence is required. Another question is whether unintentional or subconscious discrimination, even if insufficient to constitute a "discriminatory purpose" under *McCleskey*, is sufficient to warrant relief under the RJA; the broad language of the statute suggests that it may be.[32]

Relief

If a judge rules in a defendant's favor on an RJA claim prior to trial, the court must "order that a death sentence not be sought" against the defendant.[33] In other words, the court must order that the case proceed as a noncapital first-degree murder case.

Appeal

The RJA does not contain any provisions concerning appellate review. If a judge rules in a defendant's favor on an RJA claim prior to trial, it appears that the state has no right to appeal, as none of the conditions in G.S. 15A-1445 are satisfied. However, the state may nonetheless be able to seek interlocutory review by the appellate division through a petition for a writ of certiorari.[34] If a judge rules in the state's favor prior to trial, it seems that a defendant might similarly seek interlocutory review through a petition for a writ of certiorari or might seek review of the order after final judgment, as a defendant normally would do.

---

standard would be applied). The considerations behind the rule of lenity may also support such an interpretation. *See generally* State v. Abshire, 363 N.C. 322, 332 (2009) ("The rule of lenity requires that we strictly construe ambiguous criminal statutes.").

30. G.S. 15A-2011(e).

31. 481 U.S. 279, 297 (1987).

32. *See, e.g.,* G.S. 15A-2010 ("No person shall be subject to or given a sentence of death . . . pursuant to any judgment that was sought or obtained on the basis of race."); G.S. 15A-2011(a) ("A finding that race was the basis of the decision to seek or impose a death sentence may be established if the court finds that race was a significant factor in decisions to seek or impose the death penalty in the defendant's case at the time the death sentence was sought or imposed."). The state may argue that a sentence of death may only be "sought . . . on the basis of race" if a prosecutor consciously decided to pursue the death penalty on the basis of race. The only order issued so far under the amended RJA concludes that unintentional discrimination warrants relief. 12/13/12 Order, *Golphin*, cited in full *supra* note 9, at 19–23.

33. G.S. 15A-2011(g).

34. Rule 21(a)(1) of the North Carolina Rules of Appellate Procedure provides that th e writ "may be issued . . . to permit review of the judgments and orders of trial tribunals . . . when no right of appeal from an interlocutory order exists"). *See* State v. Defoe, 364 N.C. 29 (2010) (reviewing trial judge's denial of the defendant's motion to strike the death penalty via writ of certiorari). *Cf.* State v. Osterhoudt, __N.C. App. __, 731 S.E.2d 454 (2012) (reviewing superior court's order concerning suppression issue in DWI case through writ of certiorari).

C. Defendants Who May Be Entitled to Proceed under the Original RJA

Ex Post Facto Considerations

Defendants charged with murders that took place during the period when the original RJA was in effect may argue that the Ex Post Facto Clause of the federal Constitution[35] requires that their RJA claims be heard under the original RJA, notwithstanding the provision of the amended RJA that states that it applies to "all capital trials held prior to, on, or after the effective date of [the amendment]."[36]

Generally, the Ex Post Facto Clause prohibits any statute that "punishes as a crime an act previously committed, which was innocent when done; which makes more burdensome the punishment for a crime, after its commission, or which deprives one charged with crime of any defense available according to law at the time when the act was committed."[37] Defendants charged with murders that took place while the original RJA was in effect may argue that because the amended RJA narrows the protection of the original RJA, it effectively deprives them of a defense available at the time the charged offense was committed.

In analyzing the possible ex post facto constraints on the application of the amended RJA, it is helpful to divide capital defendants into three classes based on the date of the charged offense:

- **Offense dates prior to August 11, 2009.** These defendants allegedly committed murder prior to the enactment of the original RJA. The protections offered by the amended RJA, although less substantial than the protections offered by the original RJA, are no less than what was available to these defendants at the time of their alleged crimes. Therefore, there is no ex post facto problem for these defendants.
- **Offense dates after July 2, 2012.** These defendants allegedly committed murder after the amendments to the RJA, and so they cannot argue that they are entitled to the greater protections offered by the original RJA. There is no ex post facto problem for these defendants.
- **Offense dates on or after August 11, 2009, but prior to July 2, 2012.** These defendants allegedly committed murder at a time when the original RJA was in effect. They may argue that the Ex Post Facto Clause requires that they be allowed to assert claims under the original RJA.

Defendants in the third class listed above have a colorable ex post facto argument. However, the state has a possible response: it can argue that the RJA amendments are procedural in nature; that they do not alter the quantum of punishment that attaches to the crime of first-degree murder; and that they therefore do not implicate the Ex Post Facto Clause. Some cases that may bear on the question are collected in the margin.[38] Ultimately, as with virtually everything about the RJA, the issue remains to be decided by the courts.

---

35. U.S. CONST. art. I, § 9 ("No Bill of Attainder or ex post facto Law shall be passed.").
36. S.L. 2012-136 (SB 416), § 10.
37. Beazell v. Ohio, 269 U.S. 167, 169 (1925).
38. *See* Dobbert v. Florida, 432 U.S. 282 (1977). In *Dobbert*, the defendant committed murder before, but was tried and sentenced to death after, Florida revised its capital punishment procedures. Under the old system, death was mandatory unless a majority of the jury recommended life, in which case, the judge was required to impose a life sentence. Under the new system, a jury's recommendation either way was non-binding. The new procedures were used at the defendant's trial, and the jury recommended life but was overruled by the judge. The defendant contended that this was an ex post facto violation. The United States Supreme Court ruled otherwise, finding "that the changes in the law are procedural, and, on the whole, ameliorative." *Id.* at 292 (footnote omitted). As to the procedural nature of the change, the Court stated, "[t]he new statute simply altered the

Vested Rights

Defendants who filed a claim under the original RJA may argue that they have a vested right to proceed under that version of the statute. Any defendant who filed a claim under the original RJA could make this argument, regardless of whether the murder took place before or after the enactment of the original RJA. The state is likely to argue that absent a final order or judgment under the original RJA, there is no vested right to proceed under the original RJA.[39] As of this writing, one superior court judge has ruled that defendants who filed claims under the original RJA have a vested right to proceed under it.[40]

---

methods employed in determining whether the death penalty was to be imposed; there was no change in the quantum of punishment attached to the crime." *Id.* at 293–94. *See also* State v. Ring, 65 P.3d 915 (Ariz. 2003) (after *Ring v. Arizona*, 536 U.S. 584 (2002), Arizona amended its death penalty procedures to provide for the finding of aggravating factors by a jury rather than by a judge; the defendant, who committed murder when the judge-based system was in effect, argued that applying the jury-based system at his trial would violate the Ex Post Facto Clause; the state supreme court disagreed, ruling that the change was procedural, not substantive, and so did not implicate the Clause, distinguishing *State v. Correll*, 715 P.2d 721 (1986) (retroactive application of an aggravating circumstance that did not exist at the time the defendant committed murder violated the Ex Post Facto Clause)); Hameen v. Delaware, 212 F.3d 226, 244 (3d Cir. 2000) (applying Antiterrorism and Effective Death Penalty Act deference, state court was not unreasonable in finding no ex post facto violation in retroactive application of modified capital punishment statute; the change was "procedural"). *But see* Murtishaw v. Woodford, 255 F.3d 926, 961 (9th Cir. 2001) (the defendant committed murder during the time period when California's 1977 death penalty statute was in effect; after an initial conviction and appeal, he was resentenced for the crime in 1983, under the 1978 revision of California's statutes; the Ninth Circuit found an ex post facto problem because "[u]nder the 1977 statute the jury would have had discretion to reject the death penalty even if it found that the aggravating factors outweighed the mitigating factors" while "under the . . . 1978 statute the jury did not have this discretion").

39. There are many North Carolina cases on vested rights. *See, e.g.*, Gardner v. Gardner, 300 N.C. 715 (1980) (finding a vested right to a venue determination in a divorce case); Smith v. Mercer, 276 N.C. 329 (1970) (defendant in a wrongful death action had a vested right to have the plaintiff's claim adjudicated under more restrictive 1968 wrongful death statutes rather than more expansive 1969 statutes, where the death took place in 1968 but the claim was not brought until 1969; the statutory change could not retroactively place a new duty on the defendant); Bowen v. Mabry, 154 N.C. App. 734 (2002) (a new statute changed the rule in equitable distribution actions to provide that such actions would no longer automatically be dismissed upon the death of a spouse; in the case at bar, one spouse had died prior to the enactment of the new statute, though a dismissal had not yet been ordered; the court ruled that the other spouse had no vested right to the dismissal and that the new statute could apply retroactively to bar it); *and* State v. Morehead, 46 N.C. App. 39, 43 (1980) (no vested right was impaired by changes to the speedy trial statute because "[t]here is no vested right in procedure[,] and statutes affecting procedural matters may be given retroactive effect or applied to pending litigation").

40. 12/13/12 Order, *Golphin*, cited in full *supra* note 9, at 35. The court gave several additional reasons for applying the original RJA to the defendants' claims, including that "[t]he legislature simply failed to specify that the amended RJA applies instead of the original RJA to claims filed under that law." *Id.* at 32–33.

Case Index

I

J

K

L

M

N

O

P

R

S

T

U

W

Descriptive Word Index

Page numbers in italics indicate a table, chart, or figure

E

F

G

H

I

J

K

L

M

N

O

P

Q

R

www.ingramcontent.com/pod-product-compliance
Lightning Source LLC
LaVergne TN
LVHW080031210926
848481LV00011B/3153